Plant-Based Cookbook For Beginners

Table Of Contents

Introduction

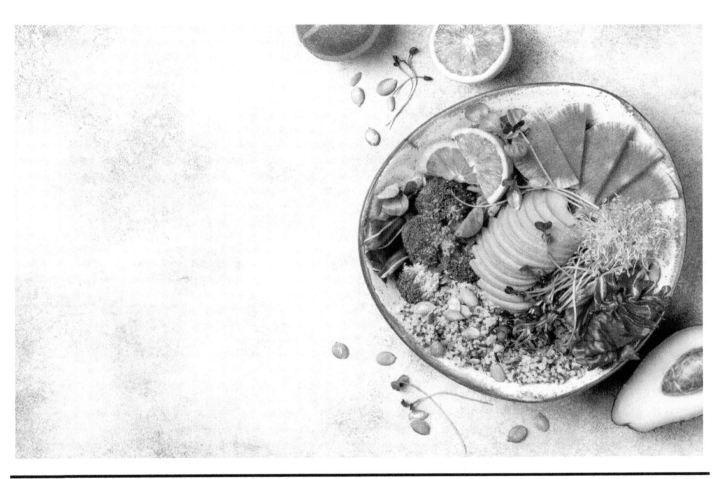

What Is the Plant-Based Diet?

A plant-based diet is a plant-centered nutrition program that includes all fruits, vegetables, grains (such as rice), legumes (such as beans), nuts and seeds. This type of diet excludes animal products such as meat, seafood, eggs or dairy.

A plant-based diet has many benefits. The following points will give you an idea of what to expect: lose weight naturally; experience improved cardiovascular health; reduce the risk of developing heart disease or type 2 diabetes; reduce cholesterol levels naturally; maintain blood sugar levels even when carbohydrate intake is high.

A plant-based diet does not have to be difficult or complicated. However, it is important to make sure you get the right nutrients and vitamins. The most important elements are: protein, calcium, iron and zinc.

Protein is a building block for your body and aids in muscle growth and repair. A protein deficiency can cause anemia, fatigue, hair loss or poor growth in children. When looking for additional protein sources, look for foods such as beans, peas and lentils as vegetarian protein sources. For meat eaters, eggs are also an excellent source of plant-based protein. Calcium is necessary for bone structure and development. Iron is necessary for oxygen transport in body tissues and improves cognitive function. Zinc is a mineral that contributes to immune system response, wound healing, bone growth and normal carbohydrate metabolism.

There are many other nutrients you can get from a plant-based diet. Vitamin A is important for immune system function and vision, vitamin B1 (thiamine) supports energy metabolism in cells, vitamin B2 (riboflavin) supports energy production, niacin (B3), folic acid, pantothenic acid (B5), vitamin C, which supports iron absorption, and several other vitamins, such as vitamin D, which supports bone health.

Plant-based diets are a popular part of today's lifestyle and health. If you want to learn more about the benefits of a plant-based diet, consider the following:

1. Metabolic Advantage (Auckland, New Zealand): this is an online help for programmed weight loss that offers various products and consulting services in order to promote healthy eating habits. Services include coaching, nutrition packages, trainers and intermittent fasting plans available through the website.

2. Plant-Based Diet (New York): The Plant-Based Diet is a registered non-profit food education organization dedicated to promoting safe and sustainable diets through public health campaigns and workshops that explore plant-based nutrition from every possible angle. The Plant-Based Diet also offers free resources on its website for both beginners and experienced plant-based diet advocates.

The Plant-Based Journey (London): This is a free six-month online course for those interested in learning more about the health benefits of a plant-based diet. It is led by Dr. Melanie Brown, scientific advisor to the Vegan Society, and is designed to help you explore how this way of life can work for you.

4. Meatless Monday (Washington, D. C.): Meatless Monday is a non-profit organization whose mission is to help reduce global warming, hunger and poverty by encouraging people to eat more plant-based foods. Their motto is "1 day a week, eliminate meat."

5. The China Study (California): This is an online resource that provides free access to The China Study, a groundbreaking book by Dr. T. Colin Campbell and his son Dr. Thomas M. Campbell II that describes the relationship between nutrition and heart disease, diabetes and cancer with detailed information on diet and lifestyle changes that have been shown to prevent and reverse these diseases.

6. McDougall Program (California): This is a free 12-week online program that gives you the tools you need to make a difference in your health. It offers an email support group (for participants who have completed the program) and resources to help and guide you on this journey to wellness.

Health Benefits of Plant-Based Diet

• Lower risk for heart disease

• Lower risk for diabetes

• Lower risk for strokes

• Decrease in cholesterol levels

• Decrease in saturated fat levels in the bloodstream, which decreases chances of developing clogged arteries.

A plant-based diet is rich in potassium and low in sodium. It is rich in antioxidants, vitamins, minerals and fiber. The goal of this diet is to provide you with the essential vitamins and nutrients your body needs while avoiding the unnecessary saturated fats and processed sugars that make up the usual American diet.

According to a recent Science Daily article "A new study by UCLA researchers found that people who live on a plant-based diet have an environmental footprint three times smaller than people who follow an average American diet."

Benefits of Plant-Based Protein Powder

Eating plant-based proteins can be a powerful tool to improve your health and propel you toward a more balanced and sustainable lifestyle.

Most people think that the way to get enough protein is to eat meat, but animal meat contains a lot of unhealthy fats and large amounts of animal protein.

At the same time, plant-based proteins, such as soy, beans and quinoa, are rich in healthy dietary fiber and essential nutrients such as iron and calcium. Plant-based protein sources also promote a more sustainable food model that does not endanger the environment.

However, keep in mind that not all plant-based proteins are the same. So to reap the full benefits of plant protein power, be sure to take a look at the following four nutritional powerhouses:

Sunflower seeds are an excellent source of essential fatty acids and vitamin E, which help maintain a healthy complexion. Sunflower seeds are also an excellent source of vitamin B12, which helps maintain energy levels and reduce depression and fatigue.

Peanut butter is a great source of niacin, an essential vitamin that helps protect the skin from harmful UV rays. It is also rich in folate and protein, which keep the body strong and resilient.

Tofu, or soybean curd, has the highest levels of plant-based protein - one cup contains 20 grams - as well as calcium and iron. Tofu is also a great source of healthy omega-3s.

Quinoa, like tofu, is an excellent source of plant-based protein. In fact, it contains more protein by volume than any other grain. Quinoa also provides a healthy blend of vitamins and minerals that are essential for producing the optimal skin type.

The main benefits provided by the power of plant-based proteins include:

Builds muscle and burns fat - When you eat a diet high in carbohydrates and low in fat, you may start to feel sluggish and flabby. However, by increasing your protein intake, especially the high-quality protein found in plant-based foods, you can consume fewer carbohydrates and still have long-term energy.

Boosts energy and metabolism - When it comes to improving metabolism, protein is an elusive little nutrient. It boosts your energy by speeding up your metabolism as it helps burn fat and build muscle.

Improves skin quality - Healthy, glowing skin is the result of many factors, such as age, genetics and lifestyle. However, good nutrition plays a very important role in maintaining smooth, beautiful skin from the inside out. A diet rich in vitamins and minerals can help improve the complexion and at the same time ensure that deficiencies do not occur.

Aids digestion and weight loss - While consuming too much animal protein can lead to digestive problems, plant proteins are easier to digest.

There are no side effects from consuming too much plant protein as there would be with animal meat. And as for weight loss, research studies have shown that eating more plant-based protein results in a reduction in body fat percentage and a decrease in appetite.

Reduces hunger and improves mood - Since many of the foods consumed today are high in carbohydrates and processed, they can lead to cravings throughout the day and an increased appetite. This leads to overeating and, over time, weight gain. Eating plenty of protein-rich foods can help you feel more satiated for longer, which will help you avoid unhealthy snacking and weight gain.

At the same time, the power of plant proteins can also improve your mood. Low levels of serotonin in the brain have been linked to depression and irritability. Eating foods rich in serotonin and other mood-enhancing nutrients can help put you in a better mood and keep your body happy.

The Ideal Plant-Based Cuisine

To supplement your plant-based diet you're also going to need some basic tools for your kitchen.

Blender - many of the foods need to be pureed or made into a smoothie. A blender with at least three speeds is the best choice.

Food processor - a good food processor with a paddle attachment as well as other blending attachments is a good choice. It should have at least three speeds and a pulse mode. If you can, get a food processor with a blender jug - two appliances in one!

Salad bowls: you should have at least two salad bowls of different sizes and some smaller plates to serve the salad.

Mixing bowls: one large, one medium and one small bowl are essential in any kitchen. Especially when preparing homemade sauces.

Blender: a good full-size blender is a must in every kitchen. They are magical utensils that can fluff egg substitutes to their peak and remove lumps from any sauce.

Frying pans: large and medium nonstick pans are best; make sure they have lids.

Pans: at least three pans of different sizes, from small to large, with lids.

Cheese grater: one or two cheese graters with regular and fine grating sides.

Vegetable peeler: one or two sharp potato peelers are a must in any kitchen.

Julienne peeler: a julienne peeler is very useful for working with fresh vegetables or soups.

Wooden spoon: No kitchen is complete without a handy wooden spoon. A few of different sizes are an even better choice for the kitchen. Better yet, get a bamboo spoon, as it is more sustainable than wood, usually.

Sharp knives - you always need a knife block with smooth, serrated edges of all shapes and sizes.

Cutting boards - you need various shapes and sizes of cutting boards for cutting different foods. Look for a bamboo version.

Baking trays and baking sheets - you'll need a few different sized baking sheets, loaf pans, pie plates, cake pans and roasting dishes.

Airtight sealable containers: you'll need to invest in a few airtight sealable containers of different shapes and sizes that you can use in the fridge, freezer and cupboard.

Try buying some bottles for storing sauces and trail mixes as well.

21-Day Meal Plan

hoo

	Monday	Tuesday	Wednesday	Thursday	Friday	Saturday	Sunday
Breakfast	Max Power Smoothie	Chai Chia Smoothie	Trope-Kale Breeze	Hydration Station	Mango Madness	Chocolate PB Smoothie	Pink Panther Smoothie
Lunch	Black Bean Lentil Salad	Cabbage Salad with Seitan	Chickpeas Avocado Salad	Cold Peanut Noodle Salad	Butternut Squash Black Rice Bean Salad	Arugula Beans Salad	Spring Salad
Dinner	Cannellini Pesto Spaghetti	Spicy Eggplant Penne	Creamed Kimchi Pasta	Roasted Ragu with Whole Wheat Linguine	Penne with Swiss Chard and Olives	Indonesia Green Noodle Salad	Noodles with Red Lentil Curry
Dessert	Zesty orange-cranberry energy bites	Chocolate and walnut farfalle	Almond-date energy bites	Pumpkin Pie Cups (Pressure Cooker)	Granola-stuffed baked apples	Better pecan bars	Chocolate-almond bars

Week 2

	Monday	Tuesday	Wednesday	Thursday	Friday	Saturday	Sunday
Breakfast	Banana Nut Smoothie	Overnight Oats On the Go	Oatmeal Breakfast Cookies	Sunshine Muffins	Applesauce Crumble Muffins	Baked Banana French Toast with Raspberry Syrup	Cinnamon Apple Toast
Lunch	Tomato Lentil Salad	White Bean & Tomato Salad	Avocado & White Bean Salad	Brussels Sprouts Salad	Wedge Salad	Chef Salad	Radish Avocado Salad
Dinner	Tomato and Black Bean Rotini	Lemony Broccoli Penne	Singapore Rice Noodles	Ponzu Pea Rice Noodle Salad	Thai Tofu Noodles	Sesame Soba Noodles with Vegetables	Lemon Bow Tie Pasta
Dessert	Coconut and almond truffles	Pecan and date-stuffed roasted pears	Lime-macerated mangos	Fudgy brownies (pressure cooker)	Chocolate-banana fudge	Chocolate–almond butter truffles	Chocolate macaroons

Week 3

	Monday	Tuesday	Wednesday	Thursday	Friday	Saturday	Sunday
Breakfast	Muesli and Berries Bowl	Chocolate Quinoa Breakfast Bowl	Fruit Salad with Zesty Citrus Couscous	Fruity Granola	Chickpea Scramble	Roasted Veg with Creamy Avocado Dip	Spinach Artichoke Quiche
Lunch	Mix Grain Salad	Quinoa and Chickpea Salad	Rice and Tofu Salad	Kidney Bean and Pomegranate Salad	Corn and Bean Salad	Cherry Tomato Couscous Salad	Spicy Watermelon Tomato Salad
Dinner	Shiitake and Bean Sprout Ramen	Spinach Roselle Provençale	Sumptuous Shiitake Udo Noodles	Tomato and Artichoke Rigatoni	Tomato Spaghetti	Noodle Salad with Spinach	Garlic & White Wine Pasta
Dessert	Chocolate pudding	Avocado pudding	Almond butter brownies	Raspberry chia pudding	Chocolate fudge	Quick Chocó brownie	Cinnamon Coconut Chips

Measurement Conversion

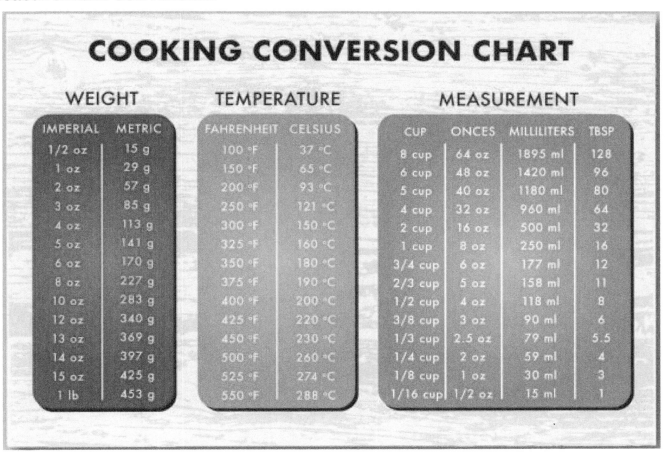

CHAPTER 1:

Breakfast

1. Max Power Smoothie

Preparation Time: 5 minutes

Cooking Time: 0 minutes

Servings: 3-4 cups

Ingredients:

- 1 banana
- ¼ cup rolled oats or 1 scoop plant protein powder
- 1 tablespoon flaxseed or chia seeds
- 1 cup raspberries or other berries
- 1 cup chopped mango (frozen or fresh)
- ½ cup non-dairy milk (optional)
- 1 cup water

Bonus Boosters (Optional)

- 2 tablespoons fresh parsley, or basil, chopped
- 1 cup chopped fresh kale, spinach, collards, or other green
- 1 carrot, peeled
- 1 tablespoon grated fresh ginger

Directions:

1. Purée everything in a blender until smooth, adding more water (or non-dairy milk) if needed.
2. Add none, some, or all of the bonus boosters, as desired. Purée until blended.

Make ahead: Buy extra bananas so that when they ripen you can peel them and put them in the freezer. Frozen bananas make for max creaminess in your smoothie.

Nutrition Per Serving (3 to 4 cups)

Calories: 550; Total fat: 9g; Carbs: 116g; Fiber: 29g; Protein: 13g

2. Chai Chia Smoothie

Preparation Time: 5 minutes

Cooking Time: 0 minutes

Servings: 3 cups

Ingredients:

- 1 banana
- ½ cup coconut milk
- 1 cup water
- 1 cup alfalfa sprouts (optional)
- 1 to 2 soft Medjool dates, pitted
- 1 tablespoon chia seeds, or ground flax or hemp hearts
- ¼ teaspoon ground cinnamon
- Pinch ground cardamom
- 1 tablespoon grated fresh ginger or ¼ teaspoon ground ginger

Directions:

1. Purée everything in a blender until smooth, adding more water (or coconut milk) if needed.
2. Did you know? Although dates are super sweet, they don't cause a large blood sugar spike. They're great to boost sweetness while also boosting your intake of fiber and potassium.

Nutrition Per Serving (3 cups)

Calories: 477; Total fat: 29g; Carbs: 57g; Fiber: 14g; Protein: 8g

3. Trope-Kale Breeze

Preparation Time: 5 minutes

Cooking Time: 0 minutes

Servings: 3-4 cups

Ingredients:

- 1 cup chopped pineapple (frozen or fresh)
- 1 cup chopped mango (frozen or fresh)
- ½ to 1 cup chopped kale
- ½ avocado
- ½ cup coconut milk
- 1 cup water or coconut water
- 1 teaspoon matcha green tea powder (optional)

Directions:

1. Purée everything in a blender until smooth, adding more water (or coconut milk) if needed.

Did you know? Matcha green tea powder contains catechins, which minimize inflammation and maximize fat-burning potential.

Nutrition Per Serving (3 to 4 cups)

Nutrition: Calories: 566; Total fat: 36g; Carbs: 66g; Fiber: 12g; Protein: 8g

4. Hydration Station

Preparation Time: 5 minutes

Cooking Time: 0 minutes

Servings: 3-4 cups

Ingredients:

- 1 banana
- 1 orange, peeled and sectioned, or 1 cup pure orange juice
- 1 cup strawberries (frozen or fresh)
- 1 cup chopped cucumber
- ½ cup coconut water
- 1 cup water
- ½ cup ice

Bonus Boosters (Optional)

- 1 cup chopped spinach
- ¼ cup fresh mint, chopped

Directions:

1. Purée everything in a blender until smooth, adding more water if needed.
2. Add bonus boosters, as desired. Purée until blended.

Make ahead: Pour your smoothie in an insulated travel mug or thermos to keep it chilled if you're on the go.

Nutrition Per Serving (3 to 4 cups)

Calories: 320; Total fat: 3g; Carbs: 76g; Fiber: 13g; Protein: 6g

5. Mango Madness

Preparation Time: 5 minutes

Cooking Time: 0 minutes

Servings: 3-4 cups

Ingredients:

- 1 banana
- 1 cup chopped mango (frozen or fresh)
- 1 cup chopped peach (frozen or fresh)
- 1 cup strawberries
- 1 carrot, peeled and chopped (optional)
- 1 cup water

Directions:

1. Purée everything in a blender until smooth, adding more water if needed.

Options: If you can't find frozen peaches and fresh ones are not in season, use extra mango or strawberries, or try cantaloupe.

Nutrition Per Serving (3 to 4 cups)

Calories: 376; Total fat: 2g; Carbs: 95g; Fiber: 14g; Protein: 5g

6. Chocolate PB Smoothie

Preparation Time: 5 minutes

Cooking Time: 0 minutes

Servings: 3-4 cups

Ingredients:

- 1 banana
- ¼ cup rolled oats or 1 scoop plant protein powder
- 1 tablespoon flaxseed or chia seeds
- 1 tablespoon unsweetened cocoa powder
- 1 tablespoon peanut butter, or almond or sunflower seed butter
- 1 tablespoon maple syrup (optional)
- 1 cup alfalfa sprouts or spinach, chopped (optional)
- ½ cup non-dairy milk (optional)
- 1 cup water

Bonus Boosters (Optional)

- 1 teaspoon maca powder
- 1 teaspoon cocoa nibs

Directions:

1. Purée everything in a blender until smooth, adding more water (or non-dairy milk) if needed.
2. Add bonus boosters, as desired. Purée until blended.

Did you know? Flavones found in cocoa appear to help protect our blood vessel linings, and postmenopausal women seem to reap the most cardiovascular benefits from consuming cocoa.

Nutrition Per Serving (3 to 4 cups)

Calories: 474; Total fat: 16g; Carbs: 79g; Fiber: 18g; Protein: 13g

7. Pink Panther Smoothie

Preparation Time: 5 minutes

Cooking Time: 0 minutes

Servings: 3 cups

Ingredients:

- 1 cup strawberries
- 1 cup chopped melon (any kind)
- 1 cup cranberries or raspberries
- 1 tablespoon chia seeds
- ½ cup coconut milk, or other non-dairy milk
- 1 cup water

Bonus Boosters (Optional)

- 1 teaspoon goji berries
- 2 tablespoons fresh mint, chopped

Directions:

1. Purée everything in a blender until smooth, adding more water (or coconut milk) if needed.
2. Add bonus boosters, as desired. Purée until blended.

Options: If you don't have (or don't like) coconut, try using sunflower seeds for an immune boost of zinc and selenium.

Nutrition Per Serving (3 cups)

Calories: 459; Total fat: 30g; Carbs: 52g; Fiber: 19g; Protein: 8g

8. Banana Nut Smoothie

Preparation Time: 5 minutes

Cooking Time: 0 minutes

Serving: 2 to 3 cups

Ingredients:

- 1 banana
- 1 tablespoon almond butter or sunflower seed butter

- ¼ teaspoon ground cinnamon
- Pinch ground nutmeg
- 1 to 2 tablespoons dates or maple syrup
- 1 tablespoon ground flaxseed, or chia, or hemp hearts
- ½ cup non-dairy milk (optional)
- 1 cup water

Directions:

1. Purée everything in a blender until smooth, adding more water (or non-dairy milk) if needed.

Options: You could make this a pumpkin spice smoothie by adding 1 cup cooked pumpkin and a pinch of allspice.

Nutrition Per Serving (2 to 3 cups)

Calories: 343; Total fat: 14g; Carbs: 55g; Fiber: 8g; Protein: 6g

9. Overnight Oats On the Go

Preparation Time: 5 minutes

Cooking Time: 5 minutes

Servings: 1

Ingredients:

Basic Overnight Oats

- ½ cup rolled oats, or quinoa flakes for gluten-free
- 1 tablespoon ground flaxseed, or chia seeds, or hemp hearts
- 1 tablespoon maple syrup or coconut sugar (optional)
- ¼ teaspoon ground cinnamon (optional)

Topping Options

- 1 apple, chopped, and 1 tablespoon walnuts
- 2 tablespoons dried cranberries and 1 tablespoon pumpkin seeds
- 1 pear, chopped, and 1 tablespoon cashews
- 1 cup sliced grapes and 1 tablespoon sunflower seeds
- 1 banana, sliced, and 1 tablespoon peanut butter
- 2 tablespoons raisins and 1 tablespoon hazelnuts
- 1 cup berries and 1 tablespoon unsweetened coconut flakes

Directions:

1. Mix the oats, flax, maple syrup, and cinnamon (if using) in a bowl or to-go container (a travel mug or short thermos works beautifully).
2. Pour enough cool water over the oats to submerge them, and stir to combine. Leave to soak for a minimum of half an hour or overnight.

3. Add your choice of toppings.

Quick morning option: Boil about ½ cup of water and pour over the oats. Let them soak about 5 minutes before eating.

Did you know? Cinnamon has been shown to help control blood sugar levels, improve insulin response, and reduce triglycerides, LDL (bad) cholesterol, and total cholesterol.

Nutrition Per Serving (Basic)

Calories: 244; Total fat: 6g; Carbs: 30g; Fiber: 6g; Protein: 7g

Nutrition Per Serving (Apple and Walnut version)

Calories: 401; Total fat: 15g; Carbs: 63g; Fiber: 10g; Protein: 10g

10. Oatmeal Breakfast Cookies

Preparation Time: 15 minutes

Cooking Time: 12 minutes

Servings: 5 big cookies

Ingredients:

- 1 tablespoon ground flaxseed
- 2 tablespoons almond butter or sunflower seed butter
- 2 tablespoons maple syrup
- 1 banana, mashed
- 1 teaspoon ground cinnamon
- ¼ teaspoon ground nutmeg (optional)
- Pinch sea salt
- ½ cup rolled oats
- ¼ cup raisins, or dark chocolate chips

Directions:

1. Preheat the oven to 350°F. Line a large baking sheet with parchment paper.
2. Mix the ground flax with just enough water to cover it in a small dish, and leave it to sit.
3. In a large bowl, mix the almond butter and maple syrup until creamy, then add the banana. Add the flax-water mixture.
4. Sift the cinnamon, nutmeg, and salt into a separate medium bowl, then stir into the wet mixture.
5. Add the oats and raisins, and fold in.
6. From 3 to 4 tablespoons of batter into a ball and press lightly to flatten onto the baking sheet. Repeat, spacing the cookies 2 to 3 inches apart.
7. Bake for 12 minutes, or until golden brown.
8. Store the cookies in an airtight container in the fridge, or freeze them for later.

Make ahead: The quantity here is for one person, so you don't have too many cookies lying around to tempt you. But they're great to double for a full batch of snacks.

Nutrition Per Serving (1 cookie)

Calories: 192; Total fat: 6g; Carbs: 34g; Fiber: 4g; Protein: 4g

11. Sunshine Muffins

Preparation Time: 15 minutes

Cooking Time: 30 minutes

Servings: 6 muffins

Ingredients:

- 1 teaspoon coconut oil for greasing muffin tins (optional)
- 2 tablespoons almond butter or sunflower seed butter
- ¼ cup non-dairy milk
- 1 orange, peeled
- 1 carrot, coarsely chopped
- 2 tablespoons chopped dried apricots, or other dried fruit
- 3 tablespoons molasses
- 2 tablespoons ground flaxseed
- 1 teaspoon apple cider vinegar
- 1 teaspoon pure vanilla extract
- 1/2 teaspoon ground cinnamon
- 1/2 teaspoon ground ginger (optional)
- 1/4 teaspoon ground nutmeg (optional)
- ¼ teaspoon allspice (optional)
- ¾ cup rolled oats or whole-grain flour
- 1 teaspoon baking powder
- ½ teaspoon baking soda

Mix-Ins (Optional)

- ½ cup rolled oats
- 2 tablespoons raisins or other chopped dried fruit
- 2 tablespoons sunflower seeds

Directions:

1. Preheat the oven to 350°F. Prepare a 6-cup muffin tin by rubbing the insides of the cups with coconut oil or using silicone or paper muffin cups.
2. Purée the nut butter, milk, orange, carrot, apricots, molasses, flaxseed, vinegar, vanilla, cinnamon, ginger, nutmeg, and allspice in a food processor or blender until somewhat smooth.
3. Grind the oats in a clean coffee grinder until they're the consistency of flour (or use whole-grain flour). In a large bowl, mix the oats with the baking powder and baking soda.

4. Mix the wet ingredients into the dry ingredients until just combined. Fold in the mix-ins (if using).
5. Spoon about ¼ cup of batter into each muffin cup and bake for 30 minutes, or until a toothpick inserted into the center comes out clean. The orange creates a very moist base, so the muffins may take longer than 30 minutes, depending on how heavy your muffin tin is.

Leftovers: Store the muffins in the fridge or freezer, because they are so moist. If you plan to keep them frozen, you can easily double the batch for a full dozen.

Nutrition Per Serving (1 muffin)

Calories: 287; Total fat: 12g; Carbs: 41g; Fiber: 6g; Protein: 8g

12. Applesauce Crumble Muffins

Preparation Time: 15 minutes

Cooking Time: 15 to 20 minutes

Servings: 12 muffins

Ingredients:

- 1 teaspoon coconut oil for greasing muffin tins (optional)
- 2 tablespoons nut butter or seed butter
- 1½ cup unsweetened applesauce
- 1/3 cup coconut sugar
- ½ cup non-dairy milk
- 2 tablespoons ground flaxseed
- 1 teaspoon apple cider vinegar
- 1 teaspoon pure vanilla extract
- 2 cups whole-grain flour
- 1 teaspoon baking soda
- ½ teaspoon baking powder
- 1 teaspoon ground cinnamon
- Pinch sea salt
- ½ cup walnuts, chopped

Toppings (Optional)

- ¼ cup walnuts
- ¼ cup coconut sugar
- ½ teaspoon ground cinnamon

Directions:

1. Preheat the oven to 350°F. Prepare two 6-cup muffin tins by rubbing the insides of the cups with coconut oil or using silicone or paper muffin cups.
2. In a large bowl, mix the nut butter, applesauce, coconut sugar, milk, flaxseed, vinegar, and vanilla until thoroughly combined or purée in a food processor or blender.

3. In another large bowl, sift together the flour, baking soda, baking powder, cinnamon, salt, and chopped walnuts.
4. Mix the dry ingredients into the wet ingredients until just combined.
5. Spoon about ¼ cup of batter into each muffin cup and sprinkle with the topping of your choice (if using). Bake for 15 to 20 minutes, or until a toothpick inserted into the center comes out clean. The applesauce creates a very moist base, so the muffins may take longer, depending on how heavy your muffin tins are.

Options: To make this nut-free, swap the walnuts for sunflower seeds and use sunflower seed butter.

Nutrition Per Serving (1 muffin)

Calories: 287; Total fat: 12g; Carbs: 41g; Fiber: 6g; Protein: 8g

13. Baked Banana French Toast with Raspberry Syrup

Preparation Time: 10 minutes

Cooking Time: 30 minutes

Servings: 8 slices

For The French Toast

- 1 banana
- 1 cup coconut milk
- 1 teaspoon pure vanilla extract
- ¼ teaspoon ground nutmeg
- ½ teaspoon ground cinnamon
- 1½ teaspoons arrowroot powder or flour
- Pinch sea salt
- 8 slices whole-grain bread

For The Raspberry Syrup

- 1 cup fresh or frozen raspberries, or other berries
- 2 tablespoons water, or pure fruit juice
- 1 to 2 tablespoons maple syrup or coconut sugar (optional)

Directions:

To Make The French Toast

1. Preheat the oven to 350°F.
2. In a shallow bowl, purée or mash the banana well. Mix in the coconut milk, vanilla, nutmeg, cinnamon, arrowroot, and salt.
3. Dip the slices of bread in the banana mixture, and then lay them out in a 13-by-9-inch baking dish. They should cover the bottom of the dish and can overlap a bit but shouldn't be stacked on top of each other. Pour any leftover banana mixture over the bread, and put the dish in the oven. Bake for about 30 minutes or until the tops are lightly browned.
4. Serve topped with raspberry syrup.

To Make The Raspberry Syrup

1. Heat the raspberries in a small pot with the water and the maple syrup (if using) on medium heat.
2. Leave to simmer, stirring occasionally and breaking up the berries for 15 to 20 minutes until the liquid has reduced.

Leftovers: Leftover raspberry syrup makes a great topping for simple oatmeal as a quick and delicious breakfast or as a drizzle on top of whole-grain toast smeared with natural peanut butter.

Nutrition Per Serving (1 slice with syrup)

Calories: 166; Total fat: 7g; Carbs: 23g; Fiber: 4g; Protein: 5g

14. Cinnamon Apple Toast

Preparation Time: 5 minutes

Cooking Time: 10 to 20 minutes

Servings: 2 slices

Ingredients:

- 1 to 2 teaspoons coconut oil
- ½ teaspoon ground cinnamon
- 1 tablespoon maple syrup or coconut sugar
- 1 apple, cored and thinly sliced
- 2 slices whole-grain bread

Directions:

1. In a large bowl, mix the coconut oil, cinnamon, and maple syrup together. Add the apple slices and toss with your hands to coat them.
2. To panfry the toast, place the apple slices in a medium skillet on medium-high and cook for about 5 minutes, or until slightly soft, then transfer to a plate. Cook the bread in the same skillet for 2 to 3 minutes on each side. Top the toast with the apples. Alternately, you can bake the toast. Use your hands to rub each slice of bread with some of the coconut oil mixture on both sides. Lay them on a small baking sheet, top with the coated apples, and put in the oven or toaster oven at 350°F for 15 to 20 minutes, or until the apples have softened.

Options: For a more everyday version, toast the bread, spread with nut butter, top with apple slices, and sprinkle with a pinch of cinnamon and coconut sugar.

Nutrition Per Serving (1 slice)

Calories: 187; Total fat: 8g; Carbs: 27g; Fiber: 4g; Protein: 4g

15.   Muesli and Berries Bowl

Preparation Time: 10 minutes
Cooking Time: 0 minutes
Servings: 5 cups
Ingredients:
For The Muesli

- 1 cup rolled oats
- 1 cup spelt flakes, or quinoa flakes, or more rolled oats
- 2 cups puffed cereal
- ¼ cup sunflower seeds
- ¼ cup almonds
- ¼ cup raisins
- ¼ cup dried cranberries
- ¼ cup chopped dried figs
- ¼ cup unsweetened shredded coconut
- ¼ cup non-dairy chocolate chips
- 1 to 3 teaspoons ground cinnamon

For The Bowl

- ½ cup non-dairy milk, or unsweetened applesauce
- ¾ cup muesli
- ½ cup berries

Directions:
1. Put the muesli ingredients in a container or bag and shake.
2. Combine the muesli and bowl ingredients in a bowl or to-go container.

Substitutions: Try chopped Brazil nuts, peanuts, dried cranberries, dried blueberries, dried mango, or whatever inspires you. Ginger and cardamom are interesting flavors if you want to branch out on spices.

Nutrition Per Serving (1 bowl)
Calories: 441; Total fat: 20g; Carbs: 63g; Fiber: 13g; Protein: 10g

16.   Chocolate Quinoa Breakfast Bowl

Preparation Time: 5 minutes
Cooking Time: 30 minutes
Servings: 2
Ingredients:

- 1 cup quinoa
- 1 teaspoon ground cinnamon
- 1 cup non-dairy milk
- 1 cup water
- 1 large banana

- 2 to 3 tablespoons unsweetened cocoa powder or carob
- 1 to 2 tablespoons almond butter or other nut or seed butter
- 1 tablespoon ground flaxseed, or chia or hemp seeds
- 2 tablespoons walnuts
- ¼ cup raspberries

Directions:
1. Put the quinoa, cinnamon, milk, and water in a medium pot. Bring to a boil over high heat, then turn down low and simmer, covered, for 25 to 30 minutes.
2. While the quinoa is simmering, purée or mash the banana in a medium bowl and stir in the cocoa powder, almond butter, and flaxseed.
3. To serve, spoon 1 cup of cooked quinoa into a bowl, top with half the pudding and half the walnuts and raspberries.

Make ahead: This is a great way to use leftover quinoa or plan ahead and make extra quinoa for dinner, so you can whip this together on a weekday morning as quickly as you would a smoothie.

Nutrition Per Serving (1 bowl)
Calories: 392; Total fat: 19g; Carbs: 49g; Fiber: 10g; Protein: 12g

17. Fruit Salad with Zesty Citrus Couscous

Preparation Time: 5 minutes
Cooking Time: 5 minutes
Serving: 1
Ingredients:

- 1 orange, zested and juiced
- ¼ cup whole-wheat couscous, or corn couscous
- 1 cup assorted berries (strawberries, blackberries, blueberries)
- ½ cup cubed or balled melon (cantaloupe or honeydew)
- 1 tablespoon maple syrup or coconut sugar (optional)
- 1 tablespoon fresh mint, minced (optional)
- 1 tablespoon unsweetened coconut flakes

Directions:
1. Put the orange juice in a small pot, add half the zest, and bring to a boil.
2. Put the dry couscous in a small bowl and pour the boiling orange juice over it. If there isn't enough juice to fully submerge the couscous, add just enough boiling water to do so. Cover the

bowl with a plate or seal with wrap, and let steep for 5 minutes.

3. In a medium bowl, toss the berries and melon with the maple syrup (if using) and the rest of the zest. You can either keep the fruit cool or heat it lightly in the small pot you used for the orange juice.

4. When the couscous is soft, remove the cover and fluff it with a fork. Top with fruit, fresh mint, and coconut.

Options: This would also be fantastic with cooked quinoa instead of couscous. Just leave it to marinate with the orange juice while you prepare the fruit.

Nutrition Per Serving

Calories: 496; Total fat: 10g; Carbs: 97g; Fiber: 14g; Protein: 11g

18.   Fruity Granola

Preparation Time: 15 minutes

Cooking Time: 45 minutes

Servings: 5 cups

Ingredients:

- 2 cups rolled oats
- ¾ cup whole-grain flour
- 1 tablespoon ground cinnamon
- 1 teaspoon ground ginger (optional)
- ½ cup sunflower seeds, or walnuts, chopped
- ½ cup almonds, chopped
- ½ cup pumpkin seeds
- ½ cup unsweetened shredded coconut
- 1¼ cup pure fruit juice (cranberry, apple, or something similar)
- ½ cup raisins, or dried cranberries
- ½ cup goji berries (optional)

Directions:

1. Preheat the oven to 350°F.
2. Mix the oats, flour, cinnamon, ginger, sunflower seeds, almonds, pumpkin seeds, and coconut in a large bowl.
3. Sprinkle the juice over the mixture, and stir until it's just moistened. You might need a bit more or a bit less liquid, depending on how much your oats and flour absorb.
4. Spread the granola on a large baking sheet (the more spread out it is, the better), and put it in the oven. After about 15 minutes, use a spatula to turn the granola so that the middle gets dried out. Let the granola bake until it's as crunchy as you want it, about 30 minutes more.

5. Take the granola out of the oven and stir in the raisins and goji berries (if using).
6. Store leftovers in an airtight container for up to 2 weeks.

Leftovers: Serve with non-dairy milk and fresh fruit, use as a topper for morning porridge or a smoothie bowl to add a bit of crunch, or make a granola parfait by layering with non-dairy yogurt or puréed banana.

Nutrition Per Serving (½ cup)

Calories: 398; Total fat: 25g; Carbs: 39g; Fiber: 8g; Protein: 11g

19.   Chickpea Scramble

Preparation Time: 5 minutes

Cooking Time: 15 minutes

Servings: 1

Ingredients:

- 1 teaspoon olive oil, or 1 tablespoon vegetable broth or water
- ½ cup mushrooms, sliced
- Pinch sea salt - ½ cup chopped zucchini
- ½ cup chickpeas (cooked or canned)
- 1 teaspoon smoked paprika or regular paprika
- 1 teaspoon turmeric
- 1 tablespoon nutritional yeast (optional)
- Freshly ground black pepper
- ½ cup cherry tomatoes, chopped
- ¼ cup fresh parsley, chopped

Directions:

1. Heat a large skillet to medium-high. Once the skillet is hot, add the olive oil and mushrooms, along with the sea salt to help them soften, and sauté, stirring occasionally, for 7 to 8 minutes.
2. Add the zucchini to the skillet.
3. If you're using canned chickpeas, rinse and drain them. Mash the chickpeas with a potato masher, fork, or your fingers. Add them to the skillet and cook until they are heated through.
4. Sprinkle the paprika, turmeric, and nutritional yeast over the chickpeas, and stir to combine.
5. Toss in the black pepper, cherry tomatoes, and fresh parsley at the end, just to warm, reserving a small bit of parsley to use as garnish.

Did You Know? Nutritional yeast is a yellow flaky seasoning with a savory and salty flavor. Most regular grocery stores carry it these days. Vegans often use it to add a cheesy or deeply savory taste to foods like popcorn.

Nutrition Per Serving

Calories: 265; Total fat: 8g; Carbs: 37g; Fiber: 12g; Protein: 16g

20. Roasted Veg with Creamy Avocado Dip

Preparation Time: 10 minutes

Cooking Time: 30 minutes

Servings: 2

Ingredients:

For The Avocado Dip

- 1 avocado
- 1 tablespoon apple cider vinegar
- ¼ to ½ cup water
- 2 tablespoons nutritional yeast
- 1 teaspoon dried dill or 1 tablespoon fresh dill
- Pinch sea salt

For The Roasted Veg

- 1 small sweet potato, peeled and cubed
- 2 small beets, peeled and cubed
- 2 small carrots, peeled and cubed
- 1 teaspoon sea salt
- 1 teaspoon dried oregano
- ¼ teaspoon cayenne pepper
- Pinch freshly ground black pepper

Directions:

To Make The Avocado Dip

1. In a blender, purée the avocado with the other dip ingredients, using just enough water to get a smooth, creamy texture. Alternately, you can mash the avocado thoroughly in a large bowl, then stir in the rest of the dip ingredients.

To Make The Roasted Veg

1. Preheat the oven to 350°F.
2. Put the sweet potato, beets, and carrots in a large pot with a small amount of water, and bring to a boil over high heat. Boil for 15 minutes until they're just barely soft, then drain. Sprinkle the salt, oregano, cayenne, and pepper over them and stir gently to combine. (Use more or less cayenne depending on your taste.)
3. Spread the vegetables on a large baking sheet and roast them in the oven for 10 to 15 minutes until they've browned around the edges.
4. Serve the veg with the avocado dip on the side.

Make ahead: Make the roasted veg in large batches so that you have them on hand through the week to add to salads, bowls, and wraps.

Nutrition Per Serving

Calories: 335; Total fat: 12g; Carbs: 51g; Fiber: 16g; Protein: 11g

21. Spinach Artichoke Quiche

Preparation Time: 10 minutes

Cooking Time: 55 minutes

Servings: 4

Ingredients

- 14 oz. tofu, soft
- 14 oz. of artichokes, chopped
- 2 cups spinach
- ½ of a large onion, peeled, chopped
- 1 lemon, juiced
- 1 teaspoon minced garlic
- ¼ teaspoon salt
- ¼ teaspoon ground black pepper
- 1 teaspoon dried basil - ½ teaspoon turmeric
- 1 tablespoon coconut oil
- 1 teaspoon Dijon mustard
- ½ cup nutritional yeast
- 2 large tortillas, cut in half

Directions:

1. Switch on the oven, then set it to 350°f and let it preheat.
2. Take a pie plate, grease it with oil, place tortilla to cover the bottom and sides of the plate, and bake for 10 to 15 minutes until baked.
3. Meanwhile, take a large pan, place it over medium heat, add oil and when hot, add onion and fry for 5 minutes.
4. Then add garlic, cook for 1 minute until fragrant, stir in spinach and cook for 4 minutes until the spinach has wilted, set aside when done.
5. Place tofu in a food processor, add all the spices, yeast, and lemon juice, and pulse for 2 minutes until smooth.
6. Then add the cooked onion mixture and artichokes, blend for 15 to 25 times until combined, and then pour the mixture over the crust on the pie plate.
7. Bake quiche for 45 minutes until done, then cut it into wedges and serve.

Nutrition Per Serving

Calories: 105, Fat 4.7 g, Carbs 25 g, Protein 9.3 g, Fiber 0.7 g

22. Pumpkin Muffins

Preparation Time: 15 minutes

Cooking Time: 30 minutes

Servings: 9

Ingredients

- 2 tablespoons mashed ripe banana

- 3 flax eggs
- 1 teaspoon vanilla extract, unsweetened
- ¼ cup maple syrup - ¼ cup olive oil
- 2/3 cup coconut sugar
- 3/4 cup pumpkin puree
- 1 ¼ teaspoon pumpkin pie spice
- ¼ teaspoon sea salt
- ½ teaspoon ground cinnamon
- 2 teaspoons baking soda
- ½ cup water - ½ cup almond meal
- 1 cup gluten-free flour blend
- 3/4 cup rolled oats

Ingredients for the Crumble

- 2 tablespoons chopped pecans
- 3 ½ tablespoons gluten-free flour blend
- 3 tablespoons coconut sugar
- 1/8 teaspoon cinnamon
- 1/8 teaspoon pumpkin pie spice
- 1 ¼ tablespoon coconut oil

Directions:

1. Switch on the oven, then set it to 350°f and let it preheat.
2. Meanwhile, prepare the muffin batter and for this, place the first seven ingredients in a bowl and whisk until combined.
3. Then whisk in the next five ingredients until mixed and gradually beat in the remaining ingredients until incorporated and smooth batter comes together.
4. Prepare crumble, and for this, place all of its ingredients in a bowl and stir until combined.
5. Distribute the batter evenly between ten muffin tins lined with muffin liners, top with prepared crumble, and then bake for 30 minutes until muffins are set and the tops are golden brown.
6. When done, let muffins cool for 5 minutes, then take them out to cool completely and serve.

Nutrition Per Serving

Calories: 329, Fat 12.7 g, Carbs 52.6 g, Protein 4.6 g, Fiber 5 g

23.   Tomato and Asparagus Quiche

Preparation Time: 40 minutes

Cooking Time: 35 minutes

Servings: 12

Ingredients for the Dough:

- 2 cups whole wheat flour
- ½ teaspoon salt

- 3/4 cup vegan margarine
- 1/3 cup water

Ingredients for the Filling:

- 14 oz. silken tofu
- 6 cherry tomatoes, halved
- 2 green onions, cut into rings
- 10 sun-dried tomatoes in oil, chopped
- 7 oz. green asparagus, diced
- 1 ½ tablespoons herb de Provence
- 1 tablespoon cornstarch
- 1 teaspoon turmeric
- 3 tablespoons olive oil

Directions:

1. Switch on the oven, then set it to 350°f and let it preheat.
2. Prepare the dough and for this, take a bowl, place all the ingredients for it, beat until incorporated, then knead for 5 minutes until smooth, and refrigerate the dough for 30 minutes.
3. Meanwhile, take a skillet pan, place it over medium heat, add 1 tablespoon oil and when hot, add green onion and cook for 2 minutes. Set aside until required.
4. Place a pot half full with salty water over medium heat, bring it to boil, then add asparagus and boil for 3 minutes until tender. Drain and set aside until required.
5. Take a medium bowl, add tofu along with herbs de Provence, starch, turmeric, and oil, whisk until smooth and then fold in tomatoes, green onion, and asparagus until mixed.
6. Divide the prepared dough into twelve sections, take a muffin tray, line twelve cups with baking cups, and then press a dough ball at the bottom of each cup and all the way up.
7. Fill the cups with prepared tofu mixture, top with tomatoes, and bake for 35 minutes until cooked.
8. Serve straight away.

Nutrition Per Serving

Calories: 206, Fat 14 g, Carbs 16 g, Protein 4 g, Fiber 2 g

24.   Simple Vegan Breakfast Hash

Preparation Time: 10 minutes

Cooking Time: 25 minutes

Servings: 4

Ingredients for the Potatoes:

- 1 large sweet potato, peeled, diced
- 3 medium potatoes, peeled, diced
- 1 tablespoon onion powder

- 2 teaspoons sea salt
- 1 tablespoon garlic powder
- 1 teaspoon ground black pepper
- 1 teaspoon dried thyme
- ¼ cup olive oil

Ingredients for The Skillet Mixture:

- 1 medium onion, peeled, diced
- 5 cloves of garlic, peeled, minced
- ¼ teaspoon of sea salt
- ¼ teaspoon ground black pepper
- 1 teaspoon olive oil

Directions:

1. Switch on the oven, then set it to 450°f and let it preheat.
2. Meanwhile, take a casserole dish, add all the ingredients for the potatoes, toss until coated, and then cook for 20 minutes until crispy, stirring halfway.
3. Then take a skillet pan, place it over medium heat, add oil and when hot, add onion and garlic, season with salt and black pepper and cook for 5 minutes until browned.
4. When potatoes have roasted, add garlic and cooked onion mixture, stir until combined, and serve.

Nutrition Per Serving

Calories: 212, Fat 10 g, Carbs 28 g, Protein 3 g, Fiber 4 g

25. Chickpeas On Toast

Preparation Time: 5 minutes
Cooking Time: 15 minutes
Servings: 6
Ingredients

- 14-oz cooked chickpeas
- 1 cup baby spinach
- ½ cup chopped white onion
- 1 cup crushed tomatoes
- ½ teaspoon minced garlic
- ¼ teaspoon ground black pepper
- ½ teaspoon brown sugar
- 1 teaspoon smoked paprika powder
- 1/3 teaspoon sea salt
- 1 tablespoon olive oil
- 6 slices of gluten-free bread, toasted

Directions:

1. Take a frying pan, place it over medium heat, add oil and when hot, add onion and cook for 2 minutes.

2. Then stir in garlic, cook for 30 seconds until fragrant, stir in paprika and continue cooking for 10 seconds.
3. Add tomatoes, stir, bring the mixture to simmer, season with black pepper, sugar, and salt, and then stir in chickpeas.
4. Stir in spinach, cook for 2 minutes until leaves have wilted, then remove the pan from heat and taste to adjust seasoning.
5. Serve cooked chickpeas on toasted bread.

Nutrition Per Serving

Calories: 305, Fat 7.6 g, Carbs 45 g, Protein 13 g, Fiber 8 g

26. Blueberry Muffins

Preparation Time: 5 minutes
Cooking Time: 15 minutes
Servings: 12
Ingredients

- 2 cups fresh blueberries
- 2 cups all-purpose flour
- 2 ½ teaspoons baking powder
- ½ teaspoon salt
- ¼ teaspoon baking soda
- ½ cup and 2 tablespoon sugar
- Zest of 1 lemon
- 1 teaspoon apple cider vinegar
- ¼ cup and 2 tablespoons canola oil
- 1 cup of soy milk
- 1 teaspoon vanilla extract, unsweetened

Directions:

1. Switch on the oven, then set it to 450°f and let it preheat. Meanwhile, take a small bowl, add vinegar and milk, whisk until combined, and let it stand to curdle.
2. Take a large bowl, add flour, salt, baking powder, and soda, and stir until mixed. Whisk in sugar, lemon zest, oil, and vanilla into soy milk mixture, then gradually whisk in flour mixture until incorporated and fold in berries until combined. Take a twelve cups muffin tray, grease them with oil, distribute the prepared batter in them and bake for 25 minutes until done and the tops are browned. Let muffins cool for 5 minutes, then cool them completely and serve.

Nutrition Per Serving

Calories: 160, Fat 5 g, Carbs 25 g, Protein 2 g, Fiber 2 g

27. Ultimate Breakfast Sandwich

Preparation Time: 40 minutes
Cooking Time: 10 minutes
Servings: 4
Ingredients for the Tofu:

- 12 ounces tofu, extra-firm, pressed, drain
- ½ teaspoon garlic powder
- 1 teaspoon liquid smoke
- 2 tablespoons nutritional yeast
- 1 teaspoon Sirach sauce
- 2 tablespoons soy sauce
- 2 tablespoons olive oil
- 2 tablespoons water

Ingredients for the Vegan Breakfast Sandwich:

- 1 large tomato, sliced
- 4 English muffins, halved, toasted
- 1 avocado, mashed

Directions:

1. Prepare tofu, and for this, cut tofu into 4 slices and set aside. Stir together the remaining ingredients of tofu, pour the mixture into a bag, then add tofu pieces, toss until coated, and marinate for 30 minutes. Take a skillet pan, place it over medium-high heat, add tofu slices along with the marinade and cook for 5 minutes per side.
2. Prepare sandwich and for this, spread mashed avocado on the inner of the muffin, top with a slice of tofu, layer with a tomato slice, and then serve.

Nutrition Per Serving
Calories: 277, Fat 9.1 g, Carbs 33.1 g, Protein 16.1 g, Fiber 3.6 g

28. Waffles with Fruits

Preparation Time: 10 minutes
Cooking Time: 20 minutes
Servings: 4
Ingredients

- 1 ¼ cup all-purpose flour
- 2 teaspoons baking powder
- 3 tablespoons sugar
- ¼ teaspoon salt
- 2 teaspoons vanilla extract, unsweetened
- 2 tablespoons coconut oil
- 1 ¼ cup soy milk
- Sliced fruits as desired
- 1 cup Vegan whipping cream

Directions:

1. Switch on the waffle maker and let it preheat. Meanwhile, place flour in a bowl, stir in salt, baking powder, and sugar, and whisk in remaining ingredients, except for topping, until incorporated.
2. Ladle the batter into the waffle maker and cook until firm and brown.
3. When done, top waffles with fruits and whipped cream and serve.

Nutrition Per Serving
Calories: 277, Fat 8.3 g, Carbs 42.5 g, Protein 6.2 g, Fiber 1.5 g

29. Scrambled Tofu Breakfast Burrito

Preparation Time: 15 minutes
Cooking Time: 20 minutes
Servings: 4
Ingredients

- 4 large tortillas
- 1 medium avocado, chopped
- Cilantro as needed
- Salsa as needed

Ingredients for the Tofu:

- 12-ounce tofu, extra-firm, pressed
- ¼ cup minced parsley
- 1 ½ teaspoons minced garlic
- 1 teaspoon nutritional yeast
- ¼ teaspoon sea salt
- ½ teaspoon red chili powder
- ½ teaspoon cumin
- 1 teaspoon olive oil
- 1 tablespoon hummus

Ingredients for the Vegetables:

- 5 baby potatoes, chopped
- 1 medium red bell pepper, sliced
- 2 cups chopped kale
- ½ teaspoon ground cumin
- 1/8 teaspoon sea salt
- ½ teaspoon red chili powder
- 1 teaspoon oil

Directions:

1. Switch on the oven, then set it to 400°f and let it preheat.
2. Take a baking sheet, add potato and bell pepper, drizzle with oil, season with all the spices, toss

until coated, and bake for 15 minutes until tender and nicely browned.

3. Then add kale to the potatoes, cook for 5 minutes, and set aside until required.

4. In the meantime, take a skillet pan, place it over medium heat, add oil and when hot add tofu, crumble it well and cook for 10 minutes until lightly browned.

5. In the meantime, take a small bowl, add hummus and the remaining ingredients for the tofu and stir until combined.

6. Add hummus mixture into tofu, stir and cook for 3 minutes, set aside until required.

7. Assemble the burritos and for this, distribute roasted vegetables on the tortilla, top with tofu, avocado, cilantro, and salsa, roll and then serve.

Nutrition Per Serving

Calories: 441, Fat 19.6 g, Carbs 53.5 g, Protein 16.5 g, Fiber 8 g

30. Pancake

Preparation Time: 10 minutes
Cooking Time: 18 minutes
Servings: 4
Ingredients:
Dry Ingredients:

- 1 cup buckwheat flour
- 1/8 teaspoon salt
- ½ teaspoon gluten-free baking powder
- ½ teaspoon baking soda

Wet Ingredients:

- 1 tablespoon almond butter
- 2 tablespoons maple syrup
- 1 tablespoon lime juice
- 1 cup coconut milk, unsweetened

Directions:

1. Take a medium bowl, add all the dry ingredients and stir until mixed.

2. Take another bowl, place all the wet ingredients, whisk until combined, and then gradually whisk in the dry ingredients mixture until smooth and incorporated.

3. Take a frying pan, place it over medium heat, add 2 teaspoons oil and when hot, drop in batter and cook for 3 minutes per side until cooked and lightly browned.

4. Serve pancakes and fruits and maple syrup.

Nutrition Per Serving

Calories: 148, Fat 8.2 g, Carbs 15 g, Protein 4.6 g, Fiber 1.7 g.

31. Honey Buckwheat Coconut Porridge

Preparation Time: 20 minutes
Cooking Time: 15 minutes
Servings: 2
Ingredients

- ¼ cup buckwheat, toasted, ground
- 1 tablespoon coconut, shredded
- 2 tablespoons pecans, chopped
- ½ cup + 2 tablespoons coconut milk
- 1 tablespoon raw honey
- ¾ teaspoon vanilla
- ¾ cup of water
- 2 tablespoons currants
- 1 drizzle coconut syrup

Directions:

1. In a small pot, boil the coconut milk, honey, vanilla, and water. Stir in the ground buckwheat, then reduce the heat to low.

2. Cook for 10 minutes, covered. Add extra liquid during the cooking if needed.

3. Transfer to a bowl and serve with shredded coconut, pecans, currants, and a drizzle of coconut syrup.

Nutrition Per Serving

Calories: 268, Fat 19.86 g, Carbs 22.33 g, Protein 3.64 g, Fiber 4.1 g.

32. Tempeh and Potato

Preparation Time: 30 minutes
Cooking Time: 20 minutes
Servings: 4
Ingredients:

- 1 package (8 oz) tempeh, finely diced
- 4 red potatoes
- 6 leaves Lacinato kale, stemmed, chopped
- 2 tablespoons olive oil
- 1 medium onion, chopped
- 1 medium green bell pepper, diced
- 1 teaspoon smoked paprika
- 1 teaspoon seasoning, salt-free
- Ground pepper, salt, to taste

Directions:

1. Microwave the potatoes until done but still firm. Finely chop them when cool.

2. Preheat oil in a skillet over medium heat. Sauté onions until translucent. Add tempeh, potatoes and bell pepper,

and sauté, stirring constantly, over medium-high heat until golden brown.

3. Stir in the kale and seasoning, then cook, stirring constantly until the mixture is a bit browned. Occasionally add water to prevent sticking if necessary.

4. Sprinkle with pepper and salt to taste. Serve hot.

Nutrition Per Serving

Calories: 342, Fat 7.41 g, Carbs 64.1 g, Protein 7.84 g, Fiber 7.4 g.

33. Breakfast French Toast

Preparation Time: 5 minutes

Cooking Time: 6 minutes

Servings: 1

Ingredients

- 2 slices bread, gluten-free
- 2 teaspoons cinnamon
- 2 tablespoons flaxseed, ground
- 6 oz. soy milk
- 2 teaspoons vanilla extract
- 1 scoop vegan protein powder

Directions:

1. Mix cinnamon, flaxseed, soy milk, vanilla extract, and protein powder in a deep baking dish. Deep the bread slices into the mixture to coat.

2. Preheat a non-stick frying pan over medium heat and toast the bread for 3 minutes per side. Enjoy!

Nutrition Per Serving

Calories: 506, Fat 15.99 g, Carbs 52.99 g, Protein 35.24g, Fiber 12.5 g.

34. Dairy-Free Pumpkin Pancakes

Preparation Time: 10 minutes

Cooking Time: 10 minutes

Servings: 12

Ingredients

- 1-cup all-purpose flour
- 2 teaspoons baking powder
- ½ cup pumpkin puree
- 1 egg
- 3 tablespoons chia seeds
- 3 tablespoons coconut oil, melted, slightly cooled
- 1 cup almond milk
- 2 teaspoons vanilla extract
- 1 tablespoon white vinegar
- 1 tablespoon maple syrup
- 1 teaspoon pumpkin pie spice
- ½ teaspoon kosher salt

Directions:

1. Combine almond milk and vinegar in a bowl. Let it rest for 5 minutes.

2. Mix flour, baking powder, baking soda, chia seeds, pumpkin pie spice, and salt in a separate bowl.

3. Whisk eggs into the almond milk, then stir in pumpkin puree, coconut oil, vanilla, and maple syrup.

4. Pour the wet ingredients into the dry ingredients and mix until blended. Add in more almond milk if the batter is thick.

5. Place a non-stick frying pan over medium heat. Scoop out 1/3 of the batter and pour it into the pan. Cook for 1 minute, then flip to the other side and cook until golden brown. Do this with the remaining batter and serve.

Nutrition Per Serving

Calories: 124, Fat 6.99 g, Carbs 12.34 g, Protein 3.43g, Fiber 0.7 g.

35. Protein Blueberry Bars

Preparation Time: 1 hour

Cooking Time: 5 minutes

Servings: 16

Ingredients

- ½ cup dried blueberries
- 1 ½ cup rolled oats
- ¾ cup whole almonds
- 1/3 cup ground flaxseed
- 1/3 cup walnuts
- ¼ cup sunflower seeds
- ½ cup pistachios
- 1/3 cup pepitas
- ¼ cup apple sauce
- 1/3 cup maple syrup
- 1 cup almond butter

Directions:

1. In a bowl, mix rolled oats, blueberries, almonds, flaxseed, walnuts, sunflower seeds, pistachios and pepitas together.

2. Stir in apple sauce and maple syrup. Mix in almond butter, then pour the batter into a baking sheet lined with parchment paper (paper should be big enough to cover and hang over the baking sheet edges). Firmly press down the batter using your palms, then spread evenly.

3. Refrigerate for 1 hour. Remove from the freezer afterward and lift the batter from the pan by lifting from the paper. Place on a working surface and gently remove the paper. Cut the dough into 16 bars and serve.

Nutrition Per Serving

Calories: 221, Fat 15.96 g, Carbs 18.26 g, Protein 7.77g, Fiber 5 g.

36. Chickpea Scramble Breakfast Basin

Preparation Time:

Cooking Time: 10 minutes

Servings: 2

Ingredients

For chickpea scramble:

- 1 can (15 oz.) chickpeas
- A drizzle olive oil
- ¼ white onion, diced
- 2 garlic cloves, minced
- ½ teaspoon turmeric
- ½ teaspoon pepper
- ½ teaspoon salt

For breakfast basin:

- • 1 avocado, wedged
- Greens, combined
- Handful parsley, minced
- Handful cilantro, minced

Directions:

For chickpea scramble:

1. Scoop out the chickpeas and a little bit of its water into a bowl. Slightly mash the chickpeas using a fork, intentionally omitting some. Stir in the turmeric, pepper, and salt until adequately combined.

2. Sauté onions in olive oil until soft, then add garlic and cook for 1 minute. Stir in the chickpeas and sauté for 5 minutes.

For breakfast basin and Serving:

1. Get 2 breakfast basins. Layer the bottom of the basins with the combined greens. Top with chickpea scramble, parsley, and cilantro. Enjoy with avocado wedges.

Nutrition Per Serving

Calories: 348, Fat 18.3 g, Carbs 39.63 g, Protein 11.42g, Fiber 15.2 g.

37. Quinoa, Oats, Hazelnut and Blueberry Salad

Preparation Time: 10 minutes

Cooking Time: 35 minutes

Servings: 8

Ingredients

- 1 cup golden quinoa, dry
- 1 cup oats, cut into pieces
- 2 cups blueberries
- 2 cups hazelnuts, roughly chopped, toasted
- ½ cup dry millet
- 2 large lemons, zested, juiced
- 3 tablespoons olive oil, divided
- ½ cup maple syrup
- 1 cup Greek yogurt

- 1 (1-inch) piece fresh ginger, peeled, cut
- ¼ teaspoon nutmeg

Directions:

1. Combine quinoa, oats and millet in a large bowl. Rinse, drain and set aside.

2. Add one tablespoon olive oil into a saucepan and place over medium-high heat. Cook the rinsed grains in it for 3 minutes. Add 4 ½ cups water and salt. Add the zest of 1 lemon and ginger.

3. When the mixture boils, cover the pot and cook in reduced heat for 20 minutes. Remove from heat. Let it rest for 5 minutes. Uncover and fluff with a fork. Discard the ginger and layer the grains on a large baking sheet. Let cool for 30 minutes.

4. Transfer the grains into a large bowl and mix in the remaining lemon zest.

5. Combine the juice of both lemons with the remaining olive oil in a separate bowl. Stir in the yogurt, maple syrup, and nutmeg. Pour the mixture into the grains and stir. Mix in the blueberries and hazelnuts. Refrigerate overnight, then serve.

Nutrition Per Serving

Calories: 522, Fat 28.49g, Carbs 64.34g, Protein 11.93g, Fiber 8.7g.

38. Chia Flaxseed Waffles

Preparation Time: 15 minutes

Cooking Time: 10 minutes

Servings: 8

Ingredients:

- 2 cups ground golden flaxseed
- 2 tsp cinnamon
- 10 tsp ground chia seed
- 15 tbsp warm water
- 1/3 cup coconut oil, melted
- 1/2 cup water
- 1 tbsp baking powder - 1 tsp sea salt

Directions:

1. Preheat the waffle iron.

2. In a small bowl, mix ground chia seed and warm water.

3. In a large bowl, mix ground flaxseed, sea salt, and baking powder. Set aside.

4. Add melted coconut oil, chia seed mixture, and water into the blender and blend for 30 seconds.

5. Transfer the coconut oil mixture into the flaxseed mixture and mix well. Add cinnamon and stir well. Scoop the waffle mixture into the hot waffle iron and cook on each side for 3-5 minutes. Serve and enjoy.

Nutrition Per Serving: Calories 240; Fat 20.6 g; Carbohydrates 12.9 g; Sugar 0 g; Protein 7 g; Cholesterol 0 mg

39. Flax Almond Muffins

Preparation Time: 10 minutes

Cooking Time: 35 minutes

Servings: 6

Ingredients:

- 1 tsp cinnamon
- 2 tbsp coconut flour
- 20 drops liquid stevia
- 1/4 cup water
- 1/4 tsp vanilla extract
- 1/4 tsp baking soda
- 1/2 tsp baking powder
- 1/4 cup almond flour
- 1/2 cup ground flax
- 2 tbsp ground chia

Directions:

1. Preheat the oven to 350°F/ 176°C.
2. Spray muffin tray with cooking spray and set aside.
3. In a small bowl, add 6 tablespoons of water and ground chia. Mix well and set aside.
4. In a mixing bowl, add ground flax, baking soda, baking powder, cinnamon, coconut flour, and almond flour, and mix well.
5. Add chia seed mixture, vanilla, water, and liquid stevia and stir well to combine.
6. Pour mixture into the prepared muffin tray and bake in preheated oven for 35 minutes.
7. Serve and enjoy.

Nutrition Per Serving: Calories 92; Fat 6.3 g; Carbohydrates 6.9 g; Sugar 0.4 g; Protein 3.7 g; Cholesterol 0 mg

40. Whole Wheat Pizza with Summer Produce

Preparation Time: 15 minutes

Cooking Time: 15 minutes

Servings: 2

Ingredients

- 1-pound whole wheat pizza dough
- 4 ounces goat cheese - 2/3 cup blueberries
- 2 ears corn, husked - 2 yellow squash, sliced
- 2 tbsp olive oil

Directions:

1. Preheat the oven to 450°F.

2. Roll the dough out to make a pizza crust.

3. Crumble the cheese on the crust. Spread remaining ingredients, then drizzle with olive oil.

4. Bake for about 15 minutes. Serve.

Nutrition: Calories 470 Carbohydrates 66 g Fat 18 g Protein 17 g

41. Chives Avocado Mix

Preparation Time: 5 minutes

Cooking Time: 0 minutes

Servings: 4

Ingredients:

- 2 avocados, peeled, pitted and roughly cubed
- 1 tomato, cubed
- 1 cucumber, sliced
- 1 celery stalk, chopped
- 2 tablespoons avocado oil
- 1 tablespoon lime juice
- Salt and black pepper to the taste
- 2 scallions, chopped
- ½ teaspoon cayenne pepper
- 1 tablespoon chives, chopped

Directions:

1. In a bowl, combine the avocados with the tomato, cucumber and the other ingredients, toss, divide between plates and serve for breakfast.

Nutrition: Calories 232, Fat 20.7g, Fiber 8g, Carbs 13.2g, Protein 2.9g

42. Zucchini Pan

Preparation Time: 5 minutes

Cooking Time: 15 minutes

Servings: 4

Ingredients:

- 2 shallots, chopped
- 1 tablespoon olive oil
- 3 zucchinis, roughly cubed
- 2 garlic cloves, minced
- 2 sun-dried tomatoes, chopped
- 1 tablespoon capers, drained
- Salt and black pepper to the taste
- 1 tablespoon dill, chopped

Directions:

1. Heat a pan with the oil over medium heat, add the shallots, garlic and tomatoes and sauté for 5 minutes.
2. Add the zucchinis and the other ingredients, toss, cook over medium heat for 10 minutes more, divide between plates and serve.

Nutrition: Calories 73, Fat 4g, Fiber 2.6g, Carbs 9.2g, Protein 2.8g

43. Chili Spinach and Zucchini Pan

Preparation Time: 5 minutes
Cooking Time: 15 minutes
Servings: 4
Ingredients:

- 1-pound baby spinach
- 1 tablespoon olive oil
- 2 zucchinis, sliced
- 1 tomato, cubed
- 2 shallots, chopped
- 1 tablespoon lime juice
- 2 garlic cloves, minced
- 2 teaspoons red chili flakes
- 1 teaspoon chili powder
- Salt and black pepper to the taste

Directions:

1. Heat a pan with the oil over medium heat, add the shallots, garlic, chili powder and chili flakes, stir and sauté for 5 minutes.
2. Add the spinach, zucchinis and the other ingredients, toss, cook over medium heat for 10 minutes more, divide into bowls, and serve for breakfast.

Nutrition:

Calories 85, Fat 4.3g, Fiber 4.1g, Carbs 10.6g, Protein 4.9g

44. Basil Tomato and Cabbage Bowls

Preparation Time: 5 minutes
Cooking Time: 0 minutes
Servings: 4
Ingredients:

- 1-pound cherry tomatoes, halved
- 1 cup red cabbage, shredded
- 2 tablespoons balsamic vinegar
- 2 shallots, chopped
- 1 tablespoon avocado oil
- Salt and black pepper to the taste
- 1 tablespoon basil, chopped

Directions:

1. In a bowl, combine the cabbage with the tomatoes and the other ingredients, toss and serve for breakfast.

Nutrition: Calories 35, Fat 0.7g, Fiber 2g, Carbs 6.6g, Protein 1.4g

45. Spinach and Zucchini Hash

Preparation Time: 5 minutes
Cooking Time: 15 minutes
Servings: 4
Ingredients:

- 2 zucchinis, cubed
- 2 cups baby spinach
- A pinch of salt and black pepper
- 1 tablespoon olive oil
- 1 teaspoon chili powder
- 1 teaspoon rosemary, dried
- ½ cup coconut cream
- 1 tablespoon chives, chopped

Directions:

1. Heat a pan with the oil over medium heat, add the zucchinis and the chili powder, stir and cook for 5 minutes.
2. Add the rest of the ingredients, toss, cook the mix for 10 minutes more, divide between plates and serve for breakfast.

Nutrition: Calories 121, Fat 11.1g, Fiber 2.5g, Carbs 6.1g, Protein 2.4g

46. Tomato and Zucchini Fritters

Preparation Time: 5 minutes
Cooking Time: 10 minutes
Servings: 4
Ingredients:

- 1-pound zucchinis, grated
- 2 tomatoes, cubed
- 2 garlic cloves, minced
- Salt and black pepper to the taste
- 1 tablespoon coconut flour
- 1 tablespoon flaxseed mixed with 2 tablespoons water
- 1 tablespoon dill, chopped
- 2 tablespoons olive oil

Directions:

1. In a bowl, mix the zucchinis with the tomatoes and the other ingredients except for the oil, stir well, shape medium fritters out of this mix and flatten them
2. Heat a pan with the oil over medium heat, add the fritters, cook them for 5 minutes on each side, divide between plates and serve for breakfast.

Nutrition: Calories 111, Fat 8.2g, Fiber 3.4g, Carbs 9g, Protein 2.8g

47. Peppers Casserole

Preparation Time: 10 minutes

Cooking Time: 25 minutes

Servings: 4

Ingredients:

- 1-pound mixed bell peppers, cut into strips
- Salt and black pepper to the taste
- 4 scallions, chopped
- ½ teaspoon cumin, ground
- ½ teaspoon oregano, dried
- ½ teaspoon basil, dried
- 2 garlic cloves, minced
- 1 tablespoon avocado oil
- 2 tomatoes, cubed
- 1 cup cashew cheese, grated
- 2 tablespoons parsley, chopped

Directions:

1. Heat a pan with the oil over medium heat, add the scallions and the garlic and sauté for 5 minutes.
2. Add the rest of the ingredients except the cheese, stir and cook for 5 minutes more.
3. Sprinkle the cashew cheese on top and bake everything at 380 degrees F for 15 minutes.
4. Divide the mix between plates and serve for breakfast.

Nutrition: Calories 85, Fat 3.6g, Fiber 3.9g, Carbs 11.8g, Protein 3.3g

48. Eggplant and Broccoli Casserole

Preparation Time: 10 minutes

Cooking Time: 35 minutes

Servings: 4

Ingredients:

- 1-pound eggplants, roughly cubed
- 1 cup broccoli florets
- 1 cup cashew cheese, shredded
- ¼ cup almond milk - 2 scallions, chopped
- 1 tablespoon olive oil
- 2 tablespoons flaxseed mixed with 2 tablespoons water - 1 tablespoon cilantro, chopped
- Salt and black pepper to the taste

Directions:

1. In a roasting pan, combine the eggplants with the broccoli and the other ingredients except for the cashew cheese and the almond milk and toss.

2. In a bowl, combine the milk with the cashew cheese, stir, pour over the eggplant mix, spread, introduce the pan in the oven and bake at 380 degrees F for 35 minutes.
3. Cool the casserole down, slice and serve.

Nutrition:

Calories 161, Fat 11.4g, Fiber 6.6g, Carbs 12.8g, Protein 4.2g

49. Creamy Avocado and Nuts Bowls

Preparation Time: 5 minutes

Cooking Time: 0 minutes

Servings: 4

Ingredients:

- 1 tablespoon walnuts, chopped
- 1 tablespoon pine nuts, toasted
- 2 avocados, peeled, pitted and roughly cubed
- 1 tablespoon lime juice
- 1 tablespoon avocado oil
- Salt and black pepper to the taste
- ¼ cup coconut cream

Directions:

1. In a bowl, combine the avocados with the nuts and the other ingredients, toss, divide into smaller bowls and serve for breakfast.

Nutrition: Calories 273, Fat 26.3g, Fiber 7.5g, Carbs 11.1g, Protein 3.1g

50. Avocado and Watermelon Salad

Preparation Time: 5 minutes

Cooking Time: 0 minutes

Servings: 4

Ingredients:

- 2 cups watermelon, peeled and roughly cubed
- 2 avocados, peeled, pitted and roughly cubed
- 1 tablespoon lime juice
- 1 tablespoon avocado oil
- ¼ cup almonds, chopped

Directions:

1. In a bowl, combine the watermelon with the avocados and the other ingredients, toss and serve for breakfast.

Nutrition: Calories 270, Fat 23.1g, Fiber 3g, Carbs 16.7g, Protein 3.7g

51. Chia and Coconut Pudding

Preparation Time: 10 minutes

Cooking Time: 0 minutes

Servings: 4

Ingredients:

- ¼ cup walnuts, chopped
- 2 cups coconut milk
- ¼ cup coconut flakes
- 3 tablespoons chia seeds
- 1 tablespoon stevia
- 1 teaspoon almond extract

Directions:

1. In a bowl, combine the milk with the coconut flakes and the other ingredients, toss, leave aside for 10 minutes and serve for breakfast.

Nutrition: Calories 414, Fat 39.2g, Fiber 8.5g, Carbs 14.3g, Protein 7.1g

52. Tomato and Cucumber Salad

Preparation Time: 5 minutes

Cooking Time: 0 minutes

Servings: 4

Ingredients:

- 2 cups cherry tomatoes, halved
- 2 cucumbers, sliced
- 1 tablespoon lime juice
- A pinch of salt and black pepper
- 1 tablespoon olive oil
- ½ cup kalamata olives, pitted and halved
- 1 tablespoon chives, chopped

Directions:

1. In a bowl, combine the tomatoes with the cucumbers and the other ingredients, toss, and serve for breakfast.

Nutrition: Calories 91, Fat 5.7g, Fiber 2.5g, Carbs 11g, Protein 2g

53. Walnuts and Olives Bowls

Preparation Time: 5 minutes

Cooking Time: 0 minutes

Servings: 4

Ingredients:

- 1 cup walnuts, roughly chopped
- 1 cup black olives, pitted and halved
- 1 cup green olives, pitted and halved
- 1 tablespoon lime juice
- 1 teaspoon chili powder
- 1 teaspoon rosemary, dried
- 1 teaspoon cumin, ground
- 2 spring onions, chopped
- 1 tablespoon cilantro, chopped
- A pinch of salt and black pepper
- 2 tablespoons avocado oil

Directions:

1. In a bowl, mix olives with the walnuts and the other ingredients, toss, divide into smaller bowls and serve for breakfast.

Nutrition: Calories 260, Fat 24g, Fiber 4.5g, Carbs 8.5g, Protein 8.4g

54. Kale and Broccoli Pan

Preparation Time: 5 minutes

Cooking Time: 12 minutes

Servings: 4

Ingredients:

- 1 cup broccoli florets
- 2 shallots, chopped
- 1 tablespoon olive oil
- 1 teaspoon sweet paprika
- 1 teaspoon turmeric powder
- 1 cup kale, torn
- Salt and black pepper to the taste
- ¼ cup cashew cheese, grated
- 2 tablespoons chives, chopped

Directions:

1. Heat a pan with the oil over medium heat, add the shallots and sauté for 2 minutes.
2. Add the broccoli, kale and the other ingredients, toss, cook for 10 minutes more, divide between plates and serve.

Nutrition: Calories 63, Fat 4.4g, Fiber 1.3g, Carbs 5.3g, Protein 1.8g

55. Spinach and Berries Salad

Preparation Time: 5 minutes

Cooking Time: 0 minutes

Servings: 4

Ingredients:

- 1 cup baby spinach
- 1 cup blackberries
- 1 cup blueberries
- 1 tablespoon avocado oil
- 1 tablespoon balsamic vinegar
- 1 tablespoon parsley, chopped
- ½ cup pine nuts, chopped
- Salt and black pepper to the taste

Directions:

1. In a salad bowl, combine the spinach with the berries and the other ingredients, toss and serve for breakfast.

Nutrition: Calories 158, Fat 12.4g, Fiber 3.8g, Carbs 11.5g, Protein 3.4g

56. Cauliflower Hash

Preparation Time: 10 minutes

Cooking Time: 15 minutes

Servings: 4

Ingredients:

- 2 cups cauliflower florets, roughly chopped
- ½ teaspoon basil, dried
- 1 teaspoon sage, dried
- 2 spring onions, chopped
- 1 tablespoon avocado oil
- ½ cup coconut cream
- ½ teaspoon sweet paprika
- Salt and black pepper to the taste
- 1 tablespoon cilantro, chopped

Directions:

1. Heat a pan with the oil over medium heat, add the onions and sauté for 5 minutes.
2. Add the cauliflower and the other ingredients, toss, cook everything for 10 minutes more, divide between plates, and serve for breakfast.

Nutrition:

Calories 90, Fat 7.7g, Fiber 2.4g, Carbs 5.3g, Protein 1.9g

57. Spinach and Green Beans Casserole

Preparation Time: 10 minutes

Cooking Time: 40 minutes

Servings: 4

Ingredients:

- 1-pound green beans, trimmed and halved
- 4 scallions, chopped
- 1 tablespoon coconut oil, melted
- 1 cup baby spinach
- 2 tablespoons flaxseed mixed with 3 tablespoons water
- ½ cup cashew cheese, grated
- Salt and black pepper to the taste
- ½ teaspoon thyme, chopped

Directions:

1. Heat a pan with the oil over medium heat, add the scallions and sauté for 5 minutes.

2. Add the green beans and the other ingredients except for the cheese, stir and cook for 5 minutes more.
3. Sprinkle the cheese on top and bake the mix at 390 degrees F for 30 minutes.
4. Divide the mix between plates and serve.

Nutrition: Calories 273, Fat 13.7g, Fiber 0.2g, Carbs 2.2g, Protein 1.5g

58. Spiced Zucchini and Eggplant Bowls

Preparation Time: 10 minutes

Cooking Time: 15 minutes

Servings: 4

Ingredients:

- 1 tablespoon olive oil
- 4 scallions, chopped
- 2 zucchinis, cubed
- 1 eggplant, cubed
- 1 tablespoon cilantro, chopped
- 1 teaspoon rosemary, dried
- 1 teaspoon allspice, ground
- 1 teaspoon nutmeg, ground
- ¼ cup coconut cream
- Salt and black pepper to the taste
- 1 tablespoon chives, chopped

Directions:

1. Heat a pan with the oil over medium heat, add the scallions, allspice and the nutmeg and sauté for 5 minutes.
2. Add the zucchini is, eggplant, and the other ingredients, toss, cook over medium heat for 10 minutes, divide into bowls and serve for breakfast,

Nutrition: Calories 242, Fat 6.4g, Fiber 2g, Carbs 10g, Protein 2g

59. Blueberry and Banana Smoothie

Preparation Time: 10 minutes

Cooking Time: 0 minutes

Serving: 4

Ingredients

- 1 cup of blueberries, frozen
- 1 whole banana
- ½ a cup of almond milk
- 1 tablespoon of almond butter
- Water as needed

Directions

1. Add the listed ingredients to your blender and blend well until you have a smoothie-like texture

2. Chill and serve

3. Enjoy!

Nutrition Per Serving: Calories: 321 Fat: 11g Carbohydrates: 55g Protein: 5g

60.   Lemon and Rosemary Iced Tea

Preparation Time: 1 minute

Cooking Time: 5 minutes

Serving: 4

Ingredients

- 4 cups of water
- 4 earl grey tea bags
- ¼ cup of sugar
- 2 lemons
- 1 sprig rosemary

Directions

1. Peel two lemons and keep them on the side

2. Take a medium-sized saucepan and place it over medium heat, add water, sugar, and lemon peels

3. Bring the mix to a boil

4. Remove from heat and add rosemary and tea into the mix

5. Cover saucepan and steep for 5 minutes

6. Add the juice of peeled lemons to the mixture

7. Strain and chill

8. Enjoy!

Nutrition Per Serving:

Calories: 88 Fat: 2g Carbohydrates: 14g Protein: 2g

61.   Lavender and Mint Ice Tea

Preparation Time: 1 minute

Cooking Time: 5 minutes

Serving: 4

Ingredients

- 8 cups of water
- ¼ cup dried lavender buds
- ¼ cup mint

Directions

1. Add mint and lavender to the pot, keep it on the side

2. Add in 8 cups of boiling water to the pot, sweeten as needed

3. Cover and let it steep for 10 minutes

4. Strain and chill

5. Serve and enjoy!

Nutrition Per Serving:

Calories: 120 Fat: 0g Carbohydrates: 8g Protein: 1g

62.   Thai Iced Tea

Preparation Time: 1 minute

Cooking Time: 5 minutes

Serving: 4

Ingredients

- 4 cups of water
- 1 can of light coconut milk
- ¼ cup maple syrup
- ¼ cup muscovite sugar
- 1 teaspoon vanilla sugar
- 1 teaspoon vanilla extract

Directions

1. Take a large-sized saucepan and place it over medium heat, bring water to a boil

2. Remove heat and add tea, let it steep for 5 minutes

3. Strain the tea into a bowl and add maple syrup and vanilla extract, whisk well

4. Set it in the fridge and let it chill

5. Serve as needed with a topping of coconut milk

6. Enjoy!

Nutrition Per Serving:

Calories: 100 Fat: 3g Carbohydrates: 14g Protein: 3g

63.   Healthy Coffee Smoothie

Preparation Time: 10 minutes

Cooking Time: 0 minutes

Serving: 1

Ingredients:

- 1 tablespoon chia seeds
- 2 cups strongly brewed coffee, chilled
- 1-ounce Macadamia Nuts
- 1-2 packets Stevia, optional
- 1 tablespoon MCT oil

Directions

1. Add all the listed ingredients to a blender.

2. Blend on high until smooth and creamy.

3. Enjoy your smoothie.

Nutrition Per Serving:

Calories: 395 Fat: 39g Carbohydrates: 11g Protein: 5.2g

64.   Berry   and   Strawberry Smoothie

Preparation Time: 10 minutes

Cooking Time: 0 minutes

Servings: 3

Ingredients

- 1 cup crushed ice
- ½ cup unsweetened almond milk
- ½ cup frozen raspberries
- ½ cup strawberries

- 1 tablespoon coconut oil
- ½ teaspoon fresh vanilla bean extract

Directions:

1. Add the listed ingredients to a blender

2. Blend on low until everything is incorporated well

3. Increase to high speed and blend until smooth

4. Add a few drops of liquid stevia for extra taste

5. Divide into 3 servings and enjoy!

Nutrition Per Serving:

Calories: 232 Fat: 22g Carbohydrates: 16g Protein: 3g

65.   Mint Flavored Pear Smoothie

Preparation Time: 5 minutes

Cooking Time: 0 minutes

Serving: 2

Ingredients

- ¼ honeydew
- 2 green pears, ripe
- ½ an apple, juiced
- 1 cup of ice cubes
- ½ cup fresh mint leaves

Directions:

1. Add the listed ingredients to your blender and blend until smooth

2. Serve chilled!

Nutrition Per Serving: Calories: 200 Fat: 10g Carbohydrates: 14g Protein 2g

66.   Epic Pineapple Juice

Preparation Time: 10 minutes

Cooking Time: 0 minutes

Serving: 4

Ingredients

- 4 cups of fresh pineapple, chopped
- 1 pinch of salt
- 1 ½ cup of water

Directions:

1. Add the listed ingredients to your blender and blend well until you have a smoothie-like texture

2. Chill and serve

3. Enjoy!

Nutrition Per Serving: Calories: 82 Fat: 0.2g Carbohydrates: 21g Protein: 21

67.   Chilled Watermelon Smoothie

Preparation Time: 5 minutes

Cooking Time: 0 minutes

Servings: 2

Ingredients

- 1 cup watermelon chunks
- ½ cup of coconut water
- 1 and ½ teaspoons of lime juice

- 4 mint leaves
- 4 ice cubes

Directions:

1. Add the listed ingredients to your blender and blend until smooth

2. Serve chilled!

Nutrition Per Serving: Calories: 200 Fat: 10g Carbohydrates: 14g Protein 2g

68.   The Mocha Shake

Preparation Time: 10 minutes

Cooking Time: 0 minutes

Serving: 1

Ingredients:

- 1 cup whole almond milk
- 2 tablespoons cocoa powder
- 2 pack stevia - 1 cup brewed coffee, chilled
- 1 tablespoon coconut oil

Directions:

1. Add listed ingredients to a blender

2. Blend until you have a smooth and creamy texture

3. Serve chilled and enjoy!

Nutrition (Per Serving) Calories: 293 Fat: 23g Carbohydrates: 19g Protein: 10g

69.   Cinnamon Chiller

Preparation Time: 10 minutes

Cooking Time: 0 minutes

Servings: 1

Ingredients:

- 1 cup unsweetened almond milk
- 2 tablespoons vanilla protein powder
- ½ teaspoon cinnamon
- ¼ teaspoon vanilla extract
- 1 tablespoon chia seeds - 1 cup ice cubes

Directions:

1. Add listed ingredients to a blender

2. Blend until you have a smooth and creamy texture

3. Serve chilled and enjoy!

Nutrition Per Serving: Calories: 145 Fat: 4g Carbohydrates: 1.6g Protein: 0.6g

70.   Sensational   Strawberry Medley

Preparation Time: 5 minutes

Cooking Time: 0 minutes

Serving: 2

Ingredients

- 1-2 handfuls baby greens

- 3 medium kale leaves
- 5-8 mint leaves
- 1-inch piece ginger, peeled
- 1 avocado
- 1 cup strawberries
- 6-8 ounces coconut water + 6-8 ounces filtered water
- Fresh juice of one lime
- 1-2 teaspoon olive oil

Directions:

1. Add all the listed ingredients to your blender
2. Blend until smooth
3. Add a few ice cubes and serve the smoothie
4. Enjoy!

Nutrition (Per Serving) Calories: 200 Fat: 10g Carbohydrates: 14g Protein 2g

71. Alkaline Strawberry Smoothie

Preparation Time: 5 minutes

Cooking Time: 0 minutes

Servings: 2

Ingredients

- ½ cup of organic strawberries/blueberries
- Half a banana
- 2 cups of coconut water
- ½ inch ginger
- Juice of 2 grapefruits

Directions:

1. Add all the listed ingredients to your blender
2. Blend until smooth
3. Add a few ice cubes and serve the smoothie
4. Enjoy!

Nutrition Per Serving: Calories: 200 Fat: 10g Carbohydrates: 14g Protein 2g

72. Awesome Orange Smoothie

Preparation Time: 5 minutes

Cooking Time: 0 minutes

Servings: 2

Ingredients

- 1 orange, peeled
- ¼ cup fat-free yogurt
- 2 tablespoons frozen orange juice concentrate
- ¼ teaspoon vanilla extract
- 4 ice cubes

Directions:

1. Add the listed ingredients to your blender and blend until smooth
2. Serve chilled!

Nutrition Per Serving: Calories: 200 Fat: 10g Carbohydrates: 14g Protein 2g

73. Pineapple and Coconut Milk Smoothie

Preparation Time: 5 minutes

Cooking Time: 0 minutes

Servings: 2

Ingredients

- ¼ cup pineapple, frozen
- ¾ cup of coconut milk

Directions:

1. Add the listed ingredients to a blender and blend well on high
2. Once the mixture is smooth, pour the smoothie into a tall glass and serve
3. Chill and enjoy it!

Nutrition Per Serving: Calories: 200 Fat: 10g Carbohydrates: 14g Protein 2g

74. Sweet Potato and Almond Smoothie

Preparation Time: 5 minutes

Cooking Time: 0 minutes

Servings: 2

Ingredients

- 1 cup sweet potato, chopped
- 1 cup almond milk
- ¼ teaspoon nutmeg
- ¼ teaspoon ground cinnamon
- 1 teaspoon flaxseed
- 1 small avocado, cubed
- Few spinach leaves, torn

Toppings

- A handful of crushed almonds
- A handful of crushed cashews
- 3 tablespoons orange juice

Directions

1. Blend all the ingredients until smooth
2. Add a few ice cubes to make it chilled
3. Add your desired toppings
4. Enjoy!

Nutrition Per Serving: Calories: 200 Fat: 10g Carbohydrates: 14g Protein 2g

75. The Sunshine Offering

Preparation Time: 5 minutes

Cooking Time: 0 minutes

Servings: 2

Ingredients

- 2 cups of fresh spinach
- 1 and ½ cups of almond milk
- ½ cup of coconut water
- 3 cups of fresh pineapple
- 2 tablespoons of coconut unsweetened flakes

Directions:

1. Add all the listed ingredients to your blender

2. Blend until smooth

3. Add a few ice cubes and serve the smoothie

4. Enjoy!

Nutrition Per Serving: Calories: 200 Fat: 10g Carbohydrates: 14g Protein 2g

76. Strawberry and Rhubarb Smoothie

Preparation Time: 5 minutes

Cooking Time: 3 minutes

Servings: 1

Ingredients

- 1 rhubarb stalk, chopped
- 1 cup fresh strawberries, sliced
- ½ cup plain Greek yogurt
- Pinch of ground cinnamon
- 3 ice cubes

Directions:

1. Take a small saucepan and fill it with water over high heat

2. Bring to boil and add rhubarb, boil for 3 minutes

3. Drain and transfer to a blender

4. Add strawberries, honey, yogurt, and cinnamon, and pulse the mixture until smooth

5. Add ice cubes and blend until thick and has no lumps

6. Pour into a glass and enjoy chilled

Nutrition Per Serving: Calories: 295 Fat: 8g Carbohydrates: 56g Protein: 6g

77. Vanilla Hemp Drink

Preparation Time: 10 minutes

Cooking Time: 0 minutes

Servings: 1

Ingredients:

- 1 cup of water
- 1 cup unsweetened hemp almond milk, vanilla

- 1 ½ tablespoon coconut oil, unrefined
- ½ cup frozen blueberries, mixed
- 4 cups leafy greens, kale, and spinach
- 1 tablespoon flaxseed
- 1 tablespoon almond butter

Directions:

1. Add listed ingredients to a blender

2. Blend until you have a smooth and creamy texture

3. Serve chilled and enjoy!

Nutrition Per Serving: Calories: 250 Fat: 20g Carbohydrates: 10g Protein: 7g

78. Minty Cherry Smoothie

Preparation Time: 5 minutes

Cooking Time: 0 minutes

Servings: 2

Ingredients

- ¾ cup cherries
- 1 teaspoon mint
- ½ cup almond milk
- ½ cup kale
- ½ teaspoon fresh vanilla

Directions:

1. Wash and cut cherries

2. Take the pits out

3. Add cherries to the blender

4. Pour almond milk

5. Wash the mint and put two sprigs in a blender

6. Separate the leaves of kale from the stems

7. Put kale in a blender

8. Press vanilla bean and cut lengthwise with a knife

9. Scoop out your desired amount of vanilla and add to the blender

10. Blend until smooth

11. Serve chilled and enjoy!

Nutrition Per Serving: Calories: 200 Fat: 10g Carbohydrates: 14g Protein 2g

79. Hot Pink Smoothie

Preparation Time: 5 minutes

Cooking Time: 0 minutes

Servings: 1

Ingredients:

- 1 clementine, peeled, segmented
- 1/2 frozen banana
- 1 small beet, peeled, chopped
- 1/8 teaspoon sea salt
- 1/2 cup raspberries

- 1 tablespoon chia seeds
- 1/4 teaspoon vanilla extract, unsweetened
- 2 tablespoons almond butter
- 1 cup almond milk, unsweetened

Directions:

1. Place all the ingredients in the order in a food processor or blender and then pulse for 2 to 3 minutes at high speed until smooth.
2. Pour the smoothie into a glass and then serve.

Nutrition: Calories: 278 Fat: 5.6 g Carbs: 37.2 g Protein: 6.2 g Fiber: 13.2 g

80. Maca Caramel Frap

Preparation Time: 5 minutes

Cooking Time: 0 minutes

Servings: 4

Ingredients:

- 1/2 of frozen banana, sliced
- 1/4 cup cashews, soaked for 4 hours
- 2 Medjool dates, pitted
- 1 teaspoon maca powder
- 1/8 teaspoon sea salt
- 1/2 teaspoon vanilla extract, unsweetened
- 1/4 cup almond milk, unsweetened
- 1/4 cup cold coffee, brewed

Directions

1. Place all the ingredients in the order in a food processor or blender and then pulse for 2 to 3 minutes at high speed until smooth.
2. Pour the smoothie into a glass and then serve.

Nutrition: Calories: 450 Fat: 170 g Carbs: 64 g Protein: 7 g Fiber: 0 g

81. Peanut Butter Vanilla Green Shake

Preparation Time: 5 minutes

Cooking Time: 0 minutes

Servings: 1

Ingredients:

- 1 teaspoon flax seeds
- 1 frozen banana
- 1 cup baby spinach
- 1/8 teaspoon sea salt
- 1/2 teaspoon ground cinnamon
- 1/4 teaspoon vanilla extract, unsweetened
- 2 tablespoons peanut butter, unsweetened
- 1/4 cup ice
- 1 cup coconut milk, unsweetened

Directions:

1. Place all the ingredients in the order in a food processor or blender and then pulse for 2 to 3 minutes at high speed until smooth.
2. Pour the smoothie into a glass and then serve.

Nutrition: Calories: 298 Fat: 11 g Carbs: 32 g Protein: 24 g Fiber: 8 g

82. Green Colada

Preparation Time: 5 minutes

Cooking Time: 0 minutes

Servings: 1

Ingredients:

- 1/2 cup frozen pineapple chunks
- 1/2 banana
- 1/2 teaspoon spirulina powder
- 1/4 teaspoon vanilla extract, unsweetened
- 1 cup of coconut milk

Directions

1. Place all the ingredients in the order in a food processor or blender and then pulse for 2 to 3 minutes at high speed until smooth.
2. Pour the smoothie into a glass and then serve.

Nutrition: Calories: 127 Fat: 3 g Carbs: 25 g Protein: 3 g Fiber: 4 g

83. Chocolate Oat Smoothie

Preparation Time: 5 minutes

Cooking Time: 0 minutes

Servings: 1

Ingredients:

- 1/4 cup rolled oats
- 1 1/2 tablespoon cocoa powder, unsweetened
- 1 teaspoon flax seeds
- 1 large frozen banana
- 1/8 teaspoon sea salt
- 1/8 teaspoon cinnamon
- 1/4 teaspoon vanilla extract, unsweetened
- 2 tablespoons almond butter
- 1 cup coconut milk, unsweetened

Directions:

1. Place all the ingredients in the order in a food processor or blender and then pulse for 2 to 3 minutes at high speed until smooth.
2. Pour the smoothie into a glass and then serve.

Nutrition: Calories: 262 Fat: 7.3 g Carbs: 50.4 g Protein: 8.1 g Fiber: 9.6 g

84. Peach Crumble Shake

Preparation Time: 5 minutes
Cooking Time: 0 minutes
Servings: 1
Ingredients:

- 1 tablespoon chia seeds
- ¼ cup rolled oats
- 2 peaches, pitted, sliced
- ¾ teaspoon ground cinnamon
- 1 Medjool date, pitted
- ½ teaspoon vanilla extract, unsweetened
- 2 tablespoons lemon juice
- ½ cup of water
- 1 tablespoon coconut butter
- 1 cup coconut milk, unsweetened

Directions:

1. Place all the ingredients in the order in a food processor or blender and then pulse for 2 to 3 minutes at high speed until smooth.
2. Pour the smoothie into a glass and then serve.

Nutrition: Calories: 270 Fat: 4 g Carbs: 28 g Protein: 25 g Fiber: 3 g

85. Wild Ginger Green Smoothie

Preparation Time: 5 minutes
Cooking Time: 0 minutes
Servings: 1
Ingredients:

- 1/2 cup pineapple chunks, frozen
- 1/2 cup chopped kale - 1/2 frozen banana
- 1 tablespoon lime juice
- 2 inches ginger, peeled, chopped
- 1/2 cup coconut milk, unsweetened
- 1/2 cup coconut water

Directions:

1. Place all the ingredients in the order in a food processor or blender and then pulse for 2 to 3 minutes at high speed until smooth.
2. Pour the smoothie into a glass and then serve.

Nutrition: Calories: 331 Fat: 14 g Carbs: 40 g Protein: 16 g Fiber: 9 g

86. Berry Beet Velvet Smoothie

Preparation Time: 5 minutes
Cooking Time: 0 minutes
Servings: 1
Ingredients:

- 1/2 of frozen banana
- 1 cup mixed red berries
- 1 Medjool date, pitted
- 1 small beet, peeled, chopped
- 1 tablespoon cacao powder
- 1 teaspoon chia seeds
- 1/4 teaspoon vanilla extract, unsweetened
- 1/2 teaspoon lemon juice
- 2 teaspoons coconut butter
- 1 cup coconut milk, unsweetened

Directions:

1. Place all the ingredients in the order in a food processor or blender and then pulse for 2 to 3 minutes at high speed until smooth.
2. Pour the smoothie into a glass and then serve.

Nutrition: Calories: 234 Fat: 5 g Carbs: 42 g Protein: 11 g Fiber: 7 g

87. Spiced Strawberry Smoothie

Preparation Time: 5 minutes
Cooking Time: 0 minutes
Servings: 1
Ingredients:

- 1 tablespoon goji berries, soaked
- 1 cup strawberries
- 1/8 teaspoon sea salt
- 1 frozen banana
- 1 Medjool date, pitted
- 1 scoop vanilla-flavored whey protein
- 2 tablespoons lemon juice
- ¼ teaspoon ground ginger
- ½ teaspoon ground cinnamon
- 1 tablespoon almond butter
- 1 cup almond milk, unsweetened

Directions:

1. Place all the ingredients in the order in a food processor or blender and then pulse for 2 to 3 minutes at high speed until smooth.
2. Pour the smoothie into a glass and then serve.

Nutrition: Calories: 182 Fat: 1.3 g Carbs: 34 g Protein: 6.4 g Fiber: 0.7 g

88. Banana Bread Shake with Walnut Milk

Preparation Time: 5 minutes
Cooking Time: 0 minutes
Servings: 2
Ingredients:

- 2 cups sliced frozen bananas

- 3 cups walnut milk
- 1/8 teaspoon grated nutmeg
- 1 tablespoon maple syrup
- 1 teaspoon ground cinnamon
- 1/2 teaspoon vanilla extract, unsweetened
- 2 tablespoons cacao nibs

Directions:

1. Place all the ingredients in the order in a food processor or blender and then pulse for 2 to 3 minutes at high speed until smooth.
2. Pour the smoothie into two glasses and then serve.

Nutrition: Calories: 339.8 Fat: 19 g Carbs: 39 g Protein: 4.3 g Fiber: 1 g

89. Double Chocolate Hazelnut Espresso Shake

Preparation Time: 5 minutes

Cooking Time: 0 minutes

Servings: 1

Ingredients:

- 1 frozen banana, sliced
- 1/4 cup roasted hazelnuts
- 4 Medjool dates, pitted, soaked
- 2 tablespoons cacao nibs, unsweetened
- 1 1/2 tablespoons cacao powder, unsweetened
- 1/8 teaspoon sea salt
- 1 teaspoon vanilla extract, unsweetened
- 1 cup almond milk, unsweetened
- 1/2 cup ice
- 4 ounces espresso, chilled

Directions:

1. Place all the ingredients in the order in a food processor or blender and then pulse for 2 to 3 minutes at high speed until smooth.
2. Pour the smoothie into a glass and then serve.

Nutrition: Calories: 210 Fat: 5 g Carbs: 27 g Protein: 16.8 g Fiber: 0.2 g

90. Strawberry, Banana and Coconut Shake

Preparation Time: 5 minutes

Cooking Time: 0 minutes

Servings: 1

Ingredients:

- 1 tablespoon coconut flakes
- 1 1/2 cups frozen banana slices
- 8 strawberries, sliced

- 1/2 cup coconut milk, unsweetened
- 1/4 cup strawberries for topping

Directions:

1. Place all the ingredients in the order in a food processor or blender, except for the topping, and then pulse for 2 to 3 minutes at high speed until smooth.
2. Pour the smoothie into a glass and then serve.

Nutrition: Calories: 335 Fat: 5 g Carbs: 75 g Protein: 4 g Fiber: 9 g

91. Tropical Vibes Green Smoothie

Preparation Time: 5 minutes

Cooking Time: 0 minutes

Servings: 1

Ingredients:

- 2 stalks of kale, ripped
- 1 frozen banana
- 1 mango, peeled, pitted, chopped
- 1/8 teaspoon sea salt
- ¼ cup of coconut yogurt
- ½ teaspoon vanilla extract, unsweetened
- 1 tablespoon ginger juice
- ½ cup of orange juice
- ½ cup of coconut water

Directions:

1. Place all the ingredients in the order in a food processor or blender and then pulse for 2 to 3 minutes at high speed until smooth.
2. Pour the smoothie into a glass and then serve.

Nutrition: Calories: 197.5 Fat: 1.3 g Carbs: 30 g Protein: 16.3 g Fiber: 4.8 g

92. Peanut Butter and Mocha Smoothie

Preparation Time: 5 minutes

Cooking Time: 0 minutes

Servings: 1

Ingredients:

- 1 frozen banana, chopped
- 1 scoop of chocolate protein powder
- 2 tablespoons rolled oats
- 1/8 teaspoon sea salt
- ¼ teaspoon vanilla extract, unsweetened
- 1 teaspoon cocoa powder, unsweetened
- 2 tablespoons peanut butter
- 1 shot of espresso
- ½ cup almond milk, unsweetened

Directions:

1. Place all the ingredients in the order in a food processor or blender and then pulse for 2 to 3 minutes at high speed until smooth.
2. Pour the smoothie into a glass and then serve.

Nutrition: Calories: 380 Fat: 14 g Carbs: 29 g Protein: 38 g Fiber: 4 g

93. Tahini Shake with Cinnamon and Lime

Preparation Time: 5 minutes

Cooking Time: 0 minutes

Servings: 1

Ingredients:

- 1 frozen banana
- 2 tablespoons tahini
- 1/8 teaspoon sea salt
- ¾ teaspoon ground cinnamon
- ¼ teaspoon vanilla extract, unsweetened
- 2 teaspoons lime juice
- 1 cup almond milk, unsweetened

Directions:

1. Place all the ingredients in the order in a food processor or blender and then pulse for 2 to 3 minutes at high speed until smooth.
2. Pour the smoothie into a glass and then serve.

Nutrition: Calories: 225 Fat: 15 g Carbs: 22 g Protein: 6 g Fiber: 8 g

94. Fig Oatmeal Bake

Preparation Time: 5 minutes

Cooking Time: 15 minutes

Servings: 4

Ingredients:

- 2 fresh figs, sliced
- 5 dried figs, chopped
- 4 tablespoons chopped walnuts
- 1 ½ cups oats
- 1 teaspoon cinnamon
- 2 tablespoons agave syrup
- 1 teaspoon baking powder
- 2 tablespoons unsalted butter, melted
- 3 tablespoons flaxseed egg
- ¾ cup of coconut milk

Directions:

1. Switch on the oven, then set it to 350°F and let it preheat.

2. Meanwhile, take a bowl, place all the ingredients in it, except for fresh figs, and stir until combined.
3. Take an 8-inch square pan, line it with a parchment sheet, spoon in the prepared mixture, top with fig slices, and bake for 30 minutes until cooked and set.
4. Serve straight away

Nutrition: Calories: 372.8 Fat: 9.2 g Carbs: 65.6 g Protein: 11.6 g Fiber: 11.1 g

95. Vegan Breakfast Sandwich

Preparation Time: 15 minutes

Cooking Time: 8 minutes

Servings: 3

Ingredients:

- 1 cup of spinach
- 6 slices of pickle
- 14 oz tofu, extra-firm, pressed
- 2 medium tomatoes, sliced
- 1/2 teaspoon garlic powder
- ¼ teaspoon ground black pepper
- 1/2 teaspoon black salt
- 1 teaspoon turmeric
- 1 tablespoon coconut oil
- 2 tablespoons vegan mayo
- 3 slices of vegan cheese
- 6 slices of gluten-free bread, toasted

Directions:

1. Cut tofu into six slices, and then season each side with garlic, black pepper, salt, and turmeric.
2. Take a skillet pan, place it over medium heat, add oil and when hot, add seasoned tofu slices in it, season side down, and cook for 3 minutes until crispy and light brown.
3. Then flip the tofu slices and continue cooking for 3 minutes until browned and crispy.
4. When done, transfer tofu slices on a baking sheet, in the form of a set of two slices side by side, then top each set with a cheese slice and broil for 3 minutes until cheese has melted.
5. Spread mayonnaise on both sides of slices, top with two slices of tofu, cheese on the side, top with spinach, tomatoes, pickles, and then close the sandwich.
6. Cut the sandwich into half and then serve.

Nutrition: Calories: 364 Fat: 12 g Carbs: 51 g Protein: 16 g Fiber: 3 g

96. Vegan Fried Egg

Preparation Time: 5 minutes
Cooking Time: 8 minutes
Servings: 4
Ingredients:

- 1 block of firm tofu, firm, pressed, drained
- ½ teaspoon ground black pepper
- ½ teaspoon salt
- 1 tablespoon vegan butter
- 1 cup vegan toast dipping sauce

Directions:

1. Cut tofu into four slices, and then shape them into a rough circle using a cookie cutter.
2. Take a frying pan, place it over medium heat, add butter and when it melts, add prepared tofu slices in a single layer and cook for 3 minutes per side until light brown.
3. Transfer tofu to serving dishes, make a small hole in the middle of tofu by using a small cookie cutter, and fill the hole with dipping sauce.
4. Garnish eggs with black pepper and sauce and then serve.

Nutrition: Calories: 86 Fat: 9 g Carbs: 0.5 g Protein: 2 g Fiber: 0 g

97. Sweet Crepes

Preparation Time: 5 minutes
Cooking Time: 8 minutes
Servings: 5
Ingredients:

- 1 cup of water
- 1 banana
- 1/2 cup oat flour
- 1/2 cup brown rice flour
- 1 teaspoon baking powder
- 1 tablespoon coconut sugar
- 1/8 teaspoon salt

Directions:

1. Take a blender, place all the ingredients except for sugar and salt, and pulse for 1 minute until smooth.
2. Take a skillet pan, place it over medium-high heat, grease it with oil and when hot, pour in ¼ cup of batter, spread it as thin as possible, and cook for 2 to 3 minutes per side until golden brown.
3. Cook the remaining crepes in the same manner, then sprinkle with sugar and salt and serve.

Nutrition: Calories: 160.1 Fat: 4.3 g Carbs: 22 g Protein: 8.3 g Fiber: 0.6 g

98. Tofu Scramble

Preparation Time: 5 minutes
Cooking Time: 18 minutes
Servings: 4
Ingredients:
For The Spice Mix:

- 1 teaspoon black salt
- 1/4 teaspoon garlic powder
- 1 teaspoon red chili powder
- 1 teaspoon ground cumin
- 3/4 teaspoons turmeric
- 2 tablespoons nutritional yeast

For The Tofu Scramble:

- 2 cups cooked black beans
- 16 ounces tofu, firm, pressed, drained
- 1 chopped red pepper
- 1 1/2 cups sliced button mushrooms
- 1/2 of white onion, chopped
- 1 teaspoon minced garlic
- 1 tablespoon olive oil

Directions:

1. Take a skillet pan, place it over medium-high heat, add oil and when hot, add onion, pepper, mushrooms, and garlic and cook for 8 minutes until golden.
2. Meanwhile, prepare the spice mix and for this, place all its ingredients in a bowl and stir until combined.
3. When vegetables have cooked, add tofu in it, crumble it, then add black beans, sprinkle with prepared spice mix, stir and cook for 8 minutes until hot.
4. Serve straight away.

Nutrition:
Calories: 175 Fat: 9 g Carbs: 10 g Protein: 14 g Fiber: 3 g

CHAPTER 2:

Salads

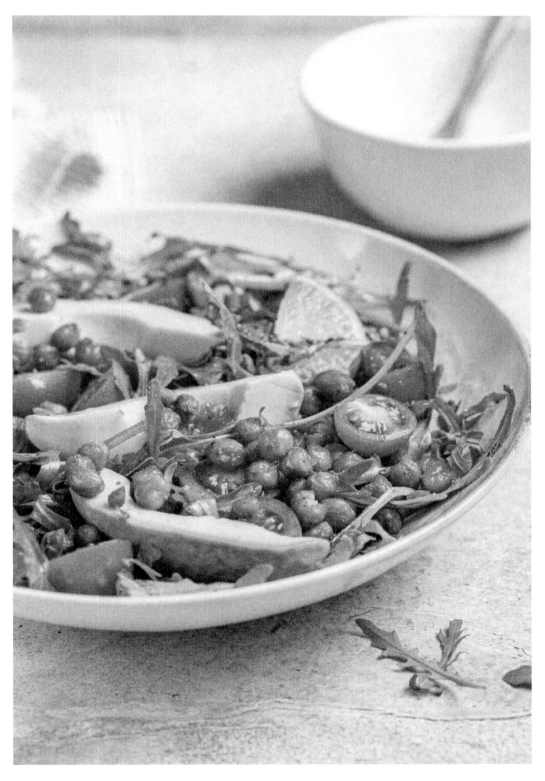

99. Black Bean Lentil Salad

Preparation Time: 10 minutes
Cooking Time: 20 minutes
Servings: 5
Ingredients:

- 1 Red Bell Pepper, diced
- 2/3 cup Cilantro
- 1 cup Green Lentils
- 2 Roma Tomatoes, diced
- ½ of 1 Red Onion, small & diced
- 15 oz. Black Beans

For dressing:

- ½ tsp. Oregano
- Juice of 1 Lime
- 1/8 tsp. Salt
- 2 tbsp. Olive Oil
- 1 tsp. Cumin
- 1 tsp. Dijon Mustard
- 2 Garlic cloves

Directions:

1. To begin with, cook the lentils in a large pan over medium heat following the manufacturer's instructions. Tip: The lentils should be cooked to firm but not mushy.
2. In the meantime, mix all the ingredients needed to make the dressing in a small bowl until combined well.
3. After that, combine the beans with the bell pepper, red onion cilantro, and red onion. Spoon on the dressing.
4. Toss well and serve immediately.

Tip: If desired, you can add your choice of seasoning like cayenne pepper, etc.

Nutrition Per Serving

Calories: 285 Kcal Protein: 15g Carbohydrates: 41g Fat: 6g

100. Cabbage Salad with Seitan

Preparation Time: 5 minutes
Cooking Time: 55 minutes
Servings: 4
Ingredients:
For the dressing:

- 1/3 cup Mango Chutney
- 1/3 cup Peanut Butter, natural & creamy

For the salad:

- 1 Cucumber, small & cut into half thin moons
- 1 tbsp. Olive Oil
- 3 Green Onions, sliced thinly
- 18 oz. Seitan, sliced into strips
- 6 cups Red Cabbage, shredded
- 3 Garlic Cloves, minced
- ¾ tsp. Curry Powder, mild

Directions

1. First, to make the dressing you need to combine the chutney, 1/3 cup water, and peanut butter in a high-speed blender.
2. Blend the mixture until it becomes smooth. Set the dressing aside.
3. After that, take a large skillet and heat it over medium heat.
4. Stir in one tablespoon of olive oil and then the seitan.
5. Add salt if needed and sauté the seitan for 5 to 7 minutes or until it becomes brown.
6. Next, spoon in the garlic and the remaining olive oil.
7. Cook for a further 30 seconds and then add the curry powder.
8. Sauté for 2 minutes and remove from the heat.
9. Finally, add the cabbage and cucumber along with the dressing in a large mixing bowl.
10. Top it with the seitan and green onions.
11. Serve immediately.

Tip: If preferred, you can add carrots also.

Nutrition Per Serving:

Calories: 330 Kcal Protein: 15g Carbohydrates: 32g Fat: 19g

101. Chickpeas Avocado Salad

Preparation Time: 10 minutes
Cooking Time: 20 minutes
Servings: 4
Ingredients:
For the salad:

- 1 ½ tbsp. Tahini
- 30 Cherry Tomatoes, sliced
- 4 ½ cups Chickpeas, cooked
- 1 Avocado, medium & diced
- 1 cup Quinoa, dried - ¼ tsp. Salt
- ½ of 1 Red Onion, medium & diced
- 1/3 cup Water
- 2 tbsp. Lemon Juice
- Pepper, as needed
- 1 ½ tsp. Dijon Mustard
- ½ cup Cilantro, packed

Directions:

1. To make this healthy salad, you first need to cook the quinoa by following the instructions given on the packet.
2. Next, take 1/3 of the chickpeas and place in a high-speed blender along with the water, lemon juice, pepper, Dijon mustard, and salt.
3. Blend for a minute or until you get a creamy consistency.
4. Now, toss the cooked quinoa, cherry tomatoes, red onion, avocado, and cilantro into a large mixing bowl.
5. Drizzle the dressing over it and serve immediately.

Tip: If preferred, you can add carrots also.

Nutrition Per Serving:

Calories: 604 Kcal Protein: 25g Carbohydrates: 90g Fat: 17g

102. Cold Peanut Noodle Salad

Preparation Time: 20 minutes
Cooking Time: 5 minutes
Servings: 2
Ingredients:
For the salad:

- 8 oz. Rice Noodles
- ½ tsp. Black Sesame Seeds
- 1 cup Carrots, shredded
- ½ of 1 Red Bell Pepper, sliced thinly
- 1/3 cup Peanuts, chopped
- 2 Scallions, chopped

For the peanut dressing:

- 2 tbsp. Hot Water
- 1/3 cup Peanut Butter, creamy
- 2 Garlic cloves, minced
- 3 tbsp. Sriracha
- 1 tbsp. Rice Vinegar

Directions:

1. First, cook the noodles by following the instructions given on the packet.
2. Drain the excess water and then rinse it under cold water. Keep aside.
3. After that, combine all the ingredients needed to make the dressing in a small bowl until mixed well. Set it aside.
4. Mix the noodles with all the remaining ingredients and dressing.
5. Combine and then place in the refrigerator until you're ready to serve.

Tip: If preferred, you can use habanero sauce instead of sriracha.

Nutrition Per Serving:

Calories: 604 Kcal Protein: 25g Carbohydrates: 90g Fat: 17g

103. Butternut Squash Black Rice Bean Salad

Preparation Time: 10 minutes
Cooking Time: 25 minutes
Servings: 8
Ingredients:
For the salad:

- 1 lb. Butternut Squash, chopped
- 2 tbsp. Olive Oil
- 2 cups Black Rice, dried
- 10 oz. Mushrooms, sliced
- ¼ cup Cranberries, dried
- 6 oz. Spinach, fresh & chopped
- ¼ cup Pumpkin Seeds
- 15 oz. White Beans, cooked
- Black Pepper, as needed

For the peanut dressing:

- 1 cup Coconut Cream
- ¼ cup Extra Virgin Olive Oil
- 2 tbsp. Curry Paste
- ¼ cup Almond Milk
- 1/3 cup Rice Vinegar

Directions:

1. Preheat the oven to 400°F.
2. After that, put the squash, pepper, and olive oil in a baking pan.
3. Toss them once or twice so that the oil and pepper coat the squash well.
4. Now, roast the squash for 10 to 15 minutes or until cooked. Set it aside.
5. In the meantime, cook the black rice until al dente. Keep it aside.
6. Next, mix all the ingredients needed to make the peanut dressing in another bowl until smooth.
7. Finally, combine the roasted squash, cooked rice, and the remaining ingredients in a large bowl.
8. Spoon the dressing over the ingredients and serve immediately.

Tip: If possible, use red curry paste.

Nutrition Per Serving:

Calories: 618 Kcal Protein: 22.2g Carbohydrates: 85.1g Fat: 24.1g

104. Arugula Beans Salad

Preparation Time: 10 minutes

Cooking Time: 25 minutes

Servings: 8

Ingredients:

For the salad:

- 15 oz. Lentils, cooked
- 4 tbsp. Capers
- 15 oz. Green Kidney Beans
- 2 handfuls of Arugula

For the dressing:

- 1 tbsp. Balsamic Vinegar
- 1 tbsp. Caper Brine
- 1 tbsp. Tahini
- 2 tbsp. Hot Sauce
- 2 tbsp. Peanut Butter
- 1 tbsp. Tamari

Directions

1. Begin by placing all the ingredients needed to make the dressing in a medium bowl and whisk it well until combined.
2. After that, combine the arugula, capers, kidney beans, and lentils in a large bowl. Pour the dressing over it.
3. Serve and enjoy.

Tip: Instead of green beans, you can also use red beans.

Nutrition Per Serving:

Calories: 543 Kcal Protein: 36g Carbohydrates: 85.4g Fat: 36g

105. Spring Salad

Preparation Time: 10 minutes

Cooking Time: 10 minutes

Servings: 1

Ingredients:

For the salad:

- 2 tbsp. Pepitas
- 2 cups Spring Mix Greens
- 1 tbsp. Hemp Hearts
- ½ cup Hummus
- ¼ cup Sun-dried Tomatoes
- 1 Watermelon Radish, sliced thinly
- 2 Carrots, medium & julienned
- 1/3 English Cucumber, cubed

Directions:

1. First, place all the ingredients in a large mixing bowl and toss them well.

2. Serve immediately.

Tip: If desired, you can use microgreens also.

Nutrition Per Serving:

Calories: 629 Kcal Protein: 31g Carbohydrates: 63g Fat: 33g

106. Tomato Lentil Salad

Preparation Time: 10 minutes

Cooking Time: 30 minutes

Servings: 6

Ingredients:

For the salad:

- 1 tbsp. Olive Oil, divided
- 2 tbsp. Extra Virgin Olive Oil
- ¼ tsp. Crushed Red Pepper
- 1 cup Green Lentil
- 1 Head of Garlic
- 2 tbsp. Lemon Juice
- 1 ½ cup Grape Tomatoes, halved
- ½ cup Red Pepper, diced
- 1 cup Red Onion, sliced
- Salt & Pepper, as needed
- 2 ¾ cup Vegetable Broth
- ½ cup Celery, diced

Directions:

1. Preheat the oven to 375°F.
2. Next, slice the top of the garlic head and put it in foil.
3. Brush half of the olive oil on the garlic and close the foil.
4. Then, place the tomatoes and onion in a single layer on a parchment paper-lined baking sheet.
5. Spoon the olive oil over the tomato-onion mixture. Sprinkle salt and pepper over it.
6. Now, cook for 28 to 30 minutes or until slightly dried.
7. After that, open the foil and allow the garlic to cool.
8. Take the garlic cloves from the head and keep them in a bowl while breaking the garlic.
9. Meanwhile, bring the broth mixture to a boil and stir in lentils to it.
10. Lower the heat and simmer for 28 to 30 minutes or until tender.
11. Drain the lentils and set them aside.
12. Meanwhile, whisk all the ingredients in a small bowl together until combined well.

13. Finally, add the tomatoes, celery, red pepper, tomatoes, and red onion. Spoon the dressing and serve immediately.

Tip: Instead of roasted tomatoes, you can also use sundried tomatoes.

Nutrition Per Serving:

Calories: 194 Kcal Protein: 8g Carbohydrates: 23g Fat: 7g

107. White Bean & Tomato Salad

Preparation Time: 5 minutes

Cooking Time: 5 minutes

Servings: 4

Ingredients:

For the dressing:

- 3 tbsp freshly squeezed lemon juice
- ¼ cup olive oil
- 1 garlic clove, minced
- ¼ tsp salt
- 1/8 tsp black pepper

For the salad:

- 2 (15 oz) cans white beans, drained and rinsed
- 2 cups cherry tomatoes, quartered
- ½ small red onion, sliced
- 1 garlic clove, minced
- ½ cup chopped fresh parsley

Directions:

1. Mix the dressing's ingredients in a large bowl until well-combined and add the white beans, garlic, tomatoes, onion, and parsley.
2. Coat the salad with the dressing.
3. Serve immediately.

108. Avocado & White Bean Salad

Preparation Time: 10 minutes

Cooking Time: 10 minutes

Servings: 2 to 4

Ingredients:

- 1 Avocado, chopped
- 1 Roma Tomato, chopped
- 14 oz. White Beans
- ¼ of 1 Sweet Onion, chopped

For the vinaigrette:

- ¼ cup Lemon Juice
- 1 ½ tbsp. Olive Oil
- Salt & Pepper, to taste
- Fresh Basil, as needed, for garnish
- 1 tsp. Mustard
- ½ tsp. Garlic, finely chopped

Directions:

1. First, whisk together all the ingredients needed to make the dressing in a small bowl until combined well.
2. Next, toss all the ingredients in a large mixing bowl and set it aside.
3. Pour the vinaigrette over the salad and place it in the refrigerator until you're ready to serve.
4. Serve and enjoy.

Tip: You can avoid onion if you desire.

Nutrition Per Serving:

Calories: 452Kcal Protein: 13.3g Carbohydrates: 39.7g Fat: 28.7g

109. Brussels Sprouts Salad

Preparation Time: 5 minutes

Cooking Time: 15 minutes

Servings: 3 cups

Ingredients:

- 14 ounces of shredded Brussels sprouts
- 1 ¼ cup of grated parmesan cheese
- 1/3 cup of raw hazelnuts*
- 2 tablespoons of extra virgin olive oil
- 1 ½ teaspoon of ground pepper
- 1 teaspoon of sea salt
- Pinch of crushed red pepper
- Zest of 1 lemon

Directions:

1. Toast nuts for better taste. Put them on a skillet on medium heat. Toast for 3–5 minutes, stirring frequently. After that, let it cool for a few minutes.

2. Put a large skillet on medium heat. Add olive oil, red pepper with ground pepper, and cook for 30–60 seconds.

3. Add Brussels sprouts into the skillet and cook for about 2 minutes, without stirring, until they start softening.

4. Spread some salt and continue cooking for 2 minutes more, until Brussels sprouts start becoming lightly golden-brown.

5. Pour over the cooked Brussels sprouts into a medium bowl. Add parmesan, hazelnuts, and lemon zest.

6. Serve immediately and enjoy!

Nutrition:

Calories: 225; Fat: 6g; Protein: 5.5g; Carbohydrates: 39.5g

110. Wedge Salad

Preparation Time: 15 minutes

Cooking Time: 0 minutes

Servings: 4

Ingredients:

- 2 carrots, finely diced

- 2 tablespoons low-sodium soy sauce or tamari
- 2 teaspoons pure maple syrup
- ½ teaspoon smoked paprika
- 2 ripe avocados
- ¼ cup cashews
- 2 tablespoons apple cider vinegar
- 1 tablespoon nutritional yeast
- 1 teaspoon spirulina powder (optional)
- 1 small red onion, sliced
- 1 cup cherry or grape tomatoes, halved
- 1 head iceberg lettuce, cut into 4 wedges
- Freshly ground black pepper

Directions:

1. Place the carrots in a small bowl and let sit for 10 minutes.

2. In a measuring cup, whisk together the soy sauce, maple syrup, and paprika and pour it over the carrots. Set aside.

3. Cut the avocados in half and remove the pits. Dice the flesh of one of the avocado halves in the peel, then gently scoop it out into a small bowl. Set aside.

4. Scoop the flesh from the 3 remaining avocado halves into a blender. Add the cashews, vinegar, nutritional yeast, and spirulina (if using) and purée until very smooth, creamy, and pourable. Add 1 to 2 tablespoons of water, if necessary, to reach the right consistency. Pour the dressing into a medium bowl.

5. Add the onion, tomatoes, and carrots (along with the liquid in the bowl) to the bowl with the dressing and stir to combine. Gently fold the diced avocado into the dressing.

6. Place a wedge of lettuce on each of the four salad plates. Dress the lettuce by spooning about ½ cup of dressing over each wedge, then repeat until the dressing is used up. Sprinkle a pinch or two of black pepper over each salad and serve.

Nutrition: Calories: 289; Fat: 4g; Protein: 8g; Carbohydrates: 29g

111. Chef Salad

Preparation Time: 15 minutes
Cooking Time: 15 minutes
Servings: 4
Ingredients:

- 6 fingerling potatoes, unpeeled, cut in half
- 2 teaspoons smoked paprika, divided
- ½ teaspoon ground turmeric
- ½ teaspoon freshly ground black pepper
- ¼ teaspoon black salt
- 2 cups fresh or drained canned pineapple chunks

- 1 small cucumber, unpeeled, cut into ¼-inch dice - 1 tablespoon rice vinegar
- 6 ounces silken tofu
- 1 tablespoon lime juice
- 2 garlic cloves, peeled
- 2 teaspoons tomato powder
- 2 heads romaine lettuce, chopped

Directions:

1. Fill a large saucepan with about 2 inches of water, insert a steamer basket, and bring to a boil over high heat. Lower the heat to medium-high and place the potatoes in the steamer. Cover and steam for 15 minutes. Transfer the potatoes to a small bowl, sprinkle with 1 teaspoon of paprika, turmeric, pepper, and black salt and toss until evenly coated. Place in the refrigerator to chill.

2. In a small bowl, combine the pineapple and remaining 1 teaspoon of paprika until evenly coated. Set aside.

3. In another small bowl, combine the cucumber and vinegar. Set aside.

4. In a food processor or blender, combine the tofu, lime juice, garlic, and tomato powder and purée until thick and creamy. Remove the food processor blade, add the cucumber-vinegar mixture, and stir to combine.

5. Place the lettuce in a large bowl. Pour the tofu dressing over the lettuce and toss until evenly coated.

6. Portion the salad into four large salad bowls. Top each bowl with three pieces of potato and ½ cup of pineapple mixture, then serve.

Nutrition: Calories: 219; Fat: 1. g; Protein: 11g; Carbohydrates: 43g

112. Radish Avocado Salad

Preparation Time: 10 minutes
Cooking Time: 0 minutes
Servings: 2
Ingredients:

- 6 shredded carrots
- 6 ounces diced radishes
- 1 diced avocado - 1/3 cup ponzu

Directions:

1. Place all the ingredients together in a serving bowl and toss. Enjoy!

Nutrition: Calories: 292; Fat: 18g; Carbohydrates: 29g; Protein: 7g

113. Mint Coriander Nutty Salad

Preparation Time: 10 minutes
Cooking Time: 0 minutes
Servings: 2
Ingredients:

- ½ cup Almond whole

- ½ cup Peanuts, roasted
- 2 cups Cabbage, sliced
- 2 Cucumber, diced
- 2 Carrot, diced
- 1 Lime, juiced
- 2 Onions, diced
- 2 Tomatoes, diced
- ½ Sea salt
- ½ Coriander
- ¼ Mint

Directions:

1. Place all the ingredients together in a large bowl.

2. Combine them well and serve.

Nutrition: Calories: 150; Fat: 2g; Carbohydrates: 12g; Protein: 5g

114.   Mix Grain Salad

Preparation Time: 20 minutes

Cooking Time: 20 minutes

Servings: 6

Ingredients:

Dressing

- ¼ cup fresh lime juice
- 2 tablespoons maple syrup
- 1 tablespoon Dijon mustard
- ½ teaspoon ground cumin
- 1 teaspoon garlic powder
- Salt and ground black pepper, to taste
- ½ cup extra-virgin olive oil

Salad

- 2 cups fresh mango, peeled, pitted, and cubed
- 2 tablespoons fresh lime juice, divided
- 2 avocados, peeled, pitted, and cubed
- Pinch of salt
- 1 cup cooked quinoa
- 2 (14-ounce) cans black beans, rinsed and drained
- 1 (15¼-ounce) can corn, rinsed and drained
- 1 small red onion, chopped
- 1 jalapeño, seeded and chopped finely
- ½ cup fresh cilantro, chopped
- 6 cups romaine lettuce, shredded

Directions:

1. For the dressing: in a blender, add all the ingredients (except oil) and pulse until well combined.

2. While the motor is running, gradually add the oil and pulse until smooth.

3. For the salad: in a bowl, add the mango and 1 tablespoon of lime juice and toss to coat well.

4. In another bowl, add the avocado, a pinch of salt, and remaining lime juice and toss to coat well.

5. In a large serving bowl, add the mango, avocado, and remaining salad ingredients and mix.

6. Place the dressing and toss to coat well.

7. Serve immediately.

Nutrition: Calories: 631; Protein: 16g; Carbohydrates: 73g; Fat: 33g

115.   Quinoa and Chickpea Salad

Preparation Time: 20 minutes

Cooking Time: 0 minutes

Servings: 4

Ingredients:

- 2 cups cooked quinoa
- 1½ cups canned red kidney beans, rinsed and drained
- 3 cups fresh baby spinach
- 1/4 cup sun-dried tomatoes, chopped
- ¼ cup fresh dill
- ¼ cup fresh parsley
- ½ cup sunflower seeds
- ¼ cup walnuts, chopped
- 3 tablespoons fresh lemon juice
- Salt and ground black pepper, as required

Directions:

1. In a large bowl, add all the ingredients and toss to coat well.

2. Serve immediately.

Nutrition: Calories: 489; Fat: 13g; Carbohydrates: 73g; Protein: 23g

116.   Rice and Tofu Salad

Preparation Time: 15 minutes

Cooking Time: 0 minutes

Servings: 4

Ingredients:

Salad

- 1 (12-ounce) package firm tofu, pressed, drained, and sliced
- 1½ cups cooked brown rice
- 3 large tomatoes, peeled and chopped
- ¼ cup fresh basil leaves

Dressing

- 3 scallions, chopped

- 2 tablespoons black sesame seeds, toasted
- 2 tablespoons low-sodium soy sauce
- ½ teaspoon sesame oil, toasted
- Drop of hot pepper sauce as deisred
- 1 tablespoon maple syrup
- ¼ teaspoon red chili powder

Directions:

1. In a large serving bowl, place all the ingredients and toss to coat well.

2. Serve immediately.

Nutrition: Calories: 393; Fat: 8.6g; Carbohydrates: 67g; Protein: 15g

117. Kidney Bean and Pomegranate Salad

Preparation Time: 15 minutes

Cooking Time: 0 minutes

Servings: 3

Ingredients:

- 2 cups canned white kidney beans, rinsed and drained
- 1 cup fresh pomegranate seeds
- 1/3 cup scallion (green part), chopped finely
- 2 tablespoons fresh parsley, chopped
- 1 tablespoon fresh lime juice
- Salt and ground black pepper, as required

Directions:

1. In a large serving bowl, place all the ingredients and toss to coat well.

2. Serve immediately.

Nutrition: Calories: 180; Protein: 12g; Carbohydrates: 35g; Fat: 0g

118. Corn and Bean Salad

Preparation Time: 15 minutes

Cooking Time: 0 minutes

Servings: 8

Ingredients:

Salad

- 1 (10-ounce) package frozen corn kernels, thawed
- 3 (15-ounce) cans black beans, rinsed and drained
- 2 large red bell peppers, seeded and chopped
- 1 large red onion, chopped

Dressing

- ¼ cup fresh cilantro, minced
- 1 garlic clove, minced

- 1 tablespoon maple syrup
- ½ cup balsamic vinegar - ½ cup olive oil
- 1 tablespoon fresh lime juice
- 1 tablespoon fresh lemon juice
- ½ teaspoon red pepper flakes, crushed
- Salt and ground black pepper, as required

Directions:

1. For the salad: add all the ingredients in a large serving bowl and mix well.

2. For the dressing: add all the ingredients in a bowl and beat until well combined.

3. Place the dressing over the salad and gently toss to coat well.

4. Serve immediately.

Nutrition: Calories: 310; Fat: 14g; Carbohydrates: 36g; Protein: 10g

119. Cherry Tomato Couscous Salad

Preparation Time: 5 minutes

Cooking Time: 15 minutes

Servings: 5

Ingredients:

- 1 cup couscous
- ½ cup small fresh basil leaves
- 2 tablespoons minced shallots
- 8-ounce sliced cherry tomatoes
- 1 tablespoon olive oil - 3 tablespoons vinegar
- ¾ teaspoon ground black pepper
- ½ teaspoon salt

Directions:

1. In a saucepan, add water and salt and bring it to a boil. Now toast couscous in a small pan cook it over medium flame. Cook it for around 7 minutes and move it in a circular motion. Add it immediately to the salty boiling water and cook for an additional 6 minutes and drain and rinse it. Now take a bowl and mix all the remaining ingredients and cooked couscous.

2. Mix them well and serve them after 15 minutes.

Nutrition: Calories: 95; Fat: 2.86g; Carbohydrates: 15.95g; Protein: 1.91g

120. Spicy Watermelon Tomato Salad

Preparation Time: 20 minutes

Cooking Time: 0 minutes

Servings: 8

Ingredients:

- 1 diced yellow tomato

- 2 cups diced seeded watermelon
- ¼ cup vinegar
- 1 cubed red tomato
- 2 teaspoons honey
- ¼ cup olive oil
- 2 tablespoons chili-garlic sauce
- 1 tablespoon chopped lemon basil
- ½ teaspoon salt
- ½ teaspoon black pepper

Directions:

1. Drain some moisture from watermelon and red and yellow tomatoes by spreading it over the paper towel. Now put all the ingredients, including the drained ingredients. Mix all the ingredients well and serve it.

Nutrition: Calories: 89; Fat: 7.18g; Carbohydrates: 6.2g; Protein: 0.77g

121. Health is Wealth Salad: Dash of Chickpea and Tomato

Preparation Time: 10 minutes
Cooking Time: 10 minutes
Servings: 3-4
Ingredients:

- 1 freshly chopped red pepper
- 2 cups of cooked chickpeas
- 1/3 cup of freshly chopped parsley
- 5 freshly chopped spring onions
- 1 cup of rinsed baby spinach leaves
- ½ a lemon, juiced
- 5 freshly chopped medium tomatoes
- 1 tablespoon of balsamic vinegar
- 2 tablespoons of sesame seeds
- ½ thinly sliced hot pepper
- 2 tablespoons of olive oil
- 2 tablespoons of flax seeds

Directions:

1. Thoroughly clean and chop all the vegetables. Do not chop the baby spinach.
2. In a big salad bowl, mix the chickpeas, onions, tomatoes, pepper, spinach, and parsley.
3. Toss with the sesame seeds and sprinkle the flax seeds.
4. Drizzle with olive oil, lemon juice, and balsamic vinegar. Give all of the ingredients a thorough mix.

5. Add salt and pepper to taste and serve this summer staple. It is fresh and healthy, and you cannot say no to this delicious salad.

Nutrition: Calories: 310; Fat: 14g; Carbohydrates: 36g; Protein: 10g

122. Eggplant Salad

Preparation Time: 15 minutes
Cooking Time: 25 minutes
Servings: 6
Ingredients:

- 2 eggplants
- 1 teaspoon salt
- 1 white onion, diced
- 1 teaspoon Pink salt
- 1 oz fresh cilantro
- 3 tablespoons lemon juice
- 4 tablespoons olive oil
- 1 garlic clove, peeled

Directions:

1. Cut eggplants into halves.
2. Preheat the oven to 365°F.
3. Put eggplants in the oven and cook for 25 minutes or until they are tender.
4. Meanwhile, blend the diced onion and transfer it to the cheesecloth.
5. Pour olive oil and lemon juice into the bowl.
6. Squeeze blended onion in the oil mixture.
7. Add salt.
8. Chop cilantro and grind garlic.
9. Add ingredients in the oily mixture too. Stir it.
10. Remove the eggplants from the oven and chill them a little.
11. Remove the flesh from the eggplants and transfer it to the salad bowl.
12. Add oil mixture and stir gently.

Nutrition: Calories: 292; Fat: 17.32g; Carbohydrates: 26.99g; Protein: 10.51g

123. Tricolored Salad

Preparation Time: 10 minutes
Cooking Time: 0 minutes
Servings: 5
Ingredients:

- 1 avocado, peeled
- ½ cup kalamata olives
- 2 tablespoons olive oil
- 1 teaspoon minced garlic
- ¼ teaspoon salt

- 2 tomatoes, chopped
- 1 teaspoon apple cider vinegar
- 6 oz Provolone cheese, chopped

Directions:

1. Mix up together salt, apple cider vinegar, minced garlic, and olive oil.
2. Cut kalamata olives into halves.
3. Slice avocado and place in a salad bowl.
4. Add olive halves, chopped tomato, and cheese.
5. Stir gently and sprinkle with olive oil mixture.

Nutrition: Calories: 257; Fat: 21.89g; Carbohydrates: 7.21g; Protein: 10.09g

124. "Potato" Salad

Preparation Time: 10 minutes
Cooking Time: 15 minutes
Servings: 4
Ingredients:

- 8 oz turnip, peeled
- 1 carrot, peeled
- 1 bay leaf
- ¼ teaspoon peppercorns
- 1 teaspoon salt
- ½ teaspoon cayenne pepper
- 1 tablespoon fresh parsley, chopped
- 3 eggs, boiled
- 3 tablespoons sour cream
- 1 tablespoon mustard
- 2 cups water, for vegetables

Directions:

1. Put turnip and carrot in the saucepan.
2. Add water, peppercorns, bay leaf, and salt.
3. Close the lid and boil vegetables for 15 minutes over high heat. The cooked vegetables should be tender.
4. Meanwhile, peel eggs and chop them.
5. Put the chopped eggs in the bowl.
6. Sprinkle them with cayenne pepper and chopped parsley.
7. In a separate bowl, stir together mustard and sour cream.
8. When the vegetables are cooked, strain them and transfer them to the salad bowl. Add mustard sauce and stir.

Nutrition:
Calories: 140; Fat: 8.78g; Carbohydrates: 6.04g; Protein: 9.08g

125. Cauliflower & Apple Salad

Preparation Time: 25 minutes
Cooking Time: 0 minutes
Servings: 4
Ingredients:

- 3 Cups Cauliflower, Chopped into Florets
- 2 Cups Baby Kale
- 1 Sweet Apple, Cored & Chopped
- ¼ Cup Basil, Fresh & Chopped
- ¼ Cup Mint, Fresh & Chopped
- ¼ Cup Parsley, Fresh & Chopped
- 1/3 Cup Scallions, Sliced Thin
- 2 Tablespoons Yellow Raisins
- 1 Tablespoon Sun-Dried Tomatoes, Chopped
- ½ Cup Miso Dressing, Optional
- ¼ Cup Roasted Pumpkin Seeds, Optional

Directions:

1. Combine everything, tossing before serving.

Interesting Facts: This vegetable is an extremely high source of vitamin A, vitamin B1, B2, and B3.

Nutrition:

Calories: 166; Fat: 7.15g; Carbohydrates: 16.43g; Protein: 11.06g

126. Corn & Black Bean Salad

Preparation Time: 10 minutes
Cooking Time: 0 minutes
Servings: 6
Ingredients:

- ¼ Cup Cilantro, Fresh & Chopped
- 1 Can Corn, Drained (10 Ounces)
- 1/8 Cup Red Onion, Chopped
- 1 Can Black Beans, Drained (15 Ounces)
- 1 Tomato, Chopped
- 3 Tablespoons Lemon Juice, Fresh
- 2 Tablespoons Olive Oil
- Sea Salt & Black Pepper to Taste

Directions:

1. Mix everything together, and then refrigerate until cool. Serve cold.

Nutrition:

Calories: 64; Fat: 2.95g; Carbohydrates: 10.03g; Protein: 1.08g

127. Spinach & Orange Salad

Preparation Time: 15 minutes
Cooking Time: 0 minutes
Servings: 6
Ingredients:

- ¼ -1/3 Cup Vegan Dressing
- 3 Oranges, Medium, Peeled, Seeded & Sectioned
- ¾ lb. Spinach, Fresh & Torn
- 1 Red Onion, Medium, Sliced & Separated into Rings

Directions:

1. Toss everything together and serve with dressing.

Nutrition:

Calories: 33; Fat: 0.39g; Carbohydrates: 6.52g; Protein: 1.75g

128. Red Pepper & Broccoli Salad

Preparation Time: 15 minutes
Cooking Time: 0 minutes
Servings: 2
Ingredients:

- Lettuce Salad Mix
- 1 Head Broccoli, Chopped into Florets
- 1 Red Pepper, Seeded & Chopped

Dressing:

- 3 Tablespoons White Wine Vinegar
- 1 Teaspoon Dijon Mustard
- 1 Clove Garlic, Peeled & Chopped Fine
- ½ Teaspoon Black Pepper
- ½ Teaspoon Sea Salt, Fine
- 2 Tablespoons Olive Oil
- 1 Tablespoon Parsley, Chopped

Directions:

1. In boiling water, boil the broccoli, drain the broccoli on a paper towel.
2. Whisk together all dressing ingredients.
3. Toss ingredients together before serving.

Nutrition:

Calories: 153; Fat: 13.93g; Carbohydrates: 5.95g; Protein: 1.98g

129. Lentil Potato Salad

Preparation Time: 35 minutes
Cooking Time: 0 minutes
Servings: 2
Ingredients:

- ½ Cup Beluga Lentils
- 8 Fingerling Potatoes
- 1 Cup Scallions, Sliced Thin
- ¼ Cup Cherry Tomatoes, Halved
- ¼ Cup Lemon Vinaigrette
- Sea Salt & Black Pepper to Taste

Directions:

1. Bring two cups of water to simmer in a pot, adding your lentils. Cook for twenty to twenty-five minutes, and then drain. Your lentils should be tender.
2. Reduce to a simmer, cook for fifteen minutes, and then drain. Halve your potatoes once they're cool enough to touch.
3. Put your lentils on a serving plate, and then top with scallions, potatoes, and tomatoes. Drizzle with your vinaigrette, and season with salt and pepper.

Nutrition:

Calories: 1189; Fat: 1.65g; Carbohydrates: 270.19g; Protein: 33.02g

130. Black Bean & Corn Salad with Avocado

Preparation Time: 20 minutes
Cooking Time: 0 minutes
Servings: 6
Ingredients:

- 1 1/2 cups corn kernels, cooked & frozen or canned
- 1/2 cup olive oil
- 1 minced clove garlic
- 1/3 cup lime juice, fresh
- 1 avocado (peeled, pitted & diced)
- 1/8 tsp. cayenne pepper
- 2 cans black beans (approximately 15 oz.)
- 6 thinly sliced green onions
- 1/2 cup chopped cilantro, fresh
- 2 chopped tomatoes
- 1 chopped red bell pepper
- Chili powder
- 1/2 tsp. salt

Directions:

1. In a small jar, place the olive oil, lime juice, garlic, cayenne, and salt.
2. Cover with lid; shake until all the ingredients under the jar are mixed well.
3. Toss the green onions, corn, beans, bell pepper, avocado, tomatoes, and cilantro together in a large bowl or plastic container with a cover.

4. Shake the lime dressing for a second time and transfer it over the salad ingredients.

5. Stir salad to coat the beans and vegetables with the dressing; cover & refrigerate.

6. To blend the flavors completely, let this sit for a moment.

7. Remove the container from the refrigerator from time to time; turn upside down & back gently a couple of times to reorganize the dressing.

Nutrition:

Calories: 433; Fat: 42.31g; Carbohydrates: 270.19g; Protein: 33.02g

131. Summer Chickpea Salad

Preparation Time: 15 minutes

Cooking Time: 0 minutes

Servings: 4

Ingredients:

- 1 ½ Cup Cherry Tomatoes, Halved
- 1 Cup English Cucumber, Slices
- 1 Cup Chickpeas, Canned, Unsalted, Drained & Rinsed
- ¼ Cup Red Onion, Slivered
- 2 Tablespoons Olive Oil
- 1 ½ Tablespoon Lemon Juice, Fresh
- 1 ½ Tablespoon Lemon Juice, Fresh
- Sea Salt & Black Pepper to Taste

Directions:

1. Mix everything together, and toss to combine before serving.

Nutrition:

Calories: 139; Fat: 7.88g; Carbohydrates: 14.3g; Protein: 4.02g

132. Edamame Salad

Preparation Time: 15 minutes

Cooking Time: 0 minutes

Servings: 1

Ingredients:

- ¼ Cup Red Onion, Chopped
- 1 Cup Corn Kernels, Fresh
- 1 Cup Edamame Beans, Shelled & Thawed
- 1 Red Bell Pepper, Chopped
- 2-3 Tablespoons Lime Juice, Fresh
- 5-6 Basil Leaves, Fresh & Sliced
- 5-6 Mint Leaves, Fresh & Sliced
- Sea Salt & Black Pepper to Taste

Directions:

1. Place everything into a Mason jar, and then seal the jar tightly. Shake well before serving.

Nutrition:

Calories: 202; Fat: 3.24g; Carbohydrates: 44.2g; Protein: 7.89g

133. Fruity Kale Salad

Preparation Time: 30 minutes

Cooking Time: 0 minutes

Servings: 4

Ingredients: Salad:

- 10 Ounces Baby Kale
- ½ Cup Pomegranate Arils
- 1 Tablespoon Olive Oil
- 1 Apple, Sliced

Dressing:

- 3 Tablespoons Apple Cider Vinegar
- 3 Tablespoons Olive Oil
- 1 Tablespoon Tahini Sauce (Optional)
- Sea Salt & Black Pepper to Taste

Directions:

1. Wash and dry the kale. If kale is too expensive, you can also use lettuce, arugula or spinach. Take the stems out, and chop.

2. Combine all of your salad ingredients together.

3. Combine all of your dressing ingredients together before drizzling it over the salad to serve.

Nutrition:

Calories: 183; Fat: 14.04g; Carbohydrates: 15.56g; Protein: 1.01g

134. Olive & Fennel Salad

Preparation Time: 5 minutes

Cooking Time: 0 minutes

Servings: 3

Ingredients:

- 6 Tablespoons Olive Oil
- 3 Fennel Bulbs, Trimmed, Cored & Quartered
- 2 Tablespoons Parsley, Fresh & Chopped
- 1 Lemon, Juiced & Zested
- 12 Black Olives
- Sea Salt & Black Pepper to Taste

Directions:

1. Grease your baking dish, and then place your fennel in it. Make sure the cut side is up.

2. Mix your lemon zest, lemon juice, salt, pepper and oil, pouring it over your fennel.

3. Sprinkle your olives over it and bake at 400F.
4. Serve with parsley.

Nutrition:

Calories: 338; Fat: 29.08g; Carbohydrates: 20.73g; Protein: 3.47g

135. Avocado & Radish Salad

Preparation Time: 10 minutes

Cooking Time: 0 minutes

Servings: 2

Ingredients:

- 1 Avocado, Sliced - 6 Radishes, Sliced
- 2 Tomatoes, Sliced
- 1 Lettuce Head, Leaves Separated
- ½ Red Onion, Peeled & Sliced

Dressing:

- ½ Cup Olive Oil
- ¼ Cup Lime Juice, Fresh
- ¼ Cup Apple Cider Vinegar
- 3 Cloves Garlic, Chopped Fine
- Sea Salt & Black Pepper to Taste

Directions:

1. Spread your lettuce leaves on a platter, and then layer with your onion, tomatoes, avocado and radishes.
2. Whisk your dressing ingredients together before drizzling them over your salad.

Nutrition:

Calories: 915; Fat: 70.44g; Carbohydrates: 71.82g; Protein: 12.54g

136. Zucchini & Lemon Salad

Preparation Time: 3 Hours 10 minutes

Cooking Time: 0 minutes

Servings: 2

Ingredients:

- 1 Green Zucchini, Sliced into Rounds
- 1 Yellow Squash, Zucchini, Sliced into Rounds
- 1 Clove Garlic, Peeled & Chopped
- 2 Tablespoons Olive Oil 2 Tablespoons Basil, Fresh
- 1 Lemon, Juiced & Zested ¼ Cup Coconut Milk
- Sea Salt & Black Pepper to Taste

Directions:

1. Refrigerate all ingredients for three hours before serving.

Nutrition:

Calories: 207; Fat: 20.81g; Carbohydrates: 6.34g; Protein: 1.5g

137. Watercress & Blood Orange Salad

Preparation Time: 10 minutes

Cooking Time: 0 minutes

Servings: 4

Ingredients:

- 1 Tablespoon Hazelnuts, Toasted & Chopped
- 2 Blood Oranges (or Navel Oranges)
- 3 Cups watercress, Stems Removed
- 1/8 Teaspoon Sea Salt, Fine
- 1 Tablespoon Lemon Juice, Fresh
- 1 Tablespoon Honey, Raw
- 1 Tablespoon Water
- 2 Tablespoons Chives, Fresh

Directions:

1. Whisk your oil, honey, lemon juice, chives, salt and water together. Add in your watercress, tossing until it's coated.
2. Arrange the mixture onto salad plates, and top with orange slices. Drizzle with remaining liquid, and sprinkle with hazelnuts.

Nutrition:

Calories: 201; Fat: 17.51g; Carbohydrates: 9.79g; Protein: 4.96g

138. Parsley Salad

Preparation Time: 30 minutes

Cooking Time: 0 minutes

Servings: 8

Ingredients:

- 3 Lemons, Juiced
- 150 Grams Flat Leaf Parsley, Chopped Fine
- 1 Cup Boiled Water - 5 Tablespoons Olive Oil
- Sea Salt & Black Pepper to Taste
- 6 Green Onions, Chopped Fine
- 1 Cup Bulgur
- 4 Tomatoes, Chopped Fine

Directions:

1. Add your Bulgur to your water, and mix well. Put a towel on top of it to steam it. Keep it to the side, and then chop your spring onions, tomatoes and parsley. Put them in your salad bowl.
2. Pour your juice into the mixture, and then add in your olive oil, salt and pepper.
3. Put this mixture over your bulgur to serve.

Nutrition:

Calories: 530; Fat: 17.81g; Carbohydrates: 82.66g; Protein: 35.35g

CHAPTER 3:

Soups

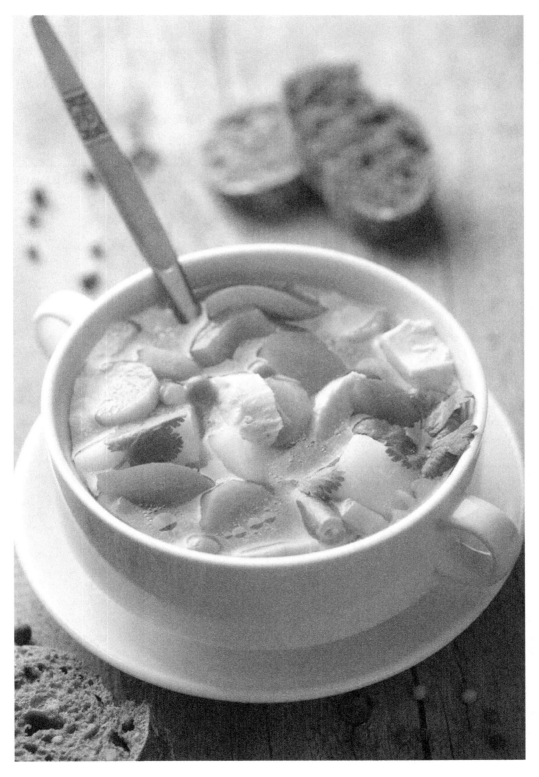

139. Classic Vegetable Soup

Preparation Time: 10 minutes
Cooking Time: 20 minutes
Servings: 4 To 6
Ingredients:

- 1 tablespoon red miso paste
- 2 cups diced onion
- 1 cup diced carrots
- 1 cup diced russet potatoes
- 3 garlic cloves, minced
- ½ teaspoon dried basil
- ½ teaspoon dried oregano
- ½ teaspoon dried thyme
- 3 cups Vegetable Broth
- 1 cup chopped frozen or fresh green beans
- 1 cup diced tomato

Directions:

1. In a large saucepan, bring ¼ cup of water to a simmer over medium-high heat. Add the miso and whisk until thick and smooth. Add the onion, carrots, potatoes, garlic, basil, oregano, thyme, and broth, and bring to a boil. Lower the heat to medium-low, cover, and simmer for 10 minutes.

2. Add the green beans and tomato and bring back to a boil. Lower the heat, cover, and simmer for 5 minutes more, then serve.

ALLERGEN TIP: To make this soy-free, sauté the vegetables with 2 teaspoons of Spicy Umami Blend instead of the miso paste.

Nutrition Per Serving (2 CUPS): Calories: 103; Saturated Fat: 0g; Total Fat: 1g; Protein: 4g; Total Carbs: 23g; Fiber: 4g; Sodium: 190mg

140. Cream of Miso Mushroom Stew

Preparation Time: 10 minutes
Cooking Time: 15 minutes
Servings: 4 To 6
Ingredients:

- 1 tablespoon low-sodium soy sauce or tamari
- 1 cup julienned green onions
- 2 cups sliced mushrooms (shiitake, oyster, or baby bella)
- 2 cups Miso Cream Sauce
- 2 cups Vegetable Broth
- 1 tablespoon rice vinegar

Directions:

1. In a large saucepan, heat the soy sauce over medium-high heat. Add the green onions and mushrooms and sauté until tender, 3 to 5 minutes. Add the miso cream sauce and sauté until it begins to thicken, about 3 minutes.

2. Add the broth and bring it to a boil. Lower the heat to low and simmer, stirring occasionally, for 10 minutes.

3. Remove from the heat. Stir in the vinegar and serve.

SWAP IT: I call for green onions because they are easy to find, but negi (Japanese leeks), leeks, or bunching onions are great substitutes.

ALLERGEN TIP: Use gluten-free tamari or coconut aminos and be sure to use a gluten-free miso paste in your Miso Cream Sauce.

Nutrition Per Serving (1½ CUPS):

Calories: 156; Saturated Fat: 1g; Total Fat: 7g; Protein: 8g; Total Carbs: 13g; Fiber: 2g; Sodium: 476mg

141. Chickpea Noodle Soup

Preparation Time: 10 minutes
Cooking Time: 25 minutes
Servings: 4 To 6
Ingredients:

- 4 ounces dried soba noodles
- 4 cups Vegetable Broth, divided
- 2 cups diced onions
- 1 cup chopped carrots
- 1 cup chopped celery
- 3 garlic cloves, finely diced
- ½ teaspoon dried parsley
- ½ teaspoon dried sage
- ½ teaspoon dried thyme
- ½ teaspoon freshly ground black or white pepper
- 1 (15-ounce) can chickpeas, drained and rinsed
- ¼ cup chopped fresh parsley, for garnish (optional)

Directions:

1. In a large saucepan, bring 4 cups of water to a boil over high heat. Add the soba noodles and cook, stirring occasionally, until just tender, 4 to 5 minutes. Drain in a colander and rinse well under cold water. Set aside.

2. In the same saucepan, heat ¼ cup of broth over medium-high heat. Add the onions, carrots, celery, garlic, parsley, sage, thyme, and pepper, and sauté for 5 minutes, or until the carrots are fork-tender.

3. Add the chickpeas and remaining 3¾ cups of broth and bring to a boil. Lower the heat to low, cover, and simmer for 15 minutes.

4. Serve garnished with parsley, if desired.

INGREDIENT TIP: I love using soba noodles in Spring Rolls with Pistachio Sauce or as a grain addition to a salad. Make an entire package at once, use what you need for this soup, and store the rest in an airtight container in the refrigerator for up to 5 days.

Nutrition Per Serving (1 CUP):

Calories: 266; Saturated Fat: 0g; Total Fat: 3g; Protein: 12g; Total Carbs: 53g; Fiber: 8g; Sodium: 351mg

142. Tangy Tomato Soup

Preparation Time: 5 minutes

Cooking Time: 30 minutes

Servings: 4

Ingredients:

- 1 large sweet onion, coarsely chopped
- 1 (28-ounce) can diced tomatoes
- 1 (28-ounce) can crushed tomatoes
- 1 cup Vegetable Broth
- 2 teaspoons dried tarragon
- 1 Medjool date, pitted and chopped (optional)
- ¼ cup balsamic vinegar

Directions:

1. In a large saucepan, dry sauté the onion over medium-high heat, stirring frequently, until just beginning to brown, 8 to 10 minutes. Add the diced and crushed tomatoes, broth, and tarragon, and bring to a boil.

2. Lower the heat to medium-low and simmer, stirring frequently, for 20 minutes.

3. Add the date and use an immersion blender to purée the soup directly in the pan until smooth (or transfer the soup to a standing blender and carefully purée, then return the soup to the pan).

4. Pour in the vinegar, quickly stir, and serve hot.

SWAP IT: No tarragon? No problem! Use ¼ teaspoon ground fennel seed and ¼ teaspoon ground anise seed.

Nutrition Per Serving (2 CUPS):

Calories: 153; Saturated Fat: 0g; Total Fat: 1g; Protein: 6g; Total Carbs: 35g; Fiber: 9g; Sodium: 408mg

143. Yellow Potato Soup

Preparation Time: 10 minutes

Cooking Time: 25 minutes

Servings: 4

Ingredients:

- 3 cups cubed potatoes (any kind)
- 1 cup diced onion
- 1 cup chopped carrots
- ½ teaspoon chipotle chile powder
- ½ teaspoon ground cinnamon

- ½ teaspoon sea salt, or 1 teaspoon Spicy Umami Blend
- ½ teaspoon ground turmeric
- ¼ teaspoon cayenne pepper
- 2 cups diced Anjou pear
- ½ cup dried yellow split peas
- 4 cups Vegetable Broth
- ½ teaspoon freshly ground black pepper

Directions:

1. In a large saucepan, combine the potatoes, onion, carrots, chipotle powder, cinnamon, salt, turmeric, and cayenne and dry sauté over medium-high heat for 5 minutes.

2. Add the pear, split peas, and broth, and bring to a boil. Lower the heat to medium-low, cover, and simmer until the split peas are tender, 15 to 20 minutes.

3. Serve garnished with black pepper.

INGREDIENT TIP: You want a very firm pear for this soup, which is why I specifically call for the Anjou variety. Asian pears are fairly firm and work great, too.

Nutrition Per Serving (2 CUPS):

Calories: 252; Saturated Fat: 0g; Total Fat: 1g; Protein: 9g; Total Carbs: 55g; Fiber: 13g; Sodium: 181mg

144. Greens and Grains Soup

Preparation Time: 5 minutes

Cooking Time: 35 minutes

Servings: 6

Ingredients:

- 2 cups sliced onions
- 1 cup diced carrots
- 1 cup diced celery
- 1 cup dry farro
- 1 teaspoon dried basil
- 1 teaspoon dried oregano
- ½ teaspoon dried rosemary
- ½ teaspoon dried thyme
- 1 (15-ounce) can diced tomatoes
- 1 (15-ounce) can white kidney beans, drained and rinsed
- 5 ounces arugula
- 3 tablespoons lemon juice

Directions:

1. In a large saucepan, combine the onions, carrots, and celery and dry sauté over medium-high heat, stirring occasionally, until the carrots are softened, about 5 minutes.

2. Add the farro and stir until coated. Add the basil, oregano, rosemary, thyme, and 4 cups water and bring to a boil. Lower the heat to low, cover, and simmer for 30 minutes.

3. Add the tomatoes and beans, raise the heat to medium-high, and bring back to a boil.

4. Add the arugula and lemon juice and cook, stirring, until the arugula is a deep green and lightly wilted, 1 to 2 minutes more.

5. Remove from the heat and serve.

SWAP IT: Wheat berries or pearled barley can be substituted for the farro and cooked for the same amount of time.

Nutrition Per Serving (2 CUPS):

Calories: 183; Saturated Fat: 0g; Total Fat: 1g; Protein: 9g; Total Carbs: 38g; Fiber: 9g; Sodium: 122mg

145. Herby Split Pea Soup
Preparation Time: 5 minutes
Cooking Time: 30 minutes
Servings: 4
Ingredients:
- ¼ cup Vegetable Broth - 2 large carrots, diced
- 2 large celery stalks, diced
- 1 small russet potato, unpeeled, cubed
- 1 cup dried split peas
- 1 tablespoon herbes de Provence
- ½ teaspoon sea salt, or 1½ teaspoons Spicy Umami Blend

Directions:

1. In a large saucepan, heat the broth over medium-high heat. Add the carrots, celery, potato, and sauté for 5 minutes.

2. Add the split peas, herbes de Provence, and 2 cups water, and bring to a boil. Lower the heat to medium-low, cover, and cook for 25 minutes.

3. Stir in the salt and serve.

APPLIANCE TIP: Combine all the ingredients in a multicooker like an Instant Pot or a pressure cooker and cook for 15 minutes on high pressure, then use a quick pressure release.

Nutrition Per Serving (1 CUP):

Calories: 227; Saturated Fat: 0g; Total Fat: 1g; Protein: 13g; Total Carbs: 43g; Fiber: 15g; Sodium: 205mg

146. Moroccan Eggplant Stew
Preparation Time: 5 minutes
Cooking Time: 15 minutes
Servings: 4
Ingredients:
- 2 teaspoons Spicy Umami Blend
- 1 leek, white part only, thinly sliced and rinsed well
- 1 medium eggplant, diced
- 2 cups chopped mushrooms
- 1 tablespoon paprika
- 2 teaspoons ground cumin
- 1 teaspoon ground cinnamon
- 1 (15-ounce) can chickpeas, drained and rinsed
- 1 (15-ounce) can diced tomatoes
- 1 cup Vegetable Broth

Directions:

1. In a large saucepan, combine the umami blend and 3 tablespoons of water and heat over medium-high heat until bubbling. Add the leek, eggplant, mushrooms, paprika, cumin, and cinnamon and sauté, stirring frequently, for 8 to 10 minutes. If the mixture begins to stick, add water 1 teaspoon at a time as needed.

2. Add the chickpeas, tomatoes, and broth and bring to a boil. Lower the heat to medium-low, cover, and simmer for 10 minutes.

3. Remove from the heat and serve.

SWAP IT: Instead of canned tomatoes, you can use 2 cups chopped fresh tomatoes and add an extra ½ cup vegetable broth.

Nutrition Per Serving (2 CUPS):

Calories: 200; Saturated Fat: 0g; Total Fat: 3g; Protein: 10g; Total Carbs: 37g; Fiber: 13g; Sodium: 315mg

147. Minestrone in minutes
Preparation Time: 5 minutes
Cooking Time: 15 minutes
Servings: 4 To 6
Ingredients:
- 1 cup diced red onion
- ½ cup diced carrot
- ½ cup diced celery
- 2 to 3 garlic cloves, minced
- 2 teaspoons dried basil
- 1 (15.5-ounce) can cannellini beans, drained and rinsed
- 1 (15.5-ounce) can red beans, drained and rinsed
- 1 (15-ounce) can no-salt tomato sauce
- 3 cups Vegetable Broth
- 1 cup diced mushrooms
- ½ teaspoon red pepper flakes
- 3 tablespoons lemon juice

Directions:

1. In a large saucepan, heat ¼ cup of water over medium-high heat. Add the onion, carrot, celery, and garlic and cook until the vegetables begin to soften, about 3 minutes.

2. Add the basil, cannellini beans, red beans, tomato sauce, broth, mushrooms, and red pepper flakes, stir well, and bring to a boil.

3. Lower the heat to medium-low and cook, stirring occasionally, for about 10 minutes. Remove from the heat and serve.

SWAP IT: Skip the mushrooms and use 1 cup of frozen or fresh vegetables. Zucchini, green beans, and peas are all tasty and add a pop of color.

Nutrition Per Serving (1½ CUPS):

Calories: 267; Saturated Fat: 0g; Total Fat: 1g; Protein: 17g; Total Carbs: 50g; Fiber: 15g; Sodium: 37mg

148. 3-Bean Chili

Preparation Time: 10 minutes

Cooking Time: 25 minutes

Servings: 6

Ingredients:

- 1 cup diced onion
- 3 teaspoons minced garlic
- 1 teaspoon chipotle chile powder
- 1 teaspoon paprika
- 1 teaspoon chili powder
- 1 teaspoon ground cumin
- ½ teaspoon red pepper flakes
- 1 (14-ounce) can black beans, drained and rinsed
- 1 (14-ounce) can kidney beans, drained and rinsed
- 1 (14-ounce) can pinto beans, drained and rinsed
- 1 (14.5-ounce) can fire-roasted diced tomatoes
- 2 teaspoons tomato paste
- 3 cups Vegetable Broth
- 1 to 2 tablespoons diced jalapeño (optional)
- ½ teaspoon sea salt, or 1 teaspoon Spicy Umami Blend
- ½ teaspoon freshly ground black pepper
- 2 tablespoons lime juice

Directions:

1. In a large saucepan, heat 2 tablespoons of water over medium-high heat. Add the onion and garlic and sauté until the onion is translucent, 5 minutes. Add the chipotle powder, paprika, chili powder, cumin, and red pepper flakes and stir well. Add the black beans, kidney beans, pinto beans, diced tomatoes, tomato paste, broth,

jalapeño (if using), salt, and black pepper, and bring to a boil.

2. Lower the heat to low, cover, and simmer for 15 minutes.

3. Stir in the lime juice just before serving.

INGREDIENT TIP: Substitute 1½ cups cooked beans for each 14-ounce can.

PAIR IT: Try ladling this chili over some BBQ Baked French Fries and drizzle a little Cheesy Chickpea Sauce on top.

Nutrition Per Serving (2 CUPS):

Calories: 220; Saturated Fat: 0g; Total Fat: 2g; Protein: 13g; Total Carbs: 40g; Fiber: 6g; Sodium: 336mg

149. White Chili

Preparation Time: 5 minutes

Cooking Time: 25 minutes

Servings: 6

Ingredients:

- 1 large onion, chopped
- 4 garlic cloves, minced
- 2 (4-ounce) cans chopped green chiles
- 1 tablespoon ground cumin
- 1 tablespoon dried oregano
- 2 teaspoons cayenne pepper
- 1 (15-ounce) can cannellini or great northern beans, drained and rinsed
- 1 (15-ounce) can black-eyed peas, drained and rinsed
- 4 cups Vegetable Broth
- 1 teaspoon salt, or 1 tablespoon Spicy Umami Blend

Directions:

1. In a large saucepan, combine the onion, garlic, green chiles, and ¼ cup water and sauté over medium-high heat until the onion is tender, about 5 minutes.

2. Add the cumin, oregano, cayenne, cannellini beans, black-eyed peas, broth, and salt, and bring to a boil.

3. Lower the heat to medium-low, cover, and simmer for 15 minutes. Remove from the heat and serve.

SMART SHOPPING: In love with black-eyed peas? Stock up! Buy several bags of the frozen variety and keep them in your freezer.

Nutrition Per Serving (1 CUP):

Calories: 138; Saturated Fat: 0g; Total Fat: 1g; Protein: 9g; Total Carbs: 26g; Fiber: 8g; Sodium: 38mg

150. Hot-And-Sour Tofu Soup

Preparation Time: 5 minutes
Cooking Time: 15 minutes
Servings: 2
Ingredients:

- ¼ cup low-sodium soy sauce
- 2 teaspoons red or yellow miso paste
- 2 teaspoons Red Chili Paste
- 1 teaspoon minced garlic
- 2 teaspoons minced fresh ginger
- 1 cup sliced mushrooms
- 12 ounces silken tofu
- ¼ cup crushed peanuts (optional)
- ¼ cup chopped green onions

Directions:

1. In a large saucepan, heat the soy sauce over medium-high heat until it just begins to bubble. Add the miso and whisk and mash it with a fork to create a thick slurry. Add the chili paste, garlic, and ginger and cook, stirring frequently, for 3 minutes.

2. Add the mushrooms and 3 cups water and bring to a boil.

3. Lower the heat to medium-low and add the tofu, crumbling it with your fingers and dropping it into the pan. Cover and simmer for 10 minutes.

4. Divide the crushed peanuts (if using) and green onions between two large bowls. Ladle half the soup into each bowl and serve.

VEGGIE BOOST: Add 1 cup of your favorite frozen veggies (corn, peas, or green beans are nice options) when you crumble in the tofu.

Nutrition Per Serving (2 CUPS):

Calories: 147; Saturated Fat: 1g; Total Fat: 7g; Protein: 16g; Total Carbs: 9g; Fiber: 2g; Sodium: 1,165mg

151. Spicy Refried Bean Stew

Preparation Time: 5 minutes
Cooking Time: 30 minutes
Servings: 6
Ingredients:

- 1¼ cup Vegetable Broth, divided
- 1 small onion, halved and thinly sliced
- 1 small jalapeño, seeded and finely diced
- 2 garlic cloves, minced
- ½ to 1 teaspoon chili powder
- ½ teaspoon chipotle or ancho chile powder
- 1 teaspoon Spicy Umami Blend
- 1 (15-ounce) can pinto beans, drained and rinsed
- 1 (15-ounce) can vegetarian refried beans
- 1 (14.5-ounce) can no-salt-added diced tomatoes

Directions:

1. In a large saucepan, heat ¼ cup of broth over medium-high heat. Add the onion, jalapeño, garlic, chili powder, chipotle powder, and umami blend and cook, stirring occasionally, until the onion is tender, about 5 minutes.

2. Add the pinto beans, refried beans, tomatoes, 1 cup water, and the remaining 1 cup of broth, stir well, and bring to a boil.

3. Lower the heat to low, cover, and simmer for 20 minutes. Remove from the heat and serve.

PROTEIN BOOST: For a "meaty" chili, swap the canned pinto beans for ½ cup TVP (textured vegetable protein) or 6 ounces extra-firm tofu crumbled.

INGREDIENT TIP: Use refried pinto or black beans. You can also use 1½ cup of cooked pinto beans instead of canned, if you have purchased them frozen or in bulk.

Nutrition Per Serving (1½ CUPS):

Calories: 150; Saturated Fat: 0g; Total Fat: 1g; Protein: 9g; Total Carbs: 27g; Fiber: 8g; Sodium: 154mg

152. Sweet Potato Stew

Preparation Time: 10 minutes
Cooking Time: 40 minutes
Servings: 6
Ingredients:

- ¼ cup balsamic vinegar
- 1 large sweet potato, cut into bite-size pieces
- 1 cup diced onion
- ½ cup chopped carrot
- ½ cup chopped celery
- 2 teaspoons dried thyme
- 1 teaspoon dried oregano
- 1-pound Brussels sprouts, halved and thinly sliced
- 1 (15-ounce) can black beans, drained and rinsed
- 3 cups Vegetable Broth
- 1 bay leaf
- 1 teaspoon Spicy Umami Blend
- ½ teaspoon freshly ground black pepper

Directions:

1. In a large saucepan, heat the vinegar over medium-high heat. Add the sweet potato, onion, carrot, celery, thyme, and oregano, and sauté until the sweet potato brightens in color and the onion is tender, about 5 minutes.

2. Add the Brussels sprouts, black beans, broth, bay leaf, umami blend, and pepper, stir well, and bring to a boil.

3. Lower the heat to medium-low and simmer, stirring occasionally, until the sweet potatoes are tender, about 30 minutes. Remove from the heat, discard the bay leaf, and serve.

APPLIANCE TIP: To make this in a multicooker, use the Sauté function for step 1. Add the rest of the ingredients to the pot and cook on low pressure for 8 minutes, then use a natural pressure release.

INGREDIENT TIP: Use 1½ cup of cooked black beans instead of canned.

Nutrition Per Serving (2 CUPS):

Calories: 134; Saturated Fat: 0g; Total Fat: 1g; Protein: 7g; Total Carbs: 27g; Fiber: 8g; Sodium: 49mg

153. Oyster (Mushroom) Stew

Preparation Time: 10 minutes

Cooking Time: 25 minutes

Servings: 2

Ingredients:

- ¾ cup unsweetened plant-based milk, divided, plus more if needed
- 1-pound oyster mushrooms, trimmed and cut into thick slices
- 1 small yellow or sweet onion, diced
- 3 garlic cloves, minced
- 2 teaspoons dried sage
- 1 (15-ounce) can cannellini or great northern beans, drained and rinsed
- ¼ cup Miso Cream Sauce
- 1 tablespoon low-sodium soy sauce
- 2 cups Vegetable Broth, divided
- 2 teaspoons Red Chili Paste

Directions:

1. In a large saucepan, heat ½ cup of plant-based milk over medium-high heat. Add the mushrooms, onion, garlic, and sage and cook until the mushrooms begin to brown, 5 to 8 minutes.

2. Meanwhile, in a blender, combine the beans, miso cream sauce, and remaining ¼ cup of milk and purée until smooth and easy to pour. Add more milk a little at a time, if needed, to reach the desired consistency.

3. Transfer the bean purée to the saucepan and stir well. Add 1 cup of broth and bring to a boil, stirring frequently. Add the remaining 1 cup of broth and stir well. Lower the heat to medium-low, cover, and simmer for 10 minutes.

4. Stir in the chili paste just before serving.

CHANGE IT UP: You can turn this into a cream of mushroom soup easily. Reserve about ½ cup of browned mushrooms. Use an immersion blender to purée the stew directly in the pot (or transfer it to a standing blender), then stir in the reserved browned mushrooms and serve.

ALLERGEN TIP: To make a gluten-free version, be sure to use a nut or seed milk, and replace the soy sauce with tamari that is labeled "gluten-free" or coconut aminos.

Nutrition Per Serving (2 CUPS):

Calories: 323; Saturated Fat: 1g; Total Fat: 4g; Protein: 23g; Total Carbs: 54g; Fiber: 16g; Sodium: 382mg

154. New England Corn Chowder

Preparation Time: 5 minutes

Cooking Time: 20 minutes

Servings: 6

Ingredients:

- 1-pound fingerling potatoes, unpeeled, cut in half
- 3 tablespoons aquafaba (see Tip)
- 1¾ cup fresh, canned, or frozen corn kernels (14 ounces)
- 1 teaspoon chili powder
- 1 small sweet onion, diced
- 2 cups Vegetable Broth
- 2 cups unsweetened plant-based milk, divided
- 1 teaspoon dried thyme
- 1 teaspoon dried basil
- ½ teaspoon freshly ground black pepper
- ½ teaspoon paprika

Directions:

1. Place the potatoes in a large saucepan, cover with water, and bring to a boil over medium-high heat. Lower the heat to medium and simmer until the potatoes are tender, 10 to 15 minutes.

2. While the potatoes are cooking, in a large saucepan, heat the aquafaba over medium-high heat. Add the corn and chili powder and cook until the corn begins to brown, about 10 minutes.

3. Drain the potatoes and roughly mash them with a potato masher, leaving some chunks. Set aside.

4. Add the onion, vegetable broth, 1 cup of plant-based milk, thyme, basil, and pepper to the pan with the corn and bring to a boil.

5. Add the mashed potatoes and remaining 1 cup of milk, stir to combine, and return to a boil. Lower the heat to low and simmer for 5 minutes, then serve.

MAKE IT FASTER: Opt for fire-roasted frozen corn, omit the aquafaba and chili powder, and skip step 2.

Nutrition Per Serving (1½ CUPS):

Calories: 187; Saturated Fat: 0g; Total Fat: 2g; Protein: 7g; Total Carbs: 38g; Fiber: 5g; Sodium: 67mg

155. Mushroom and Quinoa "Gumbo"

Preparation Time: 15 To 30 minutes
Cooking Time: 30 minutes
Servings: 6
Ingredients:

- 2 cups chopped portobello mushrooms
- ¼ cup balsamic vinegar
- 1 cup chopped onion
- 1 cup chopped green bell pepper
- 1 cup chopped celery
- 1 tablespoon file powder
- 1 tablespoon tomato powder, or 2 teaspoons tomato paste
- 1 teaspoon dried basil
- 1 teaspoon cayenne pepper
- 1 teaspoon dried thyme
- 3 cups Vegetable Broth, divided
- ½ cup dry quinoa, rinsed and drained
- 4 cups chopped mustard greens

Directions:

1. In a large skillet, combine the mushrooms and vinegar. Set aside to marinate for 15 to 30 minutes.

2. Place the skillet over medium-high heat and cook the mushrooms for 3 minutes. Add the onion, bell pepper, and celery, and cook for 3 minutes more. Add the file, stir to coat the vegetables, and cook, stirring frequently, for 5 minutes more.

3. Add the tomato powder, basil, cayenne, thyme, 2 cups of broth, and the quinoa, and bring to a boil.

4. Lower the heat to medium-low, cover, and cook until the quinoa is tender, about 15 minutes.

5. Raise the heat to medium-high, add the mustard greens and remaining 1 cup of broth, stir to combine, and bring the mixture back to a boil.

6. Lower the heat to low, cover, and simmer for 5 minutes more. Remove from the heat and serve.

INGREDIENT TIP: Filé powder is a fantastic salt-free spice that you can use in all kinds of recipes, stews, soup, and sauces. It thickens and creates a slightly sweet contrast in savory dishes.

SWAP IT: Use arugula or spinach instead of mustard greens.

Nutrition Per Serving (2 CUPS):

Calories: 97; Saturated Fat: 0g; Total Fat: 1g; Protein: 4g; Total Carbs: 18g; Fiber: 4g; Sodium: 29mg

156. Asparagus & Green Peas Soup

Preparation Time: 15 minutes
Cooking Time: 25 minutes
Servings: 4
Ingredients

- 12 ounces fresh asparagus, trimmed
- 4 tablespoons avocado oil, divided
- 2 cups fresh peas, shelled
- 4 garlic cloves, minced
- 1 medium shallot, sliced thinly
- Salt and ground black pepper, to taste
- 1½ cups vegetable broth
- 2 cups unsweetened soy milk
- 2 tablespoons nutritional yeast
- 1 tablespoon fresh lemon juice

Directions:

1. Preheat your oven to 400°F.

2. Place the asparagus spears, 2 tablespoons of oil, salt, and black pepper onto a baking sheet, and toss to coat well.

3. Then, arrange the asparagus spears in a single layer.

4. Roast for about 15 minutes.

5. Remove the baking sheet from the oven and set it aside.

6. Heat the remaining oil over medium heat and sauté the shallot, garlic, salt, and black pepper for about 2–3 minutes.

7. Add peas, broth, and almond milk and bring to a boil.

8. Remove the pan of soup from heat and set it aside to cool slightly.

9. Transfer the soup into a blender along with asparagus in 2 batches and pulse until smooth.

10. Return the soup to the pan over medium heat and bring to a gentle simmer.

11. Add nutritional yeast and whisk until well combined.

12. Cook for about 3–4 minutes or until heated completely.

13. Stir in lemon juice, salt, and black pepper, and remove from heat.

14. Serve hot.

Nutrition Per Serving:

Calories: 228; Fat: 16.67g; Carbs: 15.18g; Protein: 6.45g

157. Black Beans Stew

Preparation Time: 10 minutes
Cooking Time: 30 minutes
Servings: 4
Ingredients

- 1 tablespoon olive oil

- 2 small onions, chopped
- 5 garlic cloves, chopped finely
- 1 teaspoon of dried oregano
- 1 teaspoon ground cumin
- ½ teaspoon ground ginger
- Salt and ground black pepper, to taste
- 1 (14-ounce) can diced tomatoes
- 2 (13½-ounce) cans black beans, rinsed and drained
- ½ cup vegetable broth

Directions:

1. Heat the olive oil in a pan over medium heat and cook the onion for about 5–7 minutes, stirring frequently.

2. Add garlic, oregano, spices, salt, and black pepper, and cook for about 1 minute.

3. Add the tomatoes and cook for about 1–2 minutes.

4. Add in the beans and broth and bring to a boil.

5. Now, adjust the heat to medium-low and simmer, covered for about 15 minutes.

6. Serve hot.

Nutrition: Calories 247 Total Fat 5.5 g Saturated Fat 0.6 g Cholesterol 0 mg Sodium 698 mg Total Carbs 39.4 g Fiber 13.5 g Sugar 4.4 g Protein 13 g

158. Sniffle Soup

Preparation Time: 5 minutes

Cooking Time: 33 minutes

Servings: 6

Ingredients

- 1½ tbsp plus 4 cups water, divided
- 1½ cups onion, diced
- 1 cup carrot, diced
- 1 cup celery, diced
- 3 large cloves garlic, minced
- 1 tsp paprika
- 1 tsp mild curry powder
- ½ tsp sea salt
- ¼ tsp dried thyme
- ¼ tsp ground black pepper
- 2 cups dried red lentils
- 3 cups vegetable stock
- 1½ tbsp apple cider vinegar

Directions:

1. Heat a large pot over medium heat.

2. Add all ingredients to the pot and stir occasionally.

3. Cook for 8 minutes.

4. Increase heat and bring it to a boil.

5. Once it is boiled, let it simmer for 25 minutes.

6. Serve and enjoy.

Nutrition: Calories 293, total fat 1g, saturated fat 0.1g, cholesterol 0mg, sodium 222mg, total carbohydrate 53.2g, dietary fiber 23.1g, total sugars 7.4g, protein 18.5g, vitamin d 0mcg, calcium 90mg, iron 6mg, potassium 912mg

159. Butternut Squash Soup

Preparation Time: 15 minutes

Cooking Time: 25 minutes

Servings: 6

Ingredients:

- 2 tbsp. olive oil - 1 cup onion, chopped
- 1 cup cilantro
- 1 ginger, sliced thinly
- 2 cups pears, chopped
- ½ tsp. ground coriander
- Salt to taste
- 2 ½ lb. butternut squash, cubed
- 1 tsp. lime zest
- 26 oz. coconut milk
- 1 tbsp. lime juice
- ½ cup plain yogurt

Directions:

1. Pour the oil into a pan over medium heat.
2. Add the onion, cilantro, ginger, pears, coriander and salt.
3. Stir and cook for 5 minutes.
4. Transfer to a pressure cooker.
5. Stir in the squash and lime zest.
6. Pour in the coconut milk.
7. Cook on high for 20 minutes.
8. Release pressure naturally.
9. Stir in the lime juice.
10. Transfer to a blender.
11. Pulse until smooth.
12. Reheat and stir in yogurt before serving.

Nutrition: Calories 274 Total Fat 14 g Saturated Fat 8 g Cholesterol 3 mg Sodium 438 mg Total Carbohydrate 36 g Dietary Fiber 6 g Protein 5 g Total Sugars 11 g Potassium 715 mg

160. Lemon & Strawberry Soup

Preparation Time: 4 hours and 10 minutes

Cooking Time: 0 minutes

Servings: 4

Ingredients:

- 1 cup buttermilk

- 3 cups strawberries, sliced
- 1 tsp. lemon thyme
- 2 tsp. lemon zest
- 2 tbsp. honey

Directions:
1. Blend the buttermilk and strawberries in your food processor.
2. Transfer this mixture to a bowl.
3. Add the thyme and lemon zest.
4. Chill in the refrigerator for 4 hours.
5. Strain the soup and stir in the honey.
6. Serve in bowls.

Nutrition: Calories 92 Total Fat 1 g Saturated Fat 0 g Cholesterol 2 mg Sodium 66 mg Total Carbohydrate 20 g Dietary Fiber 2 g Protein 3 g Total Sugars 17 g Potassium 266 mg

161. Tomato Soup with Kale & White Beans

Preparation Time: 5 minutes
Cooking Time: 7 minutes
Servings: 4
Ingredients:

- 28 oz. tomato soup
- 1 tbsp. olive oil
- 3 cups kale, chopped
- 14 oz. cannellini beans, rinsed and drained
- 1 tsp. garlic, crushed and minced
- ¼ cup Parmesan cheese, grated

Directions:
1. Pour the soup into a pan over medium heat.
2. Add the oil and cook the kale for 2 minutes.
3. Stir in the beans and garlic.
4. Simmer for 5 minutes.
5. Sprinkle with Parmesan cheese before serving.

Nutrition: Calories 200 Total Fat 6 g Saturated Fat 1 g Cholesterol 4 mg Sodium 355 mg Total Carbohydrate 29 g Dietary Fiber 6 g Protein 9 g Total Sugars 1 g Potassium 257 mg

162. Bursting Black Bean Soup

Preparation Time: 2 hours and 10 minutes
Cooking Time: 6 hours
Servings: 6
Ingredients:

- 1 pound of black beans, uncooked
- 1/4 cup of lentils, uncooked
- 1 medium-sized carrot, peeled and chopped
- 2 medium-sized green bell peppers, cored and chopped
- 1 stalk of celery, chopped
- 28 ounces of diced tomatoes
- 2 jalapeno pepper, seeded and minced
- 1 large red onion, peeled and chopped
- 3 teaspoons of minced garlic
- 1 tablespoon of salt
- 1/2 teaspoon ground black pepper
- 2 tablespoons of red chili powder
- 2 teaspoons of ground cumin
- 1/2 teaspoon of dried oregano
- 3 tablespoons of apple cider vinegar
- 1/2 cup of brown rice, uncooked
- 3 quarts of water, divided

Directions:
1. Place a large pot over medium-high heat, add the beans, pour in 1 1/2 quarts of water, and boil it.
2. Let it boil for 10 minutes, then remove the pot from the heat, let it stand for 1 hour, and then cover the pot.
3. Drain the beans and add them to a 6-quarts slow cooker.
4. Pour in the remaining 1 1/2 quarts of water and cover it with the lid.
5. Plug in the slow cooker and let it cook for 3 hours at the high setting or until it gets soft.
6. When the beans are done, add the remaining ingredients except for the rice and continue cooking for 3 hours on the low heat setting.
7. When it is 30 minutes left to finish, add the rice to the slow cooker and let it cook.
8. When done, using an immersion blender process half of the soup and then serve.

Nutrition:
Calories: 116, Carbohydrates: 19g, Protein: 5.6g, Fat: 1.5g, Fiber: 4g.

163. Yummy Lentil Rice Soup

Preparation Time: 15 minutes
Cooking Time: 4 hours
Servings: 6
Ingredients:

- 2 cups of brown rice, uncooked
- 2 cups of lentils, uncooked
- 1/2 cup of chopped celery
- 1 cup of chopped carrots
- 1 cup of sliced mushrooms

- 1/2 of a medium-sized white onion, peeled and chopped
- 1 teaspoon of minced garlic
- 1 tablespoon of salt
- 1/2 teaspoon of ground black pepper
- 1 cup of vegetable broth
- 8 cups of water

Directions:

1. Using a 6-quarts slow cooker, place all the ingredients except for mushrooms and stir until it mixes properly.
2. Cover with lid, plug in the slow cooker, and let it cook for 3 to 4 hours at the high setting or until it is cooked thoroughly.
3. Pour in the mushrooms, stir and continue cooking for 1 hour at the low heat setting or until it is done.
4. Serve right away.

Nutrition:

Calories: 226, Carbohydrates: 41g, Protein: 13g, Fat: 2g, Fiber: 12g.

164. Tangy Corn Chowder

Preparation Time: 15 minutes

Cooking Time: 5 hours

Servings: 6

Ingredients:

- 24 ounces of cooked kernel corn
- 3 medium-sized potatoes, peeled and diced
- 2 red chile peppers, minced
- 1 large white onion, peeled and diced
- 1 teaspoon of minced garlic
- 2 teaspoons of salt
- 1/2 teaspoon of ground black pepper
- 1 tablespoon of red chili powder
- 1 tablespoon of dried parsley
- 1/4 cup of vegan margarine
- 14 fluid ounces of soy milk
- 1 lime, juiced
- 24 fluid ounces of vegetable broth

Directions:

1. Using a 6-quarts slow cooker, place all the ingredients except for the soy milk, margarine, and lime juice.
2. Stir properly and cover it with the lid.
3. Then plug in the slow cooker and let it cook for 3 to 4 hours at the high setting or until it is cooked thoroughly.

4. When done, process the mixture with an immersion blender or until it gets smooth.
5. Pour in the milk, margarine and stir properly.
6. Continue cooking the soup for 1 hour at the low heat setting.
7. Drizzle it with the lime juice and serve.

Nutrition:

Calories: 237, Carbohydrates: 18g, Protein: 7.4g, Fat: 15g, Fiber: 2.2g.

165. Healthy Cabbage Soup

Preparation Time: 15 minutes

Cooking Time: 4 hours

Servings: 6

Ingredients:

- 5 cups of shredded cabbage
- 3 medium-sized carrots, peeled and chopped
- 3 1/2 cups of diced tomatoes
- 1 medium-sized white onion, chopped
- 2 teaspoons of minced garlic
- 1 teaspoon of salt
- 1 teaspoon of dried oregano
- 1 tablespoon of dried parsley
- 1 1/2 cups of tomato sauce
- 5 cups of vegetable broth

Directions:

1. Using a 6-quarts slow cooker, place all the ingredients and stir properly.
2. Cover it with the lid, plug in the slow cooker, and let it cook for 4 hours at the high heat setting or until the vegetables are tender.
3. Serve right away.

Nutrition:

Calories: 150, Carbohydrates: 4g, Protein: 20g, Fat: 5g, Fiber: 2g.

166. Chunky Potato Soup

Preparation Time: 10 minutes

Cooking Time: 6 hours

Servings: 6

Ingredients:

- 1 medium-sized carrot, grated
- 6 medium-sized potatoes, peeled and diced
- 2 stalks of celery, diced
- 1 medium-sized white onion, peeled and diced
- 2 teaspoons of minced garlic
- 1 1/2 teaspoons of salt
- 1 teaspoon of ground black pepper

- 1 1/2 teaspoons of dried sage
- 1 teaspoon of dried thyme
- 2 tablespoons of olive oil
- 2 bay leaves
- 8 1/2 cups of vegetable water

Directions:

1. Using a 6-quarts slow cooker, place all the ingredients and stir properly.
2. Cover it with the lid, plug in the slow cooker, and let it cook for 6 hours at the high heat setting or until the potatoes are tender.
3. Serve right away.

Nutrition:

Calories: 200, Carbohydrates: 26g, Protein: 6g, Fat: 8g, Fiber: 2g.

167. Yogurt Soup with Rice

Preparation Time: 15 minutes

Cooking Time: 48 minutes

Servings: 6

Ingredients:

- ½ cup brown rice, rinsed and drained
- 1 egg - 4 cups yogurt
- 3 tbsp. rice flour - 3 cups water
- ½ cup mint, chopped
- ½ cup cilantro, chopped
- ½ cup dill, chopped
- ½ cup parsley, chopped
- 2 cups arugula - Salt to taste

Directions:

1. Combine the rice, egg, yogurt, and flour in a pot.
2. Put it over medium heat and cook for 1 minute, stirring frequently.
3. Pour in the water and increase the heat to boil.
4. Reduce heat and simmer for 45 minutes.
5. Add the arugula, herbs and salt.
6. Cook for 2 minutes.
7. Add more water to adjust consistency.

Nutrition: Calories 186, Total Fat 7 g, Saturated Fat 4 g Cholesterol 52 mg, Sodium 486 mg, Total Carbohydrate 24 g Dietary Fiber 2g, Protein 9g, Total Sugars 8g, Potassium 365 mg

168. Zucchini Soup

Preparation Time: 5 minutes

Cooking Time: 15 minutes

Servings: 4

Ingredients:

- 3 cups chicken broth

- 1 tbsp. tarragon, chopped
- 3 zucchinis, sliced
- 3 oz. cheddar cheese
- Salt and pepper to taste

Directions:

1. Pour the broth into a pot.
2. Stir in the tarragon and zucchini.
3. Bring to a boil and then simmer for 10 minutes.
4. Transfer to a blender and blend until smooth.
5. Put it back on the stove and stir in cheese.
6. Season with salt and pepper.

Nutrition: Calories 110, Total Fat 5 g, Saturated Fat 3 g Cholesterol 15 mg, Sodium 757 mg, Total Carbohydrate 7 g Dietary Fiber 2 g, Protein 10 g, Total Sugars 4g Potassium 606 mg

169. Hearty Vegetarian Lasagna Soup

Preparation Time: 20 minutes

Cooking Time: 7 hours

Servings: 10

Ingredients:

- 12 ounces of lasagna noodles
- 4 cups of spinach leaves
- 2 cups of brown mushrooms, sliced
- 2 medium-sized zucchinis, stemmed and sliced
- 28 ounces of crushed tomatoes
- 1 medium-sized white onion, peeled and diced
- 2 teaspoons of minced garlic
- 1 tablespoon of dried basil
- 2 bay leaves
- 2 teaspoons of salt
- 1/8 teaspoon of red pepper flakes
- 2 teaspoons of ground black pepper
- 2 teaspoons of dried oregano
- 15-ounce of tomato sauce
- 6 cups of vegetable broth

Directions:

1. Grease a 6-quarts slow cooker and place all the ingredients in it except for the lasagna and spinach.
2. Cover the top, plug in the slow cooker; adjust the cooking time to 7 hours and let it cook on the low heat setting or until it is properly done.
3. In the meantime, cook the lasagna noodles in the boiling water for 7 to 10 minutes or until it gets soft.

4. Then drain and set it aside until the slow cooker is done cooking.

5. When it is done, add the lasagna noodles into the soup along with the spinach and continue cooking for 10 to 15 minutes or until the spinach leaves wilt.

6. Using a ladle, serve it in a bowl.

Nutrition: Calories: 188, Carbohydrates: 13g, Protein: 18g, Fat: 9g, Fiber: 0g.

170. Chunky Black Lentil Veggie Soup

Preparation Time: 35 minutes

Cooking Time: 4 hours

Servings: 8

Ingredients:

- 1 1/2 cups of black lentils, uncooked
- 2 small turnips, peeled and diced
- 10 medium-sized carrots, peeled and diced
- 1 medium-sized green bell pepper, cored and diced
- 3 cups of diced tomatoes
- 1 medium-sized white onion, peeled and diced
- 2 tablespoons of minced ginger
- 1 teaspoon of minced garlic
- 1 teaspoon of salt
- 1/2 teaspoon of ground coriander
- 1/2 teaspoon of ground cumin
- 3 tablespoons of unsalted butter
- 32 fluid ounces of vegetable broth
- 32 fluid ounces of water

Directions:

1. Using a medium-sized microwave, cover the bowl, place the lentils, and pour in the water.

2. Microwave lentils for 10 minutes or until softened, stirring after 5 minutes.

3. Drain lentils and add to a 6-quarts slow cooker along with remaining ingredients and stir until just mix.

4. Cover with top, plug in slow cooker; adjust cooking time to 6 hours and let cook on low heat setting or until carrots are tender.

5. Serve straight away.

Nutrition:

Calories: 90, Carbohydrates: 15g, Protein: 3g, Fat: 2g, Fiber: 3g.

171. Lovely Parsnip & Split Pea Soup

Preparation Time: 10 minutes

Cooking Time: 5 hours

Servings: 8

Ingredients:

- 1 tablespoon of olive oil
- 2 large parsnips, peeled and chopped
- 2 large carrots, peeled and chopped
- 1 medium-sized white onion, peeled and diced
- 1 1/2 teaspoon of minced garlic
- 2 1/4 cups of dried green split peas, rinsed
- 1 teaspoon of salt
- 1/2 teaspoon of ground black pepper
- 1 teaspoon of dried thyme
- 2 bay leaves
- 6 cups of vegetable broth
- 1 teaspoon of liquid smoke

Directions:

1. Place a medium-sized non-stick skillet pan over an average pressure of heat, add the oil and let it heat.

2. Add the parsnip, carrot, onion, garlic and let it cook for 5 minutes or until it is heated.

3. Transfer this mixture into a 6-quarts slow cooker and add the remaining ingredients.

4. Stir until mixed properly and cover the top.

5. Plug in the slow cooker; adjust the cooking time to 5 hours and let it cook on the high heat setting or until the peas and vegetables get soft.

6. When done, remove the bay leaf from the soup and blend it with a submersion blender or until the soup reaches your desired state.

7. Add the seasoning and serve.

Nutrition:

Calories: 199, Carbohydrates: 21g, Protein: 18g, Fat: 5g, Fiber: 8g.

172. Incredible Tomato Basil Soup

Preparation Time: 1 hour and 10 minutes

Cooking Time: 5 hours

Servings: 6

Ingredients:

- 1 cup of chopped celery
- 1 cup of chopped carrots
- 74 ounces of whole tomatoes, canned
- 2 cups of chopped white onion
- 2 teaspoons of minced garlic

- 1 tablespoon of salt
- 1/2 teaspoon of ground white pepper
- 1/4 cup of basil leaves and more for garnishing
- 1 bay leaf
- 32 fluid ounces of vegetable broth
- 1/2 cup of grated Parmesan cheese

Directions:

1. Using an 8 quart or larger slow cooker, place all the ingredients.
2. Stir until it mixes properly and cover the top.
3. Plug in the slow cooker; adjust the cooking time to 5 hours and let it cook on the high heat setting or until the vegetables are tender.
4. Blend the soup with a submersion blender or until the soup reaches your desired state.
5. Garnish it with cheese, basil leaves, and serve.

Nutrition:
Calories: 210, Carbohydrates: 11g, Protein: 12g, Fat: 10g, Fiber: 3g.

173. Spicy Cajun Boiled Peanuts

Preparation Time: 5 minutes
Cooking Time: 8 hours
Servings: 15
Ingredients:

- 5 pounds of peanuts, raw and in shells
- 6-ounce of dry crab boil
- 4-ounce of jalapeno peppers, sliced
- 2-ounce of vegetable broth

Directions:

1. Take a 6-quarts slow cooker, place the ingredients in it and cover it with water.
2. Stir properly and cover the top.
3. Plug in the slow cooker; adjust the cooking time to 8 hours and let it cook on the low heat setting or until the peanuts are soft and float on top of the cooking liquid.
4. Drain the nuts and serve right away.

Nutrition:
Calories: 309, Carbohydrates: 5g, Protein: 0g, Fat: 26g, Fiber: 0g.

174. Comfort Soup

Preparation Time: 5 minutes
Cooking Time: 35 minutes
Servings: 5-6
Ingredients:

- ½ cup of freshly diced onion
- 1 teaspoon of paprika

- ½ tablespoon of water
- 3 ½ cups of water
- 1 cup of freshly diced carrots
- 3 freshly minced large cloves of garlic
- 1 cup of freshly diced celery
- 1 teaspoon of mild curry powder
- 2 cups of dried red lentils
- ½ teaspoon of sea salt
- Freshly ground black pepper to taste
- ¼ teaspoon of dried thyme
- 3 cups of vegetable stock
- 1 – 1 ½ teaspoons of lemon juice/apple cider vinegar
- 2 teaspoons of freshly chopped rosemary

Directions:

1. Put a large pot on the stove over medium heat.
2. Add 1 ½ teaspoon of water along with celery, onion, carrot, paprika, garlic, curry powder, sea salt, black pepper, and thyme.
3. After all the herbs and spices are inside the pot, cover them and cook for about 7-8 minutes, stirring occasionally so that the spices do not burn.
4. Rinse the lentils and add them to 3 ½ cups of water. Stir into the stock.
5. Cover the pot and allow everything to simmer for 12-15 minutes.
6. Add the rosemary and simmer for another 10 minutes. You will know that your soup is ready when the lentils are fully softened.
7. Add the vinegar and some more water if you want a thinner liquid.
8. Serve the soup with your favorite bread.
9. If you do not have fresh rosemary, you can also add dried rosemary. In that case, add it with the rest of the herbs and spices at the beginning. You can use ½ to 1 teaspoon of dried rosemary.

Nutrition: Fat – 5 g Protein – 7.6 g Carbohydrate – 23 g

175. Tangy Chickpea Soup with a Hint of Lemon

Preparation Time: 10 minutes
Cooking Time: 30 minutes
Servings: 6
Ingredients:

- 2 cups of freshly diced onion
- 3 freshly minced large garlic cloves
- Water
- ½ cup of freshly diced celery

- ¾ teaspoon of sea salt
- Freshly ground black pepper to taste
- 1 teaspoon of mustard seeds
- ½ teaspoon of dried oregano
- 1 teaspoon of cumin seeds
- ½ teaspoon of paprika
- 1 ½ teaspoon of dried thyme
- 3 ½ cups of cooked chickpeas
- 1 cup of dried red lentils
- 3 cups of vegetable stock
- 2 dried bay leaves
- 2 cups of freshly chopped tomatoes or zucchini
- 2 cups of water
- ¼ to 1/3 cup of fresh lemon juice

Directions:

1. Put a large pot on the stove on medium heat.

2. Add onion, water, salt, celery, garlic, pepper, cumin, and mustard seeds along with thyme, oregano, and paprika. Stir everything to combine well.

3. Cover the pot and cook for about 7 minutes, stirring occasionally.

4. Rinse the lentils.

5. Add the lentils along with 2 ½ cups of chickpeas, zucchini/tomatoes, stock, bay leaves, and water. Stir everything to combine well.

6. Increase the heat to bring to a boil.

7. Once the ingredients start to boil, cover the pot, lower the heat, and simmer for 20-25 minutes.

8. You will know that the soup is ready when the lentils are tender.

9. After removing the bay leaves, add the lemon juice.

10. Once the ingredients have cooled down, use a hand blender to puree the ingredients, but keep a somewhat coarse texture instead of having a smooth puree.

11. Add the remaining chickpeas. Taste the soup and adjust the salt, pepper, and lemon juice to taste.

12. Enjoy this amazing soup with your favorite bread.

Nutrition: Fat – 2.8 g Protein – 7.1 g Carbohydrate – 31.1 g

176. **Lentil Soup the Vegan Way**

Preparation Time: 5 minutes

Cooking Time: 20 minutes

Servings: 4

Ingredients:

- 2 tablespoons of water
- 4 stalks of thinly sliced celery
- 2 cloves of freshly minced garlic

- 4 thinly sliced large carrots
- Sea salt to taste
- 2 freshly diced small shallots
- Pepper to taste
- 3 cups of red/yellow baby potatoes
- 2 cups of chopped sturdy greens
- 4 cups of vegetable broth
- 1 cup of uncooked brown or green lentils
- Fresh rosemary/thyme as desired

Directions:

1. Put a large pot over medium heat. Once the pot is hot enough, add the shallots, garlic, celery, and carrots to the water. Season the veggies with a little bit of pepper and salt.

2. Sauté the veggies for 5 minutes until they are tender. You will know that the veggies are ready when they have turned golden brown. Be careful with the garlic, because it can easily burn.

3. Add the potatoes and some more seasoning. Cook for 2 minutes.

4. Mix the vegetable broth with the rosemary. Now Increase the heat to medium-high. Allow the veggies to be on a rolling simmer. Add the lentils and give everything a thorough stir.

5. Once it starts to simmer again, decrease the heat and simmer for about 20 minutes without a cover. You will know that the veggies are ready when both the lentils and potatoes are soft

6. Add the greens. Cook for 4 minutes until they wilt. You can adjust the flavor with seasonings.

7. Enjoy this with rice or flatbread. The leftovers are equally tasty, so store them well to enjoy on a day when you are not in the mood to cook.

Nutrition: Fat – 8.3 g Carbohydrates – 52.7 g Protein – 8.4 g

177. **Quinoa Soup with a Dash of Kale**

Preparation Time: 15 minutes

Cooking Time: 45 minutes

Servings: 4-6

Ingredients:

- 3 carrots freshly peeled and chopped
- 3 tablespoons of extra virgin olive oil
- 6 freshly minced or pressed garlic cloves
- 2 freshly chopped celery stalks
- 1 freshly chopped medium-sized white or yellow onion

- 1-2 cups of seasonal veggies: butternut squash, yellow squash, zucchini, sweet potato, bell pepper
- ½ teaspoon of dried thyme
- 1 cup of rinsed quinoa
- 1 can of diced tomatoes
- 2 cups of water
- 2 bay leaves
- 4 cups of vegetable broth
- 1 teaspoon of salt
- Freshly ground black pepper to taste
- 1 cup of freshly chopped kale or collard greens
- Red pepper flakes to taste
- 1-2 teaspoons of lemon juice
- 1 can of rinsed and dried great northern beans or chickpeas
- Freshly grated parmesan cheese as desired

Directions:

1. On medium heat, warm the olive oil in a soup pot. Once the oil starts to shimmer, start adding the carrot, onion, celery, and seasonal veggies, along with salt. Cook everything until the onion softens. You will know that the veggies have become tender when the onions become translucent. This will take about 6-8 minutes.

2. Add the thyme and garlic to the veggies. After cooking for about 1 minute, it will turn fragrant. Add the diced tomatoes and cook everything for a few more minutes.

3. Add the quinoa, water, and broth.

4. Add the bay leaves along with 1 teaspoon of salt and red pepper flakes. Increase the heat and bring everything to a boil. Cover the pot partially and lower the heat so that the ingredients continue to simmer.

5. Simmer for about 25 minutes.

6. Uncover the pot, and add the greens and beans. Simmer for another 5 minutes. Let the greens soften a bit.

7. Remove the pot from the heat, and remove the bay leaves. Add 1 teaspoon of lemon juice.

8. Taste the soup and add salt and pepper to taste. Divide the warm, hearty soup equally in bowls and top with parmesan cheese. Dig in and enjoy a bowl full of happiness.

Nutrition: Fat – 7.8 g Protein – 4.7 g Carbohydrate – 28.4 g

178. Amazing Chickpea and Noodle Soup

Preparation Time: 10 minutes
Cooking Time: 20 minutes
Servings: 4
Ingredients:

- 1 freshly diced celery stalk
- ¼ cup of 'chicken' seasoning
- 1 cup of freshly diced onion
- 3 cloves of freshly crushed garlic
- 2 cups of cooked chickpeas
- 4 cups of vegetable broth
- Freshly chopped cilantro
- 2 freshly cubed medium-size potatoes
- Salt
- 2 freshly sliced carrots
- ½ teaspoon of dried thyme
- Pepper
- 2 cups of water
- 6 ounces of gluten-free spaghetti

'Chicken' seasoning

- 1 tablespoon of garlic powder
- 2 teaspoons of sea salt
- 1 1/3 cup of nutritional yeast
- 3 tablespoons of onion powder
- 1 teaspoon of oregano
- ½ teaspoon of turmeric
- 1 ½ tablespoon of dried basil

Directions:

1. Put a pot on medium heat and sauté the onion. It will soften within 3 minutes.

2. Add celery, potato, and carrots and sauté for another 3 minutes

3. Add the 'chicken' seasoning to the garlic, thyme, water, and vegetable broth.

4. Simmer the mix on medium-high heat. Cook the veggies for about 20 minutes until they soften.

5. Add the cooked pasta and chickpeas.

6. Add salt and pepper to taste.

7. Put the fresh cilantro on top and enjoy the fresh soup!

Nutrition: Fat – 8.3 g Carbohydrates – 52.7 g Protein – 8.4 g

CHAPTER 4:

Stews & Chilies

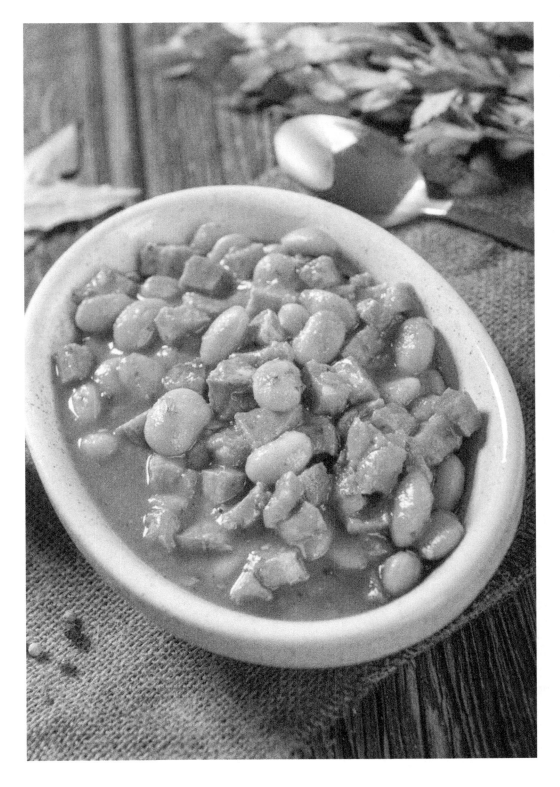

179. Spanish Chickpea and Sweet Potato Stew

Preparation Time: 5 minutes

Cooking Time: 35 minutes

Servings: 4

Ingredients:

- 14 ounces cooked chickpeas
- 1 small sweet potato, peeled, cut into ½-inch cubes
- 1 medium red onion, sliced
- 3 ounces baby spinach
- 14 ounces crushed tomatoes
- 2 teaspoons minced garlic
- 1 teaspoon salt
- 1 1/2 teaspoons ground cumin
- 2 teaspoons harissa paste
- 2 teaspoons maple syrup
- ½ teaspoon ground black pepper
- 2 teaspoons sugar
- 1 tablespoon olive oil
- 1/2 cup vegetable stock
- 2 tablespoons chopped parsley
- 1-ounce slivered almonds, toasted
- Brown rice, cooked, for serving

Directions:

1. Take a large saucepan, place it over low heat, add oil and when hot, add onion and garlic and cook for 5 minutes.

2. Then add sweet potatoes, season with cumin, stir in the harissa paste and cook for 2 minutes until toasted.

3. Switch heat to medium-low level, add tomatoes and chickpeas, pour in vegetable stock, stir in maple syrup and sugar and simmer for 25 minutes until potatoes have softened, stirring every 10 minutes.

4. Then add spinach, cook for 1 minute until its leaves have wilted, and season with salt and black pepper.

5. When done, distribute cooked rice between bowls, top with stew, garnish with parsley and almonds and serve.

Nutrition: Calories: 348 Fat: 16.5 g Carbs: 41.2 g Protein: 7.2 g Fiber: 5.3 g

180. Pomegranate and Walnut Stew

Preparation Time: 10 minutes

Cooking Time: 55 minutes

Servings: 6

Ingredients:

- 1 head of cauliflower, cut into florets
- 1 medium white onion, peeled, diced
- 1 1/2 cups California walnuts, toasted
- 1 cup yellow split peas
- 1 1/2 tablespoons honey
- ¼ teaspoon salt
- ½ teaspoon turmeric
- ½ teaspoon cinnamon
- 2 tablespoons olive oil, separated
- 4 cups pomegranate juice
- 2 tablespoons chopped parsley
- 2 tablespoons chopped walnuts for garnishing

Directions:

1. Take a medium saute pan, place it over medium heat, add walnuts, cook for 5 minutes until toasted and then cool for 5 minutes.

2. Transfer walnuts to the food processor, pulse for 2 minutes until ground, and set aside until required.

3. Take a large saute pan, place it over medium heat, add 1 tablespoon oil and when hot, add onion and cook for 5 minutes until softened.

4. Switch heat to medium-low heat, then add lentils and walnuts, stir in cinnamon, salt, and turmeric, pour in honey and pomegranate, stir until mixed and simmer the mixture for 40 minutes until the sauce has reduced by half and lentils have softened.

5. Meanwhile, place cauliflower florets in a food processor and then pulse for 2 minutes until the mixture resembles rice.

6. Take a medium to saute pan, place it over medium heat, add remaining oil and when hot, add cauliflower rice, cook for 5 minutes until softened, and then season with salt.

7. Serve cooked pomegranate and walnut sauce with cooked cauliflower rice and garnish with walnuts and parsley.

Nutrition: Calories: 439 Fat: 25 g Carbs: 67 g Protein: 21 g Fiber: 3 g

181. Fennel and Chickpeas Provençal

Preparation Time: 10 minutes

Cooking Time: 50 minutes

Servings: 4

Ingredients:

- 15 ounces cooked chickpeas
- 3 fennel bulbs, sliced
- 1 medium onion, peeled, sliced
- 15 ounces diced tomatoes
- 10 black olives, pitted, cured
- 10 Kalamata olives, pitted

- 1 ½ teaspoon minced garlic
- 1 teaspoon salt
- 1/8 teaspoon ground black pepper
- 1 teaspoon Herbes de Provence
- 1/2 teaspoon red pepper flakes
- 2 tablespoons olive oil
- 1/2 cup water
- 2 tablespoons chopped parsley

Directions:

1. Take a saucepan, place it over medium-high heat, add oil and when hot, add onion, fennel, and garlic, and cook for 20 minutes until softened.

2. Then add the remaining ingredients except for olives and chickpeas, bring the mixture to boil, switch heat to medium-low level, and simmer for 15 minutes.

3. Then add remaining ingredients, cook for 10 minutes until hot, garnish stew with parsley and serve.

Nutrition: Calories: 395 Fat: 13 g Carbs: 56 g Protein: 16 g Fiber: 13 g

182. African Peanut Lentil Soup

Preparation Time: 10 minutes

Cooking Time: 25 minutes

Servings: 3

Ingredients:

- 1/2 cup red lentils
- 1/2 medium white onion, sliced
- 2 medium tomatoes, chopped
- 1/2 cup baby spinach
- 1/2 cup sliced zucchini
- 1/2 cup sliced sweet potatoes
- ½ cup sliced potatoes
- ½ cup broccoli florets
- 2 teaspoons minced garlic
- 1 inch of ginger, grated
- 1 tablespoon tomato paste
- 1/4 teaspoon ground black pepper
- 1 teaspoon salt
- 1 ½ teaspoon ground cumin
- 2 teaspoons ground coriander
- 2 tablespoons peanuts
- 1 teaspoon Harissa Spice Blend
- 1 tablespoon sambal oelek
- 1/4 cup almond butter - 1 teaspoon olive oil
- 1 teaspoon lemon juice
- 2 ½ cups vegetable stock

Directions:

1. Take a large saucepan, place it over medium heat, add oil and when hot, add onion and cook for 5 minutes until translucent.

2. Meanwhile, place tomatoes in a blender, add garlic, ginger and sambal oelek along with all the spices, and pulse until pureed.

3. Pour this mixture into the onions, cook for 5 minutes, then add remaining ingredients except for spinach, peanuts and lemon juice, and simmer for 15 minutes.

4. Taste to adjust the seasoning, stir in spinach, and cook for 5 minutes until cooked.

5. Ladle soup into bowls, garnish with lime juice and peanuts and serve.

Nutrition: Calories: 411 Fat: 17 g Carbs: 50 g Protein: 20 g Fiber: 18 g

183. White Bean Stew

Preparation Time: 5 minutes

Cooking Time: 10 hours and 10 minutes

Servings: 10

Ingredients:

- 2 cups chopped spinach
- 28 ounces diced tomatoes
- 2 pounds white beans, dried
- 2 cups chopped chard
- 2 large carrots, peeled, diced
- 2 cups chopped kale
- 3 large celery stalks, diced
- 1 medium white onion, peeled, diced
- 1 ½ teaspoon minced garlic
- 2 tablespoons salt
- 1 teaspoon dried rosemary
- ½ teaspoon Ground black pepper, to taste
- 1 teaspoon dried thyme
- 1 teaspoon dried oregano
- 1 bay leaf
- 10 cups water

Directions:

1. Switch on the slow cooker, add all the ingredients in it, except for kale, chard, and spinach and stir until combined.

2. Shut the cooker with a lid and cook for 10 hours at a low heat setting until thoroughly cooked.

3. When done, stir in kale, chard, and spinach, and cook for 10 minutes until leaves wilt.

4. Serve straight away.

Nutrition: Calories: 109 Fat: 2.4 g Carbs: 17.8 g Protein: 5.3 g Fiber: 6 g

184. Vegetarian Gumbo

Preparation Time: 10 minutes

Cooking Time: 45 minutes

Servings: 4

Ingredients:

- 1 1/2 cups diced zucchini
- 16-ounces cooked red beans
- 4 cups sliced okra
- 1 1/2 cup diced green pepper
- 1 1/2 cup chopped white onion
- 1 1/2 cup diced red bell pepper
- 8 cremini mushrooms, quartered
- 1 cup sliced celery
- 3 teaspoons minced garlic
- 1 medium tomato, chopped
- 1 teaspoon red pepper flakes
- 1 teaspoon dried thyme
- 3 tablespoons all-purpose flour
- 1 tablespoon smoked paprika
- 1 teaspoon dried oregano
- 1/4 teaspoon nutmeg
- 1 teaspoon soy sauce
- 1 1/2 teaspoon liquid smoke
- 2 tablespoons mustard
- 1 tablespoon apple cider vinegar
- 1 tablespoon Worcestershire sauce, vegetarian
- 1/2 teaspoon hot sauce
- 3 tablespoons olive oil
- 4 cups vegetable stock
- 1/2 cup sliced green onion
- 4 cups cooked jasmine rice

Directions:

1. Take a Dutch oven, place it over medium heat, add oil and flour and cook for 5 minutes until fragrant.

2. Switch heat to the medium low level, and continue cooking for 20 minutes until the roux becomes dark brown, stirring constantly.

3. Meanwhile, place the tomato in a food processor, add garlic and onion along with remaining ingredients, except for stock, zucchini, celery, mushroom, green and red bell pepper, and pulse for 2 minutes until smooth.

4. Pour the mixture into the pan, return the pan over medium-high heat, stir until mixed, and cook for 5 minutes until all the liquid has evaporated.

5. Stir in stock, bring it to simmer, then add remaining vegetables and simmer for 20 minutes until tender.

6. Garnish gumbo with green onions and serve with rice.

Nutrition: Calories: 160 Fat: 7.3 g Carbs: 20 g Protein: 7 g Fiber: 5.7 g

185. Black Bean and Quinoa Stew

Preparation Time: 10 minutes

Cooking Time: 6 hours

Servings: 6

Ingredients:

- 1-pound black beans, dried, soaked overnight
- 3/4 cup quinoa, uncooked
- 1 medium red bell pepper, cored, chopped
- 1 medium red onion, peeled, diced
- 1 medium green bell pepper, cored, chopped
- 28-ounce diced tomatoes
- 2 dried chipotle peppers
- 1 ½ teaspoon minced garlic
- 2/3 teaspoon sea salt
- 2 teaspoons red chili powder
- 1/3 teaspoon ground black pepper
- 1 teaspoon coriander powder
- 1 dried cinnamon stick
- 1/4 cup cilantro
- 7 cups of water

Directions:

1. Switch on the slow cooker, add all the ingredients in it, except for salt, and stir until mixed.

2. Shut the cooker with a lid and cook for 6 hours at a high heat setting until cooked.

3. When done, stir salt into the stew until mixed, remove cinnamon sticks and serve.

Nutrition: Calories: 308 Fat: 2 g Carbs: 70 g Protein: 23 g Fiber: 32 g

186. Root Vegetable Stew

Preparation Time: 10 minutes

Cooking Time: 8 hours and 10 minutes

Servings: 6

Ingredients:

- 2 cups chopped kale
- 1 large white onion, peeled, chopped
- 1-pound parsnips, peeled, chopped
- 1-pound potatoes, peeled, chopped
- 2 celery ribs, chopped
- 1-pound butternut squash, peeled, deseeded, chopped - 1-pound carrots, peeled, chopped
- 3 teaspoons minced garlic
- 1-pound sweet potatoes, peeled, chopped

- 1 bay leaf - 1 teaspoon ground black pepper
- 1/2 teaspoon sea salt
- 1 tablespoon chopped sage
- 3 cups vegetable broth

Directions:

1. Switch on the slow cooker, add all the ingredients in it, except for the kale, and stir until mixed.

2. Shut the cooker with a lid and cook for 8 hours at a low heat setting until cooked.

3. When done, add kale into the stew, stir until mixed, and cook for 10 minutes until leaves have wilted.

4. Serve straight away.

Nutrition: Calories: 120 Fat: 1 g Carbs: 28 g Protein: 4 g Fiber: 6 g

187. Bean and Mushroom Chili

Preparation Time: 15 minutes

Cooking Time: 38 minutes

Servings: 6

Ingredients:

- 1 large onion, peeled and chopped
- 1-pound (454 g) button mushrooms, chopped
- 6 cloves garlic, peeled and minced
- 1 tablespoon ground cumin
- 4 teaspoons ground fennel
- 1 tablespoon ancho chile powder
- ½ teaspoon cayenne pepper
- 1 tablespoon unsweetened cocoa powder
- 4 cups cooked pinto beans, drained and rinsed
- 1 (28-ounce / 794-g) can diced tomatoes
- Salt, to taste (optional)

Directions:

1. Put the mushrooms and onion in a saucepan and sauté over medium heat for 10 minutes.

2. Add the garlic, cumin, fennel, chile powder, cayenne pepper, and cocoa powder, and cook for 3 minutes.

3. Add the beans, tomatoes, and 2 cups of water and simmer, covered, for 25 minutes. Season with salt, if desired. Serve immediately.

Nutrition Per Serving

Calories: 436, Fat: 2g, Carbs: 97g, Protein: 19g, Fiber: 23g

188. 5-Bean Chili

Preparation Time: 10 minutes

Cooking Time: 1 hour

Servings: 8

Ingredients:

- 2 (26- to 28-ounce / 737- to 794-g) cans diced tomatoes

- 1 (19-ounce / 539-g) can red kidney beans, drained and rinsed
- 1 (19-ounce / 539-g) can white kidney beans, drained and rinsed
- 1 (19-ounce / 539-g) can chickpeas, drained and rinsed
- 1 (19-ounce / 539-g) can black beans, drained and rinsed
- 1 (19-ounce / 539-g) can pinto beans, drained and rinsed
- 2 1/2 cups fresh mushrooms, sliced
- 1 medium red bell pepper, chopped
- 1 large yellow onion, chopped
- 1 cup corn, canned or frozen
- 1½ tablespoons chili powder
- 1 teaspoon ground cumin
- ½ teaspoon freshly ground black pepper
- ½ teaspoon pink Himalayan salt
- ¼ teaspoon cayenne pepper
- ¼ teaspoon garlic powder

Directions:

1. Combine all the ingredients in a large pot over medium heat. Cover the pot with a lid and cook, stirring occasionally, for 45 to 60 minutes.

2. Serve as is, or on a bed of brown rice, quinoa, or with a fresh avocado. If you have leftovers or you're doing meal prep, store them in reusable containers in the refrigerator for up to 5 days or freeze for up to 2 months.

Nutrition Per Serving

Calories: 756 Fat: 5g carbs: 139g protein: 41g fiber: 44g

189. Mushroom & Wild Rice Stew

Preparation Time: 10 minutes

Cooking Time: 50 minutes

Servings: 6

Ingredients

- 1 to 2 teaspoons olive oil
- 2 cups chopped mushrooms
- ½ to 1 teaspoon salt
- 1 onion, chopped, or 1 teaspoon onion powder
- 3 or 4 garlic cloves, minced, or ½ teaspoon garlic powder
- 1 tablespoon dried herbs
- ¾ cup brown rice
- ¼ cup wild rice or additional brown rice
- 3 cups water
- 3 Vegetable Broth or store-bought broth

- 2 to 4 tablespoons balsamic vinegar (optional)
- Freshly ground black pepper
- 1 cup frozen peas, thawed
- 1 cup unsweetened nondairy milk (optional)
- 1 to 2 cups chopped greens, such as spinach, kale, or chard

Directions:

1. Heat the olive oil in a large soup pot over medium-high heat.

2. Add the mushrooms and a pinch of salt, and sauté for about 4 minutes until the mushrooms are softened. Add the onion and garlic (if using fresh), and sauté for 1 to 2 minutes more. Stir in the dried herbs (plus the onion powder and/or garlic powder, if using), white or brown rice, wild rice, water, vegetable broth, vinegar (if using), and salt and pepper to taste. Bring to a boil, turn the heat to low, and cover the pot. Simmer the soup for 15 minutes (for white rice) or 45 minutes (for brown rice). Turn off the heat and stir in the peas, milk (if using), and greens. Let the greens wilt before serving.

3. Leftovers will keep in an airtight container for up to 1 week in the refrigerator or up to 1 month in the freezer.

Nutrition Per Serving (2 cups)

Calories: 201; Protein: 6g; Total fat: 3g; Saturated fat: 0g; Carbohydrates: 44g; Fiber: 4g

190. Ethiopian Cabbage, Carrot, and Potato Stew

Preparation Time: 10 minutes

Cooking Time: 20 minutes

Servings: 6

Ingredients

- 3 russet potatoes, peeled and cut into ½-inch cubes
- 2 tablespoons olive oil
- 6 carrots, peeled, halved lengthwise, and cut into ½-inch slices
- 1 onion, chopped
- 4 garlic cloves, minced
- 1 tablespoon ground turmeric
- 1 teaspoon ground cumin
- 1 teaspoon ground ginger
- 1½ teaspoons sea salt
- 1½ cups low-sodium vegetable broth, divided
- 4 cups shredded or thinly sliced green cabbage

Directions:

1. Bring a large pot of water to a boil over medium-high heat.

2. Add the potatoes and cook for 10 minutes, or until fork-tender. Drain and set aside. While the potatoes are cooking, heat the oil in a large skillet over medium-high heat. Add the carrots and onion and sauté for 5 minutes. Add the garlic, turmeric, cumin, ginger, and salt and sauté for 1 additional minute, until fragrant. Add the cooked potatoes and 1 cup of broth to the skillet, bring to a boil and reduce to a simmer. Scatter the cabbage on top of the potatoes. Cover and simmer for 3 minutes.

3. Mix the cabbage into the potatoes, add the remaining ½ cup of broth, cover, and simmer for 5 more minutes, or until the cabbage is wilted and tender. Stir the cabbage from time to time while cooking to incorporate it with the other ingredients as it continues to wilt.

Nutrition: Calories: 216 Fat: 5.03g Carbohydrates: 39.85g Fiber: 3.6g Sugar: 3.94g Protein: 5.12g Sodium: 630mg

191. Balsamic Lentil Stew

Preparation Time: 10 minutes

Cooking Time: 30 minutes

Servings: 5

Ingredients

- 1 teaspoon olive oil
- 4 carrots, peeled and chopped
- 1 onion, chopped
- 3 garlic cloves, minced
- 2 tablespoons balsamic vinegar
- 4 Vegetable Broth or water
- 1 (28-ounce) can crushed tomatoes
- 1 tablespoon sugar
- 2 cups dried lentils or 2 (15-ounce) cans lentils, drained and rinsed
- 1 teaspoon salt
- Freshly ground black pepper

Directions:

1. Heat the olive oil in a large soup pot over medium heat. Add the carrots, onion, and garlic and sauté for about 5 minutes until the vegetables are softened. Pour in the vinegar, and let it sizzle to deglaze the bottom of the pot. Add the vegetable broth, tomatoes, sugar, and lentils.

2. Bring to a boil, then reduce the heat to low. Simmer for about 25 minutes until the lentils are soft. Add the salt and season to taste with pepper. Leftovers will keep in an airtight container for up to 1 week in the refrigerator or up to 1 month in the freezer.

Nutrition Per Serving (2 cups) Calories: 353; Protein: 22g; Total fat: 2g; Saturated fat: 0g; Carbohydrates: 67g; Fiber: 27g

192. Winter Stew

Preparation Time: 10 minutes
Cooking Time: 20 minutes
Servings: 6
Ingredients:

- ½ cup red lentils
- 1 cup mushrooms, chopped
- 1 yellow onion, chopped
- 2 sweet potatoes, chopped
- 1 carrot, chopped
- ½ cup red kidney beans, canned
- 1 tablespoon tomato paste
- 2 cups of water
- ½ cup almond milk
- 1 teaspoon salt
- ½ teaspoon peppercorns
- 1 teaspoon olive oil

Directions:

1. Cook mushrooms with onion and olive oil on Saute mode for 10 minutes.
2. Then add red lentils, sweet potatoes, carrot, red kidney beans, tomato paste, almond milk, water, salt, and peppercorns.
3. Mix up the ingredients gently.
4. Close and seal the lid.
5. Set High-pressure mode and cook the stew for 10 minutes. Then allow natural pressure release.
6. Mix up the cooked stew carefully.
Nutrition: Calories 177, Fat 5.9g, fiber 8.6g, carbs 23.8g, protein 8.8

193. Vegan "Beef" Stew

Preparation Time: 10 minutes
Cooking Time: 45 minutes
Servings: 2
Ingredients:

- ½ yellow onion, chopped roughly
- 1 oz celery stalk, chopped
- ¼ cup carrot, chopped
- 1 garlic clove, diced
- 1 tablespoon tomato sauce
- ¼ cup green peas
- 1 tomato, chopped
- 1 cup vegetable stock
- 1 teaspoon salt - 1 teaspoon thyme
- 2 Yukon potatoes

Directions:

1. Chop Yukon potatoes roughly and transfer them to the instant pot.
2. Add celery stalk, yellow onion, carrot, garlic, tomato sauce, green peas, tomato, salt, thyme, and mix up.
3. Then add vegetable stock and close the lid.
4. Set Sauté mode and cook the stew for 45 minutes.
5. When the time is over, check if all the ingredients are cooked and mix up the stew gently.
Nutrition: Calories 100, Fat 1.2g, Fiber 4.5g, Carbs 22.4g, Protein 3g

194. Egyptian Stew

Preparation Time: 10 minutes
Cooking Time: 12 minutes
Servings: 5
Ingredients:

- 1 tablespoon tomato paste
- 1 tablespoon olive oil
- 1 tablespoon red pepper
- 1 teaspoon paprika
- 4 potatoes, peeled, chopped
- 2 cups lentils
- 6 cups of water
- 1 teaspoon salt
- 1 cup fresh dill, chopped
- 3 tablespoons lemon juice

Directions:

1. Place tomato paste, paprika, potatoes, lentils, water, and salt in the instant pot.
2. Close and seal the lid.
3. After this, set Manual mode and cook the stew for 12 minutes.
4. Then use quick pressure release.
5. Open the lid and add lemon juice. Mix it up.
6. Transfer the stew to the serving bowls.
7. Then mix up together red pepper and olive oil.
8. Pour the mixture over the stew.
9. Garnish the meal with fresh dill.
Nutrition: Calories 451, Fat 4.4g, Fiber 29.5g, Carbs 81.1g, Protein 25.1g

195. Moroccan Stew

Preparation Time: 10 minutes
Cooking Time: 18 minutes
Servings: 4
Ingredients:

- 1 cup butternut squash, chopped
- ½ cup chickpeas, canned

- 1 teaspoon turmeric
- 1 teaspoon sage
- 1 teaspoon ground coriander
- 1 teaspoon thyme
- 1 teaspoon harissa
- 1 teaspoon ground ginger
- ¼ teaspoon saffron
- 1 lemon slice
- 1 teaspoon salt
- 1 teaspoon tomato paste
- 2 cups of water

Directions:

1. In the instant pot, combine water, tomato paste, salt, saffron, ground ginger, harissa, thyme, ground coriander, sage, turmeric, and canned chickpeas.

2. Add butternut squash and mix the ingredients.

3. Add lemon slice and close the lid.

4. Set Manual mode (high pressure) and cook the stew for 8 minutes. Then allow natural pressure release for 10 minutes more.

5. Open the lid and chill the stew till room temperature.

Nutrition: Calories 117, Fat 1.9g, Fiber 5.5g, Carbs 21.1, protein 5.5g

196. Peas and Carrot Stew

Preparation Time: 5 minutes
Cooking Time: 15 minutes
Servings: 5
Ingredients:

- 3 potatoes, peeled, chopped
- 2 carrots, chopped
- 1 cup green peas, frozen
- 2 cups of water
- 1 tablespoon tomato paste
- 1 teaspoon salt
- 1 teaspoon cayenne pepper

Directions:

1. Place carrots, potatoes, and green peas in the instant pot.

2. Then in the separated bowl, combine tomato paste, water, salt, and cayenne pepper.

3. Whisk the liquid until it gets a light red color, and then pour it into the instant pot.

4. Close and seal the lid. Cook the stew on Manual mode for 10 minutes.

5. Then allow natural pressure release for 5 minutes.

Nutrition: Calories 125, Fat 0.3g, Fiber 5.4g, Carbs 27.5g, Protein 4.1g

197. Mediterranean Vegan Stew

Preparation Time: 10 minutes
Cooking Time: 35 minutes
Servings: 4
Ingredients:

- ¼ cup white cabbage, shredded
- 1 potato, chopped
- ½ cup corn kernels
- 1 sweet pepper, chopped
- ½ cup fresh parsley
- 1 cup tomatoes, chopped
- ¼ cup green beans, chopped
- 1 ½ cup water
- 1 teaspoon salt
- 1 tablespoon coconut cream
- 1 teaspoon white pepper

Directions:

1. Place all the ingredients in the instant pot and mix them up.

2. After this, close the lid and sir Saute mode.

3. Cook the stew for 35 minutes.

4. When the time is over, open the lid and mix the stew well.

5. Check if all the ingredients are cooked and close the lid.

6. Let the stew rest for 10-15 minutes before serving.

Nutrition: Calories 83, Fat 1.4g, Fiber 3.2g, Carbs 16.8g, Protein 2.8g

198. African Pineapple Peanut Stew

Preparation Time: 30 minutes
Cooking Time: 10 minutes
Servings: 4
Ingredients:

- 4 cups sliced kale
- 1 cup chopped onion
- 1/2 cup peanut butter
- 1 tbsp. hot pepper sauce or 1 tbsp. Tabasco sauce
- 2 minced garlic cloves
- 1/2 cup chopped cilantro
- 2 cups pineapple, undrained, canned & crushed
- 1 tbsp. vegetable oil

Directions:

1. In a saucepan (preferably covered), sauté the garlic and onions in the oil until the onions are lightly browned, approximately 10 minutes, stirring often.

2. Wash the kale till the time the onions are sautéed.

3. Get rid of the stems. Mound the leaves on a cutting surface & slice crosswise into slices (preferably 1" thick).

4. Now put the pineapple and juice into the onions & bring to a simmer. Stir the kale in, cover, and simmer until just tender, stirring frequently, for approximately 5 minutes.

5. Mix in the hot pepper sauce, peanut butter & simmer for more 5 minutes.

6. Add salt according to your taste.

Nutrition:

382 Calories, 20.3 g Total Fat, 0 mg Cholesterol, 27.6 g Total Carbohydrate, 5 g Dietary Fiber, 11.4 g Protein

199. Cauliflower Stew

Preparation Time: 15 minutes

Cooking Time: 50 minutes

Servings: 4

Ingredients

- 1 fresh green chili, seeded and chopped
- 1 teaspoon ground coriander
- 1¼ cups homemade vegetable broth
- Salt and black pepper, to taste
- 1 teaspoon fresh ginger root, minced
- ½ teaspoon cayenne pepper
- 2 tablespoons lemon juice, freshly squeezed
- 2 tablespoons fresh cilantro, chopped
- 2 tablespoons olive oil
- 3 large garlic cloves, minced
- 1 teaspoon ground cumin
- 2 cups fresh tomatoes, finely chopped
- 1 bay leaf
- 1 medium yellow onion, chopped
- ½ teaspoon dried thyme, crushed
- 1 medium head cauliflower, cut into florets
- 2 tablespoons sugar-free tomato paste

Directions:

1. Heat olive oil in a large Dutch oven over medium heat and add onion.

2. Sauté for about 4 minutes and add garlic, ginger, green chili, thyme and spices.

3. Sauté for about 1 minute and stir in the tomatoes.

4. Cook for about 3 minutes, stirring constantly, and add the cauliflower.

5. Cook for about 2 minutes and stir in the bay leaf, tomato paste and broth.

6. Increase the heat and bring it to a boil.

7. Reduce the heat to low and allow to simmer, covered for about 40 minutes.

8. Squeeze in the lemon juice, salt and black pepper, and discard the bay leaf.

9. Garnishing with cilantro and serve hot.

Nutrition: Calories: 13 net carbs: 6.2g Fat: 8.5g carbohydrates: 10.5g Fiber: 2.3g sugar: 5.4g Protein: 5.4g sodium: 617mg

200. Mushroom Stew

Preparation Time: 15 minutes

Cooking Time: 17 minutes

Servings: 4

Ingredients

- ¼ cup fresh cilantro, chopped
- 3 small garlic cloves, minced
- 2 tablespoons fresh lime juice
- ¼ pound fresh shiitake mushrooms, sliced
- ¼ pound fresh portobello mushrooms, sliced
- 1 small yellow onion, chopped
- Salt and black pepper, to taste
- ½ pound fresh button mushrooms, sliced
- ½ cup coconut milk, unsweetened
- ¼ cup homemade vegetable broth
- 2 tablespoons olive oil
- 2 tablespoons fresh lemon juice
- 1 tablespoon fresh parsley, chopped

Directions:

1. Heat olive oil in a large skillet over medium heat and add garlic and onions.

2. Sauté for about 5 minutes and stir in the mushrooms, salt and black pepper.

3. Cook for about 7 minutes and stir in the broth and coconut milk.

4. Bring to a boil and allow to simmer for about 5 minutes.

5. Whisk in the lemon juice and parsley and dish out to serve hot.

Nutrition: Calories: 185 net carbs: 8.3g Fat: 14.6g carbohydrates: 12.8g Fiber: 2.5g sugar: 4.3g Protein: 4.6g sodium: 128mg

201. Tofu and Veggies Stew

Preparation Time: 15 minutes

Cooking Time: 15 minutes

Servings: 8

Ingredients

- 1 (16-ounce) jar roasted red peppers, rinsed, drained and chopped
- 1 jalapeño pepper, seeded and chopped

- 2 cups homemade vegetable broth
- 1 medium red bell pepper, seeded and thinly sliced
- 1 medium yellow bell pepper, seeded and thinly sliced
- 1 (16-ounce) package extra-firm tofu, drained, pressed and cubed
- Salt and black pepper, to taste
- 2 cups water
- 1 medium green bell pepper, seeded and thinly sliced
- 1 (10-ounce) package frozen baby spinach, thawed
- ¼ cup fresh basil leaves, chopped

Directions:

1. Put the garlic sauce, jalapeño pepper and roasted red peppers in a food processor and pulse until smooth.

2. Add the puree, broth and water in a large pan over medium-high heat and bring to a boil.

3. Stir in the bell peppers and tofu and reduce the heat.

4. Cook for about 5 minutes and add the spinach.

5. Cook for 5 more minutes and season with salt and black pepper.

6. Remove from heat and garnish with basil to serve hot.

Nutrition: Calories: 90 net carbs: 3.4g Fat: 4g carbohydrates: 7.4g Fiber: 2g sugar: 3.9g Protein: 8.5g sodium: 359mg

202. Bell Pepper and Spinach Stew

Preparation Time: 15 minutes

Cooking Time: 15 minutes

Servings: 5

Ingredients

- 4 cups water
- ½ cup sour cream
- 2 tablespoons garlic, peeled
- 1 jalapeño pepper, seeded and chopped
- 1 (16-ounce) jar roasted red peppers, rinsed, drained and chopped
- 2 cups vegetable broth
- 2 cups water
- 1 medium green bell pepper, seeded and thinly sliced
- 1 medium red bell pepper, seeded and thinly sliced
- 1 (10-ounce) package frozen baby spinach, thawed

Directions:

1. Put garlic, jalapeño pepper and roasted red peppers in a food processor and pulse until smooth.

2. Put the puree, broth and water in a large pan over medium-high heat and bring to a boil.

3. Stir in the bell peppers and tofu and reduce the heat.

4. Cook for about 5 minutes and add the spinach.

5. Cook for 5 more minutes and dish out to serve hot.

Nutrition: Calories: 119 net carbs: 7.9g Fat: 5.9g carbohydrates: 13.1g Fiber: 3.2g sugar: 6.4g Protein: 5.8g sodium: 586mg

203. Potato and Chickpeas Stew

Preparation Time: 15 minutes

Cooking Time: 35 minutes

Servings: 6

Ingredients

- 2 tablespoons olive oil
- 1 teaspoon fresh ginger, minced
- 2 garlic cloves, minced
- 1 teaspoon ground cumin
- 2 large potatoes, scrubbed and cubed
- 2 (15-ounce) cans chickpeas, rinsed and drained
- 2 cups vegetable broth
- ¼ cup fresh cilantro, chopped
- 1 onion, chopped
- 1 tablespoon hot curry powder
- ¼ teaspoon ground turmeric
- 2 (15-ounce) cans diced tomatoes with liquid
- Salt and black pepper, to taste

Directions:

1. Heat olive oil in a large pan over medium heat and add onions.

2. Sauté for about 4 minutes and add ginger, garlic, curry powder and spices.

3. Sauté for about 1 minute and stir in the potatoes.

4. Cook for about 5 minutes and stir in the remaining ingredients except for the cilantro.

5. Reduce the heat to medium-low and cover the lid.

6. Let it simmer for about 25 minutes and dish it out in a bowl.

7. Garnish with cilantro and serve hot.

Nutrition: Calories: 691net carbs: 81.7gFat: 14.2g carbohydrates: 113.6g Fiber: 29.9g sugar: 21.4g Protein: 32.7g sodium: 308mg

204. Squash and Beans Stew

Preparation Time: 15 minutes

Cooking Time: 1 hour 10 minutes

Servings: 8

Ingredients

- 2 large white onions, chopped
- 2 tablespoons ground cinnamon
- 8 large tomatoes, seeded and chopped finely
- 4 tablespoons vegetable oil
- 8 garlic cloves, minced
- 2 tablespoons red chili powder
- 2 tablespoons cumin seeds, toasted
- 2 cups canned pinto beans
- 3 cups water
- Salt and black pepper, to taste
- 2 medium acorn squash, peeled and chopped
- 4 tablespoons fresh lemon juice

Directions:

1. Heat olive oil in a large pan over medium heat and add onions.

2. Sauté for about 4 minutes and add garlic and spices.

3. Sauté for about 1 minute and stir in the tomatoes.

4. Cook for about 3 minutes and add beans, squash and water.

5. Bring to a boil and reduce the heat to medium-low.

6. Cover the lid and allow to simmer for about 1 hour.

7. Stir in the lemon juice, salt and black pepper and dish out in a bowl to serve hot.

Nutrition: Calories: 340 net carbs: 40.3g Fat: 8.7g carbohydrates: 56.2g Fiber: 13.9g sugar: 7.8g Protein: 14g sodium: 46mg

205. Hearty Vegetable Stew

Preparation Time: 30 minutes

Cooking Time: 25 minutes

Servings: 6

Ingredients

- ¼ cup portobello mushrooms, sliced
- 1 teaspoon rosemary, dried
- 2 carrots, chopped
- 2 ribs celery, chopped
- 2 potatoes, chopped
- 2 tomatoes, diced
- 1 teaspoon Italian seasoning
- 1 large onion, chopped
- 1 small onion, minced
- 1 clove garlic, minced
- 1 rib celery, minced
- 1 carrot, minced
- ¼ cup vegetable broth
- ¼ cup button mushrooms, sliced
- ½ cup red wine
- 3 cups low sodium vegetable broth
- ½ teaspoon salt
- ¼ teaspoon black pepper
- ½ cup tomato sauce
- 1 tablespoon balsamic vinegar
- 1 tablespoon cornstarch
- 1 cup peas, frozen

Directions:

1. Heat ¼ cup vegetable broth in a pot and add minced onion, celery, and carrots.

2. Cook for about 5 minutes on high heat until they soften and then add the large onion to it.

3. Cook for about 4 minutes and stir in the mushrooms.

4. Cook for about 5 minutes until the liquid comes out.

5. Season with Italian seasoning and rosemary.

6. Add the wine to the pot afterwards and cook for about 3 minutes.

7. Stir in the tomatoes, tomato sauce, and broth and cook for 3 more minutes.

8. Add the remaining chopped veggies, turn the flame high and boil the contents in the pot.

9. Add the rest of the seasonings to the pot and bring to a boil.

10. Stir in the peas to the pot and mix well until combined.

11. Whisk the cornstarch with some water and add it to the pot.

12. Allow it to simmer for about 4 minutes until it is thickened.

13. Dish out to serve hot and delve into the delicious blend.

Nutrition: Calories: 137 net carbs: 19.2 g Fat: 0.7g carbohydrates: 26.3g Fiber: 5.1g sugar: 7.2g Protein: 14.1g sodium: 563mg

206. Barley Lentil Stew

Preparation Time: 5 minutes

Cooking Time: 50 minutes

Servings: 3

Ingredients

- ½ onion, chopped
- 2 stalks celery, chopped
- 1 carrot, diced
- 1 tablespoon olive oil

- 3 cups vegetable stock
- 2 small red potatoes, skin on, chopped
- ¼ cup dry, uncooked barley
- ¾ cup cooked lentils

Directions:

1. Place a large pot over medium-high heat and add the oil. Once it is heated, add the vegetables and sauté for three to four minutes, until slightly softened.

2. Add the vegetable stock and the potatoes and bring the pot to a boil.

3. Reduce the heat to a simmer and add the barley and lentils.

4. Simmer gently for 45 minutes, adding water if needed until the barley is plump and soft.

5. Serve hot.

Nutrition: Calories 367, total fat 5.8g, saturated fat 0.9g, cholesterol 0mg, sodium 85mg, total carbohydrate 63.1g, dietary fiber 20.8g, total sugars 4.9g, protein 17.3g, vitamin d 0mcg, calcium 59mg, iron 5mg, potassium 1165mg

207. Fruits Stew

Preparation Time: 10 minutes

Cooking Time: 10 minutes

Servings: 4

Ingredients:

- 1 avocado, peeled, pitted and sliced
- 1 cup plums, stoned and halved
- 2 cups water
- 2 teaspoons vanilla extract
- 1 tablespoon lemon juice
- 2 tablespoons stevia

Directions:

1. In a pan, combine the avocado with the plums, water and the other ingredients, bring to a simmer and cook over medium heat for 10 minutes.

2. Divide the mix into bowls and serve cold.

Nutrition: calories 178, fat 4.4, fiber 2, carbs 3, protein 5

208. Quinoa and Black Bean Chili

Preparation Time: 10 minutes

Cooking Time: 32 minutes

Servings: 10

Ingredients:

- 1 cup quinoa, cooked
- 38 ounces cooked black beans
- 1 medium white onion, peeled, chopped
- 1 cup of frozen corn

- 1 green bell pepper, deseeded, chopped
- 1 zucchini, chopped
- 1 tablespoon minced chipotle peppers in adobo sauce
- 1 red bell pepper, deseeded, chopped
- 1 jalapeno pepper, deseeded, minced
- 28 ounces crushed tomatoes
- 2 teaspoons minced garlic
- 1/3 teaspoon ground black pepper
- ¾ teaspoon salt
- 1 teaspoon dried oregano
- 1 tablespoon red chili powder
- 1 tablespoon ground cumin
- 1 tablespoon olive oil
- 1/4 cup chopped cilantro

Directions:

1. Take a large pot, place it over medium heat, add oil and when hot, add onion and cook for 5 minutes.

2. Then stir in garlic, cumin, and chili powder, cook for 1 minute, add remaining ingredients except for corn and quinoa, stir well and simmer for 20 minutes at medium-low heat until cooked.

3. Then stir in corn and quinoa, cook for 5 minutes until hot and then top with cilantro.

4. Serve straight away.

Nutrition: Calories: 233 Fat: 3.5 g Carbs: 42 g Protein: 11.5 g Fiber: 11.8 g

209. Mushroom, Lentil, and Barley Stew

Preparation Time: 10 minutes

Cooking Time: 6 hours

Servings: 8

Ingredients:

- 3/4 cup pearl barley
- 2 cups sliced button mushrooms
- 3/4 cup dry lentils
- 1-ounce dried shiitake mushrooms
- 2 teaspoons minced garlic
- 1/4 cup dried onion flakes
- 2 teaspoons ground black pepper
- 1 teaspoon dried basil
- 2 ½ teaspoons salt
- 2 teaspoons dried savory
- 3 bay leaves
- 2 quarts vegetable broth

Directions:

1. Switch on the slow cooker, place all the ingredients in it, and stir until combined.
2. Shut with lid and cook the stew for 6 hours at a high heat setting until cooked.
3. Serve straight away.

Nutrition: Calories: 213 Fat: 1.2 g Carbs: 44 g Protein: 8.4 g Fiber: 9 g

210. Sweet Potato, Kale and Peanut Stew

Preparation Time: 10 minutes
Cooking Time: 45 minutes
Servings: 3
Ingredients:

- 1/4 cup red lentils
- 2 medium sweet potatoes, peeled, cubed
- 1 medium white onion, peeled, diced
- 1 cup kale, chopped - 2 tomatoes, diced
- 1/4 cup chopped green onion
- 1 teaspoon minced garlic
- 1 inch of ginger, grated
- 2 tablespoons toasted peanuts
- ¼ teaspoon ground black pepper
- 1 teaspoon ground cumin
- 1/2 teaspoon turmeric
- 1/8 teaspoon cayenne pepper
- 1 tablespoon peanut butter
- 1 1/2 cups vegetable broth
- 2 teaspoons coconut oil

Directions:

1. Take a medium pot, place it on medium heat, add oil and when it melts, add onions and cook for 5 minutes.
2. Then stir in ginger and garlic, cook for 2 minutes until fragrant, add lentils and potatoes along with all the spices, and stir until mixed.
3. Stir in tomatoes, pour in the broth, bring the mixture to boil, then switch heat to the low level and simmer for 30 minutes until cooked.
4. Then stir in peanut butter until incorporated and then puree by using an immersion blender until half-pureed.
5. Return stew over low heat, stir in kale, cook for 5 minutes until its leaves wilt, and then season with black pepper and salt. Garnish the stew with peanuts and green onions and then serve.

Nutrition: Calories: 401 Fat: 6.7 g Carbs: 77.3 g Protein: 10.8 g Fiber: 16 g

211. Vegetarian Irish Stew

Preparation Time: 5 minutes
Cooking Time: 38 minutes
Servings: 6
Ingredients:

- 1 cup textured vegetable protein, chunks
- ½ cup split red lentils
- 2 medium onions, peeled, sliced
- 1 cup sliced parsnip
- 2 cups sliced mushrooms
- 1 cup diced celery,
- 1/4 cup flour
- 4 cups vegetable stock
- 1 cup rutabaga
- 1 bay leaf
- ½ cup fresh parsley
- 1 teaspoon sugar
- ¼ teaspoon ground black pepper
- 1/4 cup soy sauce
- ¼ teaspoon thyme
- 2 teaspoons marmite
- ¼ teaspoon rosemary
- 2/3 teaspoon salt
- ¼ teaspoon marjoram

Directions:

1. Take a large soup pot, place it over medium heat, add oil and when it gets hot, add onions and cook for 5 minutes until softened.
2. Then switch heat to the low level, sprinkle with flour, stir well, add remaining ingredients, stir until combined, and simmer for 30 minutes until vegetables have cooked.
3. When done, season the stew with salt and black pepper, and then serve.

Nutrition: Calories: 117.4 Fat: 4 g Carbs: 22.8 g Protein: 6.5 g Fiber: 7.3 g

212. White Bean and Cabbage Stew

Preparation Time: 5 minutes
Cooking Time: 8 hours
Servings: 4
Ingredients:

- 3 cups cooked great northern beans
- 2 pounds potatoes, peeled, cut into large dice
- 1 large white onion, peeled, chopped
- ½ head of cabbage, chopped
- 3 ribs celery, chopped

- 4 medium carrots, peeled, sliced
- 14.5 ounces diced tomatoes
- 1/3 cup pearled barley
- 1 teaspoon minced garlic
- ½ teaspoon ground black pepper
- 1 bay leaf
- 1 teaspoon dried thyme
- ½ teaspoon crushed rosemary
- 1 teaspoon salt
- ½ teaspoon caraway seeds
- 1 tablespoon chopped parsley
- 8 cups vegetable broth

Directions:

2. Switch on the slow cooker, then add all the ingredients except for salt, parsley, tomatoes, and beans and stir until mixed.
3. Shut the slow cooker with a lid, and cook for 7 hours at a low heat setting until cooked.
4. Then stir in the remaining ingredients, stir until combined, and continue cooking for 1 hour.
5. Serve straight away

Nutrition: Calories: 150 Fat: 0.7 g Carbs: 27 g Protein: 7 g Fiber: 9.4 g

213. Spinach and Cannellini Bean Stew

Preparation Time: 10 minutes
Cooking Time: 15 minutes
Servings: 6
Ingredients:

- 28 ounces cooked cannellini beans
- 24 ounces tomato passata
- 17 ounces spinach chopped
- ¼ teaspoon ground black pepper
- 2/3 teaspoon salt
- 1 ¼ teaspoon curry powder
- 1 cup cashew butter
- ¼ teaspoon cardamom
- 2 tablespoons olive oil
- 1 teaspoon salt
- ¼ cup cashews
- 2 tablespoons chopped basil
- 2 tablespoons chopped parsley

Directions:

1. Take a large saucepan, place it over medium heat, add 1 tablespoon oil and when hot, add spinach and cook for 3 minutes until fried.

2. Then stir in butter and tomato passata until well mixed, bring the mixture to a near boil, add beans, and season with ¼ teaspoon curry powder, black pepper, and salt.
3. Take a small saucepan, place it over medium heat, add remaining oil, stir in cashew, stir in salt and curry powder and cook for 4 minutes until roasted, set aside until required.
4. Transfer cooked stew into a bowl, top with roasted cashews, basil, and parsley, and then serve.

Nutrition: Calories: 242 Fat: 10.2 g Carbs: 31 g Protein: 11 g Fiber: 8.5 g

214. Cabbage Stew

Preparation Time: 10 minutes
Cooking Time: 50 minutes
Servings: 6
Ingredients:

- 12 ounces cooked Cannellini beans
- 8 ounces smoked tofu, firm, sliced
- 1 medium cabbage, chopped
- 1 large white onion, peeled, julienned
- 2 ½ teaspoon minced garlic
- 1 tablespoon sweet paprika
- 5 tablespoons tomato paste
- 3 teaspoons smoked paprika
- 1/3 teaspoon ground black pepper
- 2 teaspoons dried thyme
- 2/3 teaspoon salt
- ½ tsp ground coriander
- 3 bay leaves - 4 tablespoons olive oil
- 1 cup vegetable broth

Directions:

1. Take a large saucepan, place it over medium heat, add 3 tablespoons oil and when hot, add onion and garlic and cook for 3 minutes or until sauté.
2. Add cabbage, pour in water, simmer for 10 minutes or until softened, then stir in all the spices and continue cooking for 30 minutes.
3. Add beans and tomato paste, pour in water, stir until mixed and cook for 15 minutes until thoroughly cooked.
4. Take a separate skillet pan, add 1 tablespoon oil and when hot, add tofu slices and cook for 5 minutes until golden brown on both sides.
5. Serve cooked cabbage stew with fried tofu.

Nutrition: Calories: 182 Fat: 8.3 g Carbs: 27 g Protein: 5.5 g Fiber: 9.4 g

215. Kimchi Stew

Preparation Time: 10 minutes
Cooking Time: 25 minutes
Servings: 4
Ingredients:

- 1-pound tofu, extra-firm, pressed, cut into 1-inch pieces
- 4 cups Napa cabbage kimchi, vegan, chopped
- 1 small white onion, peeled, diced
- 2 cups sliced shiitake mushroom caps
- 1 ½ teaspoon minced garlic
- 2 tablespoons soy sauce
- 2 tablespoons olive oil, divided
- 4 cups vegetable broth
- 2 tablespoons chopped scallions

Directions:

1. Take a large pot, place it over medium heat, add 1 tablespoon oil and when hot, add tofu pieces in a single layer and cook for 10 minutes until browned on all sides.
2. When cooked, transfer tofu pieces to a plate, add remaining oil to the pot and when hot, add onion and cook for 5 minutes until soft.
3. Stir in garlic, cook for 1 minute until fragrant, stir in kimchi, continue cooking for 2 minutes, then add mushrooms and pour in broth.
4. Switch heat to medium-high level, bring the mixture to boil, then switch heat to medium-low level and simmer for 10 minutes until mushrooms are softened.
5. Stir in tofu, taste to adjust seasoning, and garnish with scallions.
6. Serve straight away.

Nutrition: Calories: 153 Fat: 8.2 g Carbs: 25 g Protein: 8.4 g Fiber: 2.6 g

216. Spicy Bean Stew

Preparation Time: 5 minutes
Cooking Time: 50 minutes
Servings: 4
Ingredients:

- 7 ounces cooked black eye beans
- 14 ounces chopped tomatoes
- 2 medium carrots, peeled, diced
- 7 ounces cooked kidney beans
- 1 leek, diced
- ½ a chili, chopped
- 1 teaspoon minced garlic
- 1/3 teaspoon ground black pepper
- 2/3 teaspoon salt
- 1 teaspoon red chili powder
- 1 lemon, juiced
- 3 tablespoons white wine
- 1 tablespoon olive oil
- 1 2/3 cups vegetable stock

Directions:

1. Take a large saucepan, place it over medium-high heat, add oil and when hot, add leeks and cook for 8 minutes or until softened.
2. Then add carrots, continue cooking for 4 minutes, stir in chili and garlic, pour in the wine, and continue cooking for 2 minutes.
3. Add tomatoes, stir in lemon juice, pour in the stock and bring the mixture to boil.
4. Switch heat to medium level, simmer for 35 minutes until stew has thickened, then add both beans along with remaining ingredients and cook for 5 minutes until hot.
5. Serve straight away.

Nutrition: Calories: 114 Fat: 1.6 g Carbs: 19 g Protein: 6 g Fiber: 8.4 g

217. Eggplant, Onion and Tomato Stew

Preparation Time: 5 minutes
Cooking Time: 5 minutes
Servings: 4
Ingredients:

- 3 1/2 cups cubed eggplant
- 1 cup diced white onion
- 2 cups diced tomatoes
- 1 teaspoon ground cumin
- 1/8 teaspoon ground cayenne pepper
- 1 teaspoon salt
- 1 cup tomato sauce
- 1/2 cup water

Directions:

1. Switch on the instant pot, place all the ingredients in it, stir until mixed, and seal the pot.
2. Press the 'manual' button and cook for 5 minutes at a high-pressure setting until cooked.
3. When done, do a quick pressure release, open the instant pot, and stir the stew.
4. Serve straight away.

Nutrition: Calories: 88 Fat: 1 g Carbs: 21 g Protein: 3 g Fiber: 6 g

218. Brussel Sprouts Stew

Preparation Time: 10 minutes
Cooking Time: 55 minutes
Servings: 4
Ingredients:

- 35 ounces Brussels sprouts
- 5 medium potatoes, peeled, chopped
- 1 medium onion, peeled, chopped
- 2 carrots, peeled, cubed
- 2 teaspoon smoked paprika
- 1/8 teaspoon ground black pepper
- 1/8 teaspoon salt
- 3 tablespoons caraway seeds
- 1/2 teaspoon red chili powder
- 1 tablespoon nutmeg
- 1 tablespoon olive oil
- 4 ½ cups hot vegetable stock

Directions:

1. Take a large pot, place it over medium-high heat, add oil and when hot, add onion and cook for 1 minute.
2. Then add carrot and potato, cook for 2 minutes, then add Brussel sprouts and cook for 5 minutes.
3. Stir in all the spices, pour in vegetable stock, bring the mixture to boil, switch heat to medium-low and simmer for 45 minutes until cooked and the stew reaches to desired thickness.
4. Serve straight away.

Nutrition: Calories: 156 Fat: 3 g Carbs: 22 g Protein: 12 g Fiber: 5.11 g

219. Portobello Mushroom Stew

Preparation Time: 10 minutes
Cooking Time: 8 hours
Servings: 4
Ingredients:

- 8 cups vegetable broth
- 1 cup dried wild mushrooms
- 1 cup dried chickpeas
- 3 cups chopped potato
- 2 cups chopped carrots
- 1 cup corn kernels
- 2 cups diced white onions
- 1 tablespoon minced parsley
- 3 cups chopped zucchini
- 1 tablespoon minced rosemary
- 1 1/2 teaspoon ground black pepper
- 1 teaspoon dried sage
- 2/3 teaspoon salt
- 1 teaspoon dried oregano
- 3 tablespoons soy sauce
- 1 1/2 teaspoons liquid smoke
- 8 ounces tomato paste

Directions:

1. Switch on the slow cooker, add all the ingredients to it, and stir until mixed.
2. Shut the cooker with a lid and cook for 10 hours at a high heat setting until cooked.
3. Serve straight away.

Nutrition: Calories: 447 Fat: 36 g Carbs: 24 g Protein: 11 g Fiber: 2 g

CHAPTER 5:

Wraps and Spreads

220. Buffalo Chickpea Wraps

Preparation Time: 20 minutes
Cooking Time: 5 minutes
Servings: 4
Ingredients:

- ¼ cup plus 2 tablespoons hummus
- 2 tablespoons lemon juice
- 1½ tablespoons maple syrup
- 1 to 2 tablespoons hot water
- 1 head Romaine lettuce, chopped
- 1 15-ounce can chickpeas, drained, rinsed and patted dry
- 4 tablespoons hot sauce, divided
- 1 tablespoon olive or coconut oil
- ¼ teaspoon garlic powder
- 1 pinch sea salt
- 4 wheat tortillas
- ¼ cup cherry tomatoes, diced
- ¼ cup red onion, diced
- ¼ of a ripe avocado, thinly sliced

Directions:

1. Mix the hummus with the lemon juice and maple syrup in a large bowl. Use a whisk and add the hot water a little at a time until it is thick but spreadable.

2. Add the Romaine lettuce and toss to coat. Set aside.

3. Pour the prepared chickpeas into another bowl. Add three tablespoons of the hot sauce, olive oil, garlic powder and salt; toss to coat.

4. Heat a metal skillet (cast iron works the best) over medium heat and add the chickpea mixture. Sauté for three to five minutes and mash gently with a spoon.

5. Once the chickpea mixture is slightly dried out, remove it from the heat and add the rest of the hot sauce. Stir it in well and set it aside.

6. Lay the tortillas on a clean, flat surface and spread a quarter cup of buffalo chickpeas on top. Top with tomatoes, onion and avocado (optional) and wrap.

Nutrition: Calories 254 Carbohydrates 39.4 g Fat 6.7 g Protein 9.1 g

221. Coconut Veggie Wraps

Preparation Time: 5 minutes
Cooking Time: 15 minutes
Servings: 5
Ingredients:

- 1½ cup shredded carrots
- 1 red bell pepper, seeded, thinly sliced
- 2½ cups kale
- 1 ripe avocado, thinly sliced
- 1 cup fresh cilantro, chopped
- 5 coconut wraps
- 2/3 cups hummus
- 6½ cups green curry paste

Directions:

1. Slice, chop and shred all the vegetables.

2. Lay a coconut wrap on a clean flat surface and spread two tablespoons of the hummus and one tablespoon of the green curry paste on top of the end closest to you.

3. Place some carrots, bell pepper, kale and cilantro on the wrap and start rolling it up, starting from the edge closest to you. Roll tightly and fold in the ends.

4. Place the wrap, seam down, on a plate to serve.

Nutrition: Calories 236 Carbohydrates 23.6 g Fat 14.3 g Protein 5.5 g

222. Spicy Hummus and Apple Wrap

Preparation Time: 10 minutes
Cooking Time: 15 minutes
Servings: 1
Ingredients:

- 3 to 4 tablespoons hummus
- 2 tablespoons mild salsa
- ½ cup broccoli slaw
- ½ teaspoon fresh lemon juice
- 2 teaspoons plain yogurt
- salt and pepper to taste
- 1 tortilla
- Lettuce leaves
- ½ Granny Smith or another tart apple, cored and thinly sliced

Directions:

1. In a small bowl, mix the hummus with the salsa. Set the bowl aside.

2. In a large bowl, mix the broccoli slaw, lemon juice and yogurt. Season with salt and pepper.

3. Lay the tortilla on a flat surface and spread it on the hummus mixture.

4. Lay down some lettuce leaves on top of the hummus.

5. On the upper half of the tortilla, place a pile of the broccoli slaw mixture and cover with the apples.

6. Fold and wrap.

Nutrition: Calories 121 Carbohydrates 27 g Fat 2 g Protein 4 g

223. **Sun-dried Tomato Spread**

Preparation Time: 20 minutes

Cooking Time: 15 minutes

Servings: 16

Ingredients:

- 1 cup sun-dried tomatoes
- 1 cup raw cashews
- Water for soaking tomatoes and cashews just enough to submerge
- ½ cup water
- 1 clove garlic, minced
- 1 green onion, chopped
- 5 large basil leaves
- ½ teaspoon lemon juice
- ¼ teaspoon salt
- 1 dash pepper
- Hulled sunflower seeds as desired

Directions:

1. Soak tomatoes and cashews for 30 minutes in separate bowls, with enough water to cover them. Drain and pat dry.

2. Put the tomatoes and cashews in a food processor and puree them, drizzling the water in as it purees to make a smooth, creamy paste.

3. Add the garlic, onion, basil leaves, lemon juice, salt and pepper, and mix thoroughly.

4. Scrape into a bowl, cover, and refrigerate overnight.

5. Spread on bread or toast and sprinkle with sunflower seeds for a little added crunch.

Nutrition: Calories 60 Carbohydrates 5.6 g Fat 4.2 g Protein 1.2 g

224. **Sweet Potato Sandwich Spread**

Preparation Time: 10 minutes

Cooking Time: 15 minutes

Servings: 4

Ingredients:

- 1 large sweet potato baked, peeled
- 1 teaspoon cumin - 1 teaspoon chili powder
- 1 teaspoon garlic powder
- Salt and pepper to taste
- 2 slices whole-wheat bread
- 1 to 2 tablespoons pinto beans, drained
- Lettuce as deired

Directions:

1. Bake and peel the sweet potato and mash it in a bowl. If it is too thick, add a little almond or coconut milk.

2. Mix in the cumin, chili powder, garlic powder, salt and pepper.

3. Spread the mixture on a slice of bread and spoon some beans on top.

4. Top with lettuce leaves and the other slice of bread.

Nutrition: Calories 253 Carbohydrates 49 g Fat 6 g Protein 8 g

225. **Shawarma**

Preparation Time: 20 minutes

Cooking Time: 15 minutes

Servings: 4

Ingredients:

- 1/4 cup tahini
- 1/4 cup water
- 2 tablespoons freshly squeezed lemon juice
- 1 teaspoon garlic powder
- 2 teaspoons vegetable oil
- 1 small red onion, thinly sliced
- 1-pound Seitan, or store-bought seitan, thinly sliced
- 1/2 teaspoon ground cumin
- 1/2 teaspoon ground turmeric
- 1/2 teaspoon paprika
- 1/4 teaspoon salt
- ¼ teaspoon freshly ground black pepper
- 4 pitas, or flatbreads of choice
- 1 large tomato, sliced
- 1 cup sliced cucumber
- 2 cups sliced romaine lettuce

Directions:

1. In a small bowl, whisk the tahini, water, lemon juice, and garlic powder to blend. Set aside.

2. In a large pan over medium-high heat, heat the vegetable oil. Add the red onion and cook for about 5 minutes, stirring frequently, until it begins to soften and brown.

3. Add the seitan, cumin, turmeric, paprika, salt, and pepper. Cook, stirring frequently, for about 10 minutes until the seitan browns and some of the edges get crispy.

4. To assemble the sandwiches, stuff each pita with some of the seitan mixture. Add tomato and cucumber slices and romaine lettuce. Drizzle each with the tahini dressing.

5. Substitution tip: Swap store-bought vegan beef for the seitan, if you prefer. You can also use sliced portobello mushrooms to keep your shawarma veggie-centric.

Nutrition: Calories: 354 Fat: 12g Carbs: 41g Protein: 20g

226. Chipotle Seitan Taquitos

Preparation Time: 15 minutes

Cooking Time: 15 minutes

Servings: 12

Ingredients:

- ½ cup Cashew Cream Cheese, or store-bought non-dairy cream cheese
- 2 canned chipotle peppers in adobo sauce, minced, sauce reserved
- 12 (6-inch) corn tortillas
- 1-pound Seitan, or store-bought seitan, cut into slices

Directions:

1. Preheat the oven to 400°F. Have a large baking dish or sheet nearby.

2. In a small bowl, stir together the cashew cream cheese, chipotle peppers, and 2 tablespoons of the reserved adobo sauce.

3. Place a tortilla on a clean surface and spread a line (about 2 teaspoons) of the chipotle cream cheese mixture down the middle. Top with a few slices of seitan. Roll up the tortilla as tightly as possible and place it, seam-side down, in the baking dish. Repeat with the remaining tortillas.

4. Bake for 15 minutes or until the tortillas are crisp.

Fun fact: Chipotles are not their type of pepper. They're dried, smoked jalapeños. When buying them for this recipe, look for chipotles in adobo sauce, which come in small cans found in the grocery store's Mexican food section. You'll need both the peppers and the sauce.

Nutrition: Calories: 193 Fat: 7g Carbs: 25g Protein: 8g;

227. Mediterranean Chickpea Wraps

Preparation Time: 15 minutes

Cooking Time: 0 minutes

Servings: 4

Ingredients:

- 1/4 cup extra-virgin olive oil
- 2 tablespoons freshly squeezed lemon juice
- 1 teaspoon dried dill
- 1 teaspoon dried oregano
- 1/4 teaspoon salt
- 1 (15-oz.) can chickpeas, drained and rinsed, or 1½ cups cooked chickpeas
- ½ cup Tofu Feta, or store-bought non-dairy feta
- 1 cup chopped cucumber
- 1 large tomato, diced
- ¼ cup diced red onion
- 2 cups fresh baby spinach
- 4 (12-inch) tortillas, or flatbreads of choice

Directions:

1. In a small bowl, whisk the olive oil, lemon juice, dill, oregano, and salt to combine.

2. In a large bowl, gently toss together the chickpeas, feta, cucumber, tomato, and red onion. Add the dressing and toss to combine.

3. Assemble the wraps by placing ½ cup of spinach on each tortilla and topping it with ¼ of the chickpea mixture. Roll up the wrap, tucking in the sides as you go.

Substitution tip: If you'd like to keep your wraps gluten-free and you can't find gluten-free flatbread, use collard greens. You'll need 4 large collard leaves. Cut off the stem from each and shave off the thick part of the stem that's left in the center with a sharp knife. Assemble the wrap the way you would a tortilla, by filling it with the spinach and chickpea mixture and rolling the leaf, tucking in the sides as you go.

Nutrition: Calories: 623 Fat: 25g Carbs: 80g Protein: 20g;

228. Barbecue Chickpea Burgers with Slaw

Preparation Time: 15 minutes

Cooking Time: 25 minutes

Servings: 4

Ingredients:

- 1 cup rolled oats
- 1 (15-oz.) can chickpeas, drained and rinsed, or 1½ cup cooked chickpeas (see here)
- ½ cup Barbecue Sauce, or store-bought vegan barbecue sauce, divided
- 1 garlic clove, minced
- ½ teaspoon salt
- ½ teaspoon freshly ground black pepper
- 2 cups shredded cabbage
- 2 carrots, grated or shredded
- ¼ cup Cashew Mayonnaise, or store-bought non-dairy mayonnaise
- 4 burger buns of choice

Directions:

1. Preheat the oven to 400°F. Line a large baking sheet with parchment paper.

2. In a food processor, pulse the rolled oats until they resemble a coarse meal. Add the chickpeas, ¼ cup of barbecue sauce, garlic, salt, and pepper.

3. Pulse until the chickpeas are mashed and everything is well combined. It's okay if there are a few whole chickpeas. Form the mixture into 4 patties and place them on the prepared baking sheet.

4. Bake the burgers for 20 to 25 minutes, flipping them at the halfway point. They should be golden brown and firm.

5. While the burgers bake, make the slaw. In a large bowl, stir together the cabbage, carrots, and mayonnaise.

6. Serve each burger on a bun topped with 1 tablespoon of the remaining barbecue sauce and 1/4 cup of slaw.

First-Timer tip: If you don't have a food processor, mash your chickpeas well using a potato masher or large fork. Rolled oats won't mash well by hand, so use oat flour or all-purpose flour instead. Combine the mashed chickpeas, flour, barbecue sauce, garlic, salt, and pepper in a large bowl before shaping into patties.

Nutrition: Calories: 433 Fat: 10g Carbs: 73g Protein: 13g

229. Mediterranean Veggie Wrap

Preparation Time: 15 minutes

Cooking Time: 0 minutes

Servings: 4

Ingredients:

- Whole-grain Tortillas
- 3 cups chickpeas
- ¼ onion, diced
- 1 tomato, diced
- Salt, to taste
- 4 tablespoons kalamata olives
- 1 garlic clove, minced
- 2 cups lettuce
- 2 tablespoons lemon juice
- 1 cucumber, grated
- 2 tablespoons fresh dill
- 7 oz plant-based yogurt
- 1/4 cup green pepper, diced
- Pepper, to taste

Directions:

1. Before you begin preparing this wrap, you will want to take half of your cucumber and grate it into a mixing bowl.

2. After this step is complete, lightly sprinkle the cucumber with salt to help get some of the excess water out.

3. As this process happens, you can now take your chickpeas and mash them down well with a fork.

4. With that, all set, take out a dish and combine the cucumber, yogurt, citrus juice, garlic, and dill altogether. Once this is done, season with pepper and salt to your liking.

5. When you are ready, lay out your wraps and layer your smashed chickpeas, lettuce, and the mixed vegetables. For some extra flavor, try adding some tzatziki sauce over the top before rolling up.

Nutrition: Calories: 400 Carbs: 30g Fat: 5g Proteins: 15g

230. Quick Lentil Wrap

Preparation Time: 10 minutes

Cooking Time: 30 minutes

Servings: 4

Ingredients:

- 4 Whole-grain Wraps
- 1 garlic clove, minced
- 2 tablespoons olive oil
- 1 onion, diced
- 1/3 cup cilantro
- 2 cups lentils
- 1/3 cup tomato paste

Directions:

1. Begin this recipe by taking out a skillet and place two cups of water and lentils in.

2. You will want to get everything to a boil before turning the temperature down and simmer for ten minutes or until the lentils are soft.

3. Once the lentils are cooked through, add in the tomato paste, garlic, and onion. Go ahead and cook all of these ingredients together for another five minutes before turning off the heat and seasoning to your liking.

4. Finally, lay out your wraps, spread the mixture in the center, and then roll the wrap up for lunch.

Nutrition: Calories: 400 Carbs: 50g Fat: 5g Proteins: 20g

231. Thai Vegetable and Tofu Wrap

Preparation Time: 5 minutes

Cooking Time: 30 minutes

Servings: 1

Ingredients:

- 1 cup extra-firm Tofu, diced
- 1/4 cup peanut sauce
- 1 teaspoon olive oil
- 1/3 cup cucumber, diced
- 1/3 cup carrot, shredded
- 1/4 cup cilantro
- 1 garlic cloves, minced
- 2 Whole-wheat Wrap

Directions:

1. Tofu is an excellent protein to have on hand because it is so versatile! To begin this recipe, you will want to take a skillet and place it over medium heat.

2. As it warms, add in your olive oil and begin cooking the tofu for around five minutes.

3. After five minutes, combine the garlic and cook for an additional minute. At this point, all of the liquid from the tofu should be gone.

4. Next, eliminate the skillet from the cooker and add the peanut sauce. Be sure to stir very well to help coat the tofu pieces evenly!

5. When you are set to make your wraps, spread the tofu into your wrap, top with the diced and shredded vegetables, and roll everything up together nice and tight before serving.

6. For extra flavor, feel free to add some fresh cilantro to your wrap!

Nutrition: Calories: 270 Carbs: 12g Fat: 15g Proteins: 20g

232. Plant-based Buffalo Wrap

Preparation Time: 5 minutes
Cooking Time: 15 minutes
Servings: 4
Ingredients:

- 1 teaspoon olive oil
- 2 cups kale, chopped
- ½ cup buffalo sauce
- 1 cup seitan, chopped
- 4 Whole Wheat Wraps
- 1 cup tomatoes, diced
- 1 cup cashews
- Salt, to taste
- 1/2 teaspoon dried dill
- Pepper to taste
- 1/2 teaspoon dried parsley
- 8 tablespoons almond milk
- 1 ½ tablespoons apple cider vinegar

Directions:

1. This recipe is the perfect way to get a buffalo chicken wrap without the chicken! You will want to start by making your ranch dressing.

2. You can accomplish this by taking out your blender and mixing the almond milk, apple cider vinegar, cashews, pepper, salt, parsley, and dill.

3. Once this is done, set your sauce to the side.

4. Next, you will need to get out a saucepan and place it over medium heat. Once warm, add in some olive oil and begin cooking your seitan pieces. Normally, this will take you eight minutes.

5. When the seitan is cooked through, add in the buffalo sauce and cook for another minute.

6. With these steps done, you will want to now take a moment to take the kale and mix it in a bowl with olive oil and seasoning.

7. Finally, it is time to assemble your wrap! You can do this by taking out your wrap and spreading your ranch dressing across the surface.

8. Once this is in place, begin building your wrap by layering the kale, tomato, and seitan pieces. For a final touch, add some more buffalo sauce over the top, and then wrap it up!

Nutrition: Calories: 250 Carbs: 25g Fat: 15g Proteins: 20g

233. Colorful Veggie Wrap

Preparation Time: 10 minutes
Cooking Time: 0 minutes
Servings: 4
Ingredients:

- Large Lettuce Leaves as desired
- 1 tablespoon Soy Sauce
- 1 tablespoon Olive Oil
- ½ cup Seed Butter
- 1 tablespoon Garlic Powder
- 2 tablespoons Lime Juice
- 1 cup Red Cabbage, shredded
- 1 cup Cucumber, chopped
- 1 cup Red Pepper, chopped
- 1 cup Carrot, chopped
- ¼ teaspoon Ground Ginger

Directions:

1. This wrap looks pretty and full of flavor! You can start this recipe off by making the sauce.

2. For the sauce, take out a petite bowl and combine the oil, garlic, soy sauce, juice of the lime, ground ginger, pepper flakes, and seed butter.

3. Once everything is mixed together well, place it to the side.

4. Next, it is time to build your wrap! Go ahead and lay the lettuce leaves out flat before spreading sauce across the surface.

5. Once this is in place, you will want to layer the other vegetables before rolling the leaf up and enjoying your veggie-packed wrap!

Nutrition: Calories: 250 Carbs: 15g Fat: 20g Proteins: 10g

234. BBQ Chickpea Wrap

Preparation Time: 10 minutes
Cooking Time: 0 minutes
Servings: 4
Ingredients:

- 4 Whole-wheat Tortillas
- 2 cups Coleslaw - ½ cup BBQ Sauce
- 2 cups Chickpeas

Directions:

1. Are you in a rush for lunch? You can slap this wrap together in a snap! Start by taking out a blending bowl and combine the BBQ with the chickpeas.

2. Next, you will want to lay out your tortillas and place the coleslaw and chickpeas in the center.

3. For a nice touch, wrap your tortilla up and pop it into the microwave for a few seconds to heat it before enjoying it!

Nutrition: Calories: 450 Carbs: 50g Fat: 5g Proteins: 10g

235. Chickpea and Mango Wraps

Preparation Time: 15 minutes

Cooking Time: 0 minutes

Servings: 3

Ingredients:

- 3 tablespoons tahini
- 1 tablespoon curry powder
- ¼ teaspoon sea salt (optional)
- Zest and juice of 1 lime
- 3 to 4 tablespoons water
- 1½ cups cooked chickpeas
- 1 cup diced mango
- ½ cup fresh cilantro, chopped
- 1 red bell pepper, deseeded and diced
- 3 large whole-wheat wraps
- 1½ cups shredded lettuce

Directions:

1. In a large bowl, stir together the tahini, curry powder, lime zest, lime juice and sea salt (if desired) until smooth and creamy. Whisk in 3 to 4 tablespoons of water to help thin the mixture.

2. Add the cooked chickpeas, mango, cilantro and bell pepper to the bowl. Toss until well coated.

3. On a clean work surface, lay the wraps. Divide the chickpea and mango mixture among the wraps. Spread the shredded lettuce on top and roll up tightly.

4. Serve immediately.

Nutrition: Calories: 436 Fat: 17.9g Carbs: 8.9g Protein: 15.2g

236. Tofu and Pineapple in Lettuce

Preparation Time: 2 hours

Cooking Time: 15 minutes

Servings: 4

Ingredients:

- ¼ cup low-sodium soy sauce
- 1 garlic clove, minced
- 2 tablespoons sesame oil (optional)
- 1 tablespoon coconut sugar (optional)
- 1 (14-oz. / 397-g) package extra-firm tofu, drained, cut into ½-inch cubes
- 1 small white onion, diced
- ½ pineapple, peeled, cored, cut into cubes
- Salt and ground black pepper, to taste (optional)
- 4 large lettuce leaves
- 1 tablespoon roasted sesame seeds

Directions:

1. Combine the soy sauce, garlic, sesame oil (if desired), and coconut sugar in a bowl. Stir to mix well.

2. Add the tofu cubes to the bowl of the soy sauce mixture, then press to coat well. Wrap the bowl in plastic and refrigerate to marinate for at least 2 hours.

3. Pour the marinated tofu and marinade in a skillet and heat over medium heat. Add the onion and pineapple cubes to the skillet and stir to mix well.

4. Sprinkle with salt (if desired) and pepper and sauté for 15 minutes or until the onions are lightly browned and the pineapple cubes are tender.

5. Divide the lettuce leaves among 4 plates, then top the leaves with the tofu and pineapple mixture. Sprinkle with sesame seeds and serve immediately.

Nutrition: Calories: 259 Fat: 15.4g Carbs: 20.5g Protein: 12.1g

237. Quinoa and Black Bean Lettuce Wraps

Preparation Time: 30 minutes

Cooking Time: 15 minutes

Servings: 6

Ingredients:

- 2 tablespoons avocado oil (optional)
- ¼ cup deseeded and chopped bell pepper
- ½ onion, chopped
- 2 tablespoons minced garlic
- 1 teaspoon salt (optional)
- 1 teaspoon pepper (optional)
- ½ cup cooked quinoa
- 1 cup cooked black beans
- ½ cup almond flour
- ½ teaspoon paprika
- ½ teaspoon red pepper flakes
- 6 large lettuce leaves

Directions:

1. Heat 1 tablespoon of the avocado oil (if desired) in a skillet over medium-high heat.

2. Add bell peppers, onions, garlic, salt (if desired), and pepper. Sauté for 5 minutes or until the bell peppers are tender.

3. Turn off the heat and cool for 10 minutes, then pour the vegetables into a food processor. Add the quinoa, beans, flour.

4. Sprinkle with paprika and red pepper flakes. Pulse until thick and well combined.

5. Line a baking pan with parchment paper, then shape the mixture into 6 patties with your hands and place on the baking pan.

6. Put the pan in the freezer for 5 minutes to make the patties firm.

7. Heat the remaining avocado oil (if desired) in the skillet over high heat.

8. Add the patties and cook for 6 minutes or until well browned on both sides. Flip the patties halfway through.

9. Arrange the patties in the lettuce leaves and serve immediately.

Nutrition: Calories: 200 Fat: 10.6g Carbs: 40.5g Protein: 9.5g

238. Maple Bagel Spread

Preparation Time: 10 minutes

Cooking Time: 10 minutes

Servings: 1

Ingredients:

- cream cheese as deired
- maple syrup as desired
- cinnamon as desired
- walnuts as desired

Directions:

1. Beat the cinnamon, syrup, and cream cheese in a big bowl until it becomes smooth, then mix in walnuts.

2. Let it chill until ready to serve. Serve it with bagels.

Nutrition: Calories: 586 Fat: 7g Carbs: 23g Protein: 4g

239. Hummus and Quinoa Wrap

Preparation Time: 10 minutes

Cooking Time: 10 minutes

Servings: 4

Ingredients:

- 6 Lettuce Leaves)
- 1 cup Cooked Quinoa
- ½ cup Cabbage
- ½ cup Sprouts
- 1 cup Avocado, Sliced - 1 cup Hummus

Directions:

1. For this recipe, the lettuce leaves are going to act as your wrap! When you are all set, spread the wrap out and then place the hummus and avocado into each leaf. Once this is set, layer your quinoa and cabbage on top before wrapping the leaf up and eating!

Nutrition: Calories: 280 Carbs: 40g Fat: 10g Proteins: 10g

240. Peanut and Ginger Tofu Wrap

Preparation Time: 30 minutes

Cooking Time: 10 minutes

Servings: 4 wraps

Ingredients:

Crispy Tofu

- 2 tablespoons of avocado/peanut oil
- 1 piece of 14-ounce extra-firm tofu, pressed for 30 minutes, cut into 16 spear-shaped pieces
- Peanut Ginger Spread
- 2 tablespoons of lime juice
- 1 tablespoon of water
- 6 tablespoons of creamy peanut butter
- 1 tablespoon of tamari
- 1 tablespoon of ginger juice
- 2-3 tablespoons of coconut sugar or light brown sugar

Wrap

- ¼ cup of cilantro leaves
- 4 large whole-grain tortillas or sandwich wraps
- ¼ cup of sliced green onions
- 1 freshly peeled and shredded carrot
- Lime wedges
- Sriracha/sweet chili sauce
- 1 small red bell pepper, cored and cut into thin strips

Directions

1. Put a large skillet on medium-high heat. Heat some oil and add the tofu, cooking it for 5 minutes. The tofu will be crisp and brown on both sides. Shift the tofu to a paper-lined dish so that the excess oil is absorbed.

2. Whisk all the ingredients to make the peanut spread. If you want a less thick consistency, you can add a few drops of water to the mix.

3. Start assembling the tofu, pepper strips, carrot cilantro, and green onions on top of the peanut spread on the wraps. Add a dash of lime juice followed by the sauce of your choice.

4. Your healthy wrap is ready to be eaten!

Nutrition: Fat – 22.7 g Carbohydrates – 34.1 g Protein – 22.4 g

241. Quick-Fix Veggie Wrap

Preparation Time: 15 minutes

Cooking Time: 15 minutes

Servings: 8

Ingredients:

- 1 finely diced medium red onion
- ½ freshly diced large green bell pepper
- 4 freshly minced garlic cloves
- ½ freshly diced large red bell pepper
- 1 teaspoon of curry powder
- 4 cups of shredded butter lettuce
- 4 cups of chopped veggies: cauliflower, steamed potatoes, zucchini, broccoli, carrots, and green beans
- 3 tablespoons of vegan feta
- 8 flour tortillas
- ½ cup of hummus

Directions:

1. In a large pan, sauté the curry powder, green and red bell peppers, onion, and garlic in little water for about 5 minutes.

2. To these sautéed ingredients, add the shredded lettuce and chopped veggies. Cover everything, reduce the heat, and steam for another 10 minutes.

3. On a non-stick skillet, warm the tortillas. You can also warm them in a microwave by wrapping them in a wet towel.

4. Spoon ½ cup of veggies in the middle of the tortilla and put 2 tablespoons of hummus on one side of the tortilla.

5. Fold the other side and then make a roll.

6. If you are hungry and need a quick fix, this healthy veggie wrap will never disappoint.

Nutrition: Calories: 202 per serving Fat – 5.5 g Carbohydrates – 32.6 g Protein – 7.2 g

242. Delicious Collard Wraps

Preparation Time: 15 minutes

Cooking Time: 0 minutes

Servings: 4

Ingredients:

- 4 large collard leaves
- ½ lime
- 1 teaspoon of extra virgin olive oil
- 1 red bell pepper
- 2-3 ounces of alfalfa sprouts
- 1 avocado
- ½ teaspoon of minced garlic
- 1 cup of raw pecans
- ½ teaspoon of grated ginger
- 1 tablespoon of tamari

Directions:

1. Wash the collard leaves thoroughly and cut off the white stem. Put them in warm water with a dash of lemon juice. Allow the leaves to soak for about 10 minutes. Dry the leaves with a paper towel and, with a sharp knife, cut off the central root.

2. Slice the pepper and avocado.

3. In a blender, combine the pecan, cumin, tamari, and olive oil. Pulse everything until you have a clumpy mix.

4. Spread a collard leaf and spoon the pecan mixture onto it. Top it with the red bell pepper and avocado slices. Add some lime juice. Lastly, add the alfalfa sprouts. Fold the bottom and top and then wrap on both sides.

5. Slice the wrap in half and serve it to your guests!

Nutrition: Calories: 279 per serving Fat – 26 g Carbohydrates – 11 g Protein – 4 g

243. Falafel Wrap

Preparation Time: 30 minutes

Cooking Time: 30 minutes

Servings: 6

Ingredients

For the falafel patties

- 1 (14-ounce) can chickpeas, drained and rinsed, or 1½ cups cooked
- 1 zucchini, grated
- 2 scallions, minced
- ¼ cup fresh parsley, chopped
- 2 tablespoons black olives, pitted and chopped (optional)
- 1 tablespoon tahini, or almond, cashew, or sunflower seed butter
- 1 tablespoon lemon juice or apple cider vinegar
- ½ teaspoon ground cumin
- ¼ teaspoon paprika
- ¼ teaspoon sea salt
- 1 teaspoon olive oil (optional, if frying)

For the wrap

- 1 whole-grain wrap or pita
- ¼ cup classic hummus
- ½ cup fresh greens
- 1 baked falafel patty
- ¼ cup cherry tomatoes, halved
- ¼ cup diced cucumber
- ¼ cup chopped avocado, or guacamole

- ¼ cup cooked quinoa, or tabbouleh salad (optional)

Directions

To make the falafel

1. Use a food processor to pulse the chickpeas, zucchini, scallions, parsley, and olives (if using) until roughly chopped. Just pulse—don't purée. Or use a potato masher to mash the chickpeas in a large bowl and stir in the grated and chopped veggies.

2. In a small bowl, whisk together the tahini and lemon juice and stir in the cumin, paprika, and salt. Pour this into the chickpea mixture, and stir well (or pulse the food processor) to combine. Taste and add more salt, if needed. Using your hands, form the mix into 6 patties.

3. You can either panfry or bake the patties. To panfry, heat a large skillet to medium, add 1 teaspoon of olive oil, and cook the patties for about 10 minutes on the first side. Flip, and cook another 5 to 7 minutes. To bake them, put them on a baking sheet lined with parchment paper and bake at 350°f for 30 to 40 minutes.

To make the wrap

4. Lay the wrap on a plate and spread the hummus down the center. Then lay on the greens and crumble the falafel patty on top. Add the tomatoes, cucumber, avocado, and quinoa.

5. Fold in both ends, and wrap up as tightly as you can. If you have a sandwich press, you can press the wraps for about 5 minutes. This will travel best in a reusable lunch box or reusable plastic lunch wrap.

Nutrition: (1 wrap) Calories: 546; Total Fat: 19g; Carbs: 81g; Fiber: 14g; Protein: 18g

244. **Curried Mango Chickpea Wrap**

Preparation Time: 15 minutes

Cooking Time: 0 minutes

Servings: 3

Ingredients:

- 3 tablespoons tahini
- Zest and juice of 1 lime
- 1 tablespoon curry powder
- ¼ teaspoon sea salt
- 3 to 4 tablespoons water
- 1 (14-ounce) can chickpeas, rinsed and drained, or 1½ cups cooked
- 1 cup diced mango
- 1 red bell pepper, seeded and diced small
- ½ cup fresh cilantro, chopped
- 3 large whole-grain wraps
- 1 to 2 cups shredded green leaf lettuce

Directions:

1. In a medium bowl, whisk together the tahini, lime zest and juice, curry powder, and salt until the mixture is creamy and thick.

2. Add 3 to 4 tablespoons of water to thin it out a bit. Or you can process this all in a blender. The taste should be strong and salty, to flavor the whole salad.

3. Toss the chickpeas, mango, bell pepper, and cilantro with the tahini dressing. Spoon the salad down the center of the wraps, top with shredded lettuce, and then roll up and enjoy.

Nutrition: (1 wrap) Calories: 437; total fat: 8g; carbs: 79g; fiber: 12g; protein: 15g

245. **Paprika Olives Spread**

Preparation Time: 10 minutes

Cooking Time: 0 minutes

Servings: 4

Ingredients:

- 1 cup kalamata olives, pitted and halved
- 1 cup black olives, pitted and halved
- 1 avocado, peeled, pitted and cubed
- 2 scallions, chopped
- 2 teaspoons sweet paprika
- 1 tablespoon olive oil
- 1 tablespoon lime juice
- Salt and black pepper to the taste
- ½ cup coconut cream

Directions:

1. In a blender, combine the olives with the avocado, scallions, and the other ingredients, pulse well, divide into bowls and serve for breakfast.

Nutrition: calories 287, fat 27.8, fiber 6.8, carbs 12.2, protein 2.5

246. **Korean Barbecue Tempeh Wraps**

Preparation Time: 15 minutes

Cooking Time: 25 minutes

Servings: 4

Ingredients:

For the Korean barbecue sauce:

- ¾ cup water
- 1/3 cup soy sauce
- ¼ cup maple syrup
- ¼ cup tomato paste
- 2 tablespoons gochujang
- 2 garlic cloves, minced

- 2 teaspoons ginger, grated
- 1 teaspoon sesame oil

For the Tempeh filling:
- 2 tablespoons vegetable oil
- 2-8 oz. packages tempeh, cubed
- 1 red bell pepper, thinly sliced
- 1 onion, thinly sliced
- 2 scallions, chopped
- 2 teaspoons sesame seeds

For the wraps:
- 4 large flour tortillas
- 4 large lettuce leaves
- 1 large avocado sliced

Directions:
2. Combine the Korean sauce ingredients in a bowl.
3. Place a large skillet over medium heat, add sauce and bring it to a simmer, lower the heat and let it simmer for 10 minutes.
4. Place another skillet over medium heat and add oil.
5. Add and cook tempeh for about 5 minutes.
6. Increase the heat, add bell pepper, onion and cook for 2 minutes, then lower the heat, add sauce and cook for 3 minutes. Once done, remove them from heat and set them aside.
7. Put a tortilla on a working surface, place lettuce leaves, avocado slices, and tempeh mixture on top. Wrap like a burrito to enclose the fillings inside
8. Do this for all tortillas before serving.

Nutrition: Calories: 48 Fat: 11g Carbs: 10g

247. Black Bean Wrap with Hummus

Preparation Time: 5 minutes
Cooking Time: 30 minutes
Servings: 2 Wraps
Ingredients:
- 1 Poblano Pepper, roasted
- ½ packet Spinach
- 1 Onion, chopped
- 2 Whole Grain Wraps
- ½ can Black Beans
- 1 Bell Pepper, seeded & chopped
- 4 oz. Mushrooms, sliced
- ½ cup Corn
- 8 oz. Red Bell Pepper Hummus, roasted

Directions:
1. First, preheat the oven to 450°F.
2. Next, spoon in oil into a heated skillet and stir in the onion.
3. Cook them for 2 to 3 minutes or until softened.
4. After that, stir in the bell pepper and sauté for another 3 minutes.
5. Then, add mushrooms and corn to the skillet. Sauté for 2 minutes.
6. In the meantime, spread the hummus over the wraps.
7. Now, place the sautéed vegetables, spinach, Poblano strips, and beans.
8. Roll them into a burrito and place them on a baking sheet with the seam side down.
9. Finally, bake them for 9 to 10 minutes.
10. Serve them warm.

Nutrition: Calories: 293, Proteins: 13.7g, Carbs: 42.8g, Fat: 8.8g

248. Sprout Wraps

Preparation Time: 15 min
Cooking Time: 15 minutes
Servings: 2
Ingredients:
- 2 large whole-wheat Tortillas
- ½ cup Parsley
- 2 stalks green Onion
- 1 teaspoon Black pepper
- 1 Cucumber, sliced thin
- 1 cup Bean sprouts
- ½ Salt
- 1 tablespoon Lemon juice
- 1 tablespoon Olive oil

Directions:
1. Lay out each of the tortilla wraps on a plate. Divide evenly all of the ingredients between the two tortillas, leaving about two inches on either side for rolling the tortilla up.
2. When you have added all of the ingredients to the tortilla, then fold in the sides and roll the tortilla up into a cylinder shape.

Nutrition: Calories 226, 12 g carbs, 10 g protein, 3 g fat

249. Collard Wraps

Preparation Time: 20 min
Cooking Time: 30 minutes
Servings: 4
Ingredients:
Wrap
- 4 Cherry tomatoes, cut in half

- ¼ cup black olives, sliced
- ½ cup purple onion, diced fine
- Red bell pepper, one half of one cut in julienne strips
- 1 medium-sized cucumber, cut into julienne strips
- 4 large green collard leaves

Sauce
- Black pepper, one teaspoon
- Salt, one half teaspoon
- Dill, fresh, minced, two tablespoons
- Cucumber, seeded and grated, one quarter cup
- Olive oil, two tablespoons
- White vinegar, one tablespoon
- Garlic powder, one teaspoon

Directions:
1. Place all of the ingredients on the list for the sauce in a mixing bowl and mix well. Store the dressing in the refrigerator.
2. Wash off the collard leaves and dry them and then cut off the stem from each leaf. Cover each leaf with two tablespoons of the sauce you just made.
3. In the middle of the collard leaf layer, add all of the other ingredients.
4. Fold the leaf up like a burrito by first folding the ends in and then rolling the leaf until it is all rolled. Cut into slices and serve with more dressing for dipping.

Nutrition per wrap: Calories 165, 7.36 g carbs, 6.98 g protein, 11.25 g fat

250. Lite Tuna Melt Wrap
Preparation Time: 20 minutes
Cooking Time: 20 minutes
Servings: 2
Ingredients:
Creamy tuna
- 1 (5-ounce) can chunk light tuna in water, drained
- 1/4 teaspoon black pepper
- 1/4 cup plain low-fat Greek yogurt, or clean mayo
- 1/4 teaspoon kosher or sea salt

To Assemble
- 4 large leaves butter or iceberg lettuce
- 4 pickle slices or jalapeño slices, optional
- 1 large whole wheat wrap
- 1/2 cup shredded reduced-fat cheddar cheese

Directions:
1. Mix all ingredients for creamy tuna. Spread in a broiler-safe baking dish/pan and sprinkle cheese on top. Place under broiler for one to two minutes, just until cheese melts.
2. Lay wrap flat and line with lettuce leaves. Scoop tuna with melted cheese over wrap. Top with pickles or pickled jalapeño slices, if using. Tuck under one end and roll wrap. Cut in half and serve.
Nutrition: Calories: 329 | Total Fat: 15g | Saturated Fat: 6g | Trans Fat: 0g | Cholesterol: 60mg | Sodium: 924mg | Carbohydrates: 18g | Fiber: 1g | Sugar: 2g | Protein: 30g

251. Curry Wraps
Preparation Time: 5 minutes
Cooking Time: 22 minutes
Servings: 5
Ingredients:
- 8 Chapattis
- 4 Sliced garlic cloves
- 2 Sliced onions
- 2 Tablespoons Olive oil
- 2 Tablespoons Tandoori curry paste, cubed tofu (600g)
- 3 Tbs Mint sauce
- 4 Tablespoons Yogurt
- 1 cup Shredded red cabbage head
- 1 Quartered lime

Directions:
1. We can start this out by taking out a bowl and mix the yogurt, cabbage, and mint sauce, then set it to the side.
2. Toss the tofu and the tandoori paste into a frying pan with some of the oil. Then cook this for a bit on each side to make it all golden brown. Take out of the heat when you are done with this.
3. Next, we can add the garlic and onions into the same pan and cook those for a bit. After ten minutes, add the tofu back in and cook a bit longer.
4. Heat the chapattis using the directions on the package and then fill them up with the tandoori tofu and the sauce that you made. Serve with the lime quarters.
Nutrition:
Calories: 211 Carbs: 22g Fat: 7g Protein: 19g

252. Leeks Spread
Preparation Time: 5 minutes
Cooking Time: 10 minutes
Servings: 4
Ingredients:
- 3 leeks, sliced

- 2 scallions, chopped
- 1 tablespoon avocado oil
- ¼ cup coconut cream
- Salt and black pepper to the taste
- ¼ teaspoon garlic powder
- ½ teaspoon thyme, dried
- 1 tablespoon cilantro, chopped

Directions:

1. Heat a pan with the oil over medium heat, add the scallions and the leeks and sauté for 5 minutes.
2. Add the rest of the ingredients, cook everything for 5 minutes more, blend using an immersion blender, divide into bowls and serve for breakfast.

Nutrition:

Calories 83, Fat 4.2, Fiber 2, Carbs 11.3, Protein 1.6

253. Eggplant Spread

Preparation Time: 10 minutes

Cooking Time: 25 minutes

Servings: 4

Ingredients:

- 1-pound eggplants
- 2 tablespoons olive oil
- 4 spring onions, chopped
- ½ teaspoon chili powder
- 1 tablespoon lime juice
- Salt and black pepper to the taste

Directions:

1. Arrange the eggplants in a roasting pan and bake them at 400 degrees F for 25 minutes.
2. Peel the eggplants, put them in a blender, add the rest of the ingredients, pulse well, divide them into bowls and serve for breakfast.

Nutrition:

Calories 97, Fat 7.3, Fiber 4.6, Carbs 8.9, Protein 1.5

254. Vegan Mediterranean Wraps

Preparation Time: 20-25 minutes

Cooking Time: 30-60 minutes

Servings: 2

Ingredients:

- 1 small cucumber, grate half and dice half
- 1 small tomato, diced
- 1/8 green bell pepper, diced
- 1/8 red onion, diced
- ½ jar (from a 19 ounces jar) chickpeas, drained

- 1 tablespoon chopped fresh dill
- ½ tablespoon lemon juice
- 1 cup chopped lettuce
- Salt to taste
- 2 tablespoons chopped kalamata olives
- 2 ounces soy yogurt or any other vegan yogurt
- 2 small cloves garlic, peeled, minced
- Pepper to taste
- 2 large tortillas

Directions:

1. Sprinkle a large pinch of salt over the grated cucumber and place it in a strainer. Place the strainer on top of a bowl. Let it drain for 15 minutes. Squeeze off the excess moisture.
2. To make tzatziki sauce: Add grated cucumber, dill, salt, pepper, lemon juice, garlic and yogurt into a bowl and stir.
3. Add chickpeas into a bowl and mash with a fork.
4. Mix diced cucumber, tomato, olives and lettuce into a bowl and toss.
5. Spread the tortillas on your countertop. Divide the vegetable mixture and chickpeas among the tortillas.
6. Spoon some tzatziki sauce over the chickpeas. Wrap and place with its seam side facing down.
7. Heat the wrap in a pan if desired.
8. Serve with some more tzatziki sauce if desired.

Nutrition: 1 wrap

Calories – 347, Fat – 8 g, Carbohydrate – 55 g, Fiber – 8 g, Protein – 12 g

255. Jackfruit Wrap

Preparation Time: 20-25 minutes

Cooking Time: 30-60 minutes

Servings: 2

Ingredients:

- ½ can (from a 20 ounces can) green jackfruit, drained, rinsed
- ¼ teaspoon garlic powder
- ½ teaspoon onion powder
- ¼ cup BBQ sauce
- ¼ cup vegetable broth
- Salt to taste
- 1 cup shredded Romaine lettuce
- 1 small red onion, sliced
- 1 small tomato, sliced
- Few avocado slices
- 2 large gluten-free tortillas

- For garlic aioli sauce:
- 2 tablespoons vegan mayonnaise
- 1 small clove garlic, crushed
- ¼ teaspoon lemon juice or to taste
- Salt to taste

Directions:

1. Add jackfruit into a bowl. Sprinkle onion powder and garlic powder and toss well.
2. Place a skillet over medium heat. Add broth, jackfruit, and BBQ sauce and mix well.
3. Cover and cook until jackfruit is tender. Remove the jackfruit and place it on your cutting board. Shred the jackfruit with a pair of forks.

4. Meanwhile, make the garlic aioli by mixing together all the ingredients for aioli in a bowl.
5. Warm the tortillas and place them on your countertop. Spread garlic aioli sauce on the tortillas. Divide the lettuce, tomato, avocado and onion slices among the tortillas.
6. Divide the jackfruit among the tortillas. Wrap like a burrito.
7. Cut into 2 halves and serve.

Tip: You can use any other sauce of your choice instead of garlic aioli. I keep trying a new sauce each time.

Nutrition: 1 wrap

Calories – 370, Fat – 14 g, Carbohydrate – 50 g, Fiber – NA g, Protein – 4 g

CHAPTER 6:

Pasta and Noodles

256. Cannellini Pesto Spaghetti

Preparation Time: 5 minutes

Cooking Time: 10 minutes

Servings: 4

Ingredients:

- 12 ounces (340 g) whole-grain spaghetti, cooked, drained, and kept warm, ½ cup cooking liquid reserved - 1 cup pesto
- 2 cups cooked cannellini beans, drained and rinsed

Directions:

1. Put the cooked spaghetti in a large bowl and add the pesto.

2. Add the reserved cooking liquid and beans and toss well to serve.

Nutrition Per Serving

Calories: 549 Fat: 34g carbs: 45g protein: 18g fiber: 10g

257. Spicy Eggplant Penne

Preparation Time: 15 minutes

Cooking Time: 30 minutes

Servings: 4

Ingredients:

- 1 medium yellow onion, peeled and diced
- 2 medium eggplants (about 1½ pounds / 680 g), stemmed, peeled, quartered, and cut into ½-inch pieces - 6 cloves garlic, peeled and minced
- 2 teaspoons minced oregano
- 1 teaspoon crushed red pepper flakes, or to taste
- 1 (28-ounce / 794-g) can diced tomatoes
- 2 tablespoons red wine vinegar
- Salt, to taste
- 1-pound (454 g) penne, cooked according to package directions, drained, and kept warm
- ½ cup chopped basil

Directions:

1. Place the onion in a large saucepan and sauté over medium heat for 10 minutes. Add water 1 to 2 tablespoons at a time to keep the onion from sticking to the pan. Add the eggplant and cook, stirring constantly, for 5 minutes, adding water only when the eggplant starts to stick to the pan. Add the garlic, oregano, and crushed red pepper flakes and cook for 30 seconds. Add the tomatoes and red wine vinegar and cook, covered, for 10 minutes. Season with salt.

2. Remove from the heat, add the pasta, and toss well. Garnish with basil.

Nutrition Per Serving

Calories: 105 Fat: 0.78g carbs: 24.11g protein: 4.41g fiber: 11.2g

258. Creamed Kimchi Pasta

Preparation Time: 5 minutes

Cooking Time: 4 to 5 minutes

Servings: 4 to 6

Ingredients:

- 8 ounces (227 g) dried small pasta
- 2 1/3 cups vegetable stock
- 2 garlic cloves, minced
- ½ red onion, sliced
- ½ to 1 teaspoon salt
- 1¼ cups kimchi, with any larger pieces chopped
- ½ cup coconut cream

Directions:

1. In the Instant Pot, combine the pasta, stock, garlic, red onion and salt.

2. Set the lid in place. Select the Manual mode and set the cooking time for 1 minute on High Pressure. When the timer goes off, do a quick pressure release. Carefully open the lid.

3. Select Sauté mode. Stir in the kimchi. Simmer for 3 to 4 minutes. Stir in the coconut cream and serve.

Nutrition Per Serving

Calories: 748 Fat: 80.02g carbs: 13.17g protein: 2.39g fiber: 2.5g

259. Roasted Ragu with Whole Wheat Linguine

Preparation Time: 15 minutes

Cooking Time: 45 minutes

Servings: 8

Ingredients:

- 4 beefsteak tomatoes, halved
- 1 yellow onion, cut into slices and left as rings
- 2 large zucchinis, cubed
- 2 large yellow squash, cubed
- 1 small red bell pepper, diced
- 3 garlic cloves, minced
- 1 teaspoon Italian seasoning
- ½ teaspoon freshly ground black pepper
- 1 pound (454 g) whole wheat linguine
- ¼ cup tomato paste
- 1 teaspoon red pepper flakes
- ¼ teaspoon dried oregano
- 1 tablespoon packed minced fresh Italian parsley
- 2 tablespoons fresh basil chiffonade, divided

Directions:

1. Preheat the oven to 450°F (235°C). Line 2 baking sheets with parchment paper.

2. Place the tomato halves on 1 prepared baking sheet, cut-side up. Place the onion rings on the same baking sheet.

3. Roast on the center rack for 10 minutes.

4. While the tomatoes roast, in a large bowl, toss together the zucchini, squash, bell pepper, garlic, Italian seasoning, and pepper. Spread the vegetables on the other prepared baking sheet.

5. Place the vegetables on a lower rack (but not the lowest) and bake for 15 minutes. Flip the vegetables. Remove the tomato sheet and set it aside. Move the vegetables to the center rack and roast for 15 minutes more.

6. Bring a large pot of water to a boil over high heat. Cook the pasta according to the package directions to al dente. Reserve ½ cup of the pasta water and drain the pasta. Keep the pasta in the strainer.

7. Return the pasta pot to medium heat. Transfer the roasted tomatoes and onions to the pot and stir in the tomato paste, reserved pasta water, red pepper flakes, and oregano. You can mash the tomatoes and onion using a heavy spoon for a chunky texture or purée using an immersion blender, as you like.

8. Add the pasta, roasted vegetables, parsley, and 1 tablespoon of basil to the pot. Toss to combine and coat. Serve garnished with the remaining 1 tablespoon of basil.

Nutrition Per Serving

Calories: 272 Fat: 2g carbs: 55g protein: 11g fiber: 5g

260. Penne with Swiss Chard and Olives

Preparation Time: 15 minutes

Cooking Time: 20 minutes

Servings: 4

Ingredients:

- 4 large shallots, peeled and diced small
- 2 bunches Swiss chard, ribs removed and chopped, leaves chopped
- 4 cloves garlic, peeled and minced
- 2 teaspoons minced thyme
- 1-pound (454 g) whole-grain penne, cooked according to package directions, drained, and kept warm, ½ cup cooking liquid reserved
- Salt and freshly ground black pepper, to taste
- ½ cup kalamata olives, pitted and coarsely chopped
- ½ cup dried currants

Directions:

1. Place the shallots and chard ribs in a large saucepan and sauté over medium heat for 5 minutes. Add water 1 to 2 tablespoons at a time to keep the vegetables from sticking to the pan. Add the garlic and thyme and cook for another minute. Add half of the chard leaves and a few tablespoons of the reserved pasta cooking liquid and cook until the leaves start to wilt, adding more leaves as the chard cooks down, until all the leaves are wilted, about 10 minutes.

2. Season with salt and pepper and add the olives, currants, and cooked pasta. Toss well before serving.

Nutrition Per Serving

Calories: 279 Fat: 13.27g carbs: 4.07g protein: 34.29g fiber: 1.3g

261. Indonesia Green Noodle Salad

Preparation Time: 10 minutes

Cooking Time: 8 minutes

Servings: 4

Ingredients:

- 12 ounces (340 g) brown rice noodles, cooked, drained, and rinsed until cool
- 1 cup snow peas, trimmed and sliced in half on the diagonal
- 2 medium cucumbers, peeled, halved, deseeded, and sliced thinly
- 2 heads baby bok choy, trimmed and thinly sliced
- 4 green onions, green and white parts, trimmed and thinly sliced
- 3 tablespoons sambal oelek
- ½ cup chopped cilantro
- 2 tablespoons soy sauce
- ¼ cup fresh lime juice
- ¼ cup finely chopped mint

Directions:

1. Combine all the ingredients in a large bowl and toss to coat well.

2. Serve immediately.

Nutrition Per Serving

Calories: 288 Fat: 1g carbs: 64g protein: 12g fiber: 18g

262. Noodles with Red Lentil Curry

Preparation Time: 10 minutes

Cooking Time: 37 minutes

Servings: 4

Ingredients:

- 3 cups vegetable stock
- 1 cup red lentils, rinsed
- 1 medium red onion, peeled and diced small

- 2 tablespoons plus 2 teaspoons curry powder, or to taste
- 6 cups packed baby spinach
- Zest and juice of 2 lemons
- ½ teaspoon crushed red pepper flakes (optional)
- Salt and freshly ground black pepper, to taste
- 1 pound (454 g) brown rice noodles, cooked according to package directions, drained, and kept warm
- Finely chopped cilantro

Directions:

1. Bring the vegetable stock to a boil in a medium saucepan over medium-high heat. Add the lentils and cook for 20 to 25 minutes, or until the lentils are tender but not mushy.

2. Place the onion in a large skillet and stir-fry over medium heat for 7 to 8 minutes, or until the onion starts to brown. Add water 1 to 2 tablespoons at a time to keep the onion from sticking to the pan. Stir in the curry powder and spinach and cook until the spinach wilts, about 5 minutes. Add the cooked lentils, lemon zest and juice, and crushed red pepper flakes (if using), and season with salt and pepper.

3. To serve, divide the noodles among 4 individual plates. Spoon some of the lentil sauce over the noodles and garnish with the cilantro.

Nutrition Per Serving

Calories: 1795 fat: 166.6g carbs: 72.81g protein: 23.06g fiber: 15g

263. Tomato and Black Bean Rotini

Preparation Time: 5 minutes
Cooking Time: 9 to 10 minutes
Servings: 4
Ingredients:

- 1 red onion, diced
- 1 to 2 teaspoons olive oil
- 1 to 2 teaspoons ground chipotle pepper
- 1 (28-ounce / 794-g) can crushed tomatoes
- 8 ounces (227 g) rotini
- 1 cup water
- 1½ cup fresh corn
- 1½ cups cooked black beans
- Salt and freshly ground black pepper, to taste

Directions

1. Press the Sauté button on the Instant Pot and heat the oil. Add the red onion and cook for 5 to 6 minutes, stirring occasionally, or until the onion is lightly browned.

2. Stir in the chipotle pepper, tomatoes, rotini and water.

3. Lock the lid. Select the Manual mode and set the cooking time for 4 minutes on High Pressure. Once the timer goes off, perform a natural pressure release for 4 minutes, then release any remaining pressure. Carefully open the lid.

4. Stir in the corn and black beans. Taste and season with salt and pepper.

5. Serve immediately.

Nutrition Per Serving

Calories: 410 Fat: 4.25g carbs: 81.76g protein: 15.49g fiber: 13.3g

264. Lemony Broccoli Penne

Preparation Time: 25 minutes
Cooking Time: 15 minutes
Servings: 4
Ingredients:

- 1 medium yellow onion, peeled and thinly sliced
- 1-pound (454 g) broccoli rabe, trimmed and cut into 1-inch pieces
- ¼ cup golden raisins
- Zest and juice of 2 lemons
- 4 cloves garlic, peeled and minced
- ½ teaspoon crushed red pepper flakes
- 1-pound (454 g) whole-grain penne, cooked, drained, and kept warm, ¼ cup cooking liquid reserved
- Salt and freshly ground black pepper, to taste (optional) - ¼ cup pine nuts, toasted
- ½ cup chopped basil

Directions:

1. Put the onion in a large skillet over medium-high heat and sauté for 10 minutes, or until the onion is lightly browned.

2. Add the broccoli rabe and cook, stirring frequently, until the rabe is tender, about 5 minutes.

3. Add the raisins, lemon zest and juice, garlic, crushed red pepper flakes, and the cooked pasta and reserved cooking water. Remove from the heat. Mix well and season with salt (if desired) and pepper. Serve garnished with pine nuts and basil.

Nutrition Per Serving

Calories: 278 Fat: 7g carbs: 49g protein: 8g fiber: 9g

265. Singapore Rice Noodles

Preparation Time: 20 minutes
Cooking Time: 10 minutes
Servings: 2
Ingredients:

- 1 small yellow onion, peeled and cut into ½-inch slices

- 2 medium carrots, peeled and cut into matchsticks
- 1 medium red bell pepper, seeded and cut into ½-inch slices
- 8 ounces (227 g) shiitake mushrooms, stems removed
- ½ cup vegetable stock
- 4 teaspoons low-sodium soy sauce, or to taste
- 1 tablespoon grated ginger
- 2 cloves garlic, peeled and minced
- 1 tablespoon curry powder, or to taste
- 4 ounces (113 g) brown rice noodles, cooked according to the package directions, drained, and kept warm
- Freshly ground black pepper, to taste

Directions:

1. Heat a large skillet over high heat. Add the onion, carrots, red pepper, and mushrooms and stir-fry for 3 to 4 minutes. Add water 1 to 2 tablespoons at a time to keep the vegetables from sticking to the pan. Add the vegetable broth, soy sauce, ginger, garlic, and curry powder, and cook for 3 to 4 minutes. Add the cooked noodles, toss well, and season with black pepper.

Nutrition Per Serving

Calories: 649 Fat: 55.55g carbs: 41.42g protein: 5.19g fiber: 7g

266. Ponzu Pea Rice Noodle Salad

Preparation Time: 5 minutes
Cooking Time: 10 minutes
Servings: 4
Ingredients:

- 16 cups water
- 1 pound (454 g) brown rice noodles
- ½ pound (227 g) snow peas, trimmed and cut into matchsticks
- 3 medium carrots, peeled and cut into matchsticks
- ½ cup unsweetened Ponzu sauce
- 3 green onions, white and green parts, cut into ¾-inch pieces
- ½ cup coarsely chopped cilantro

Directions:

1. Bring water to a boil in a large pot, add the rice noodles and cook for 10 minutes or until al dente.
2. Add the snow peas and carrots during the last minute of cooking.
3. Drain and rinse the mixture until cooled and place them in a large bowl.

4. Add the ponzu sauce, green onions, and cilantro. Toss well before serving.

Nutrition Per Serving

Calories: 179 Fat: 1g carbs: 39g protein: 4g fiber: 4g

267. Thai Tofu Noodles

Preparation Time: 30 minutes
Cooking Time: 20 minutes
Servings: 4
Ingredients:
Sauce:

- 3 tablespoons tamarind paste
- ¾ cup boiling water
- ¼ cup soy sauce
- 2 tablespoons rice vinegar
- 3 tablespoons date sugar (optional)
- 1 tablespoon vegetable oil (optional)
- 1/8 teaspoon cayenne pepper

Noodles:

- 8 ounces (227 g) rice noodles
- 14 ounces (397 g) extra-firm tofu, cut into ¾-inch cubes
- 1/3 cup cornstarch
- ¼ cup vegetable oil, divided (optional)
- 1 shallot, minced
- 3 garlic cloves, minced
- 6 ounces (170 g) bean sprouts
- 4 scallions, sliced thinly
- Salt, to taste (optional)
- ¼ cup minced fresh cilantro
- 2 tablespoons chopped dry-roasted peanuts
- Lime wedges, for garnish

Directions:
For the Sauce

1. Soak the tamarind paste in boiling water until softened, about 10 minutes.
2. Strain the mixture through a fine-mesh strainer, pressing on solids to extract as much pulp as possible, then discard the solids.
3. Whisk the soy sauce, vinegar, sugar (if desired), oil (if desired), and cayenne into the tamarind liquid.
For the Noodles
4. Cover the noodles with hot water in a large bowl and stir to separate. Let noodles soak until softened, about 20 minutes. Drain noodles.
5. Meanwhile, spread tofu on a paper towel-lined baking sheet and let drain for 20 minutes. Gently pat dry with paper towels.

6. Toss the drained tofu with cornstarch in a medium bowl, then transfer to a fine-mesh strainer and shake gently to remove excess cornstarch.

7. Heat 3 tablespoons of vegetable oil (if desired) in a skillet over medium-high heat until just smoking.

8. Add tofu and cook, turning constantly, until crisp and browned on all sides, 12 minutes. Transfer the tofu to a paper towel lined plate to drain.

9. Heat the remaining 1 tablespoon oil (if desired) in the skillet over medium heat until shimmering.

10. Add shallot and garlic and cook until lightly browned, about 2 minutes.

11. Whisk sauce to recombine. Add noodles and sauce to skillet, increase heat to high, and cook, tossing gently, until noodles are evenly coated, about 1 minute.

12. Add the browned tofu, bean sprouts, and scallions and cook, tossing gently, until tofu is warmed through and noodles are tender, about 2 minutes.

13. Season with salt (if desired), sprinkle with cilantro and peanuts, and serve with lime wedges.

Nutrition Per Serving

Calories: 523 Fat: 25g carbs: 62g protein: 15g fiber: 3g

268. Sesame Soba Noodles with Vegetables

Preparation Time: 15 minutes
Cooking Time: 8 minutes
Servings: 4
Ingredients:
Sauce:

- 3 tablespoons toasted sesame seeds
- 1½ tablespoons rice vinegar
- ¼ cup soy sauce
- 3 tablespoons peanut butter
- 1 tablespoon grated fresh ginger
- 1 garlic clove, minced
- 1½ tablespoons date sugar (optional)
- ¾ teaspoon unsweetened hot sauce

Noodles and Vegetables:

- 16 cups water
- 12 ounces (340 g) soba noodles
- Salt, to taste (optional)
- 6 ounces (170 g) snow peas, strings removed and halved lengthwise
- 10 radishes, trimmed, halved, and sliced thin
- 1 celery rib, sliced thinly
- 2 tablespoons toasted sesame oil (optional)
- ½ cup fresh cilantro leaves
- 1 tablespoon toasted sesame seeds

Directions:
For the Sauce

1. Process sesame seeds, vinegar, soy sauce, peanut butter, ginger, garlic, sugar (if desired), and hot sauce in a blender until smooth.

For the Noodles and Vegetables

2. Bring 16 cups of water to a boil in a large pot. Add noodles and 1 tablespoon salt (if desired) and cook, stirring often, for 8 minutes or until al dente.

3. Drain noodles, rinse with cold water, and drain again.

4. Transfer noodles to a large bowl and toss with snow peas, radishes, celery, the sauce, and oil (if desired) to coat well.

5. Sprinkle with cilantro and sesame seeds and serve.

Nutrition Per Serving

Calories: 512 Fat: 17g carbs: 77g protein: 19g fiber: 3g

269. Lemon Bow Tie Pasta

Preparation Time: 5 minutes
Cooking Time: 11 to 12 minutes
Servings: 4 to 5
Ingredients:

- 1 Vidalia onion, diced
- 2 garlic cloves, minced
- 1 tablespoon olive oil
- 3½ cups water
- 10 ounces (283 g) bow tie pasta
- Grated zest and juice of 1 lemon
- ¼ cup black olives, pitted and chopped
- Salt and freshly ground black pepper, to taste

Directions:

1. Press the Sauté button on the Instant Pot and heat the oil. Add the onion and garlic to the pot. Cook for 7 to 8 minutes, stirring occasionally, or until the onion is lightly browned.

2. Add the water and pasta.

3. Set the lid in place. Select the Manual mode and set the cooking time for 4 minutes on High Pressure. When the timer goes off, do a quick pressure release. Carefully open the lid.

4. Stir the pasta and drain any excess water. Stir in the lemon zest and juice and the olives. Season with salt and pepper.

5. Serve immediately.

Nutrition Per Serving

Calories: 127 Fat: 3.84g carbs: 22.29g protein: 2.19g fiber: 3.6g

270. Shiitake and Bean Sprout Ramen

Preparation Time: 20 minutes

Cooking Time: 1 hour 15 minutes

Servings: 4 to 6

Ingredients:

- 4 ounces (113 g) bean sprouts
- 3 tablespoons soy sauce, divided
- 4 teaspoons toasted sesame oil, divided (optional)
- 1 tablespoon rice vinegar
- 1 onion, chopped
- 1 (3-inch) piece ginger, peeled and sliced into ¼-inch thick
- 5 garlic cloves, smashed
- 8 ounces (227 g) shiitake mushrooms, stems removed and reserved, caps sliced thin
- ½ ounce (14 g) kombu
- ¼ cup mirin
- 4 cups vegetable broth
- 20 cups water, divided
- 2 tablespoons red miso
- Salt, to taste (optional)
- 12 ounces (340 g) dried ramen noodles
- 2 scallions, sliced thinly
- 1 tablespoon toasted black sesame seeds

Directions:

1. Combine the bean sprouts, 1 teaspoon soy sauce, 1 teaspoon sesame oil (if desired), and vinegar in a small bowl; set aside.

2. Heat the remaining 1 tablespoon sesame oil (if desired) in a large saucepan over medium-high heat until shimmering.

3. Stir in onion and cook until softened and lightly browned, about 6 minutes. Add ginger and garlic and cook until lightly browned, about 2 minutes.

4. Stir in mushroom stems, kombu, mirin, broth, 4 cups of water, and remaining soy sauce, and bring to a boil.

5. Reduce heat to low, cover, and simmer for 1 hour.

6. Strain broth through a fine-mesh strainer into a large bowl. Wipe the saucepan clean and return the strained broth to the saucepan.

7. Whisk miso into the broth and bring to a gentle simmer over medium heat, whisking to dissolve miso completely.

8. Stir in mushroom caps and cook until warmed through, about 1 minute; season with salt, if desired. Remove from heat and cover to keep warm.

9. Meanwhile, bring 16 cups of water to a boil in a large pot. Add the ramen noodles and 1 tablespoon salt (if desired) and cook, stirring often, until al dente, about 2 minutes.

10. Drain the noodles and divide evenly among serving bowls. Ladle soup over noodles, garnish with bean sprouts, scallions, and sesame seeds. Serve hot.

Nutrition Per Serving

Calories: 237 Fat: 5g carbs: 37g protein: 8g fiber: 4g

271. Spinach Roselle Provençale

Preparation Time: 8 minutes

Cooking Time: 12 minutes

Servings: 6

Ingredients:

- 2 (15-ounce / 425-g) cans unsweetened stewed tomatoes
- 1 (19-ounce / 539-g) can white beans, drained and rinsed
- 20 cups water
- 1 (10-ounce / 283-g) package spinach rotelle
- ¼ cup chopped fresh parsley

Directions:

1. Put the beans and tomatoes in a saucepan and heat over medium heat for 8 minutes or until the mixture has thickened and has a sauce consistency.

2. Meanwhile, bring the water to a boil in a large pot. Add the spinach rotelle and cook, uncovered, for 12 minutes.

3. Drain the rotelle and transfer it into a large bowl. Add the tomato-bean sauce and toss to coat.

4. Sprinkle with fresh parsley before serving.

Nutrition Per Serving

Calories: 40 Fat: 1g carbs: 8g protein: 2g fiber: 4g

272. Sumptuous Shiitake Udon Noodles

Preparation Time: 20 minutes

Cooking Time: 21 minutes

Servings: 4 to 6

Ingredients:

- 1 tablespoon vegetable oil (optional)
- 8 ounces (227 g) shiitake mushrooms, stemmed and sliced thinly
- ½ ounce (14 g) dried shiitake mushrooms, rinsed and minced
- ¼ cup mirin
- 3 tablespoons rice vinegar
- 3 tablespoons soy sauce
- 2 garlic cloves, smashed and peeled

- 1 (1-inch) piece ginger, peeled, halved, and smashed
- 1 teaspoon toasted sesame oil (optional)
- 18 cups water, divided
- 1 teaspoon unsweetened Asian chili-garlic sauce
- 1-pound (454 g) mustard greens, stemmed and chopped into 2-inch pieces
- Salt and ground black pepper, to taste (optional)
- 1 pound (454 g) fresh udon noodles

Directions:

1. Heat the vegetable oil (if desired) in a Dutch oven over medium-high heat until shimmering.

2. Add the mushrooms and cook, stirring occasionally, until softened and lightly browned, about 5 minutes.

3. Stir in the dried mushrooms, mirin, vinegar, soy sauce, garlic, ginger, sesame oil (if desired), 2 cups of water, and chili-garlic sauce, and bring to a simmer.

4. Reduce the heat to medium-low and simmer until liquid has reduced by half, 8 minutes. Turn off the heat, discard the garlic and ginger, cover the pot to keep warm.

5. Meanwhile, bring 16 cups of water to a boil in a large pot. Add mustard greens and 1 tablespoon salt (if desired) and cook until greens are tender, about 5 minutes.

6. Add noodles and cook until greens and noodles are tender, about 2 minutes.

7. Reserve 1/3 cup cooking water, drain noodles and greens, and return them to the pot.

8. Add sauce and reserved cooking water, and toss to combine.

9. Cook over medium-low heat, tossing constantly, until sauce clings to noodles, about 1 minute.

10. Season with salt (if desired) and pepper, and serve.

Nutrition Per Serving

Calories: 184 Fat: 3g carbs: 32g protein: 6g fiber: 3g

273. **Tomato and Artichoke Rigatoni**

Preparation Time: 20 minutes

Cooking Time: 25 minutes

Servings: 4

Ingredients:

- 5 cloves garlic, peeled and minced
- 2 large tomatoes, diced small
- ½ cup dry white wine
- 2 tablespoons unsweetened tomato paste
- 1 tablespoon oregano
- 1 (15-ounce / 425-g) can artichoke hearts (oil-free), drained and halved
- 1 cup kalamata olives, pitted and halved

- 1-pound (454 g) whole-grain rigatoni, cooked, drained, and kept warm
- Salt and freshly ground black pepper, to taste (optional)
- Chopped parsley for garnish

Directions:

1. Put the garlic in a skillet and sauté over low heat for 5 minutes.

2. Raise the heat to medium and add the tomatoes, white wine, tomato paste, and oregano and cook for 15 minutes, or until the liquid is reduced by half.

3. Add the artichokes, olives, and cooked rigatoni, mix well, and cook for another 5 minutes.

4. Season with salt (if desired) and pepper. Serve garnished with parsley.

Nutrition Per Serving

Calories: 272 Fat: 5g carbs: 54g protein: 8g fiber: 17g

274. **Tomato Spaghetti**

Preparation Time: 5 minutes

Cooking Time: 10 minutes

Servings: 4

Ingredients:

- 3 medium tomatoes, chopped
- Zest and juice of 2 lemons
- 1 cup finely chopped basil
- 6 cloves garlic, peeled and minced
- 3 ears corn, kernels removed (about 2 cups)
- 1-pound (454 g) spaghetti, cooked, drained
- Salt and freshly ground black pepper, to taste (optional)

Directions:

1. Combine the tomatoes, lemon zest and juice, basil, garlic, and corn in a large bowl.

2. Add the cooked spaghetti and toss well. Season with salt (if desired) and pepper. Serve immediately.

Nutrition Per Serving

Calories: 263 Fat: 2g carbs: 57g protein: 10g fiber: 8g

275. **Noodle Salad with Spinach**

Preparation Time: 15 minutes

Cooking Time: 10 minutes

Servings: 2

Ingredients:

- 8 ounces (227 g) spaghetti
- 1 teaspoon toasted sesame oil (optional)

Sauce:

- 1 garlic clove, finely chopped
- 2 tablespoons sesame oil (optional)

- ¼ cup almond butter
- 3 tablespoons low-sodium soy sauce
- 2 tablespoons mirin
- 2 tablespoons unseasoned rice vinegar
- 1½ tablespoons maple syrup (optional)
- ½ tablespoon fresh lime juice
- 1/8 teaspoon sriracha

Servings:

- 3 cups baby spinach
- 1 cup thinly sliced English cucumber
- ½ red bell pepper, thinly sliced
- 2 scallions, thinly sliced
- 1/3 cup coarsely chopped mint leaves
- ¼ cup coarsely chopped roasted peanuts

Directions:

1. Bring a large pot of water to a boil over medium-high heat. Add the spaghetti to the pot and cook for 10 minutes, or until al dente, stirring constantly. Drain the spaghetti and rinse in cold water. Transfer to a large bowl and toss with the sesame oil (if desired).

2. In a blender, combine all the ingredients for the sauce and blend until smooth. Pour the sauce over the spaghetti and stir until well mixed. Set in a refrigerator for 15 minutes.

3. Add all the ingredients for the serving to the bowl with the spaghetti. Toss to combine well. Serve immediately.

Nutrition Per Serving

Calories: 678 Fat: 43g carbs: 60g protein: 21g fiber: 12g

276. Garlic & White Wine Pasta

Preparation Time: 10 minutes

Cooking Time: 20 minutes

Servings: 4

Ingredients:

Brussels Sprouts

- 16 oz Brussels sprouts, halved
- 1-2 tbsp olive oil
- 1 pinch sea salt
- 1/4 tsp black pepper

Pasta

- 3 tbsp olive oil
- 4 large cloves garlic, chopped
- 1/3 cup dry white wine
- 4 tbsp arrowroot starch
- 1 3/4 cup almond milk
- 4 tbsp nutritional yeast
- Sea salt and black pepper, to taste

- 1/4 cup vegan parmesan cheese
- 10 oz vegan, gluten-free pasta

For Serving

- Garlic bread
- Simple green salad

Directions:

1. Start by preheating the oven to 400 degrees F.

2. Spread the Brussels sprouts on a baking sheet.

3. Add oil, salt, and black pepper, then give it a toss.

4. Now, boil the pasta in a pot filled with water until al dente, then drain.

5. Now, heat oil in a rimmed skillet over medium heat.

6. Add garlic and sauté for 3 minutes until golden.

7. Stir in white wine and cook for 2 minutes.

8. Whisk in arrowroot and almond milk.

9. Mix well, then blend with vegan parmesan cheese, salt, and pepper in a food processor.

10. Heat the almond milk sauce in a skillet over medium heat until it bubbles.

11. Bake the Brussels sprouts in the oven for 15 minutes until golden.

12. Toss the drained pasta with cheese sauce and Brussels sprouts in a large bowl.

13. Mix well and serve.

Nutrition: Calories 248 Total Fat 15.7 g Saturated Fat 2.7 g Cholesterol 75 mg Sodium 94 mg Total Carbs 31.4 g Fiber 0.4 g Sugar 3.1 g Protein 4.9 g

277. Eggplant Vegan Pasta

Preparation Time: 10 minutes

Cooking Time: 20 minutes

Servings: 4

Ingredients:

- 12 oz dry pasta
- 1/2 small eggplant, cubed
- 2 cups cremini mushrooms, sliced
- 3 cloves garlic, minced
- 1 1/2 cups vegan marinara sauce
- 2 cups water
- 2 tsp sea salt
- 1 tsp ground black pepper
- 3 tbsp olive oil
- Fresh parsley or basil

Directions:

1. Place the eggplant in a colander and sprinkle salt on top.

2. Let them rest for 30 minutes and rinse thoroughly.

3. Now, place a saucepan over medium-high heat.

4. Add eggplant along with olive oil and 1/3 minced garlic, and ½ teaspoon salt.

5. Stir cook for 6 minutes until golden brown, then toss in mushrooms.

6. Sauté for 2 minutes approximately, then transfer to a bowl.

7. Cook pasta with water, remaining garlic, and marinara sauce in a saucepan.

8. Add salt and black pepper to pasta to adjust seasoning.

9. After cooking it to a boil, let it simmer for 10 minutes until pasta is al dente.

10. Toss in the eggplant mixture, then garnish as desired.

11. Serve.

Nutrition: Calories 246 Total Fat 14.8 g Saturated Fat 0.7 g Cholesterol 22 mg Sodium 220 mg Total Carbs 40.3 g Fiber 2.4 g Sugar 1.2 g Protein 2.4 g

278. Tomato Pesto Pasta

Preparation Time: 10 minutes
Cooking Time: 10 minutes
Servings: 3
Ingredients:

- 10 oz gluten-free pasta
- 3 oz sun-dried tomatoes
- ¼ cup olive oil
- 1 cup fresh basil
- 4 cloves garlic
- 2 tbsp vegan parmesan cheese

Directions:

1. Start by boiling the water with salt in a saucepan.

2. Add pasta and cook until al dente, then drain.

3. Take a blender jug and add basil, garlic, vegan parmesan, olive oil, and tomatoes.

4. Blend well until it forms a puree to form the pesto.

5. Toss the cooked pasta with pesto in a salad bowl.

6. Top with parmesan and olive oil.

7. Mix well and serve.

Nutrition: Calories 338 Total Fat 3.8 g Saturated Fat 0.7 g Cholesterol 22 mg Sodium 620 mg Total Carbs 58.3 g Fiber 2.4 g Sugar 1.2 g Protein 5.4 g

279. Alfredo with Peas

Preparation Time: 10 minutes
Cooking Time: 10 minutes
Servings: 4
Ingredients:

- 2 tbsp extra virgin olive oil
- 3 cloves garlic, minced
- 4 tbsp all-purpose flour
- ¾ cup 2% milk

- 1 cup vegetable stock
- 1 tbsp pesto
- ¼ tsp salt
- ¼ tsp black pepper
- ½ cup freshly grated vegan parmesan cheese
- 1 cup green peas
- ¾ box whole grain pasta

Directions:

1. Start by cooking the pasta as per the given instructions on the box, then drain.

2. Place a saucepan over medium heat, then add garlic along with olive oil.

3. Sauté for 1 minute, then add flour while constantly whisking.

4. After 1 minute, add vegetable stock and milk.

5. Mix well until smooth, then add pesto, black pepper, parmesan cheese, and salt.

6. Continue cooking until the mixture bubbles.

7. Toss in peas and pasta.

8. Mix well and serve.

Nutrition: Calories 438 Total Fat 4.8 g Saturated Fat 1.7 g Cholesterol 12 mg Sodium 520 mg Total Carbs 52.3 g Fiber 2.3 g Sugar 1.2 g Protein 2.1 g

280. Eggplant Parmesan Pasta

Preparation Time: 10 minutes
Cooking Time: 55 minutes
Servings: 2
Ingredients:
Eggplant Parmesan

- 1 medium eggplant
- 1/4 cup unbleached all-purpose flour
- 1 cup panko bread crumbs
- 2 tbsp vegan parmesan
- 1 tsp dried oregano
- 1/4 tsp sea salt
- 1/2 cup almond milk
- 1 tsp cornstarch

Pasta

- 8 oz pasta
- 2 cups marinara sauce

Directions:

1. Start by slicing the eggplant into ½-inch thick rounds.

2. Place them in a colander and sprinkle salt over the eggplant.

3. Let them rest for 15 minutes, then squeeze the excess water out using a dish towel.

4. Prepare a baking tray by lining it with aluminum foil.

5. Preheat the oven to 400 degrees F.

6. Boil the pasta as per the given instructions on the box.

7. Now, mix almond milk with salt, oregano, vegan parmesan, and cornstarch in a bowl until smooth.

8. Dip the eggplant in the flour, then in the almond milk mixture, and then breadcrumbs.

9. Place the coated slices in the baking tray.

10. Bake the eggplant for 30 minutes.

11. Meanwhile, warm up 2 tablespoons of oil in a skillet and sear the baked slices in batches until golden on both sides.

12. Warm the marinara in a pan and spread over the cooked pasta.

13. Place the eggplant slices on top.

14. Garnish as desired.

15. Serve.

Nutrition: Calories 378 Total Fat 13.8 g Saturated Fat 0.7 g Cholesterol 2 mg Sodium 620 mg Total Carbs 43.3 g Fiber 2.4 g Sugar 1.2 g Protein 5.4 g

281. Green Chili Mac 'N' Cheese

Preparation Time: 10 minutes
Cooking Time: 27 minutes
Servings: 4
Ingredients:

- 10 oz large macaroni shells
- 1/2 medium white onion, diced
- 3-4 cloves garlic, minced
- 1 cup raw cashews
- 1 1/2 cups vegetable broth
- 1 tbsp cornstarch
- 1/2 tsp cumin
- 3/4 tsp chili powder
- 2 tbsp nutritional yeast
- 1 4-oz can dice chills
- 1 cup tortilla chips
- Fresh cilantro

Directions:

1. Finely crush the tortilla chips to get the crumbs.

2. Spread the crumbs on a baking sheet lined with a parchment sheet.

3. Season with salt and avocado oil, then toss well to evenly coat.

4. Bake the chips for 10 minutes in an oven at 350°F until golden.

5. Meanwhile, cook the macaroni as per the given instructions on the box and set it aside.

6. Take a medium skillet and place it over medium-low heat.

7. Stir in garlic, olive oil, and onion to the skillet.

8. Sauté for 7 minutes, then set it aside.

9. Transfer this garlic mixture to a blender along with the remaining ingredients except for the tortilla chips and half of the green chilies.

10. Blend this mixture until smooth, then transfer to a bowl.

11. Toss drained pasta with cashew cheese blend.

12. Garnish with reserved chilies and tortilla chips.

13. Serve.

Nutrition: Calories 304 Total Fat 30.6 g Saturated Fat 13.1 g Cholesterol 131 mg Sodium 834 mg Total Carbs 21.4 g Fiber 0.2 g Sugar 0.3 g Protein 4.6 g

282. 3-Color Pasta

Preparation Time: 10 minutes
Cooking Time: 10 minutes
Servings: 1
Ingredients:

- 1 medium carrot
- 1 small-medium zucchini
- 2 oz whole-wheat spaghetti
- 1/3-1/2 cup tomato sauce
- 3 tbsp sundried tomato spread
- Vegan parmesan cheese
- Fresh basil

Directions:

1. Start by cooking the noodles as per the given instructions on the box until al dente.

2. Pass the zucchini and carrot through a spiralizer to get the noodles.

3. Heat the tomato spread with tomato sauce in a pan.

4. Boil the carrot and zucchini noodles in the pasta water for 4 minutes until al dente.

5. Drain and toss the veggies with cooked pasta noodles and tomato mixture in a bowl.

6. Garnish as desired.

7. Serve.

Nutrition: Calories 341 Total Fat 4 g Saturated Fat 0.5 g Cholesterol 69 mg Sodium 547 mg Total Carbs 36.4 g Fiber 1.2 g Sugar 1 g Protein 10.3 g

283. Caramelized Onion Mac 'N' Cheese

Preparation Time: 10 minutes
Cooking Time: 12 minutes
Servings: 4
Ingredients:
Pasta

- 1 small-medium eggplant

- 1 tbsp olive oil
- 1 1/2 yellow onions, sliced
- 10 oz macaroni noodles
- 4 tbsp nutritional yeast
- 1 3/4 cups almond milk
- 2 tsp garlic powder
- 1 tbsp cornstarch
- Sea salt

Topping

- 1/4 cup panko bread crumbs
- 1 tbsp olive oil

Directions:

1. Slice the eggplant into ½ inch thick rounds.

2. Place them in a colander, then sprinkle salt over the eggplant.

3. Let them sit for 20 minutes until the water is fully drained (squeeze out any excess).

4. Add olive oil along with onions to a skillet placed over medium heat.

5. Stir cook for 12 minutes until caramelized, then transfer to a bowl.

6. Set your oven at high broil mode and place a rack in the top portion.

7. Cook the pasta in water until al dente, then drain.

8. Spread the eggplant on a baking sheet, then broil for 4 minutes.

9. Set them aside covered with foil for 5 minutes, then peel their skin off.

10. Blend the eggplant slices with garlic powder, salt, cornstarch, yeast, and almond milk in a food processor.

11. Once it's smooth, transfer to a bowl.

12. Heat the eggplant sauce in a pan for 5 minutes.

13. Toss in noodles along with caramelized onions.

14. Divide the mixture in the serving bowls and garnish with bread crumbs.

15. Serve.

Nutrition: Calories 248 Total Fat 15.7 g Saturated Fat 2.7 g Cholesterol 75 mg Sodium 94 mg Total Carbs 40.4 g Fiber 0.1 g Sugar 0.3 g Protein 4.9 g

284. Cheesy Garlic Pasta with Ciabatta

Preparation Time: 10 minutes

Cooking Time: 10 minutes

Servings: 4

Ingredients:

Alfredo Sauce

- 1 tbsp extra virgin olive oil
- 3 cloves garlic, minced

- 1 cup low-fat milk
- 1/2 cup veggie broth
- 2-4 tbsp flour
- 1/4 tsp salt
- 1/4 tsp black pepper
- 1/4 cup grated parmesan cheese
- 1 tbsp pesto
- 1 healthy pinch red pepper flakes
- 10-12 oz pasta, boiled

Cheesy Garlic Ciabatta Bread

- 1 ciabatta bread roll
- 2 tbsp butter
- 1 tsp garlic powder
- 1 sprinkle mozzarella and parmesan cheese

Directions:

1. Start by preheating the oven to 400 degrees F.

2. Place a large saucepan over medium heat, then add garlic and olive oil.

3. Sauté until golden, then add broth and milk.

4. Mix well, then add flour with constant mixing until smooth.

5. Toss in cheese, pesto, red pepper flakes, black pepper, and salt, then mix well.

6. Stir cook for 5 minutes, then set it aside.

7. Cook the pasta to a boil until al dente, then drain.

8. Slice the ciabatta roll in half, then butter them.

9. Further cut the roll into strips and place them on a baking sheet.

10. Sprinkle mozzarella, garlic powder, and parmesan over the strips.

11. Toast them for approximately 5 minutes in the oven.

12. Toss the pasta with prepared sauce in a large bowl.

13. Garnish with bread strips.

14. Serve.

Nutrition: Calories 301 Total Fat 12.2 g Saturated Fat 2.4 g Cholesterol 110 mg Sodium 276 mg Total Carbs 5 g Fiber 0.9 g Sugar 1.4 g Protein 28.8 g

285. Tomato Red Lentil Pasta

Preparation Time: 10 minutes

Cooking Time: 30 minutes

Servings: 6

Ingredients:

- ¼ cup extra virgin olive oil
- 1 sweet onion, chopped
- 6 cloves garlic, minced
- 1 tbsp dried basil
- 1 tbsp dried oregano

- 2 tsp ground turmeric
- Kosher salt and black pepper, to taste
- 1 28-oz can fire-roasted tomatoes
- ½ cup oil-packed sundried tomatoes, chopped
- 1 tbsp apple cider vinegar
- 1 (8-oz) box red lentil pasta
- 2 large handfuls baby spinach

Directions:

1. Start by warming up the olive oil in a large pot over medium heat.

2. Add onion and sauté for 10 minutes approximately.

3. Stir in black pepper, salt, turmeric, oregano, basil, and garlic.

4. Sauté for 1 minute, then toss tomatoes along with its juices, sundried tomatoes, and vinegar.

5. Cook for 15 minutes on a simmer, then blend using an immersion blender.

6. Toss spinach into the sauce and mix well to cook for another 5 minutes.

7. Boil the pasta as per the given instructions on the box, then drain.

8. Serve pasta with spinach mixture on top.

9. Garnish as desired.

10. Serve.

Nutrition: Calories 248 Total Fat 2.4 g Saturated Fat 0.1 g Cholesterol 320 mg Sodium 350 mg Total Carbs 32.2 g Fiber 0.7 g Sugar 0.7 g Protein 44.3 g

286. Pasta with Sun-Dried Tomato Sauce

Preparation Time: 5 minutes

Cooking Time: 10 minutes

Servings: 4

Ingredients:

- 3 cups dried fusilli or rotini pasta
- 1 large tomato, chopped
- 2/3 cup sun-dried tomatoes, chopped
- 2 cloves garlic, coarsely chopped
- ½ cup fresh parsley, coarsely chopped
- ½ cup fresh grated Parmesan cheese
- ¼ cup balsamic vinegar
- 1/3 cup extra-virgin olive oil

Directions:

1. Bring a large pot of salted water to a boil. Add the pasta and cook according to package instructions.

2. While the pasta is cooking, combine the tomato, sun-dried tomatoes, garlic, parsley, Parmesan cheese, balsamic vinegar, and olive oil in a blender. Blend until smooth.

3. Drain the pasta and transfer it to serving plates.

4. Ladle the sauce over the pasta and serve hot.

Nutrition Per Serving: Calories: 419; Total fat: 22g; Total carbs: 48g; Fiber: 7g; Sugar: 5g; Protein: 14g; Sodium: 324mg

287. Zesty Green Pea and Jalapeño Pesto Pasta

Preparation Time: 5 minutes

Cooking Time: 10 minutes

Servings: 4

Ingredients:

- 3 cups dried fusilli or rotini pasta
- 1¼ cups fresh or defrosted frozen green peas, divided
- 4 sun-dried tomatoes, chopped
- 1 cup fresh basil leaves, chopped
- ¾ cup fresh mint leaves, chopped
- 1 small onion, chopped
- 2 cloves garlic, coarsely chopped
- 1 jalapeño pepper, seeded and chopped
- 3 tablespoons lemon juice
- ¼ teaspoon salt
- ¼ teaspoon freshly ground black pepper
- 3 tablespoons extra-virgin olive oil

Directions:

1. Bring a large pot of salted water to a boil. Add the pasta and cook according to package instructions.

2. 2 minutes before the pasta is finished cooking, toss in 1 cup of the peas.

3. While the pasta is cooking, combine the remaining ¼ cup of the peas with sun-dried tomatoes, basil, mint, onion, garlic, jalapeño pepper, lemon juice, salt, pepper, and olive oil in a blender.

4. Blend until smooth. Add another tablespoon of olive oil if the mixture is too thick to process.

5. Drain the pasta and peas and toss with the pesto.

6. Serve hot or warm, or cold as a salad.

Nutrition Per Serving: Calories: 345; Total fat: 13g; Total carbs: 52g; Fiber: 10g; Sugar: 5g; Protein: 11g; Sodium: 200mg

288. Lemony Pasta with Broccoli and Chickpeas

Preparation Time: 5 minutes

Cooking Time: 10 minutes

Serving 6

Ingredients:

- 3 cups dried fusilli or rotini pasta

- 3 cups broccoli florets
- 1 (14-ounce) can chickpeas, drained and rinsed
- 1/3 cup sun-dried tomatoes, chopped
- 2 tablespoons extra-virgin olive oil
- ½ tablespoon minced garlic
- ½ teaspoon paprika
- 3 tablespoons lemon juice
- 1 teaspoon salt

Directions:

1. Bring a large pot of salted water to a boil. Add the pasta and cook according to package instructions.

2. In the last 4 minutes of the pasta cooking time, add the broccoli florets.

3. Drain the pasta and broccoli and add to a large bowl.

4. Add chickpeas, sun-dried tomatoes, olive oil, garlic, paprika, lemon juice, and salt.

5. Stir to combine and serve warm or cold.

SUBSTITUTION TIP: Instead of buying broccoli florets, use the florets and stem from a fresh head of broccoli. The stems are sweet and tender, once peeled, and have the same nutritional value as the crown. You can peel and chop the stem and add it to the pasta cooking water, just as with the florets.

Nutrition Per Serving: Calories: 270; Total fat: 7g; Total carbs: 43g; Fiber: 9g; Sugar: 5g; Protein: 10g; Sodium: 469mg

289. Penne with Indian-Style Tomato Sauce and Mushrooms

Preparation Time: 5 minutes

Cooking Time: 20 minutes

Servings: 4

Ingredients:

- 2 tablespoons extra-virgin olive oil
- 1 (8-ounce) package sliced white mushrooms
- 2 tablespoons minced fresh ginger
- 2 tablespoons minced garlic
- ½ tablespoon garam masala
- ¼ teaspoon dried red chili flakes
- 1 (28-ounce) can crushed or diced tomatoes
- ½ teaspoon salt
- 3 cups dried penne pasta

Directions:

1. In a medium saucepan, heat the olive oil over medium heat.

2. When hot, add the mushrooms and sauté for 5 minutes.

3. Add the ginger, garlic, garam masala, and red chili flakes, and stir for 3 more minutes.

4. Stir in the tomatoes and salt. Bring to a boil, being careful of splattering. Lower the heat and simmer for 10 minutes.

5. While the sauce is simmering, bring a large pot of salted water to a boil. Add the pasta and cook according to package instructions.

6. Drain the pasta, return to the pot, and stir in the tomato sauce.

7. Serve hot.

Nutrition Per Serving: Calories: 326; Total fat: 9g; Total carbs: 52g; Fiber: 9g; Sugar: 8g; Protein: 11g; Sodium: 306mg

290. Teriyaki Mushrooms and Cashews with Rice Noodles

Preparation Time: 5 minutes

Cooking Time: 20 minutes

Servings: 2

Ingredients:

- 2 cups water
- 2½ ounces rice noodles
- 3½ tablespoons sesame oil, divided
- ¼ cup raw cashews, halved or coarsely chopped
- 1 tablespoon brown sugar
- 1 tablespoon tamari or soy sauce
- 1 tablespoon rice vinegar
- ½ teaspoon dried red chili flakes
- 1 green onion, white and green parts, finely sliced
- ½ tablespoon minced garlic
- 1 tablespoon minced fresh ginger
- 1 (8-ounce) package sliced white mushrooms

Directions:

1. Bring the water to a boil in a medium saucepan. Stir in the rice noodles, cover, and remove from the heat. Let sit for 5 minutes or up to 10 minutes for wider rice noodles.

2. While the noodles are resting, heat 2 tablespoons of the sesame oil in a medium nonstick pan or wok over medium-low heat. When hot, add the cashew pieces and fry, stirring frequently, for 5 to 8 minutes, until golden brown. Remove from the pan using a slotted spoon and set aside.

3. Add 1 tablespoon of the oil to the pan and stir in the brown sugar, tamari or soy sauce, rice vinegar, red chili flakes, green onion, garlic, and ginger. Stir for 1 to 2 minutes to dissolve the sugar.

4. Increase the heat to medium-high and add the mushrooms. Cook, stirring frequently, for 5 minutes until the mushrooms begin to brown.

5. Stir in the cashew pieces and toss to combine.

6. Drain the rice noodles, stir in the remaining ½ tablespoon of the sesame oil, and transfer to serving plates. Spoon the mushrooms and cashews over each portion and serve immediately.

INGREDIENT TIP: Rice noodles range in width from very fine (rice vermicelli) to ¼-inch wide. These mushrooms will look attractive with any width of rice noodle, but wider noodles will provide a more "toothsome" experience.

Nutrition Per Serving: Calories: 438; Total fat: 28g; Total carbs: 40g; Fiber: 3g; Sugar: 7g; Protein: 9g; Sodium: 566mg

291. Linguine with Pea-Basil Pesto

Preparation Time: 5 minutes

Cooking Time: 10 minutes

Servings: 4

Ingredients:

- 8 ounces dried linguine
- 1¼ cup fresh or defrosted frozen green peas, divided
- 2 tablespoons extra-virgin olive oil
- 1 small onion, chopped
- 1 tablespoon minced garlic
- 1 jalapeño pepper, seeded and chopped
- ½ cup walnuts, chopped
- ½ cup fresh basil leaves
- ½ teaspoon salt - 2/3 cup water
- Freshly ground black pepper

Directions:

1. Bring a large pot of salted water to a boil. Add the pasta and cook according to package instructions.

2. 2 minutes before the pasta is finished cooking, toss in ½ cup of the peas.

3. While the pasta is cooking, heat the olive oil in a nonstick skillet over medium heat.

4. Add the onion, garlic, and jalapeño pepper, and stir for 3 to 4 minutes to soften the onion.

5. Stir in the remaining ¾ cup of the peas and the walnuts. Continue to stir for another minute.

6. Add the basil, salt, and water. Stir for a minute and then remove from the heat.

7. Transfer the contents of the skillet to a blender and process until smooth, adding more water if the pesto is too thick.

8. Drain the pasta and peas and rinse quickly with cold water. Return the pasta to the pot and add the pesto and black pepper. Toss gently and serve hot.

LEFTOVER TIP: Place leftover pasta in a bowl, cover with plastic wrap, and refrigerate for up to 3 days. Drizzle a little olive oil into the pasta and toss again before serving.

PER **SERVING:** Calories: 415; Total fat: 19g; Total carbs: 50g; Fiber: 10g; Sugar: 5g; Protein: 12g; Sodium: 294mg

292. Greek-Inspired Macaroni and Cheese

Preparation Time: 10 minutes

Cooking Time: 15 minutes

Servings: 6

Ingredients:

- 1-pound dried macaroni
- 2 cups fresh spinach, chopped
- 2 tablespoons unsalted butter
- 1 onion, finely chopped
- 1 tablespoon minced garlic
- 2 tablespoons all-purpose flour
- 1 (12-ounce) can evaporated milk or 2 cups heavy cream - 1 cup grated Swiss cheese
- 1 cup feta cheese, crumbled
- 1 cup pitted black or Kalamata olives, sliced or chopped
- Freshly ground black pepper (optional)

Directions:

1. Bring a large pot of salted water to a boil. Add the macaroni and cook until al dente, according to package instructions.

2. Add the spinach and cook for another few minutes.

3. Drain the pasta and spinach and return to the pot.

4. While the pasta is cooking, melt the butter over medium heat in a medium saucepan. Add the onion and garlic and stir for 5 minutes to soften the onion.

5. Add the flour to the pan and stir for another 2 minutes.

6. Whisk in the evaporated milk and bring to a slow boil over medium-high heat. Continue to whisk constantly for 3 to 4 minutes until the mixture is creamy and thickened.

7. Add the Swiss and feta cheeses and stir for 2 to 3 minutes to melt. Turn the heat off and stir in the olives.

8. Add the cheese mixture to the pasta and spinach and stir to combine. Serve hot or warm, seasoned with freshly ground black pepper, if desired.

LEFTOVER TIP: Refrigerate leftovers in a sealed container for up to 3 days. To reheat, put the macaroni and cheese in a covered oven-safe bowl or casserole dish and stir in a few tablespoons of milk. Reheat in a 350°F oven for 10 to 20 minutes before serving.

Nutrition Per Serving: Calories: 572; Total fat: 22g; Total carbs: 70g; Fiber: 4g; Sugar: 10g; Protein: 23g; Sodium: 610mg

293. Spicy Mac and Ricotta Cheese with Spinach

Preparation Time: 5 minutes

Cooking Time: 25 minutes

Servings: 4 To 6

Ingredients:

- 2 cups dried macaroni
- 2 tablespoons extra-virgin olive oil or unsalted butter
- 1 medium shallot or small yellow onion, finely chopped
- 1 (10-ounce) bag fresh spinach, chopped
- 1 large tomato, finely chopped
- 1 or 2 fresh red or green chiles, seeded and minced
- ½ teaspoon turmeric
- 2/3 teaspoon ground coriander
- ½ teaspoon ground cumin
- ¼ teaspoon cayenne pepper
- 1 cup firm ricotta cheese, crumbled or mashed
- 1 to 2 teaspoons salt

Directions:

1. Bring a large pot of salted water to a boil. Stir in the macaroni and cook until al dente, according to package instructions.

2. While the pasta is cooking, heat the olive oil in a large saucepan over medium heat. Add the shallot or onion to the pan and sauté for 4 to 5 minutes or until softened.

3. Add handfuls of the spinach, stirring frequently, until it begins to wilt.

4. Once all of the spinach has been added, stir in the tomato, chiles, turmeric, coriander, cumin, and cayenne. Simmer for 5 minutes, or until the tomato is softened and most of the liquid has evaporated.

5. Reserve 1 2/3 cups of the pasta cooking liquid and drain the pasta in a strainer.

6. Stir the reserved pasta cooking water into the sauce and bring to a gentle simmer over medium-high heat. Stir in the cooked pasta, ricotta cheese, and salt.

7. Reduce the heat to medium-low and continue to simmer for another 5 minutes, stirring occasionally.

8. Serve immediately.

SUBSTITUTION TIP: If you can't find or don't want to fuss with fresh chiles, use ¼ to ½ teaspoons of dried red chili flakes instead.

Nutrition Per Serving: Calories: 313; Total fat: 13g; Total carbs: 36g; Fiber: 4g; Sugar: 3g; Protein: 15g; Sodium: 720mg

294. Spinach Pesto Pasta

Preparation Time: 5 minutes

Cooking Time: 10 minutes

Servings: 4

Ingredients:

- 8 ounces dried linguine or fettuccini
- ¼ cup pine nuts
- 1 (5-ounce) bag fresh spinach leaves
- 2 cloves garlic, chopped
- ¼ cup extra-virgin olive oil
- ¼ cup fresh grated Parmesan cheese
- ½ tablespoon balsamic vinegar or red wine vinegar
- ½ teaspoon salt
- Freshly ground black pepper (optional)

Directions:

1. Bring a large pot of salted water to a boil. Add the pasta and cook according to package instructions.

2. While the pasta is cooking, toast the pine nuts in a small dry skillet over medium-low heat for 5 minutes, tossing or stirring frequently.

3. In a blender or food processor, combine the pine nuts, spinach, and garlic, and process until well chopped.

4. Pour in the olive oil and process for another half minute until blended.

5. Transfer the spinach pesto to a medium bowl and stir in the Parmesan cheese, balsamic vinegar, and salt.

6. Drain the pasta and rinse quickly with cold water.

7. Return the pasta to the pot and add the pesto. Toss gently and serve hot with freshly ground black pepper, if desired.

SUBSTITUTION TIP: Unsalted pistachios or almonds can be substituted for pine nuts. If they are already roasted, skip the second step.

Nutrition Per Serving: Calories: 398; Total fat: 21g; Total carbs: 45g; Fiber: 3g; Sugar: 2g; Protein: 12g; Sodium: 384mg

295. Lasagna Noodles in a Creamy Mushroom Sauce

Preparation Time: 5 minutes

Cooking Time: 25 minutes

Servings: 4

Ingredients:

- 4 tablespoons unsalted butter
- 2 medium onions, chopped
- 1 (16-ounce) package sliced white mushrooms
- 1 (14-ounce) can coconut milk or cream

- 4 tablespoons lemon juice
- 2 tablespoons fresh parsley, chopped
- 1 tablespoon all-purpose flour
- ½ teaspoon dry mustard powder
- 1 teaspoon salt
- 8 ounces dried lasagna noodles
- Freshly ground black pepper (optional)

Directions:

1. In a large saucepan or wok, melt the butter over medium heat. Add the onions and cook, stirring often, for 5 minutes to soften.

2. Raise the heat to medium-high and add the mushrooms. Cook, stirring often, for 5 minutes until lightly browned but still plump.

3. Reduce the heat to medium-low and stir in the coconut milk or cream, lemon juice, parsley, flour, dry mustard powder, and salt. Simmer without boiling for 15 minutes, stirring occasionally. If the sauce becomes too thick, stir in a little water.

4. While the sauce is simmering, break the lasagna noodles into 2- to 3-inch pieces.

5. Bring a large pot of salted water to boil. Add the noodles and cook until al dente, according to package instructions.

6. Drain the noodles and rinse quickly with cold water. Return the noodles to the pot.

7. Remove the sauce from the heat and add to the pasta. Toss gently and serve hot, seasoned with freshly ground black pepper, if desired.

INGREDIENT TIPS: Do not substitute coconut milk from a carton for canned coconut milk, as it is much waterier. Avoid oven-ready (or no-boil) lasagna noodles for this recipe.

Nutrition Per Serving: Calories: 550; Total fat: 37g; Total carbs: 48g; Fiber: 5g; Sugar: 8g; Protein: 14g; Sodium: 591mg

296. Stir-Fried, Grilled and Hashed Vegetables

Roasted Corn

Preparation Time: 5 minutes
Cooking Time: 10 minutes
Servings: 4
Ingredients:

- 4 ears of corn, husk removed
- ½ teaspoon ground black pepper
- 1 teaspoon salt
- 3 teaspoons olive oil

Directions:

1. Switch on the air fryer, insert the fryer basket, then shut it with the lid, set the frying temperature to 400 degrees F, and let it preheat for 5 minutes.

2. Meanwhile, remove husk and silk from corn, rinse them well, and pat dry.

3. Then cut the corns to fit into the fryer basket, drizzle with oil, and season with black pepper and salt.

4. Open the preheated fryer, place corns in it, close the lid and cook for 10 minutes until golden brown and cooked, turning halfway.

5. When done, the air fryer will beep, and then open the lid and transfer corn to a dish.

6. Serve straight away.

Nutrition: Calories: 175 Fat: 7.7 g Carbs: 27 g Protein: 4.8 g Fiber: 3 g

297. Plantain Chips

Preparation Time: 5 minutes
Cooking Time: 20 minutes
Servings: 2
Ingredients:

- 3 green plantains, peeled, sliced
- 1 lime, zested - ½ teaspoon garlic powder
- 1 teaspoon of sea salt
- 1/8 teaspoon red chili powder
- 2 teaspoons olive oil
- 1 cup guacamole, for serving

Directions:

1. Switch on the air fryer, insert the fryer basket, then shut it with the lid, set the frying temperature at 374 degrees F, and let it preheat for 5 minutes.

2. Meanwhile, take a large bowl, add plantain slices in it along with the remaining ingredients, except for guacamole and toss until coated.

3. Open the preheated fryer, place plantain in it, close the lid and cook for 20 minutes until golden brown and cooked, shaking every 5 minutes.

4. When done, the air fryer will beep, and then open the lid and transfer plantain chips to a dish.

5. Serve plantain chips with guacamole.

Nutrition: Calories: 220 Fat: 12 g Carbs: 25 g Protein: 1 g Fiber: 2 g

298. Roasted Garlic

Preparation Time: 10 minutes
Cooking Time: 25 minutes
Servings: 4
Ingredients:

- 1 medium head of garlic
- Olive oil spray

Directions:

1. Switch on the air fryer, insert the fryer basket, then shut it with the lid, set the frying temperature to 400 degrees F, and let it preheat for 5 minutes.

2. Meanwhile, remove excess peel from the garlic head, and then expose the top of the garlic by removing ¼-inch off the top.

3. Spray the garlic head with oil generously and then wrap with foil.

4. Open the preheated fryer, place the wrapped garlic head in it, close the lid and cook for 25 minutes until done. When done, the air fryer will beep, then open the lid, transfer garlic to a dish and let it cool for 5 minutes. Then squeeze the garlic out of its skin and serve with warmed garlic or as desired.

Nutrition: Calories: 160 Fat: 2.5 g Carbs: 27 g Protein: 6 g Fiber: 3 g

299. Maple Roasted Brussels sprouts

Preparation Time: 5 minutes
Cooking Time: 10 minutes
Servings: 2
Ingredients:

- 2 cups Brussels sprouts, ¼-inch thick sliced
- 1/4 teaspoon sea salt
- 1 tablespoon balsamic vinegar
- 1 tablespoon maple syrup

Directions:

1. Switch on the air fryer, insert the fryer basket, then shut it with the lid, set the frying temperature to 400 degrees F, and let it preheat for 5 minutes.

2. Meanwhile, take a large bowl, add Brussel sprouts in it, season with salt, drizzle with vinegar and maple syrup and toss until well coated.

3. Open the preheated fryer, place Brussel sprouts in it, close the lid and cook for 10 minutes until golden brown and cooked, shaking halfway.

4. When done, the air fryer will beep, then open the lid and transfer Brussel sprouts to a dish.

5. Serve straight away.

Nutrition: Calories: 85.3 Fat: 3.3 g Carbs: 13.1 g Protein: 2.8 g Fiber: 2.8 g

300. Roasted Butternut Squash with Mushrooms and Cranberries

Preparation Time: 5 minutes
Cooking Time: 30 minutes
Servings: 6
Ingredients:

- 4 cups diced butternut squash

- 1 cup sliced green onions
- 8 ounces button mushrooms, destemmed, quartered - ¼ cup dried cranberries

For the Sauce:

- 1 tablespoon maple syrup
- 4 cloves of garlic, peeled
- 1 tablespoon soy sauce
- 1 tablespoon balsamic vinegar
- 1 tablespoon olive oil

Directions:

1. Switch on the air fryer, insert the fryer basket, then shut it with the lid, set the frying temperature to 400 degrees F, and let it preheat for 5 minutes.

2. Meanwhile, prepare the sauce and for this, place all of its ingredients in a food processor and puree for 1 minute until blended.

3. Take a large bowl, place all the vegetables and berries, add sauce and toss until coated.

4. Open the preheated fryer, place vegetables in it, close the lid and cook for 30 minutes until golden brown and cooked, shaking every 10 minutes.

5. When done, the air fryer will beep, then open the lid, transfer vegetables and berries to a dish and garnish with some more green onions.

6. Serve straight away.

Nutrition: Calories: 128 Fat: 2.6 g Carbs: 28 g Protein: 2.2 g Fiber: 8.6 g

301. Roasted Green Beans

Preparation Time: 5 minutes
Cooking Time: 10 minutes
Servings: 2
Ingredients:

- 8 ounces green beans, trimmed
- 1 teaspoon sesame oil
- 1 tablespoon soy sauce

Directions:

1. Switch on the air fryer, insert the fryer basket, then shut it with the lid, set the frying temperature to 400 degrees F, and let it preheat for 5 minutes.

2. Meanwhile, snap the green beans in half, place them in a large bowl, add oil and soy sauce and toss until well coated.

3. Open the preheated fryer, place green beans in it, spray with olive oil, close the lid and cook for 10 minutes until golden brown and cooked, shaking halfway.

4. When done, the air fryer will beep, and then open the lid and transfer green beans to a dish. Serve straight away.

Nutrition: Calories: 33.2 Fat: 2.5 g Carbs: 2.7 g Protein: 0.7 g Fiber: 1.3

302. Shashti Peppers

Preparation Time: 5 minutes
Cooking Time: 6 minutes
Servings: 4
Ingredients:

- 20 Shashti peppers
- 1 teaspoon salt
- Olive oil spray

Directions:

1. Switch on the air fryer, insert the fryer basket, then shut it with the lid, set the frying temperature at 390 degrees F, and let it preheat for 5 minutes.

2. Open the preheated fryer, place peppers in it, spray well with olive oil, close the lid and cook for 6 minutes until cooked and lightly charred, shaking halfway.

3. When done, the air fryer will beep, open the lid, transfer peppers to a dish, and season with salt.

4. Serve straight away.

Nutrition: Calories: 21 Fat: 1 g Carbs: 5 g Protein: 1 g Fiber: 2 g

303. Baby Bok Choy

Preparation Time: 5 minutes
Cooking Time: 6 minutes
Servings: 4
Ingredients:

- 4 bunches baby bok choy
- 1 teaspoon garlic powder
- Olive oil spray

Directions:

1. Switch on the air fryer, insert the fryer basket, then shut it with the lid, set the frying temperature to 350°F, and let it preheat for 5 minutes.

2. Meanwhile, prepare the bok choy and for this, slice off the bottom, separate the leaves, rinse and drain well.

3. Open the preheated fryer, place bok choy in it, spray generously with olive oil, sprinkle with garlic powder, shake well, close the lid and cook for 6 minutes until golden brown and cooked, shaking halfway.

4. When done, the air fryer will beep, then open the lid and transfer bok choy to a dish. Serve straight away.

Nutrition: Calories: 58 Fat: 2 g Carbs: 5 g Protein: 1 g Fiber: 1 g

304. Popcorn Tofu

Preparation Time: 5 minutes
Cooking Time: 24 minutes
Servings: 4
Ingredients:

- 14 ounces tofu, extra-firm, pressed, drained
- 1 ½ cup panko bread crumbs

For the Batter:

- 1 teaspoon onion powder
- 1/2 cup cornmeal - 1/2 cup chickpea flour
- 1 teaspoon garlic powder
- 1/2 teaspoon ground black pepper
- 1/2 teaspoon salt
- 1 tablespoon Vegetarian Bouillon
- 2 tablespoons nutritional yeast
- 1 tablespoon Dijon mustard
- 3/4 cup almond milk, unsweetened

Directions:

1. Switch on the air fryer, insert the fryer basket, then shut it with the lid, set the frying temperature to 350°F, and let it preheat for 5 minutes.

2. Meanwhile, prepare the batter and for this, place all of its ingredients in a large bowl and then whisk until combined until smooth batter comes together.

3. Take a shallow dish and then place bread crumbs in it.

4. Cut tofu into bite-size pieces, dip into prepared batter and then dredge with bread crumbs until coated on both sides.

5. Open the preheated fryer, place tofu in it in a single layer, spray with olive oil, close the lid and cook for 12 minutes until golden brown and cooked, shaking halfway.

6. When done, the air fryer will beep, open the lid, transfer popcorns to a dish, and cover with foil to keep them warm.

7. Cook remaining tofu popcorns in the same manner and then serve.

Nutrition: Calories: 261 Fat: 5.5 g Carbs: 37.5 g Protein: 16 g Fiber: 4.8 g

305. Roasted Vegetable Kebabs

Preparation Time: 5 minutes
Cooking Time: 15 minutes
Servings: 8
Ingredients:

- 2 cups zucchini - 2 cups mushrooms
- 2 cups onions - 2 cups bell peppers
- 2 Tbsp olive oil
- 1 Tbsp roasted garlic & herb seasoning

Directions:

1. Cut vegetables into pieces and toss them with seasoning and oil.

2. Thread the vegetables onto skewers.

3. Grill for 15 minutes on medium heat until tender.

Nutrition: Carbohydrates – 8 g Fat – 4 g Protein – 4 g Calories – 68

306. Greek Grilled Eggplant Steaks

Preparation Time: 20 minutes
Cooking Time: 15 minutes
Servings: 6
Ingredients:

- 2 eggplants
- 8 ounces feta, diced
- 4 Roma tomatoes, diced
- 1 hothouse cucumber, diced
- 1 cup parsley, chopped - 1 Tbsp olive oil
- Kosher salt, pepper, to taste

Directions:

1. Slice eggplants into 3 thick steaks. Drizzle with oil, salt, pepper.
2. Grill the eggplant in a pan for 4 minutes per side.
3. Top eggplant steaks with remaining ingredients. Serve.

Note:

For ovo-lacto vegetarian, lacto vegetarian, Pescatarian diets.

Nutrition: Carbohydrates – 12 g Fat – 7 g Protein – 8 g Calories – 86

307. Grilled Broccoli

Preparation Time: 5 minutes
Cooking Time: 20 minutes
Servings: 6
Ingredients:

- 6 cups broccoli spears - 3 Tbsp lemon juice
- 2 Tbsp olive oil - ¼ tsp salt
- ¼ tsp pepper
- ¾ cup Parmesan cheese, grated

Directions:

1. Combine broccoli, lemon juice, oil, salt, pepper. Set aside for 30 minutes.
2. Drain marinade and add cheese to coat broccoli.
3. Grill broccoli for 10 minutes per side.

Note: For ovo-lacto vegetarian, lacto vegetarian, Pescatarian diets.

Nutrition: Carbohydrates – 5 g Fat – 8 g Protein – 6 g Calories – 107

308. Roasted Garlic Grilled Vegetables

Preparation Time: 10 minutes
Cooking Time: 15 minutes
Servings: 8
Ingredients:

- 1 ear of corn, cut into chunks
- 1 onion, sliced
- 3 bell peppers, cut into chunks
- 1 squash, sliced
- 1 cup mushroom halves
- 2 Tbsp oil
- 1 Tbsp roasted garlic & herb seasoning

Directions:

1. Combine vegetables with oil and seasoning in a large dish.
2. Put vegetables in a grill basket or grill rack.
3. Grill for 15 minutes over medium heat.

Nutrition: Carbohydrates – 8 g Fat – 4 g Protein – 4 g Calories – 68

309. Stir-fry Vegetables

Preparation Time: 15 minutes
Cooking Time: 10 minutes
Servings: 10
Ingredients:

- 1 Tbsp oil
- 1 onion, sliced
- 1 cup carrots, sliced
- 2 cups broccoli florets
- 2 cups sugar snap peas
- 1 bell pepper, cut into strips
- 1 Tbsp soy sauce
- 1 tsp garlic powder

Directions:

1. Combine onion, carrots, and oil. Stir-fry for 2 minutes. Add other vegetables, stir-fry for another 7 minutes.
2. Add soy sauce, garlic powder. Stir fry until blended.
3. Serve hot.

Nutrition: Carbohydrates – 6 g Fat – 2 g Protein – 2 g Calories – 50

310. 1-Skillet Veggie Hash

Preparation Time: 10 minutes
Cooking Time: 25 minutes
Servings: 4
Ingredients:

- 3 Tbsp olive oil
- 1 onion, diced
- 1 bell pepper, diced
- 3 cloves garlic, minced
- 1 Tbsp sage leaves, chopped
- 3 medium red potatoes, diced
- 1 15-oz can black beans

- 2 cups Swiss chard, chopped
- 1 Tbsp parsley, chopped
- Salt, pepper, to taste

Directions:

1. In a skillet, cook onion, garlic, and potato in olive oil for 20 minutes.

2. Add the beans and Swiss chard to the skillet, cook for another 3 minutes. Season with salt, pepper.

3. Top with parsley and serve.

Nutrition: Carbohydrates – 39 g Fat – 11 g Protein – 9 g Calories – 273

311. Veggie Hash

Preparation Time: 10 minutes
Cooking Time: 40 minutes
Servings: 4
Ingredients:

- 2 medium red potatoes, diced
- 1 can pinto beans
- 1 cup zucchini, chopped
- 1 cup squash, chopped
- 1 red bell pepper, chopped
- ½ cup mushrooms, sliced
- ½ tsp paprika
- Pepper, to taste

Directions:

1. Preheat the oven to 425°F.

2. Season potatoes with salt and pepper and bake on a baking sheet for 25 minutes.

3. In a baking dish, combine the remaining ingredients. Put in oven and bake next to potatoes for 15 minutes.

4. Add potatoes to a baking dish, mix well.

Nutrition: Carbohydrates – 47 g Fat – 14 g Protein – 11 g Calories – 245

312. Grilled Vegetables

Preparation Time: 10 minutes
Cooking Time: 10 minutes
Servings: 6
Ingredients:

- 3 red bell peppers, seeded and halved
- 3 yellow squash, julienned
- 3 zucchinis, sliced into rectangles
- 3 Japanese eggplant, sliced into rectangles
- 1 onion, sliced
- 12 cremini mushrooms
- 1 bunch (1 lb) asparagus, trimmed
- 12 green onions, roots cut off

- 1/4 cup + 2 tbsp olive oil
- Salt and freshly ground black pepper, to taste
- 3 tbsp balsamic vinegar
- 2 garlic cloves, minced
- 1 tsp parsley leaves, chopped
- 1 tsp fresh basil leaves, chopped
- 1/2 tsp fresh rosemary leaves, chopped

Directions

1. Start by preparing and preheating the grill over medium heat.

2. Toss all the veggies with spices, herbs, and oil in a large bowl.

3. Grease the grilling grates and spread the veggies on the grill.

4. Use a tong to flip the veggies.

5. Grill all the veggies until they are slightly charred.

6. Serve warm.

Nutrition: Calories 372 Total Fat 11.1 g Saturated Fat 5.8 g Cholesterol 610 mg Sodium 749 mg Total Carbs 16.9 g Fiber 0.2 g Sugar 0.2 g Protein 13.5 g

313. Mixed Vegetable Platter

Preparation Time: 10 minutes
Cooking Time: 10 minutes
Servings: 6
Ingredients:

- 1/4 cup olive oil
- 2 tbsp maple syrup
- 4 tsp balsamic vinegar
- 1 tsp dried oregano
- 1/2 tsp garlic powder
- 1/8 tsp pepper
- Salt, to taste
- 1 medium red onion, cut into wedges
- 1 lb fresh asparagus, trimmed
- 3 small carrots, cut in half
- 1 large sweet red pepper, cut into strips
- 1 medium yellow summer squash, cut into slices

Directions:

1. Start by whisking the first 7 ingredients in a bowl.

2. Add 3 tablespoons of this marinade to a plastic bag.

3. Toss all the veggies into the plastic bag, then seal it.

4. Shake the bag well, then marinate for 2 hours.

5. Preheat a grill over medium heat and grease its grilling grates.

6. Grill the marinated veggies for 4 minutes per side until crispy

7. Garnish with remaining marinade.

8. Serve.

Nutrition: Calories 114 Total Fat 5.7 g Saturated Fat 2.7 g Cholesterol 75 mg Sodium 94 mg Total Carbs 31.4 g Fiber 0.6 g Sugar 15 g Protein 4.1 g

314. Grilled Chopped Veggies

Preparation Time: 10 minutes

Cooking Time: 10 minutes

Servings: 4

Ingredients:

- 1 red pepper, sliced
- 1 orange bell pepper, sliced
- 1 green bell pepper, sliced
- 1 zucchini squash, sliced
- 1 red onion, quartered
- 12 oz baby portobello mushrooms
- 1 pinch salt
- 1 pinch black pepper
- 1 loaf sourdough bread, sliced
- 3 tbsp olive oil - 4 garlic cloves, minced
- Fresh basil and oregano for garnish

Vinaigrette

- 3 tbsp red wine vinegar
- 1/4 cup fresh basil, chopped
- 2 garlic cloves, minced
- 1 1/2 tbsp maple syrup
- 1 tsp Dijon mustard - 1/4 tsp salt
- 1/4 tsp black pepper
- 1/4 tsp red pepper flakes
- 1/3 cup olive oil

Directions:

1. Make basil vinaigrette by whisking together all ingredients, then set aside.

2. Preheat the grill over high heat.

3. Slice the bread into slices and brush them with a mixture of olive oil and garlic.

4. Season the vegetables with salt and black pepper.

5. Grill the veggies on the hot grill for 3 minutes per side, then transfer them to a sheet pan.

6. Grill the bread slices for 2 minutes per side.

7. Chop the cooked veggies and add them to a bowl.

8. Toss in basil vinaigrette and mix well.

9. Garnish with oregano and basil.

10. Serve with grilled bread.

Nutrition: Calories 249 Total Fat 11.9 g Saturated Fat 1.7 g Cholesterol 78 mg Sodium 79 mg Total Carbs 41.8 g Fiber 1.1 g Sugar 0.3 g Protein 1 g

315. Garlic Grilled Vegetables

Preparation Time: 10 minutes

Cooking Time: 15 minutes

Servings: 6

Ingredients:

- 1 ear corn, cut into chunks
- 1 medium red onion, wedged
- 1 small green bell pepper, diced
- 1 small red bell pepper, diced
- 1 small yellow bell pepper, diced
- 1 small yellow squash, sliced
- 1 cup mushroom halves
- 2 tbsp oil
- 1 tbsp garlic & herb seasoning

Directions:

1. Start by tossing the vegetables with seasonings and oil in a bowl.

2. Thread the veggies on skewers.

3. Prepare and preheat the grill over medium heat.

4. Grill the skewers for 15 minutes while rotating occasionally.

5. Serve warm.

Nutrition: Calories 213 Total Fat 14 g Saturated Fat 8 g Cholesterol 81 mg Sodium 162 mg Total Carbs 53 g Fiber 0.7 g Sugar 19 g Protein 12 g

316. Broccoli and Tomatoes Air Fried Stew

Preparation Time: 18 minutes

Cooking Time: 12 minutes

Servings: 4

Ingredients:

- 2 tsp. coriander seeds
- 1 broccoli head, florets separated
- 1 tbsp. olive oil
- salt and black pepper to taste
- 1 yellow onion, chopped
- 28 ounces canned tomatoes, pureed
- 1 pinch of red pepper, crushed
- 1 garlic clove, minced
- 1 small ginger piece, chopped

Directions:

1. Heat a pan suitable for your air fryer with oil over medium heat, add the onion, salt, pepper and chili, stir and cook for 7 minutes.

2. Add ginger, garlic, coriander seeds, tomatoes and broccoli, mix, place in the air fryer and cook at 360°F for 12 minutes. Divide into bowls and serve.

Nutrition: Calories: 103 Fat: 6.43 g Carbs: 11.47 g Protein: 2.38 g Fiber: 4.9 g

317. Broccoli Mix
Preparation Time: 12 min
Cooking Time: 20 minutes
Servings: 2
Ingredients:

- 2 cups vegetable broth
- 3 cups broccoli
- 1 tbsp. cumin powder
- 1 tbsp. cayenne powder
- 3 green onion
- salt to taste

Directions:
1. Add vegetable broth into the air fryer pot. Combine broccoli, cumin powder, cayenne pepper powder, green onion and salt.
2. Bake at 300°F for 20 minutes. When it's ready, serve and enjoy!

Nutrition: Calories: 1912 Fat: 219.42 g Carbs: 4.54 g Protein: 2.75 g Fiber: 2.7g

318. Brussels Sprouts and Tomatoes Mix
Preparation Time: 15 min
Cooking Time: 10 minutes
Servings: 2
Ingredients:

- salt and black pepper to taste
- 1-pound Brussels sprouts, trimmed
- 6 cherry tomatoes, halved
- 1 tbsp. olive oil
- ¼ cup green onions, chopped

Directions:
1. Spice the Brussels sprouts with salt and pepper, put them in the air fryer, and bake at 350°F for 10 minutes.
2. Transfer them to a bowl, add salt, pepper, cherry tomatoes, onions, greens and olive oil, mix well and serve.

Nutrition: Calories: 184 Fat: 7.57 g Carbs: 26.88 g Protein: 8.46 g Fiber: 9.6g

319. Chinese Bowls
Preparation Time: 25 min
Cooking Time: 15 minutes
Servings: 4
Ingredients:

- 3 tbsp. maple syrup
- 12 ounces firm tofu, cubed
- ¼ cup coconut aminos
- 2 tbsp. lime juice
- 2 tbsp. sesame oil
- 2 cups red quinoa, cooked
- 1-pound fresh Romanesco, roughly chopped
- 1 red bell pepper, chopped
- 3 carrots, chopped
- 8 ounces spinach, torn

Directions:
1. In a bowl, mix the tofu cubes with oil, maple syrup, coconut aminos and lime juice, mix, transfer to your air fryer and cook at 370°F for 15 minutes, stirring frequently.
2. Add the Romanesco, carrot, spinach, pepper and quinoa, toss, divide into bowls and serve.

Nutrition: Calories: 611 Fat: 28.93 g Carbs: 42.09 g Protein: 48.95 g Fiber: 7.4g

320. Chinese Cauliflower Rice
Preparation Time: 30 minutes
Cooking Time: 20 minutes
Servings: 4
Ingredients:

- ½ block firm tofu, cubed
- 4 tbsp. coconut aminos
- 1 cup carrot, chopped
- 1 tsp. turmeric powder
- ½ cup yellow onion, chopped
- 3 cups cauliflower, riced
- 1 tbsp. rice vinegar
- 1½ tsp. sesame oil
- ½ cup peas
- ½ cup broccoli florets, chopped
- 2 garlic cloves, minced
- 1 tbsp. ginger, minced

Directions:
1. In an enormous bowl, combine 2 tbsp. of tofu with coconut aminos, ½ cup onion, turmeric and carrot, mix to cover, transfer to the air fryer and

cook at 370°F for 10 minutes, stirring halfway through cooking.

2. In a bowl, combine the cabbage with rice - cauliflower with the rest of the coconut aminos, the sesame oil, garlic, vinegar, ginger, broccoli and peas, stir, add the tofu mixture from the fryer, mix and cook everything at 370°F for 10 minutes.

3. Divide between plates and serve.

Nutrition: Calories: 111 Fat: 5.44 g Carbs: 11.34 g Protein: 6.56 g Fiber: 3.7g

321. Chinese Long Beans Mix
Preparation Time: 20 minutes
Cooking Time: 10 minutes
Servings: 3
Ingredients:

- 1 tbsp. olive oil
- ½ tsp. coconut aminos
- 1 pinch of salt and black pepper
- 4 long beans, trimmed and sliced
- 4 garlic cloves, minced

Directions:

1. In a pan suitable for your air fryer, combine the long beans with oil, coconut aminos, salt, pepper and garlic, mix, place in your air fryer and cook at 350°F for 10 minutes.

2. Divide between plates and serve.

Nutrition: Calories: 52 Fat: 4.55 g Carbs: 2.77 g Protein: 0.56 g Fiber: 0.3g

322. Cool Tofu Mix
Preparation Time: 20 min
Cooking Time: 10 minutes
Servings: 4
Ingredients:

- 1 cup kale, torn
- 3 ounces firm tofu, pressed and crumbled
- ½ cup broccoli florets
- ¼ cup cherry tomatoes, halved
- ½ cup mushrooms, halved
- ½ cup carrot, grated
- ¼ tsp. onion powder
- ¼ cup microgreens
- ¼ tsp. garlic powder
- ½ tsp. yellow curry powder
- salt and black pepper to taste
- ¼ tsp. sweet paprika
- vegan cooking spray

Directions:

1. Heat your air fryer to 380°F, grease the pan with cooking spray, add the tofu, kale, broccoli, mushrooms, tomatoes, carrots, garlic powder, onion powder, curry, paprika, salt and pepper, mix, cover, and cook for 10 minutes.

2. Divide between plates, add the micro vegetables, mix and serve.

Nutrition: Calories: 50 Fat: 2.13 g Carbs: 4.76 g Protein: 4.52 g Fiber: 1.7g

323. Coriander Endives
Preparation Time: 20 minutes
Cooking Time: 15 minutes
Servings: 4
Ingredients:

- 1 tbsp. coriander, chopped
- 2 endives, trimmed and halved
- 1 tsp. sweet paprika
- 1 pinch of salt and black pepper
- ½ cup almonds, chopped
- 2 tbsp. olive oil
- 2 tbsp. white vinegar

Directions:

1. Toss the endive with cilantro and other ingredients in the air fryer's pan, mix, bake at 350°F for 15 minutes, divide into dishes and serve.

Nutrition: Calories: 68 Fat: 6.92 g Carbs: 1.49g Protein: 0.34 g Fiber: 0.4g

324. Garlic Eggplants
Preparation Time: 20 minutes
Cooking Time: 9 minutes
Servings: 4
Ingredients:

- 2 garlic cloves, minced
- 2 tbsp. olive oil
- 3 eggplants, halved and sliced
- 1 green onion stalk, chopped
- 1 red chili pepper, chopped
- 1 tbsp. ginger, grated
- 1 tbsp. balsamic vinegar
- 1 tbsp. coconut aminos

Directions:

1. Heat a pan suitable for your air fryer with oil over medium-high heat, add the eggplant slices and cook for 2 minutes.

2. Add the chili, garlic, green onions, ginger, coconut aminos and vinegar, place it in the air fryer and cook at 320°F for 7 minutes. Divide between plates and serve.

Nutrition: Calories: 175 Fat: 7.57 g Carbs: 26.74g Protein: 4.41 g Fiber: 12.6 g

325. Hot Cabbage Mix

Preparation Time: 30 min

Cooking Time: 20 minutes

Servings: 2

Ingredients:

- 1 yellow onion, chopped
- ½ cabbage head, chopped
- salt and black pepper to taste
- 1 dash of Tabasco sauce
- 1 cup coconut cream

Directions:

1. Place the cabbage in a pan suitable for your air fryer. Add onion, salt, pepper, Tabasco sauce and coconut cream, mix, put in the air fryer and cook at 400°F for 20 minutes.
2. Divide between plates and serve.

Nutrition: Calories: 506 Fat: 46.59 g Carbs: 23.97g Protein: 7.25 g Fiber: 6.7 g

326. Indian Potatoes

Preparation Time: 10 min

Cooking Time: 12 minutes

Servings: 3

Ingredients:

- 1 tbsp. cumin seeds
- 1 tbsp. coriander seeds
- salt and black pepper to taste
- ½ tsp. red chili powder
- ½ tsp. turmeric powder
- 1 tsp. pomegranate powder
- 2 tbsp. olive oil
- 2 tsp. fenugreek, dried
- 1 tbsp. pickled mango, chopped
- 5 potatoes, boiled, peeled, and cubed

Directions:

1. Heat a pan suitable for your fryer with oil over medium heat, add the coriander and cumin seeds, stir and cook for 2 minutes.
2. Add salt, pepper, turmeric, chili powder, pomegranate powder, mango, fenugreek and potatoes, mix, place in an air fryer and cook at 360°F for 10 minutes.

3. Divide among plates and serve hot.

Nutrition: Calories: 387 Fat: 11.34 g Carbs: 69.12g Protein: 7.36 g Fiber: 9.9 g

327. Leeks Medley

Preparation Time: 22 minutes

Cooking Time:

Servings: 4

Ingredients:

- 1 tbsp. cumin, ground
- 6 leeks, roughly chopped
- 1 tbsp. mint, chopped
- salt and black pepper to taste
- 1 tsp. garlic, minced
- 1 tbsp. parsley, chopped
- 1 drizzle of olive oil

Directions:

1. In a pan suitable for your air fryer, mix the leeks with the cumin, mint, parsley, garlic, salt, pepper and oil, mix, place in your air fryer and cook at 350°F for 12 minutes.
2. Divide the leek mixture between plates and serve.

Nutrition: Calories: 174 Fat: 5.11 g Carbs: 20.68g Protein: 12.57 g Fiber: 2.8 g

328. Mediterranean Chickpeas

Preparation Time: 10 minutes

Cooking Time: 12 minutes

Servings: 2

Ingredients:

- 3 shallots, chopped
- vegan cooking spray
- 2 garlic cloves, minced
- ½ tsp. smoked paprika
- ½ tsp. sweet paprika
- 1 tbsp. parsley, chopped
- ½ tsp. cinnamon powder
- 2 tomatoes, chopped
- salt and black pepper to taste
- 2 cups chickpeas, cooked

Directions:

1. Sprig the air fryer with cooking spray and preheat to 365°F.
2. Add the chives, garlic, sweet and smoked paprika, cinnamon, salt, pepper, tomatoes, parsley and chickpeas, mix, cover and cook for 12 minutes. Divide into bowls and serve.

Nutrition: Calories: 809 Fat: 12.7 g Carbs: 137.65g Protein: 43.29 g Fiber: 27,6 g

329. Mexican Peppers Mix

Preparation Time: 28 minutes

Cooking Time: 16 minutes

Servings: 4

Ingredients:

- ½ cup tomato juice
- 4 bell peppers, cut into medium chunks
- 2 tbsp. jarred jalapenos, chopped
- ¼ cup yellow onion, chopped
- 1 cup tomatoes, chopped
- ¼ cup green peppers, chopped
- 2 cups tomato sauce
- 2 tsp. onion powder
- 1 tsp. cumin, ground
- 1 tsp. chili powder
- ½ tsp. red pepper, crushed
- ½ tsp. garlic powder
- salt and black pepper to taste

Directions:

1. In a pan suitable for your air fryer, combine the tomato juice, jalapeño, tomatoes, onion, green peppers, salt, pepper, onion powder, red pepper, chili powder, garlic powder, oregano and cumin, mix well, mix well in your air fryer and cook at 350°F for 6 minutes

2. Add the peppers and cook at 320°F for another 10 minutes. Divide the pepper mixture between plates and serve.

Nutrition: Calories: 194 Fat: 1.5 g Carbs: 37.35g Protein: 5.59 g Fiber: 10.6 g

330. Paprika Broccoli

Preparation Time: 30 min

Cooking Time: 15 minutes

Servings: 4

Ingredients:

- juice of ½ lemon
- 1 broccoli head, florets separated
- 1 tbsp. olive oil
- 1 tbsp. sesame seeds
- salt and black pepper to taste
- 2 tsp. paprika
- 3 garlic cloves, minced

Directions:

1. In a portable bowl, toss the broccoli with the lemon juice, oil, paprika, salt, pepper, and garlic, and toss to coat.

2. Transfer in the basket of the air fryer, bake at 360°F for 15 minutes, sprinkle sesame seeds, cook another 5 minutes, divide between the plates and serve.

Nutrition: Calories: 55 Fat: 4.8 g Carbs: 3.08g Protein: 0.96 g Fiber: 0.9 g

331. Pumpkin Tasty Seeds

Preparation Time: 16 min

Cooking Time: 15 minutes

Servings: 3

Ingredients:

- 2 tbsp. olive oil
- 1 onion, chopped
- 1 carrot, chopped
- 2 cloves garlic, minced
- 2 tsp. curry powder
- salt to taste
- 4 cups vegetable broth
- 2 tbsp. pumpkin seeds
- parsley to garnish

Directions:

1. Add oil into the air fryer pot. Combine the onion, carrots, garlic, curry powder, vegetable broth, pumpkin seeds and salt. Bake at 300°F for 15 minutes.

2. When it's ready, garnish with the parsley to serve.

Nutrition: Calories: 154 Fat: 11.7 g Carbs: 11.51g Protein: 2.38 g Fiber: 2.3 g

332. Red Potatoes and Green Beans

Preparation Time: 25 minutes

Cooking Time: 15 minutes

Servings: 4

Ingredients:

- 1-pound green beans
- 1-pound red potatoes, cut into wedges
- 2 garlic cloves, minced
- ½ tsp. oregano, dried
- salt and black pepper to taste
- 2 tbsp. olive oil

Directions:

1. In a pan suitable for your air fryer, mix the potatoes with the green beans, garlic, oil, salt, pepper and oregano, mix, place in your air fryer and cook at 380°F for 15 minutes.

2. Divide between plates and serve.

Nutrition: Calories: 171 Fat: 7.47 g Carbs: 24.58g Protein: 3.74 g Fiber: 4.3 g

333. Rice and Veggies

Preparation Time: 20 minutes

Cooking Time: 10 minutes

Servings: 4

Ingredients:

- 1 tbsp. olive oil
- 2 cups rice, cooked
- salt and black pepper to taste
- 2 carrots, chopped

- 10 tbsp. coconut cream
- 4 garlic cloves, minced
- 3 small broccoli florets

Directions:

1. Heat your air fryer to 350°F, add the oil, garlic, carrots, broccoli, salt and pepper, and mix. Add the rice and coconut cream, mix, cover, and cook for 10 minutes.
2. Divide the rice and vegetables between plates and serve.

Nutrition: Calories: 362 Fat: 28.79 g Carbs: 36.79g Protein: 9.94 g Fiber: 14.3 g

334. **White Mushrooms Mix**

Preparation Time: 25 minutes

Cooking Time: 15 minutes

Servings: 2

Ingredients:

- 7 ounces snow peas
- salt and black pepper to taste
- 8 ounces white mushrooms, halved
- 1 tsp. olive oil
- 2 tbsp. coconut aminos
- 1 yellow onion, cut into rings

Directions:

1. In a portable bowl, peas with mushrooms, onion, coconut aminos, oil, salt and pepper, mix well, transfer to a saucepan suitable for your air fryer, place in the air fryer, and cook at 350°F for 15 minutes.
2. Divide between plates and serve.

Nutrition: Calories: 105 Fat: 3.06 g Carbs: 16.18g Protein: 5.8 g Fiber: 5.6 g

335. **Yam Mix**

Preparation Time: 18 minutes

Cooking Time: 8 minutes

Servings: 4

Ingredients:

- ½ tsp. cinnamon powder
- 16 ounces canned candied yams, drained
- ¼ tsp. allspice, ground
- 1 tbsp. flax meal mixed with 2 tbsp. water
- ½ cup coconut sugar
- 2 tbsp. coconut cream
- vegan cooking spray
- ½ cup maple syrup

Directions:

1. In a bowl, combine the sweet potatoes with the cinnamon and all the spices, mash with a fork and mix well.
2. Grease your air fryer with cooking spray, preheat to 400°F, and drizzle with the sweet potato mixture on the bottom.
3. Add the sugar, flax flour, coconut cream and maple syrup, mix gently, cover, and cook for 8 minutes. Divide the sweet potato mixture between plates and serve for breakfast.

Nutrition: Calories: 314 Fat: 2.89 g Carbs: 71.95g Protein: 2.1 g Fiber: 5 g

CHAPTER 7:

Stuffed and Baked Vegetables

336. Instant Savory Gigante Beans

Preparation Time: 10-30 minutes

Cooking Time: 55 minutes

Servings: 6

Ingredients

- 1 lb Gigante Beans soaked overnight
- 1/2 cup olive oil
- 1 onion sliced
- 2 cloves garlic crushed or minced
- 1 red bell pepper (cut into 1/2-inch pieces)
- 2 carrots, sliced
- 1/2 tsp salt and ground black pepper
- 2 tomatoes peeled, grated
- 1 Tbsp celery (chopped)
- 1 Tbsp tomato paste (or ketchup)
- 3/4 tsp sweet paprika
- 1 tsp oregano
- 1 cup vegetable broth

Directions:

1. Soak Gigante beans overnight.
2. Press the SAUTÉ button on your Instant Pot and heat the oil.
3. Sauté onion, garlic, sweet pepper, carrots with a pinch of salt for 3 - 4 minutes; stir occasionally.
4. Add rinsed Gigante beans into your Instant Pot along with all remaining ingredients and stir well.
5. Lock lid into place and set on the MANUAL setting for 25 minutes.
6. When the beep sounds, quick release the pressure by pressing Cancel and twisting the steam handle to the Venting position.
7. Taste and adjust seasonings to taste.
8. Serve warm or cold.
9. Keep refrigerated.

Nutrition:

Calories 502.45, Calories from Fat 173.16, Total Fat 19.63g, Saturated Fat 2.86g

337. Instant Turmeric Risotto

Preparation Time: 10-30 minutes

Cooking Time: 40 minutes

Servings: 4

Ingredients

- 4 Tbsp olive oil
- 1 cup onion
- 1 tsp minced garlic
- 2 cups long-grain rice
- 3 cups vegetable broth
- 1/2 tsp paprika (smoked)
- 1/2 tsp turmeric
- 1/2 tsp nutmeg
- 2 Tbsp fresh basil leaves chopped
- Salt and ground black pepper to taste

Directions:

1. Press the SAUTÉ button on your Instant Pot and heat the oil.
2. Sauté the onion and garlic with a pinch of salt until softened.
3. Add the rice and all remaining ingredients and stir well.
4. Lock lid into place and set on and select the "RICE" button for 10 minutes.
5. Press "Cancel" when the timer beeps and carefully flip the Quick Release valve to let the pressure out.
6. Taste and adjust seasonings to taste.
7. Serve.

Nutrition:

Calories 559.81, Calories from Fat 162.48, Total Fat 18.57g, Saturated Fat 2.4g

338. Nettle Soup with Rice

Preparation Time: 10-30 minutes

Cooking Time: 40 minutes

Servings: 5

Ingredients

- 3 Tbsp of olive oil
- 2 onions finely chopped
- 2 cloves garlic finely chopped
- Salt and freshly ground black pepper
- 4 medium potatoes cut into cubes
- 1 cup of rice
- 1 Tbsp arrowroot
- 2 cups vegetable broth
- 2 cups of water
- 1 bunch of young nettle leaves packed
- 1/2 cup fresh parsley finely chopped
- 1 tsp cumin

Directions:

1. Heat olive oil in a large pot.
2. Sauté onion and garlic with a pinch of salt until softened.
3. Add potato, rice, and arrowroot; sauté for 2 to 3 minutes.

4. Pour broth and water, stir well, cover and cook over medium heat for about 20 minutes.

5. Cook over medium heat for about 20 minutes.

6. Add young nettle leaves, parsley, and cumin; stir and cook for 5 to 7 minutes.

7. Transfer the soup to a blender and blend until combined well.

8. Taste and adjust salt and pepper.

9. Serve hot.

Nutrition:

Calories 421.76, Calories from Fat 88.32, Total Fat 9.8g, Saturated Fat 1.54g

339. Okra with Grated Tomatoes (Slow Cooker)

Preparation Time: 10-30 minutes

Cooking Time: 3 hours and 10 minutes

Servings: 4

Ingredients

- 2 lbs fresh okra cleaned
- 2 onions finely chopped
- 2 cloves garlic finely sliced
- 2 carrots sliced
- 2 ripe tomatoes grated
- 1 cup of water
- 4 Tbsp olive oil
- Salt and ground black pepper
- 1 Tbsp fresh parsley finely chopped

Directions:

1. Add okra to your Crock-Pot: sprinkle with a pinch of salt and pepper.

2. Add in chopped onion, garlic, carrots, and grated tomatoes; stir well.

3. Pour water and oil, season with salt, pepper, and give a good stir.

4. Cover and cook on LOW for 2-3 hours or until tender. Open the lid and add fresh parsley; stir.

5. Taste and adjust salt and pepper. Serve hot.

Nutrition:

Calories 223.47, Calories from Fat 123.5, Total Fat 14g, Saturated Fat 1.96g,

340. Oven-baked Smoked Lentil 'Burgers'

Preparation Time: 10-30 minutes

Cooking Time: 1 hour and 20 minutes

Servings: 6

Ingredients

- 1 1/2 cups dried lentils

- 3 cups of water
- Salt and ground black pepper to taste
- 2 Tbsp olive oil
- 1 onion finely diced
- 2 cloves minced garlic
- 1 cup button mushrooms sliced
- 2 Tbsp tomato paste
- 1/2 tsp fresh basil finely chopped
- 1 cup chopped almonds
- 3 tsp balsamic vinegar
- 3 Tbsp coconut aminos
- 1 tsp liquid smoke
- 3/4 cup silken tofu soft
- 3/4 cup corn starch

Directions:

1. Cook lentils in salted water until tender or for about 30-35 minutes; rinse, drain, and set aside.

2. Heat oil in a frying skillet and sauté onion, garlic and mushrooms for 4 to 5 minutes; stir occasionally.

3. Stir in the tomato paste, salt, basil, salt, and black pepper; cook for 2 to 3 minutes.

4. Stir in almonds, vinegar, coconut aminos, liquid smoke, and lentils.

5. Remove from heat and stir in blended tofu and corn starch.

6. Keep stirring until all ingredients are combined well.

7. Form mixture into patties and refrigerate for an hour.

8. Preheat oven to 350°F.

9. Line a baking dish with parchment paper and arrange patties on the pan.

10. Bake for 20 to 25 minutes.

11. Serve hot with buns, green salad, tomato sauce. . . etc.

Nutrition:

Calories 439.12, Calories from Fat 148.97, Total Fat 17.48g, Saturated Fat 1.71g

341. Powerful Spinach and Mustard Leaves Puree

Preparation Time: 10-30 minutes

Cooking Time: 50 minutes

Servings: 4

Ingredients

- 2 Tbsp almond butter
- 1 onion finely diced

- 2 Tbsp minced garlic
- 1 tsp salt and black pepper (or to taste)
- 1 lb mustard leaves, cleaned, rinsed
- 1 lb frozen spinach thawed
- 1 tsp coriander - 1 tsp ground cumin
- 1/2 cup almond milk

Directions:

1. Press the SAUTÉ button on your Instant Pot and heat the almond butter.
2. Sauté onion, garlic, and a pinch of salt for 2-3 minutes; stir occasionally.
3. Add spinach and the mustard greens and stir for a minute or two.
4. Season with salt and pepper, coriander, and cumin; give a good stir.
5. Lock lid into place and set on the MANUAL setting for 15 minutes.
6. Use Quick Release - turn the valve from sealing to venting to release the pressure.
7. Transfer mixture to a blender, add almond milk, and blend until smooth.
8. Taste and adjust seasonings.
9. Serve.

Nutrition:

Calories 180.53, Calories from Fat 82.69, Total Fat 10g, Saturated Fat 0.65g

342. Quinoa and Rice Stuffed Peppers (Oven-Baked)

Preparation Time: 10-30 minutes

Cooking Time: 35 minutes

Servings: 8

Ingredients

- 3/4 cup long-grain rice
- 8 bell peppers (any color)
- 2 Tbsp olive oil
- 1 onion finely diced
- 2 cloves chopped garlic
- 1 can (11 oz) crushed tomatoes
- 1 tsp cumin -. 1 tsp coriander
- 4 Tbsp ground walnuts
- 2 cups cooked quinoa
- 4 Tbsp chopped parsley
- Salt and ground black pepper to taste

Directions:

1. Preheat oven to 400°F/200°C.
2. Boil rice and drain in a colander.

3. Cut the top stem section of the pepper off, remove the remaining pith and seeds, rinse the peppers.
4. Heat oil in a large frying skillet, and sauté onion and garlic until soft.
5. Add tomatoes, cumin, ground almonds, salt, pepper, and coriander; stir well and simmer for 2 minutes stirring constantly.
6. Remove from the heat and add the rice, quinoa, and parsley; stir well. Taste and adjust salt and pepper. Fill the peppers with a mixture, and place peppers cut side-up in a baking dish; drizzle with little oil. Bake for 15 minutes. Serve warm.

Nutrition:

Calories 335.69, Calories from Fat 83.63, Total Fat 9.58g, Saturated Fat 1.2g

343. Silk Tofu Penne with Spinach

Preparation Time: 10-30 minutes

Cooking Time: 25 minutes

Servings: 4

Ingredients

- 1 lb penne, uncooked
- 12 oz of frozen spinach, thawed
- 1 cup silken tofu mashed
- 1/2 cup soy milk (unsweetened)
- 1/2 cup vegetable broth
- 1 Tbsp white wine vinegar
- 1/2 tsp Italian seasoning
- Salt and ground pepper to taste

Directions:

1. Cook penne pasta; rinse and drain in a colander.
2. Drain spinach well.
3. Place spinach with all remaining ingredients in a blender and beat until smooth.
4. Pour the spinach mixture over the pasta.
5. Taste and adjust the salt and pepper.
6. Store pasta in an airtight container in the refrigerator for 3 to 5 days.

Nutrition:

Calories 492.8, Calories from Fat 27.06, Total Fat 3.07g, Saturated Fat 0.38g

344. Slow-Cooked Butter Beans, Okra and Potatoes Stew

Preparation Time: 10-30 minutes

Cooking Time: 6 hours and 5 minutes

Servings: 6

Ingredients

- 2 cups frozen butter (lima) beans, thawed

- 1 cup frozen okra, thawed
- 2 large Russet potatoes cut into cubes
- 1 can (6 oz) whole-kernel corn, drained
- 1 large carrot sliced
- 1 green bell pepper finely chopped
- 1 cup green peas
- 1/2 cup chopped celery
- 1 medium onion finely chopped
- 2 cups vegetable broth
- 2 cans (6 oz) tomato sauce
- 1 cup of water
- 1/2 tsp salt and freshly ground black pepper

Directions:

1. Combine all ingredients in your Slow Cooker; give a good stir.
2. Cover and cook on HIGH for 6 hours.
3. Taste, adjust seasonings, and serve hot.

Nutrition:

Calories 241.71, Calories from Fat 11.22, Total Fat 1.28g, Saturated Fat 0.27g

345. Soya Minced Stuffed Eggplants

Preparation Time: 10-30 minutes
Cooking Time: 1 hour
Servings: 4
Ingredients

- 2 eggplants
- 1/3 cup sesame oil
- 1 onion finely chopped
- 2 garlic cloves minced
- 1 lb soya mince* see note
- Salt and ground black pepper
- 1/3 cup almond milk
- 2 Tbsp fresh parsley, chopped
- 1/3 cup fresh basil chopped
- 1 tsp fennel powder
- 1 cup of water
- 4 Tbsp tomato paste (fresh or canned)

Directions:

1. Rinse and slice the eggplant in half lengthwise.
2. Submerge sliced eggplant into a container with salted water.
3. Soak soya mince in water for 10 to 15 minutes.
4. Preheat the oven to 400 F.
5. Rinse eggplant and dry with a clean towel.
6. Heat oil in a large frying skillet, and sauté onion and garlic with a pinch of salt until softened.

7. Add drained soya mince, and cook over medium heat until cooked through.
8. Add all remaining ingredients (except water and tomato paste) and cook for a further 5 minutes; remove from heat.
9. Scoop out the seed part of each eggplant.
10. Spoon in the filling and arrange stuffed eggplants onto the large baking dish.
11. Dissolve tomato paste into the water and pour evenly over eggplants.
12. Bake for 20 to 25 minutes.
13. Serve warm.

Nutrition:

Calories 287.32, Calories from Fat 141.77, Total Fat 16.42g, Saturated Fat 2.02g

346. Triple Beans and Corn Salad

Preparation Time: 10-30 minutes
Cooking Time: 15 minutes
Servings: 8
Ingredients

- 1 can (15 oz) kidney beans, drained and rinsed
- 1 can (15 oz) white beans, drained and rinsed
- 1 can (15 oz) black beans, rinsed and drained
- 1 can (11 oz) frozen corn kernels thawed
- 1 green bell pepper, chopped
- 1 red onion, chopped
- 1 clove crushed garlic
- 1 Tbsp salt and ground black pepper to taste
- 1/2 cup olive oil
- 3 Tbsp red wine vinegar
- 3 Tbsp lemon juice
- 1/4 cup chopped fresh cilantro
- 1/2 Tbsp ground cumin

Directions:

1. In a large bowl, combine beans, corn, pepper, onion, and garlic.
2. Season salad with salt and pepper; stir to combine well.
3. In a separate bowl, whisk together olive oil, red wine vinegar, lemon juice, cilantro, and cumin.
4. Pour olive oil dressing over salad, and toss to combine well.
5. Refrigerate for one hour and serve.

Nutrition:

Calories 696, Calories from Fat 155.25, Total Fat 17.62g, Saturated Fat 3g

347. Vegan Raw Pistachio Flaxseed 'Burgers'

Preparation Time: 10-30 minutes

Cooking Time: 15 minutes

Servings: 4

Ingredients

- 1 cup ground flaxseed
- 1 cup pistachio finely sliced
- 2 cups cooked spinach drained
- 2 Tbsp sesame oil
- 4 cloves garlic finely sliced
- 2 Tbsp lemon juice, freshly squeezed
- Sea salt to taste

Directions:

1. Add all ingredients into a food processor or high-speed blender; process until combined well.
2. Form mixture into patties.
3. Refrigerate for one hour.
4. Serve with your favorite vegetable dip.

Nutrition:

Calories 273, Calories from Fat 184.41, Total Fat 21.6g, Saturated Fat 2.72g,

348. Vegan Red Bean 'Fricassee'

Preparation Time: 10-30 minutes

Cooking Time: 40 minutes

Servings: 4

Ingredients

- 4 Tbsp olive oil
- 1 onion finely sliced
- 2 cloves garlic finely chopped
- Salt and freshly ground black pepper to taste
- 1 can (15 oz) red beans
- 1 large carrot grated
- 1 1/2 cup vegetable broth
- 1 cup of water
- 1 can (6 oz) tomato paste
- 1 tsp ground paprika
- 1 tsp parsley

Directions:

1. Heat oil in a large pot and sauté onion and garlic with a pinch of salt until soft.
2. Add red beans together with all remaining ingredients and stir well.
3. In a separate pan, sauté onion and garlic in the olive oil.

4. Reduce heat to medium, and simmer for 25 to 30 minutes.
5. Taste and adjust salt and pepper if needed.
6. Serve hot.

Nutrition:

Calories 318.72, Calories from Fat 136.25, Total Fat 15.44g, Saturated Fat 2.31g

349. Baked Cheesy Eggplant with Marinara

Preparation Time: 5 minutes

Cooking Time: 45 minutes

Servings: 3

Ingredients

- 1 clove garlic, sliced
- 1 large eggplant
- 1 tablespoon olive oil
- 1/2 pinch salt, or as needed
- 1/4 cup and 2 tablespoons dry bread crumbs
- 1/4 cup and 2 tablespoons ricotta cheese
- 1/4 cup grated Parmesan cheese
- 1/4 cup water, plus more as needed
- 1/4 teaspoon red pepper flakes
- 1-1/2 cups prepared marinara sauce
- 1-1/2 teaspoons olive oil
- 2 tablespoons shredded pepper jack cheese
- salt and freshly ground black pepper to taste

Directions:

1. Cut eggplant crosswise into 5 pieces. Peel and chop two pieces into ½-inch cubes.
2. Lightly grease the baking pan of Instant Crisp Air Fryer with 1 tbsp olive oil for 5 minutes, heat oil at 390°F. Add half eggplant strips and cook for 2 minutes per side. Transfer to a plate.
3. Add 1 ½ tsp olive oil and add garlic. Cook for a minute. Add chopped eggplants. Season with pepper flakes and salt. Cook for 4 minutes. Lower heat to 330°F. and continues cooking eggplants until soft, around 8 minutes more.
4. Stir in water and marinara sauce. Cook for 7 minutes until heated through. Stirring every now and then. Transfer to a bowl.
5. In a bowl, whisk well pepper, salt, pepper jack cheese, Parmesan cheese, and ricotta. Evenly spread cheeses over eggplant strips and then fold in half.
6. Lay folded eggplant in a baking pan. Pour the marinara sauce on top.
7. In a small bowl, whisk well olive oil and bread crumbs. Sprinkle all over the sauce.

8. Air Frying. Lock the air fryer lid. Cook for 15 minutes at 390°F until tops are lightly browned.

9. Serve and enjoy.

Nutrition:

Calories: 405; Fat: 21.4g; Protein: 12.7g

350. Creamy Spinach Quiche

Preparation Time: 10 minutes

Cooking Time: 20 minutes

Servings: 4

Ingredients

- 1 Premade quiche crust, chilled and rolled flat to a 7-inch round
- eggs
- ¼ cup of milk
- Pinch of salt and pepper
- 1 clove of garlic, peeled and finely minced
- ½ cup of cooked spinach, drained and coarsely chopped
- ¼ cup of shredded mozzarella cheese
- ¼ cup of shredded cheddar cheese

Directions:

2. Preheat the Instant Crisp Air Fryer to 360°F.

3. Press the premade crust into a 7-inch pie tin or any appropriately sized glass or ceramic heat-safe dish. Press and trim at the edges if necessary. With a fork, pierce several holes in the dough to allow air circulation and prevent cracking of the crust while cooking.

4. In a mixing bowl, beat the eggs until fluffy and until the yolks and white are evenly combined.

5. Add milk, garlic, spinach, salt and pepper, and half the cheddar and mozzarella cheese to the eggs. Set the rest of the cheese aside for now, and stir the mixture until completely blended. Make sure the spinach is not clumped together, but rather spread among the other ingredients.

6. Pour the mixture into the pie crust slowly and carefully to avoid splashing. The mixture should almost fill the crust, but not completely – leaving a ¼ inch of crust at the edges.

7. Air Frying. Lock the air fryer lid. Set the air-fryer timer for 15 minutes. After 15 minutes, the Instant Crisp Air Fryer will shut off, the quiche will already be firm and the crust begins to brown. Sprinkle the rest of the cheddar and mozzarella cheese on top of the quiche filling. Reset the Instant Crisp Air Fryer at 360 degrees for 5 minutes. After 5 minutes, when the Instant Crisp Air Fryer shuts off, the cheese will have formed an exquisite crust on top and the quiche will be golden brown and perfect. Remove from

the Instant Crisp Air Fryer using oven mitts or tongs, and set on a heat-safe surface to cool for a few minutes before cutting.

Nutrition:

Calories: 285; Fat: 20.5g; Protein: 8.6g

351. Buttery Carrots with Pancetta

Preparation Time: 5 minutes

Cooking Time: 39 minutes

Servings: 4 - 6

Ingredients

- 4 ounces pancetta, diced
- 1 medium leek, white and pale green parts only, sliced lengthwise, washed, and thinly sliced
- ¼ cup moderately sweet white wine, such as a dry Riesling - 1-pound baby carrots
- ½ teaspoon ground black pepper
- 2 tablespoons unsalted butter, cut into small bits

Directions:

1. Put the pancetta in the Instant Crisp Air Fryer turned to the "Air Fry" function and use the Time Adjustment button to adjust the cooking time to 5 minutes. Add the leek; cook, often stirring, until softened. Pour in the wine and scrape up any browned bits at the bottom of the pot as it comes to a simmer.

2. Add the carrots and pepper; stir well. Scrape and pour the contents of the Instant Crisp Air Fryer into a 1-quart, round, high-sided soufflé or baking dish. Dot with the bits of butter. Lay a piece of parchment paper on top of the dish, then a piece of aluminum foil. Seal the foil tightly over the baking dish. Set the Instant Crisp Air Fryer rack inside, and pour in 2 cups of water. Use aluminum foil to build a sling for the baking dish; lower the baking dish into the cooker.

3. High pressure for 7 minutes. Lock the Pressure-cooking lid on the Instant Crisp Air Fryer and then cook for 7 minutes. To get a 7-minutes cook time, press the "Pressure" button and use the Time Adjustment button to adjust the cooking time to 7 minutes.

4. Pressure Release. Use the quick-release method to return the pot's pressure to normal.

5. Finish the dish. Close the Air Fryer Lid. Select BROIL, and set the time to 5 minutes. Select START to begin. Cook until the top is browned.

6. Unlock and open the pot. Use the foil sling to lift the baking dish out of the cooker. Uncover, stir well, and serve.

Nutrition:

Calories: 285; Fat: 20.5g; Protein: 8.6g

352. Stuffed Mushrooms

Preparation Time: 7 minutes

Cooking Time: 8 minutes

Servings: 12

Ingredients:

- 2 Rashers Bacon, Diced
- ½ Onion, Diced
- ½ Bell Pepper, Diced
- 1 Small Carrot, Diced
- 24 Medium Size Mushrooms (Separate the caps & stalks)
- 1 cup Shredded Cheddar Plus Extra for the Top
- ½ cup Sour Cream

Directions:

1. Chop the mushroom stalks finely and fry them up with the bacon, onion, pepper and carrot at 350°F for 8 minutes.
2. When the veggies are fairly tender, stir in the sour cream & the cheese. Keep on the heat until the cheese has melted and everything is mixed nicely.
3. Now grab the mushroom caps and heap a plop of filling on each one.
4. Place in the fryer basket and top with a little extra cheese.

Nutrition:

Calories: 285; Fat: 20.5g; Protein: 8.6g

353. Winter Vegetarian Frittata

Preparation Time: 5 minutes

Cooking Time: 30 minutes

Servings: 4

Ingredients:

- 1 leek, peeled and thinly sliced into rings
- 2 cloves garlic, finely minced
- 3 medium-sized carrots, finely chopped
- 2 tablespoons olive oil
- 6 large-sized eggs
- Sea salt and ground black pepper, to taste
- 1/2 teaspoon dried marjoram, finely minced
- 1/2 cup yellow cheese of choice

Directions:

1. Sauté the leek, garlic, and carrot in hot olive oil until they are tender and fragrant; reserve.
2. In the meantime, preheat your Instant Crisp Air Fryer to 330 degrees F.
3. In a bowl, whisk the eggs along with the salt, ground black pepper, and marjoram.

4. Then, grease the inside of your baking dish with a nonstick cooking spray. Pour the whisked eggs into the baking dish. Stir in the sautéed carrot mixture. Top with the cheese shreds.
5. Air Frying. Place the baking dish in the Instant Crisp Air Fryer cooking basket. Lock the air fryer lid. Cook for about 30 minutes and serve warm.

Nutrition:

Calories: 285; Fat: 20.5g; Protein: 8.6g

354. Braised Red Cabbage with Apples

Preparation Time: 5 minutes

Cooking Time: 54 minutes

Servings: 4

Ingredients

- 4 thin bacon slices, chopped
- 1 small red onion, chopped
- 1 medium tart green apple, such as Granny Smith, peeled, cored, and chopped
- 1 teaspoon dried thyme
- ¼ teaspoon ground allspice
- ¼ teaspoon ground mace
- 1 tablespoon packed dark brown sugar
- 1 tablespoon balsamic vinegar
- 1 medium red cabbage (about 2 pounds), cored and thinly sliced
- ½ cup chicken broth

Directions:

1. Lock the air fryer lid. Fry the bacon in the Instant Crisp Air Fryer turned to the "Air Fry" function, until crisp, about 4 minutes.
2. Add the onion to the pot; cook, often stirring, until soft, about 4 minutes. Add the apple, thyme, allspice, and mace. Cook about 1 minute, stirring all the while, until fragrant. Stir in the brown sugar and vinegar; keep stirring until bubbling, about 1 minute.
3. Add the cabbage; toss well to mix evenly with the other ingredients. Drizzle the broth over the cabbage mixture.
4. High pressure for 13 minutes. Lock the Pressure-cooking Lid on the Instant Crisp Air Fryer and then cook for 13 minutes. To get a 13-minutes cook time, press the "Pressure" button, and use the Time Adjustment button to adjust the cooking time to 13 minutes.
5. Pressure Release. Use the quick-release method to return the pot to normal pressure.
6. Unlock and open the pot.

7. Close the Air Fryer Lid. Select BROIL, and set the time to 5 minutes. Select START to begin. Cook until the top is browned.
8. Serve.

Nutrition:
Calories: 285; Fat: 20.5g; Protein: 8.6g

355. Cheddar, Squash, And Zucchini Casserole

Preparation Time: 5 minutes
Cooking Time: 30 minutes
Servings: 4
Ingredients

- 1 egg
- 5 saltine crackers, or as needed, crushed
- 2 tablespoons bread crumbs
- 1/2-pound yellow squash, sliced
- 1/2-pound zucchini, sliced
- 1/2 cup shredded Cheddar cheese
- 1-1/2 teaspoons white sugar
- 1/2 teaspoon salt
- 1/4 onion, diced
- 1/4 cup biscuit baking mix
- 1/4 cup butter

Directions:
1. Lightly grease the baking pan of Instant Crisp Air Fryer with cooking spray. Add onion, zucchini, and yellow squash. Cover pan with foil and for 15 minutes, cook at 360° F or until tender.
2. Stir in salt, sugar, egg, butter, baking mix, and cheddar cheese. Mix well. Fold in crushed crackers. Top with bread crumbs.
3. Air Frying Lock the air fryer lid. Cook for 15 minutes at 390° F until tops are lightly browned.
4. Serve and enjoy.

Nutrition:
Calories: 285; Fat: 20.5g; Protein: 8.6g

356. Fresh Tomato Basil Tart

Preparation Time: 30 minutes
Cooking Time: 55 minutes
Servings: 8
Ingredients:

- 2/3 cup whole wheat flour
- 1/3 cup flour, all purpose
- ½ cup cold butter
- 5 Tbsp cold water
- 4 tomatoes, sliced
- 3 cups mozzarella cheese, shredded

- Salt, pepper, to taste

Directions:
1. Mix the flours, butter, and water to form a dough. Refrigerate for 30 minutes.
2. Roll out the dough. Bake in a tart pan at 350°F for 15 minutes.
3. Top with cheese and tomato. Garnish with salt, pepper.
4. Bake for another 30 minutes. Serve warm.

Note:
For ovo-lacto vegetarian, lacto vegetarian, Pescatarian diets.

Nutrition: Carbohydrates – 14 g Fat – 23 g Protein – 13 g Calories – 300

357. Quinoa Stuffed Bell Peppers

Preparation Time: 15 minutes
Cooking Time: 10 minutes
Servings: 4
Ingredients:

- 4 bell peppers, halved, hollowed out
- ½ cup quinoa, cooked
- 1/3 cup sun-dried tomatoes
- 12 black olives, halved
- ½ cup baby spinach
- 2 cloves garlic, minced
- Salt, pepper, to taste

Directions:
1. Bake the hollowed-out peppers in an oven at 400°F for 10 minutes.
2. Mix the cooked quinoa with the remaining ingredients.
3. Stuff peppers. Serve.

Nutrition: Carbohydrates – 19 g Fat – 5 g Protein – 3 g Calories – 126

358. Stuffed Peppers

Preparation Time: 15 minutes
Cooking Time: 15 minutes
Servings: 6
Ingredients:

- 1 cup Kalamata olives, halved
- 6 oz. goat cheese, crumbled
- ¼ cup basil, chopped
- 2 Tbsp garlic cloves, chopped
- 1 lb sweet peppers, halved, seeded
- Salt, pepper, to taste

Directions:
1. Preheat oven to 450°F.
2. Combine all ingredients and stir well. Stuff the peppers with the mixture.

3. Broil peppers for 15 min on a baking sheet.

Note:

For ovo-lacto vegetarian, lacto vegetarian, Pescatarian diets.

Nutrition: Carbohydrates – 15 g Fat – 7 g Protein – 3 g Calories – 130

359. Roasted Vegetable Hummus Plate

Preparation Time: 15 minutes

Cooking Time: 10 minutes

Servings: 1

Ingredients:

- 4 asparagus spears
- 1 pepper, seeded, cut into strips
- 1 cup mixed salad greens
- ¼ cup hummus

Directions:

1. Preheat oven to 425°F. Combine asparagus and pepper strips with olive oil and put them on the baking sheet. Roast for about 10 minutes.

2. Put the salad greens on a serving plate, top with roasted vegetables. Dip vegetables in hummus.

Nutrition: Carbohydrates – 24 g Fat – 7 g Protein – 9 g Calories – 173

360. Stuffed Baked Potato

Preparation Time: 20 minutes

Cooking Time: 1 hour 15 minutes

Servings: 2

Ingredients:

- 2 large Russet potatoes
- ½ cup non-dairy milk
- 4 Tbsp oil-free hummus
- 1 cup cooked vegetables, chopped
- ½ tsp hot sauce
- Salt, pepper, to taste

Directions

1. Preheat oven to 375°F.

2. Bake the potatoes for 1 hour. Split in half and scoop out the flesh.

3. Mash the potato flesh with the remaining ingredients.

4. Spoon the mixture back into the potato shells.

5. Bake for 15 minutes. Serve immediately.

Nutrition: Carbohydrates – 56 g Fat – 8 g Protein – 9 g Calories – 310

361. Oil-Free Rainbow Roasted Vegetables

Preparation Time: 5 minutes

Cooking Time: 25 minutes

Servings: 4

Ingredients:

- 3 cups red bell peppers, chopped
- 2 cups carrots, chopped
- 1 2/3 cup zucchini, chopped
- 1 cup broccoli florets
- 1 cup onions, chopped
- 1 Tbsp dried thyme

Directions:

1. Preheat oven to 400°F.

2. Put the vegetables on the baking sheet, add the thyme.

3. Bake for about 25 minutes.

4. Serve or store the veggies in a sealed container.

Nutrition: Carbohydrates – 56 g Fat – 8 g Protein – 9 g Calories – 310

362. Kaftan-Style Chickpea "Meatball" Pitas

Preparation Time: 10 minutes

Cooking Time: 35 minutes

Servings: 4

Ingredients:

- 1 tablespoon unsalted butter
- ½ cup finely chopped mushrooms
- 1 (15-ounce) can chickpeas, drained and rinsed
- 2 teaspoons garlic paste or minced garlic
- 1 tablespoon dried oregano
- 1 teaspoon ground allspice
- ½ teaspoon kosher salt
- ¼ teaspoon freshly ground black pepper
- ½ cup panko
- 1 large egg
- 2 pita rounds
- 3 tablespoons Tzatziki, plus more for serving
- Cherry tomatoes, quartered, for serving
- 1 Red onion slices
- Baby spinach for serving

Directions:

1. Preheat the oven to 350°F. Line a baking sheet with parchment paper.

2. Melt the butter in a large skillet over medium heat. Add the mushrooms and sauté until softened, about 5 minutes. Add the chickpeas, garlic, oregano, allspice, salt, and pepper, and

sauté for another 5 minutes. Coarsely mash the chickpeas with a fork and place everything in a bowl to cool for 5 minutes.

3. Add the panko and egg, and stir with a metal spoon to mix well.

4. Use an ice cream scooper or large spoon to form 8 balls. Place the balls on the prepared baking sheet. Bake for 20 minutes.

5. Cut the pita rounds in half and carefully open the pockets. Spread the tzatziki in the pockets and place 2 chickpea balls, a few tomatoes, red onion, and spinach leaves inside.

6. Serve with additional tzatziki.

Nutrition Per Serving: Calories: 285; total fat: 11g; total carbs: 56g; fiber: 11g; sugar: 7g; protein: 16g; sodium: 725mg

363. Spanish Paella

Preparation Time: 15 minutes

Cooking Time: 40 minutes

Servings: 6

Ingredients:

- 1 cup short-grain rice, such as Arborio
- 1 teaspoon olive oil
- 1¾ cup vegetable broth
- 1 teaspoon kosher salt
- 1 teaspoon freshly ground black pepper
- ¾ teaspoon smoked paprika
- 4 jarred cinquillo or 2 roasted red peppers, cut into thin strips
- 1 (8-ounce) can fire-roasted tomatoes with their juices
- 1 (15-ounce) can chickpeas, drained and rinsed
- 1 cup thinly sliced scallions
- ¼ cup sliced black olives, such as Kalamata
- ¼ cup pine nuts
- ¼ cup chopped fresh parsley or cilantro

Directions:

1. Arrange an oven rack in the center of the oven and preheat the oven to 350°F.

2. In a small bowl, toss the rice in the olive oil and spread it in an even layer on a rimmed baking sheet. Toast in the oven for 5 minutes.

3. Meanwhile, in a medium saucepan over medium heat, bring the broth, salt, pepper, and paprika to a simmer.

4. Add the peppers, tomatoes, and chickpeas to the baking sheet with the toasted rice and stir to combine. Pour the broth over the rice and vegetables. Cover the baking sheet tightly with aluminum foil. Bake for 20 minutes.

5. Uncover the baking sheet and stir the rice. Scatter the scallions, olives, and pine nuts over the rice. Bake, uncovered, for another 15 minutes, or until the rice is tender, with a slightly crispy skin.

6. Transfer the mixture to a serving dish and toss with the parsley.

FLEXITARIAN TIP: Cut a ½-pound cooked Linguae Portuguese sausage link into ½-inch slices and add them in step 5. Gently press the slices down so that the rice separates around them, allowing the rice to crisp.

Nutrition Per Serving: Calories: 300; total fat: 8g; total carbs: 47g; fiber: 7g; sugar: 5g; protein: 11g; sodium: 916mg

364. Veggie and Chickpea Fajitas

Preparation Time: 15 minutes

Cooking Time: 30 minutes

Servings: 6

Ingredients:

- 2 bell peppers, any color, sliced into ¼-inch strips
- 1 large red onion, sliced into ½-inch wedges
- 2 zucchinis, sliced into ½-inch wedges
- 4 ears corn, kernels sliced off the cob (about 4 cups)
- 1 (15-ounce) can chickpeas, drained and rinsed
- 2 tablespoons olive oil
- 1 tablespoon freshly squeezed lime juice
- 2 teaspoons ground cumin
- 2 teaspoons kosher salt, divided
- 1 teaspoon garlic powder
- 1 teaspoon freshly ground black pepper, divided
- 8 (8-inch) flour tortillas

Directions:

1. Preheat the oven to 450°F. Place one oven rack in the upper third of the oven and another in the lower third. Line two baking sheets with parchment paper.

2. Place the peppers, onion, zucchini, corn kernels, and chickpeas in a large bowl. Add the olive oil, lime juice, cumin, 1 teaspoon of salt, garlic powder, and ½ teaspoon of pepper, and toss to thoroughly coat the vegetables.

3. Spread the vegetables in an even layer on the baking sheets. Be careful not to crowd the vegetables too close together, as this promotes steaming instead of roasting. Roast for 20 minutes. Stir the vegetables around a little, sprinkle with the remaining salt and pepper, and roast for another 10 minutes, or until the vegetables are tender and just a little charred on the edges.

4. Wrap the tortillas in aluminum foil. Place on one of the baking sheets for the final 5 minutes of roasting.

5. Divide the filling between the tortillas and serve. Finish as desired with your favorite toppings.

Nutrition Per Serving: Calories: 440; Total Fat: 12g; Total Carbs: 74g; Fiber: 11g; Sugar: 11g; Protein: 15g; Sodium: 1337mg

365. Acorn Squash, Sweet Potatoes, And Apples

Preparation Time: 20 minutes

Cooking Time: 20 minutes

Servings: 4

Ingredients:

- 1 acorn squash, halved, seeded, and cut into ½-inch wedges
- 2 sweet potatoes, sliced crosswise into 1-inch disks
- 2 apples, such as Honey crisp or Fuji, cored and quartered
- 1 red onion, cut into 6 wedges
- ¼ cup Miso Butter
- 2 tablespoons maple syrup
- 1½ teaspoons kosher salt, divided
- 1 cup water
- 1 cup freshly squeezed orange juice
- 1 cup quinoa
- Roasted Pumpkin Seeds or store-bought, for serving

Directions:

1. Preheat the oven to 425°F.

2. Place the squash, sweet potatoes, apples, and onion on a rimmed baking sheet.

3. In a small bowl, whisk together the miso butter, maple syrup, and 1 teaspoon of salt. Drizzle this over the vegetables and apple slices, and toss with your hands to completely coat.

4. Arrange the vegetables and apple slices in a single layer, with as much space between each other as possible. Roast until everything is tender and slightly caramelized, 15 to 18 minutes.

5. Meanwhile, in a saucepan on the stovetop, bring the water and orange juice to a boil with the remaining ½ teaspoon salt. Add the quinoa. Reduce the heat to low, cover, and cook at a low simmer until the quinoa is tender, about 15 minutes. Remove the pan from the heat, and keep it covered for 5 minutes. The quinoa will be very tender, and you will see a little curlicue in each seed when it is done.

6. Spread the cooked quinoa on a serving plate, and spoon the roasted vegetables and apple slices over it. Top with roasted pumpkin seeds.

FLEXITARIAN TIP: Add 1-pound bone-in split chicken breasts to the baking sheet, and arrange so that the breasts are directly on the pan, not on the squash or potatoes. Lightly oil the chicken and sprinkle with salt and pepper. Bake everything in a preheated 350°F oven for 40 minutes or until the internal temperature of the chicken reaches 165°F. Serve everything over the quinoa, and top with the pumpkin seeds.

Nutrition Per Serving: Calories: 447; Total Fat: 9g; Total Carbs: 85g; Fiber: 12g; Sugar: 27g; Protein: 10g; Sodium: 1261mg

366. Stuffed Roasted Sweet Potatoes

Preparation Time: 20 minutes

Cooking Time: 30 minutes

Servings: 4

Ingredients:

- 4 medium sweet potatoes, halved lengthwise
- 1 red onion, quartered
- 1½ tablespoons olive oil, divided
- ½ teaspoon kosher salt, divided
- ¼ teaspoon freshly ground black pepper
- 1 (15-ounce) can chickpeas, drained, rinsed, and dried
- ½ teaspoon smoked paprika
- ½ teaspoon ground cinnamon
- ¼ teaspoon ground cumin
- 2 cups baby spinach
- 1 avocado, peeled and diced
- ½ cup halved cherry tomatoes
- ½ cup Tzatziki

Directions:

1. Preheat the oven to 400°F. Lightly oil a baking sheet.

2. Rub the sweet potatoes and onion in 1 tablespoon of olive oil and season with ¼ teaspoon of salt and pepper. Arrange in a single layer on the baking sheet, with the potatoes cut-side down.

3. In a medium bowl, toss the chickpeas in the remaining ½ tablespoon of olive oil and ¼ teaspoon of salt. Place them on the same baking sheet with the sweet potatoes and onion.

4. Roast for 20 minutes, then flip the potatoes cut-side up and shift the onion and chickpeas around a bit. Roast for another 10 minutes, or until the sweet potatoes are tender when pierced with a fork.

5. Break up the sweet potato flesh with a fork and place it in a medium bowl, and arrange the potato skins on a serving plate. Lightly mash the sweet potato filling with a fork, and add the roasted onion and chickpeas, paprika, cinnamon, and cumin. Toss together and add spinach, avocado, and tomatoes. Toss again and scoop into the potato skins.

6. Drizzle with the tzatziki. Serve any extra sauce on the side.

Nutrition Per Serving: Calories: 482; Total Fat: 24g; Total Carbs: 56g; Fiber: 15g; Sugar: 13g; Protein: 13g; Sodium: 610mg

367. Cheesy Hash Browns Egg Bake

Preparation Time: 10 minutes

Cooking Time: 6 minutes

Servings: 6

Ingredients:

- ½ tablespoon unsalted butter, at room temperature
- 1 tablespoon olive oil
- 1 medium onion, diced
- 1 medium bell pepper, any color, diced
- 1½ teaspoons kosher salt, divided
- 1 cup baby spinach
- ½ (30-ounce) bag frozen hash brown potatoes
- 10 large eggs
- 1 cup milk
- ¼ cup sour cream
- 1 tablespoon Dijon mustard
- ¼ teaspoon freshly ground black pepper
- 1½ cups shredded sharp Cheddar cheese

Directions:

1. Preheat the oven to 375°F. Grease a 9-by-13-inch baking dish with butter.

2. Warm the oil in a medium skillet over medium heat. Add the onion, bell pepper, and ½ teaspoon of salt and sauté, stirring occasionally, until the vegetables are soft, about 5 minutes. Add the spinach and toss until wilted, about 1 minute.

3. Transfer the mixture to the baking dish. Add the hash browns, stir to combine, and spread into an even layer on the bottom of the dish.

4. In a large bowl, whisk together the eggs, milk, sour cream, mustard, remaining 1 teaspoon of salt, and pepper. Fold in the cheese. Pour the mixture over the vegetables.

5. Bake for 45 minutes, or until the top is lightly browned and a knife inserted in the middle comes out clean. Let cool for 5 minutes before slicing.

Nutrition Per Serving: Calories: 356; total fat: 26g; total carbs: 12g; fiber: 1g; sugar: 5g; protein: 20g; sodium: 945mg

368. Breakfast Taquitos Casserole

Preparation Time: 10 minutes

Cooking Time: 30 minutes

Servings: 4

Ingredients:

- 2 tablespoons unsalted butter, divided
- 1½ cups frozen hash browns
- 1 teaspoon kosher salt, divided
- ½ teaspoon freshly ground black pepper, divided
- 6 large eggs, beaten
- 6 (8-inch) flour tortillas
- 1 avocado, halved and sliced lengthwise into thin wedges
- ½ cup salsa verde
- 2/3 cup grated Cheddar cheese

Directions:

1. Preheat the oven to 400°F.

2. Melt 1 tablespoon of butter in a medium skillet over medium heat. Add the hash browns, season them with ½ teaspoon of salt and ¼ teaspoon of black pepper, and cook according to the package instructions, for about 15 minutes.

3. While the hash browns are cooking, melt the remaining 1 tablespoon of butter in another medium skillet over medium heat. Add the eggs, season with the remaining ½ teaspoon of salt and ¼ teaspoon of pepper, and scramble, for about 15 minutes.

4. Wrap the tortillas in a paper towel and warm them in the microwave for about 20 seconds so that they are more pliable.

5. Lay the tortillas on a flat surface and spoon the hash browns mixture and eggs horizontally across each tortilla, slightly below the center. Place the avocado slices over the eggs. Fold the bottom edge of each tortilla up tightly over the filling, rolling from bottom to top. Place the tortillas seam-side down in a 12-by-12-inch baking dish. Drizzle the salsa over the taquitos and sprinkle with the cheese.

6. Bake until the cheese has melted, 12 to 15 minutes.

Nutrition Per Serving: Calories: 611; total fat: 37g; total carbs: 50g; fiber: 6g; sugar: 3g; protein: 22g; sodium: 1457mg

369. Potato Gratin

Preparation Time: 10 minutes

Cooking Time: 35 minutes

Servings: 6

Ingredients:

- 2 tablespoons unsalted butter, plus more for greasing
- 2 teaspoons garlic paste or minced garlic
- 1½ cups 2% milk
- ¼ cup heavy (whipping) cream
- ¼ cup vegetable broth
- 1 red bell pepper, diced
- ¾ teaspoon kosher salt
- ¼ teaspoon freshly ground black pepper
- 2 cups shredded Gruyère or Swiss cheese, divided - 2 pounds mixed yellow Yukon Gold potatoes and sweet potatoes
- ¼ cup finely chopped fresh chives

Directions:

1. Preheat the oven to 375°F and butter a 2-quart baking dish.
2. In a medium pot, combine the butter, garlic, milk, cream, broth, bell pepper, salt, and pepper, and bring to a gentle simmer over medium heat, about 5 minutes. Be careful not to bring it to a boil. Stir in 1 cup of cheese.
3. While the liquid is coming to a simmer, slice the potatoes thinly. I use a handheld mandolin on the thinnest setting, which slices potatoes 1/8-inch-thick in about 30 seconds. You can use a chef's knife, too, but it will take longer.
4. Layer the potatoes in the prepared baking dish and pour the hot milk mixture over them. Sprinkle the remaining 1 cup of cheese on top. Bake for 30 minutes. Allow resting for 10 minutes before serving.
5. Serve with a flourish of chives.

Nutrition Per Serving: Calories: 374; total fat: 20g; total carbs: 32g; fiber: 2g; sugar: 5g; protein: 16g; sodium: 452mg

370. Swiss Chard and Orzo Gratin

Preparation Time: 10 minutes

Cooking Time: 20 minutes

Servings: 4

Ingredients:

- ½ tablespoon unsalted butter, at room temperature
- ¾ cup orzo
- 1 (15-ounce) can cannellini or other white beans, drained and rinsed - 1 tablespoon olive oil
- ½ cup chopped shallot
- ½ teaspoon kosher salt
- 1 teaspoon freshly ground black pepper
- 1 cup heavy (whipping) cream
- 1½ cups vegetable broth
- 2 large bunches Swiss chard, stems removed and leaves coarsely chopped
- ½ cup coarsely chopped jarred roasted red peppers - ¾ cup grated Parmesan cheese
- 1/3 cup Lemony Breadcrumbs

Directions:

1. Preheat the oven to 400°F. Grease a 12-by-12-inch baking dish with butter.
2. Bring a medium pot of well-salted water to a boil. Add the orzo and cook for 5 minutes. The pasta won't be done in that time, but it will finish cooking in the oven. Drain the orzo and spread it across the bottom of the baking dish.
3. Evenly spread the beans over the orzo.
4. Heat the olive oil in a medium skillet over medium heat. Add the shallot, salt, and pepper, and sauté until the shallot is completely softened, about 4 minutes. Stir in the cream and broth and bring to a boil. Reduce the heat to low and simmer until the liquid is reduced to 2 cups, about 10 minutes. Add the Swiss chard in batches, tossing to coat. Cook until the chard is wilted, about 3 minutes.
5. Pour the chard and sauce into the baking dish. Top with the roasted red peppers, followed by the cheese. Finish with a flurry of breadcrumbs.
6. Bake for 25 to 30 minutes.

INGREDIENT TIP: Swiss chard is a vitamin and mineral powerhouse, boasting high levels of vitamin K and potassium. Additionally, it's loaded with antioxidants for fighting inflammation and free-radical damage and for promoting eye health.

Nutrition Per Serving: Calories: 544; total fat: 33g; total carbs: 46g; fiber: 9g; sugar: 4g; protein: 20g; sodium: 944mg

371. Baked Cheesy Broccoli with Quinoa

Preparation Time: 15 minutes

Cooking Time: 45 minutes

Servings: 8

Ingredients:

- ½ tablespoon unsalted butter, at room temperature

- 1½ cups bite-size broccoli pieces or frozen broccoli florets
- 2 large eggs
- 1 cup whole or 2% milk
- 1 tablespoon Dijon mustard
- 1 teaspoon kosher salt
- ½ teaspoon freshly ground black pepper
- ½ yellow onion, diced
- 2 teaspoons garlic paste or 5 garlic cloves, minced
- 2 cups cooked quinoa (see here)
- 1½ cups grated Cheddar cheese
- ½ cup Lemony Breadcrumbs

Directions:

1. Preheat the oven to 350°F. Grease a 9-by-13-inch baking dish with butter.
2. Fill a medium pot with about 2 inches of water and add a steamer. Bring to a boil and add the broccoli. Steam until just tender, about 10 minutes.
3. In a large bowl, beat together the eggs, milk, mustard, salt, and pepper. Fold in the broccoli, onion, garlic, quinoa, and cheese. Pour everything into the baking dish. Top with breadcrumbs.
4. Bake for 35 to 40 minutes.

SUBSTITUTION TIP: Swap cauliflower for the broccoli, and add 1½ teaspoon of curry powder.

Nutrition Per Serving: Calories: 243; total fat: 11g; total carbs: 23g; fiber: 3g; sugar: 3g; protein: 13g; sodium: 538mg

372. Mexican Casserole

Preparation Time: 15 minutes

Cooking Time: 35 minutes

Servings: 6

Ingredients:

- Olive oil, for greasing
- 1 cup cooked quinoa (here)
- 1 (15-ounce) can black beans, drained and rinsed
- 1 cup fresh or frozen corn kernels
- 1 cup halved cherry tomatoes
- 2 bell peppers, any color, diced
- 1/3 cup chopped red onion
- 1½ tablespoons freshly squeezed lime juice
- 1½ teaspoons ground cumin
- 2 teaspoons kosher salt
- 2 cups grated Monterey Jack cheese, divided
- 2 tablespoons Roasted Pumpkin Seeds (optional)

Directions:

1. Preheat the oven to 400°F. Lightly oil a 9-by-11-inch baking dish.
2. Combine the cooked quinoa, black beans, corn, tomatoes, bell peppers, onion, lime juice, cumin, salt, and 1½ cups of cheese in a large bowl.
3. Spread evenly in the baking dish. Bake for 30 minutes.
4. Spread the remaining ½ cup of cheese over the top of the casserole. Bake for another 5 minutes.
5. Sprinkle the pumpkin seeds over the top (if using). Serve warm.

Nutrition Per Serving: Calories: 325; total fat: 14g; total carbs: 33g; fiber: 8g; sugar: 4g; protein: 18g; sodium: 1037mg

373. Curried Cauliflower Tetrazzini

Preparation Time: 15 minutes

Cooking Time: 55 minutes

Servings: 6

Ingredients:

- 2½ tablespoons unsalted butter, divided
- 1 medium cauliflower, cut into bite-size pieces, or 4 cups frozen florets
- 2 small leeks, white and light greens parts only, diced
- 2 tablespoons olive oil
- 2½ teaspoons curry powder, divided
- 2 teaspoons kosher salt, divided
- 1 teaspoon freshly ground black pepper, divided
- ½ pound spaghetti
- 3 tablespoons all-purpose flour
- 1 cup milk
- ½ cup sour cream or plain Greek yogurt
- 1 tablespoon garlic paste or minced garlic
- 1 cup grated Parmesan cheese, divided
- ½ cup Lemony Breadcrumbs

Directions:

1. Preheat the oven to 400°F. Grease a 9-by-13-inch baking dish with ½ tablespoon of butter.
2. Place the cauliflower and leeks in the baking dish and toss with the olive oil, 1½ teaspoon of curry powder, 1 teaspoon of salt, and ½ teaspoon of black pepper. Roast until the cauliflower pieces are tender and begin to brown, about 30 minutes.
3. While the cauliflower is roasting, bring a large pot of salted water to a boil. Break the spaghetti into thirds so that the noodles are all around 3 inches long. Add to the boiling water and cook according to the package instructions. Drain.

4. Melt the remaining 2 tablespoons of butter in a medium skillet over medium heat. Once it's bubbling, whisk in the flour until the butter becomes a paste. Cook, stirring constantly, for 1 minute. Gradually whisk the milk into the paste. Add the sour cream, garlic, ½ cup of Parmesan, the remaining 1 teaspoon of salt, ½ teaspoon of black pepper, and 1 teaspoon of curry powder, and whisk to thoroughly mix.

5. Fold in the cooked spaghetti. Pour this over the roasted vegetables and lightly toss it together. Top with the remaining ½ cup of Parmesan and the breadcrumbs.

6. Lower the oven temperature to 350°F and bake for 15 minutes, or until bubbly.

SUBSTITUTION TIP: Swap out the cauliflower for broccoli or butternut squash.

FLEXITARIAN TIP: Since this dish was made famous with chicken, just replace the cauliflower with 4 cups diced cooked chicken. You can eliminate the curry if you wish, but it goes well with chicken, too.

Nutrition Per Serving: Calories: 425; total fat: 18g; total carbs: 52g; fiber: 6g; sugar: 7g; protein: 17g; sodium: 1104mg

374. Baked Eggplant Parmesan

Preparation Time: 20 minutes
Cooking Time: 1 hour
Servings: 8
Ingredients:

- 2 medium eggplants
- 2 large eggs, beaten
- 1/3 cup basil pesto
- 4 cups Italian breadcrumbs
- 1 cup Parmesan cheese
- 6 cups Tomato-Mushroom Raga or 2 (24-ounce) jars tomato-based pasta sauce
- 2 cups shredded mozzarella cheese, divided

Directions:

1. Preheat the oven to 375°F. Line a baking sheet with parchment paper.

2. Slice the eggplants into ½-inch rounds.

3. In a small bowl, whisk the eggs together with the pesto. In a second small bowl, combine the breadcrumbs and Parmesan cheese.

4. Dip an eggplant slice into the egg-pesto mixture. Let the excess drip off, then dip it in the breadcrumbs and coat it on both sides. Place the slice on the baking sheet. Repeat for all the eggplant slices, and arrange them on the baking sheet in a single layer.

5. Bake the eggplant for 20 minutes. Flip the slices over and bake for 20 minutes more.

6. Increase the oven temperature to 400°F. In a 9-by-13-inch baking dish, spread just enough tomato sauce to cover the bottom. Layer half of the eggplant slices in the bottom of the baking dish. Top them with one-third of the mozzarella, followed by half of the remaining sauce. Repeat with the remaining eggplant, the second third of the cheese, and the remaining sauce. Sprinkle the remaining cheese over the top.

7. Bake for 20 minutes. Let sit for 5 minutes before serving.

INGREDIENT TIP: If you find eggplant to be too bitter for you, place the slices in a colander and generously salt them. Let them sit for 1 hour. Rinse, pat dry, and begin the recipe with step 3.

Nutrition Per Serving: Calories: 423; total fat: 14g; total carbs: 57g; fiber: 10g; sugar: 15g; protein: 19g; sodium: 1015mg

CHAPTER 8:

Rice & Grains

375. Classic Garlicky Rice

Preparation Time: 4 minutes

Cooking Time: 16 minutes

Servings: 4

Ingredients

- 4 tablespoons olive oil
- 4 cloves garlic, chopped
- 1 ½ cup white rice
- 2 ½ cups vegetable broth

Directions:

1. In a saucepan, heat the olive oil over a moderately high flame. Add in the garlic and sauté for about 1 minute or until aromatic.
2. Add in the rice and broth. Bring to a boil; immediately turn the heat to a gentle simmer.
3. Cook for about 15 minutes or until all the liquid has been absorbed. Fluff the rice with a fork, season with salt and pepper, and serve hot!

Nutrition Per Serving: Calories: 422; Fat: 15.1g; Carbs: 61.1g; Protein: 9.3g

376. Brown Rice with Vegetables and Tofu

Preparation Time: 12 minutes

Cooking Time: 33 minutes

Servings: 4

Ingredients

- 4 teaspoons sesame seeds
- 2 spring garlic stalks, minced
- 1 cup spring onions, chopped
- 1 carrot, trimmed and sliced
- 1 celery rib, sliced
- 1/4 cup dry white wine
- 10 ounces tofu, cubed
- 1 ½ cups long-grain brown rice, rinsed thoroughly
- 2 tablespoons soy sauce
- 2 tablespoons tahini
- 1 tablespoon lemon juice

Directions:

1. In a wok or large saucepan, heat 2 teaspoons of the sesame oil over medium-high heat. Now, cook the garlic, onion, carrot and celery for about 3 minutes, stirring periodically to ensure even cooking.
2. Add the wine to deglaze the pan and push the vegetables to one side of the wok. Add in the remaining sesame oil and fry the tofu for 8 minutes, stirring occasionally.

3. Bring 2 ½ cups of water to a boil over medium-high heat. Bring to a simmer and cook the rice for about 30 minutes or until it is tender; fluff the rice and stir it with the soy sauce and tahini.
4. Stir the vegetables and tofu into the hot rice; add a few drizzles of the fresh lemon juice and serve warm. Bon appétit!

Nutrition Per Serving: Calories: 410; Fat: 13.2g; Carbs: 60g; Protein: 14.3g

377. Basic Amaranth Porridge

Preparation Time: 30 minutes

Cooking Time: 5 minutes

Servings: 4

Ingredients

- 3 cups water
- 1 cup amaranth
- 1/2 cup coconut milk
- 4 tablespoons agave syrup
- A pinch of kosher salt
- A pinch of grated nutmeg

Directions:

1. Bring the water to a boil over medium-high heat; add in the amaranth and turn the heat to a simmer.
2. Let it cook for about 30 minutes, stirring periodically to prevent the amaranth from sticking to the bottom of the pan.
3. Stir in the remaining ingredients and continue to cook for 1 to 2 minutes more until cooked through. Bon appétit!

Nutrition: Per Servings: Calories: 261; Fat: 4.4g; Carbs: 49g; Protein: 7.3g

378. Country Cornbread with Spinach

Preparation Time: 25 minutes

Cooking Time: 25 minutes

Servings: 8

Ingredients:

- 1 tablespoon flaxseed meal
- 1 cup all-purpose flour
- 1 cup yellow cornmeal
- 1/2 teaspoon baking soda
- 1/2 teaspoon baking powder
- 1 teaspoon kosher salt
- 1 teaspoon brown sugar
- A pinch of grated nutmeg
- 1 ¼ cups oat milk, unsweetened

- 1 teaspoon white vinegar
- 1/2 cup olive oil
- 2 cups spinach, torn into pieces

Directions:

1. Start by preheating your oven to 420 degrees F. Now, spritz a baking pan with a nonstick cooking spray.
2. To make the flax eggs, mix the flaxseed meal with 3 tablespoons of water. Stir and let it sit for about 15 minutes.
3. In a mixing bowl, thoroughly combine the flour, cornmeal, baking soda, baking powder, salt, sugar and grated nutmeg.
4. Gradually add in the flax egg, oat milk, vinegar and olive oil, whisking constantly to avoid lumps. Afterward, fold in the spinach.
5. Scrape the batter into the prepared baking pan. Bake your cornbread for about 25 minutes or until a tester inserted in the middle comes out dry and clean.
6. Let it stand for about 10 minutes before slicing and serving. Bon appétit!

Nutrition Per Serving: Calories: 282; Fat: 15.4g; Carbs: 30g; Protein: 4.6g

379. Rice Pudding with Currants

Preparation Time: 5 minutes
Cooking Time: 40 minutes
Servings: 4
Ingredients

- 1 ½ cup water - 1 cup white rice
- 2 ½ cups oat milk, divided
- 1/2 cup white sugar
- A pinch of salt
- A pinch of grated nutmeg
- 1 teaspoon ground cinnamon
- 1/2 teaspoon vanilla extract
- 1/2 cup dried currants

Directions:

1. In a saucepan, bring the water to a boil over medium-high heat. Immediately turn the heat to a simmer, add in the rice and let it cook for about 20 minutes.
2. Add in the milk, sugar and spices and continue to cook for 20 minutes more, stirring constantly to prevent the rice from sticking to the pan.
3. Top with dried currants and serve at room temperature. Bon appétit!

Nutrition Per Serving: Calories: 423; Fat: 5.3g; Carbs: 85g; Protein: 8.8g

380. Millet Porridge with Sultanas

Preparation Time: 5 minutes
Cooking Time: 20 minutes
Servings: 3
Ingredients

- 1 cup water
- 1 cup coconut milk
- 1 cup millet, rinsed
- 1/4 teaspoon grated nutmeg
- 1/4 teaspoon ground cinnamon
- 1 teaspoon vanilla paste
- 1/4 teaspoon kosher salt
- 2 tablespoons agave syrup
- 4 tablespoons sultana raisins

Directions:

1. Place the water, milk, millet, nutmeg, cinnamon, vanilla and salt in a saucepan; bring to a boil.
2. Turn the heat to a simmer and let it cook for about 20 minutes; fluff the millet with a fork and spoon into individual bowls.
3. Serve with agave syrup and sultanas. Bon appétit!

Nutrition Per Serving: Calories: 353; Fat: 5.5g; Carbs: 65.2g; Protein: 9.8g

381. Quinoa Porridge with Dried Figs

Preparation Time: 5 minutes
Cooking Time: 20 minutes
Servings: 3
Ingredients:

- 1 cup white quinoa, rinsed
- 2 cups almond milk
- 4 tablespoons brown sugar - A pinch of salt
- 1/4 teaspoon grated nutmeg
- 1/2 teaspoon ground cinnamon
- 1/2 teaspoon vanilla extract
- 1/2 cup dried figs, chopped

Directions:

1. Place the quinoa, almond milk, sugar, salt, nutmeg, cinnamon and vanilla extract in a saucepan.
2. Bring it to a boil over medium-high heat. Turn the heat to a simmer and let it cook for about 20 minutes; fluff with a fork.
3. Divide between three serving bowls and garnish with dried figs. Bon appétit!

Nutrition Per Serving: Calories: 414; Fat: 9g; Carbs: 71.2g; Protein: 13.8g

382. Bread Pudding with Raisins

Preparation Time: 15 minutes

Cooking Time: 45 minutes

Servings: 4

Ingredients:

- 4 cups day-old bread, cubed
- 1 cup brown sugar
- 4 cups coconut milk
- 1/2 teaspoon vanilla extract
- 1 teaspoon ground cinnamon
- 2 tablespoons rum
- 1/2 cup raisins

Directions:

1. Start by preheating your oven to 360 degrees F. Lightly oil a casserole dish with a nonstick cooking spray.
2. Place the cubed bread in the prepared casserole dish.
3. In a mixing bowl, thoroughly combine the sugar, milk, vanilla, cinnamon, rum and raisins. Pour the custard evenly over the bread cubes.
4. Let it soak for about 15 minutes.
5. Bake in the preheated oven for about 45 minutes or until the top is golden and set. Bon appétit!

Nutrition Per Serving: Calories: 474; Fat: 12.2g; Carbs: 72g; Protein: 14.4g

383. Bulgur Wheat Salad

Preparation Time: 12 minutes

Cooking Time: 13 minutes

Servings: 4

Ingredients

- 1 cup bulgur wheat
- 1 ½ cups vegetable broth
- 1 teaspoon sea salt
- 1 teaspoon fresh ginger, minced
- 4 tablespoons olive oil
- 1 onion, chopped
- 8 ounces canned garbanzo beans, drained
- 2 large roasted peppers, sliced
- 2 tablespoons fresh parsley, roughly chopped

Directions:

1. In a deep saucepan, bring the bulgur wheat and vegetable broth to a simmer; let it cook, covered, for 12 to 13 minutes.
2. Let it stand for about 10 minutes and fluff with a fork.

3. Add the remaining ingredients to the cooked bulgur wheat; serve at room temperature or well-chilled. Bon appétit!

Nutrition Per Serving: Calories: 359; Fat: 15.5g; Carbs: 48.1g; Protein: 10.1g

384. Rye Porridge with Blueberry Topping

Preparation Time: 9 minutes

Cooking Time: 6 minutes

Servings: 3

Ingredients

- 1 cup rye flakes
- 1 cup water
- 1 cup coconut milk
- 1 cup fresh blueberries
- 1 tablespoon coconut oil
- 6 dates, pitted

Directions:

1. Add the rye flakes, water and coconut milk to a deep saucepan; bring to a boil over medium-high. Turn the heat to a simmer and let it cook for 5 to 6 minutes.
2. In a blender or food processor, puree the blueberries with coconut oil and dates.
3. Ladle into three bowls and garnish with the blueberry topping.
4. Bon appétit!

Nutrition Per Serving: Calories: 359; Fat: 11g; Carbs: 56.1g; Protein: 12.1g

385. Coconut Sorghum Porridge

Preparation Time: 10 minutes

Cooking Time: 15 minutes

Servings: 2

Ingredients

- 1/2 cup sorghum
- 1 cup water
- 1/2 cup coconut milk
- 1/4 teaspoon grated nutmeg
- 1/4 teaspoon ground cloves
- 1/2 teaspoon ground cinnamon
- Kosher salt, to taste
- 2 tablespoons agave syrup
- 2 tablespoons coconut flakes

Directions:

1. Place the sorghum, water, milk, nutmeg, cloves, cinnamon and kosher salt in a saucepan; simmer gently for about 15 minutes.

2. Spoon the porridge into serving bowls. Top with agave syrup and coconut flakes. Bon appétit!

Nutrition Per Serving: Calories: 289; Fat: 5.1g; Carbs: 57.8g; Protein: 7.3g

386. Dad's Aromatic Rice

Preparation Time: 5 minutes

Cooking Time: 15 minutes

Servings: 4

Ingredients

- 3 tablespoons olive oil
- 1 teaspoon garlic, minced
- 1 teaspoon dried oregano
- 1 teaspoon dried rosemary
- 1 bay leaf
- 1 ½ cup white rice
- 2 ½ cups vegetable broth
- Sea salt and cayenne pepper, to taste

Directions:

1. In a saucepan, heat the olive oil over a moderately high flame. Add in the garlic, oregano, rosemary and bay leaf; sauté for about 1 minute or until aromatic.
2. Add in the rice and broth. Bring to a boil; immediately turn the heat to a gentle simmer.
3. Cook for about 15 minutes or until all the liquid has absorbed. Fluff the rice with a fork, season with salt and pepper, and serve immediately.

Bon appétit!

Nutrition Per Serving: Calories: 384; Fat: 11.4g; Carbs: 60.4g; Protein: 8.3g

387. Everyday Savory Grits

Preparation Time: 5 minutes

Cooking Time: 30 minutes

Servings: 4

Ingredients

- 2 tablespoons vegan butter
- 1 sweet onion, chopped
- 1 teaspoon garlic, minced
- 4 cups water
- 1 cup stone-ground grits
- Sea salt and cayenne pepper, to taste

Directions:

1. In a saucepan, melt the vegan butter over medium-high heat. Once hot, cook the onion for about 3 minutes or until tender.
2. Add in the garlic and continue to sauté for 30 seconds more or until aromatic; reserve.

3. Bring the water to a boil over a moderately high heat. Stir in the grits, salt and pepper. Turn the heat to a simmer, cover, and continue to cook for about 30 minutes or until cooked through.
4. Stir in the sautéed mixture and serve warm. Bon appétit!

Nutrition Per Serving: Calories: 238; Fat: 6.5g; Carbs: 38.7g; Protein: 3.7g

388. Greek-Style Barley Salad

Preparation Time: 5 minutes

Cooking Time: 30 minutes

Servings: 4

Ingredients

- 1 cup pearl barley
- 2 ¾ cups vegetable broth
- 2 tablespoons apple cider vinegar
- 4 tablespoons extra-virgin olive oil
- 2 bell peppers, seeded and diced
- 1 shallot, chopped
- 2 ounces sun-dried tomatoes in oil, chopped
- 1/2 green olives, pitted and sliced
- 2 tablespoons fresh cilantro, roughly chopped

Directions:

1. Bring the barley and broth to a boil over medium-high heat; now, turn the heat to a simmer.
2. Continue to simmer for about 30 minutes until all the liquid has absorbed; fluff with a fork.
3. Toss the barley with the vinegar, olive oil, peppers, shallots, sun-dried tomatoes and olives; toss to combine well.
4. Garnish with fresh cilantro and serve at room temperature or well-chilled. Enjoy!

Nutrition Per Serving: Calories: 378; Fat: 15.6g; Carbs: 50g; Protein: 10.7g

389. Easy Sweet Maize Meal Porridge

Preparation Time: 5 minutes

Cooking Time: 10 minutes

Servings: 2

Ingredients

- 2 cups water
- 1/2 cup maize meal
- 1/4 teaspoon ground allspice
- 1/4 teaspoon salt
- 2 tablespoons brown sugar
- 2 tablespoons almond butter

Directions:

1. In a saucepan, bring the water to a boil; then, gradually add in the maize meal and turn the heat to a simmer.
2. Add in the ground allspice and salt. Let it cook for 10 minutes.
3. Add in the brown sugar and almond butter and gently stir to combine. Bon appétit!

Nutrition Per Serving: Calories: 278; Fat: 12.7g; Carbs: 37.2g; Protein: 3g

390. Mom's Millet Muffins

Preparation Time: 10 minutes
Cooking Time: 25 minutes
Servings: 8
Ingredients

- 2 cups whole-wheat flour
- 1/2 cup millet
- 2 teaspoons baking powder
- 1/2 teaspoon salt - 1 cup coconut milk
- 1/2 cup coconut oil, melted
- 1/2 cup agave nectar
- 1/2 teaspoon ground cinnamon
- 1/4 teaspoon ground cloves
- A pinch of grated nutmeg
- 1/2 cup dried apricots, chopped

Directions:

1. Begin by preheating your oven to 400 degrees F. Lightly oil a muffin tin with nonstick oil.
2. In a mixing bowl, mix all dry ingredients. In a separate bowl, mix the wet ingredients. Stir the milk mixture into the flour mixture; mix just until evenly moist and do not overmix your batter.
3. Fold in the apricots and scrape the batter into the prepared muffin cups.
4. Bake the muffins in the preheated oven for about 15 minutes or until a tester inserted in the center of your muffin comes out dry and clean.
5. Let it stand for 10 minutes on a wire rack before unmolding and serving. Enjoy!

Nutrition Per Serving: Calories: 367; Fat: 15.9g; Carbs: 53.7g; Protein: 6.5g

391. Ginger Brown Rice

Preparation Time: 15 minutes
Cooking Time: 30 minutes
Servings: 4
Ingredients

- 1 ½ cups brown rice, rinsed
- 2 tablespoons olive oil

- 1 teaspoon garlic, minced
- 1 (1-inch) piece ginger, peeled and minced
- 1/2 teaspoon cumin seeds
- Sea salt and ground black pepper, to taste

Directions:

1. Place the brown rice in a saucepan and cover with cold water by 2 inches. Bring to a boil.
2. Turn the heat to a simmer and continue to cook for about 30 minutes or until tender.
3. In a sauté pan, heat the olive oil over medium-high heat. Once hot, cook the garlic, ginger and cumin seeds until aromatic.
4. Stir the garlic/ginger mixture into the hot rice; season with salt and pepper and serve immediately. Bon appétit!

Nutrition Per Serving: Calories: 318; Fat: 8.8g; Carbs: 53.4g; Protein: 5.6g

392. Sweet Oatmeal "Grits"

Preparation Time: 5 minutes
Cooking Time: 15 minutes
Servings: 4
Ingredients

- 1 ½ cups steel-cut oats, soaked overnight
- 1 cup almond milk - 2 cups water
- A pinch of grated nutmeg
- A pinch of ground cloves
- A pinch of sea salt
- 4 tablespoons almonds, slivered
- 6 dates, pitted and chopped
- 6 prunes, chopped

Directions:

1. In a deep saucepan, bring the steel cut oats, almond milk and water to a boil.
2. Add in the nutmeg, cloves and salt. Immediately turn the heat to a simmer, cover, and continue to cook for about 15 minutes or until they've softened. Then, spoon the grits into four serving bowls; top them with the almonds, dates and prunes.

Bon appétit!

Nutrition Per Serving: Calories: 380; Fat: 11.1g; Carbs: 59g; Protein: 14.4g

393. Freekeh Bowl with Dried Figs

Preparation Time: 15 minutes
Cooking Time: 35 minutes
Servings: 2
Ingredients

- 1/2 cup freekeh, soaked for 30 minutes, drained

- 1 1/3 cups almond milk
- 1/4 teaspoon sea salt
- 1/4 teaspoon ground cloves
- 1/4 teaspoon ground cinnamon
- 4 tablespoons agave syrup
- 2 ounces dried figs, chopped

Directions:

1. Place the freekeh, milk, sea salt, ground cloves and cinnamon in a saucepan. Bring to a boil over medium-high heat.
2. Immediately turn the heat to a simmer for 30 to 35 minutes, stirring occasionally to promote even cooking.
3. Stir in the agave syrup and figs. Ladle the porridge into individual bowls and serve. Bon appétit!

Nutrition Per Serving: Calories: 458; Fat: 6.8g; Carbs: 90g; Protein: 12.4g

394. **Cornmeal Porridge with Maple Syrup**

Preparation Time: 5 minutes

Cooking Time: 15 minutes

Servings: 4

Ingredients

- 2 cups water
- 2 cups almond milk
- 1 cinnamon stick
- 1 vanilla bean
- 1 cup yellow cornmeal
- 1/2 cup maple syrup

Directions:

1. In a saucepan, bring the water and almond milk to a boil. Add in the cinnamon stick and vanilla bean.
2. Gradually add in the cornmeal, stirring continuously; turn the heat to a simmer. Let it simmer for about 15 minutes.
3. Drizzle the maple syrup over the porridge and serve warm. Enjoy!

Nutrition Per Serving: Calories: 328; Fat: 4.8g; Carbs: 63.4g; Protein: 6.6g

395. **Garlic and White Bean Soup**

Preparation Time: 1 hour

Cooking Time: 10 minutes

Servings: 4

Ingredients:

- 45 ounces cooked cannellini beans

- 1/4 teaspoon dried thyme
- 2 teaspoons minced garlic
- 1/8 teaspoon crushed red pepper
- 1/2 teaspoon dried rosemary
- 1/8 teaspoon ground black pepper
- 2 tablespoons olive oil
- 4 cups vegetable broth

Directions:

1. Place one-third of white beans in a food processor, then pour in 2 cups broth and pulse for 2 minutes until smooth.
2. Place a pot over medium heat, add oil and when hot, add garlic and cook for 1 minute until fragrant.
3. Add pureed beans into the pan along with the remaining beans, sprinkle with spices and herbs, pour in the broth, stir until combined, and bring the mixture to boil over medium-high heat.
4. Switch heat to medium-low level, simmer the beans for 15 minutes, and then mash them with a fork.
5. Taste the soup to adjust seasoning and then serve.

Nutrition: Calories: 222 Fat: 7 g Carbs: 13 g Protein: 11.2 g Fiber: 9.1 g

396. **Coconut Curry Lentils**

Preparation Time: 10 minutes

Cooking Time: 40 minutes

Servings: 4

Ingredients:

- 1 cup brown lentils
- 1 small white onion, peeled, chopped
- 1 teaspoon minced garlic
- 1 teaspoon grated ginger
- 3 cups baby spinach
- 1 tablespoon curry powder
- 2 tablespoons olive oil
- 13 ounces coconut milk, unsweetened
- 2 cups vegetable broth

For Servings:

- 4 cups cooked rice
- 1/4 cup chopped cilantro

Directions:

1. Place a large pot over medium heat, add oil and when hot, add ginger and garlic and cook for 1 minute until fragrant.

2. Add onion, cook for 5 minutes, stir in curry powder, cook for 1 minute until toasted, add lentils, and pour in broth.

3. Switch heat to medium-high level, bring the mixture to a boil, then switch heat to the low level and simmer for 20 minutes until tender and all the liquid is absorbed.

4. Pour in milk, stir until combined, turn heat to medium level, and simmer for 10 minutes until thickened.

5. Then remove the pot from heat, stir in spinach, let it stand for 5 minutes until its leaves wilt and then top with cilantro.

6. Serve lentils with rice.

Nutrition: Calories: 184 Fat: 3.7 g Carbs: 30 g Protein: 11.3 g Fiber: 10.7 g

397. Tomato, Kale, and White Bean Skillet

Preparation Time: 10 minutes
Cooking Time: 10 minutes
Servings: 4
Ingredients:

- 30 ounces cooked cannellini beans
- 2 ounces sun-dried tomatoes, packed in oil, chopped - 6 ounces kale, chopped
- 1 teaspoon minced garlic
- 1/4 teaspoon ground black pepper
- 1/4 teaspoon salt
- 1/2 tablespoon dried basil
- 1/8 teaspoon red pepper flakes
- 1 tablespoon apple cider vinegar
- 1 tablespoon olive oil
- 2 tablespoons oil from sun-dried tomatoes

Directions:

1. Prepare the dressing and for this, place basil, black pepper, salt, vinegar, and red pepper flakes in a small bowl, add oil from sun-dried tomatoes and whisk until combined.

2. Take a skillet pan, place it over medium heat, add olive oil and when hot, add garlic and cook for 1 minute until fragrant.

3. Add kale, splash with some water and cook for 3 minutes until kale leaves have wilted.

4. Add tomatoes and beans, stir well and cook for 3 minutes until heated.

5. Remove pan from heat, drizzle with the prepared dressing, toss until mixed and serve.

Nutrition: Calories: 264 Fat: 12 g Carbs: 38 g Protein: 9 g Fiber: 13 g

398. Chard Wraps with Millet

Preparation Time: 25 minutes
Cooking Time: 0 minutes
Servings: 4
Ingredients:

- 1 carrot, cut into ribbons
- 1/2 cup millet, cooked
- 1/2 of a large cucumber, cut into ribbons
- 1/2 cup chickpeas, cooked
- 1 cup sliced cabbage
- 1/3 cup hummus
- Mint leaves as needed for topping
- Hemp seeds as needed for topping
- 1 bunch of Swiss rainbow chard

Directions:

1. Spread hummus on one side of chard, place some of the millet, vegetables, and chickpeas on it, sprinkle with some mint leaves and hemp seeds, and wrap it like a burrito.

2. Serve straight away.

Nutrition: Calories: 152 Fat: 4.5 g Carbs: 25 g Protein: 3.5 g Fiber: 2.4 g

399. Quinoa Meatballs

Preparation Time: 10 minutes
Cooking Time: 35 minutes
Servings: 4
Ingredients:

- 1 cup quinoa, cooked
- 1 tablespoon flax meal
- 1 cup diced white onion
- 1 ½ teaspoon minced garlic
- 1/2 teaspoon salt
- 1 teaspoon dried oregano
- 1 teaspoon lemon zest
- 1 teaspoon paprika
- 1 teaspoon dried basil
- 3 tablespoons water
- 2 tablespoons olive oil
- 1 cup grated vegan mozzarella cheese
- Marinara sauce as needed for serving

Directions:

1. Place flax meal in a bowl, stir in water and set aside until required.

2. Take a large skillet pan, place it over medium heat, add 1 tablespoon oil and when hot, add onion and cook for 2 minutes.

3. Stir in all the spices and herbs, then stir in quinoa until combined and cook for 2 minutes.

4. Transfer quinoa mixture in a bowl, add flax meal mixture, lemon zest, and cheese, stir until well mixed and then shape the mixture into twelve 1 ½ inch balls.

5. Arrange balls on a baking sheet lined with parchment paper, refrigerate the balls for 30 minutes and then bake for 20 minutes at 400 degrees F.

6. Serve balls with marinara sauce.

Nutrition: Calories: 100 Fat: 100 g Carbs: 100 g Protein: 100 g Fiber: 100 g

400. Rice Stuffed Jalapeños

Preparation Time: 5 minutes
Cooking Time: 15 minutes
Servings: 6
Ingredients:

- 3 medium-sized potatoes, peeled, cubed, boiled
- 2 large carrots, peeled, chopped, boiled
- 3 tablespoons water
- 1/4 teaspoon onion powder
- 1 teaspoons salt
- 1/2 cup nutritional yeast
- 1/4 teaspoon garlic powder
- 1 lime, juiced
- 3 tablespoons water
- Cooked rice as needed
- 3 jalapeños pepper, halved
- 1 red bell pepper, sliced, for garnish
- ½ cup vegetable broth

Directions:

1. Place boiled vegetables in a food processor, pour in the broth, and pulse until smooth.

2. Add garlic powder, onion powder, salt, water, and lime juice, pulse until combined, then add yeast and blend until smooth.

3. Tip the mixture in a bowl, add rice, and stir until incorporated.

4. Cut each jalapeno into half lengthwise, brush them with oil, season them with some salt, stuff them with rice mixture and bake them for 20 minutes at 400 degrees F until done.

5. Serve straight away.

Nutrition: Calories: 148 Fat: 3.7 g Carbs: 12.2 g Protein: 2 g Fiber: 2 g

401. Pineapple Fried Rice

Preparation Time: 5 minutes
Cooking Time: 12 minutes
Servings: 2
Ingredients:

- 2 cups brown rice, cooked
- 1/2 cup sunflower seeds, toasted
- 2/3 cup green peas
- 1 teaspoon minced garlic
- 1 large red bell pepper, cored, diced
- 1 tablespoon grated ginger
- 2/3 cup pineapple chunks with juice
- 2 tablespoons coconut oil
- 1 bunch of green onions, sliced
- For the Sauce:
- 4 tablespoons soy sauce
- 1/2 cup pineapple juice
- 1/2 teaspoon sesame oil
- 1/2 a lime, juiced

Directions:

1. Take a skillet pan, place it over medium-high heat, add oil and when hot, add red bell pepper, pineapple pieces, and two-thirds of onion, cook for 5 minutes, then stir in ginger and garlic and cook for 1 minute.

2. Switch heat to the high level, add rice to the pan, stir until combined, and cook for 5 minutes.

3. When done, fold in sunflower seeds and peas and set aside until required.

4. Prepare the sauce and for this, place sesame oil in a small bowl, add soy sauce and pineapple juice and whisk until combined.

5. Drizzle sauce over rice, drizzle with lime juice, and serve straight away.

Nutrition: Calories: 179 Fat: 5.5 g Carbs: 30 g Protein: 3.3 g Fiber: 2 g

402. Lentil and Wild Rice Soup

Preparation Time: 10 minutes
Cooking Time: 40 minutes
Servings: 4
Ingredients:

- 1/2 cup cooked mixed beans
- 12 ounces cooked lentils
- 2 stalks of celery, sliced
- 1 1/2 cup mixed wild rice, cooked
- 1 large sweet potato, peeled, chopped

- 1/2 medium butternut, peeled, chopped
- 4 medium carrots, peeled, sliced
- 1 medium onion, peeled, diced
- 10 cherry tomatoes
- 1/2 red chili, deseeded, diced
- 1 ½ teaspoon minced garlic
- 1/2 teaspoon salt
- 2 teaspoons mixed dried herbs
- 1 teaspoon coconut oil
- 2 cups vegetable broth

Directions:

1. Take a large pot, place it over medium-high heat, add oil and when it melts, add onion and cook for 5 minutes.
2. Stir in garlic and chili, cook for 3 minutes, then add remaining vegetables, pour in the broth, stir and bring the mixture to a boil.
3. Switch heat to medium-low heat, cook the soup for 20 minutes, then stir in the remaining ingredients and continue cooking for 10 minutes until the soup has reached to desired thickness.
4. Serve straight away.

Nutrition: Calories: 331 Fat: 2 g Carbs: 54 g Protein: 13 g Fiber: 12 g

403. **Black Bean Meatball Salad**

Preparation Time: 10 minutes
Cooking Time: 25 minutes
Servings: 4
Ingredients:
For the Meatballs:

- 1/2 cup quinoa, cooked
- 1 cup cooked black beans
- 3 cloves of garlic, peeled
- 1 small red onion, peeled
- 1 teaspoon ground dried coriander
- 1 teaspoon ground dried cumin
- 1 teaspoon smoked paprika

For the Salad:

- 1 large sweet potato, peeled, diced
- 1 lemon, juiced
- 1 teaspoon minced garlic
- 1 cup coriander leaves
- 1/3 cup almonds
- 1/3 teaspoon ground black pepper
- ½ teaspoon salt
- 1 1/2 tablespoons olive oil

Directions:

1. Prepare the meatballs and for this, place beans and puree in a blender, pulse until pureed, and place this mixture in a medium bowl.
2. Add onion and garlic, process until chopped, add to the bean mixture, add all the spices, stir until combined, and shape the mixture into uniform balls.
3. Bake the balls on a greased baking sheet for 25 minutes at 350°F until browned.
4. Meanwhile, spread sweet potatoes on a baking sheet lined with baking paper, drizzle with ½ tablespoon oil, toss until coated, and bake for 20 minutes with the meatballs.
5. Prepare the dressing, and for this, place the remaining ingredients for the salad in a food processor and pulse until smooth.
6. Place roasted sweet potatoes in a bowl, drizzle with the dressing, toss until coated, and then top with meatballs.
7. Serve straight away.

Nutrition: Calories: 140 Fat: 8 g Carbs: 8 g Protein: 10 g Fiber: 4 g

404. **Bulgur Pancakes with a Twist**

Preparation Time: 30 minutes
Cooking Time: 20 minutes
Servings: 4
Ingredients

- 1/2 cup bulgur wheat flour
- 1/2 cup almond flour
- 1 teaspoon baking soda
- 1/2 teaspoon fine sea salt
- 1 cup full-fat coconut milk
- 1/2 teaspoon ground cinnamon
- 1/4 teaspoon ground cloves
- 4 tablespoons coconut oil
- 1/2 cup maple syrup
- 1 large-sized banana, sliced

Directions:

1. In a mixing bowl, thoroughly combine the flour, baking soda, salt, coconut milk, cinnamon, and ground cloves; let it stand for 30 minutes to soak well.
2. Heat a small amount of the coconut oil in a frying pan.
3. Fry the pancakes until the surface is golden brown.
4. Garnish with maple syrup and banana. Bon appétit!

Nutrition Per Serving: Calories: 414; Fat: 21.8g; Carbs: 51.8g; Protein: 6.5g

405. Chocolate Rye Porridge

Preparation Time: 4 minutes

Cooking Time: 6 minutes

Servings: 4

Ingredients

- 2 cups rye flakes
- 2 ½ cups almond milk
- 2 ounces dried prunes, chopped
- 2 ounces dark chocolate chunks

Directions:

1. Add the rye flakes and almond milk to a deep saucepan; bring to a boil over medium-high. Turn the heat to a simmer and let it cook for 5 to 6 minutes.
2. Remove from the heat. Fold in the chopped prunes and chocolate chunks, gently stir to combine.
3. Ladle into serving bowls and serve warm.
4. Bon appétit!

Nutrition Per Serving: Calories: 460; Fat: 13.1g; Carbs: 72.2g; Protein: 15g

406. Authentic African Mylie-Meal

Preparation Time: 5 minutes

Cooking Time: 10 minutes

Servings: 4

Ingredients

- 3 cups water
- 1 cup coconut milk
- 1 cup maize meal
- 1/3 teaspoon kosher salt
- 1/4 teaspoon grated nutmeg
- 1/4 teaspoon ground cloves
- 4 tablespoons maple syrup

Directions:

1. In a saucepan, bring the water and milk to a boil; then, gradually add in the maize meal and turn the heat to a simmer.
2. Add in the salt, nutmeg and cloves. Let it cook for 10 minutes.
3. Add in the maple syrup and gently stir to combine. Bon appétit!

Nutrition Per Serving: Calories: 336; Fat: 15.1g; Carbs: 47.9g; Protein: 4.1g

407. Teff Porridge with Dried Figs

Preparation Time: 10 minutes

Cooking Time: 20 minutes

Servings: 4

Ingredients

- 1 cup whole-grain teff
- 1 cup water
- 2 cups coconut milk
- 2 tablespoons coconut oil
- 1/2 teaspoon ground cardamom
- 1/4 teaspoon ground cinnamon
- 4 tablespoons agave syrup
- 7-8 dried figs, chopped

Directions:

1. Bring the whole-grain teff, water and coconut milk to a boil.
2. Turn the heat to a simmer and add in the coconut oil, cardamom and cinnamon.
3. Let it cook for 20 minutes or until the grain has softened and the porridge has thickened. Stir in the agave syrup and stir to combine well.
4. Top each serving bowl with chopped figs and serve warm. Bon appétit!

Nutrition Per Serving: Calories: 356; Fat: 12.1g; Carbs: 56.5g; Protein: 6.8g

408. Decadent Bread Pudding with Apricots

Preparation Time: 15 minutes

Cooking Time: 45 minutes

Servings: 4

Ingredients

- 4 cups day-old ciabatta bread, cubed
- 4 tablespoons coconut oil, melted
- 2 cups coconut milk
- 1/2 cup coconut sugar
- 4 tablespoons applesauce
- 1/4 teaspoon ground cloves
- 1/2 teaspoon ground cinnamon
- 1 teaspoon vanilla extract
- 1/3 cup dried apricots, diced

Directions:

1. Start by preheating your oven to 360 degrees F. Lightly oil a casserole dish with a nonstick cooking spray.
2. Place the cubed bread in the prepared casserole dish.

3. In a mixing bowl, thoroughly combine the coconut oil, milk, coconut sugar, applesauce, ground cloves, ground cinnamon and vanilla. Pour the custard evenly over the bread cubes; fold in the apricots.

4. Press with a wide spatula and let it soak for about 15 minutes.

5. Bake in the preheated oven for about 45 minutes or until the top is golden and set. Bon appétit!

Nutrition Per Serving: Calories: 418; Fat: 18.8g; Carbs: 56.9g; Protein: 7.3g

409. Chipotle Cilantro Rice

Preparation Time: 10 minutes

Cooking Time: 18 minutes

Servings: 2

Ingredients

- 4 tablespoons olive oil
- 1 chipotle pepper, seeded and chopped
- 1 cup jasmine rice
- 1 ½ cups vegetable broth
- 1/4 cup fresh cilantro, chopped
- Sea salt and cayenne pepper, to taste

Directions:

1. In a saucepan, heat the olive oil over a moderately high flame. Add in the pepper and rice and cook for about 3 minutes or until aromatic.

2. Pour the vegetable broth into the saucepan and bring to a boil; immediately turn the heat to a gentle simmer.

3. Cook for about 18 minutes or until all the liquid has absorbed. Fluff the rice with a fork, add in the cilantro, salt and cayenne pepper; stir to combine well. Bon appétit!

Nutrition Per Serving: Calories: 313; Fat: 15g; Carbs: 37.1g; Protein: 5.7g

410. Oat Porridge with Almonds

Preparation Time: 8 minutes

Cooking Time: 12 minutes

Servings: 2

Ingredients

- 1 cup water
- 2 cups almond milk, divided
- 1 cup rolled oats
- 2 tablespoons coconut sugar
- 1/2 vanilla essence
- 1/4 teaspoon cardamom
- 1/2 cup almonds, chopped

- 1 banana, sliced

Directions:

1. In a deep saucepan, bring the water and milk to a rapid boil. Add in the oats, cover the saucepan and turn the heat to medium.

2. Add in the coconut sugar, vanilla and cardamom. Continue to cook for about 12 minutes, stirring periodically.

3. Spoon the mixture into serving bowls; top with almonds and banana. Bon appétit!

Nutrition Per Serving: Calories: 533; Fat: 13.7g; Carbs: 85g; Protein: 21.6g

411. Aromatic Millet Bowl

Preparation Time: 10 minutes

Cooking Time: 20 minutes

Ingredients

- 1 cup water
- 1 ½ cup coconut milk
- 1 cup millet, rinsed and drained
- 1/4 teaspoon crystallized ginger
- 1/4 teaspoon ground cinnamon
- A pinch of grated nutmeg
- A pinch of Himalayan salt
- 2 tablespoons maple syrup

Directions:

1. Place the water, milk, millet, crystallized ginger cinnamon, nutmeg and salt in a saucepan; bring to a boil.

2. Turn the heat to a simmer and let it cook for about 20 minutes; fluff the millet with a fork and spoon into individual bowls.

3. Serve with maple syrup. Bon appétit!

Nutrition Per Serving: Calories: 363; Fat: 6.7g; Carbs: 63.5g; Protein: 11.6g

412. Harissa Bulgur Bowl

Preparation Time: 12 minutes

Cooking Time: 13 minutes

Servings: 4

Ingredients

- 1 cup bulgur wheat
- 1 ½ cups vegetable broth
- 2 cups sweet corn kernels, thawed
- 1 cup canned kidney beans, drained
- 1 red onion, thinly sliced
- 1 garlic clove, minced
- Sea salt and ground black pepper, to taste
- 1/4 cup harissa paste

- 1 tablespoon lemon juice
- 1 tablespoon white vinegar
- 1/4 cup extra-virgin olive oil
- 1/4 cup fresh parsley leaves, roughly chopped

Directions:

1. In a deep saucepan, bring the bulgur wheat and vegetable broth to a simmer; let it cook, covered, for 12 to 13 minutes.
2. Let it stand for 5 to 10 minutes and fluff your bulgur with a fork.
3. Add the remaining ingredients to the cooked bulgur wheat; serve warm or at room temperature. Bon appétit!

Nutrition Per Serving: Calories: 353; Fat: 15.5g; Carbs: 48.5g; Protein: 8.4g

413. Coconut Quinoa Pudding

Preparation Time: 25 minutes
Cooking Time: 20 minutes
Servings: 3
Ingredients

- 1 cup water
- 1 cup coconut milk
- 1 cup quinoa
- A pinch of kosher salt
- A pinch of ground allspice
- 1/2 teaspoon cinnamon
- 1/2 teaspoon vanilla extract
- 4 tablespoons agave syrup
- 1/2 cup coconut flakes

Directions:

1. Place the water, coconut milk, quinoa, salt, ground allspice, cinnamon and vanilla extract in a saucepan.
2. Bring it to a boil over medium-high heat. Turn the heat to a simmer and let it cook for about 20 minutes; fluff with a fork and add in the agave syrup.
3. Divide between three serving bowls and garnish with coconut flakes. Bon appétit!

Nutrition Per Serving: Calories: 391; Fat: 10.6g; Carbs: 65.2g; Protein: 11.1g

414. Cremini Mushroom Risotto

Preparation Time: 5 minutes
Cooking Time: 15 minutes
Servings: 3
Ingredients

- 3 tablespoons vegan butter
- 1 teaspoon garlic, minced
- 1 teaspoon thyme
- 1-pound Cremini mushrooms, sliced
- 1 1/2 cups white rice
- 2 ½ cups vegetable broth
- 1/4 cup dry sherry wine
- Kosher salt and ground black pepper, to taste
- 3 tablespoons fresh scallions, thinly sliced

Directions:

1. In a saucepan, melt the vegan butter over a moderately high flame. Cook the garlic and thyme for about 1 minute or until aromatic.
2. Add in the mushrooms and continue to sauté until they release the liquid or about 3 minutes.
3. Add in the rice, vegetable broth and sherry wine. Bring to a boil; immediately turn the heat to a gentle simmer.
4. Cook for about 15 minutes or until all the liquid has absorbed. Fluff the rice with a fork, season with salt and pepper, and garnish with fresh scallions.
5. Bon appétit!

Nutrition Per Serving: Calories: 513; Fat: 12.5g; Carbs: 88g; Protein: 11.7g

CHAPTER 9:

Vegetables & Side Dishes

415. Steamed Cauliflower

Preparation Time: 5 minutes

Cooking Time: 10 minutes

Servings: 6

Ingredients:

- 1 large head cauliflower
- 1 cup water
- ½ teaspoon salt
- 1 teaspoon red pepper flakes (optional)

Directions:

1. Remove any leaves from the cauliflower, and cut them into florets.
2. In a large saucepan, bring the water to a boil. Place a steamer basket over the water, and add the florets and salt. Cover and steam for 5 to 7 minutes, until tender.
3. In a large bowl, toss the cauliflower with the red pepper flakes (if using).
4. Transfer the florets to a large airtight container or 6 single-serving containers. Let cool before sealing the lids.

Nutrition: Calories: 35 Fat: 0g Protein: 3g Carbohydrates: 7g Fiber: 4g Sugar: 4g Sodium: 236mg

416. Cajun Sweet Potatoes

Preparation Time: 5 minutes

Cooking Time: 30 minutes

Servings: 4

Ingredients:

- 2 pounds sweet potatoes
- 2 teaspoons extra-virgin olive oil
- ½ teaspoon ground cayenne pepper
- ½ teaspoon smoked paprika
- ½ teaspoon dried oregano
- ½ teaspoon dried thyme
- ½ teaspoon garlic powder
- ½ teaspoon salt (optional)

Directions:

1. Preheat the oven to 400°F. Line a baking sheet with parchment paper.
2. Wash the potatoes, pat dry, and cut into ¾-inch cubes. Transfer to a large bowl, and pour the olive oil over the potatoes.
3. In a small bowl, combine the cayenne, paprika, oregano, thyme, and garlic powder. Sprinkle the spices over the potatoes and combine until the potatoes are well coated. Spread the potatoes on the prepared baking sheet in a single layer. Season with salt (if using). Roast for 30 minutes, stirring the potatoes after 15 minutes.

4. Divide the potatoes evenly among 4 single-serving containers. Let cool completely before sealing.

Nutrition: Calories: 219 Fat: 3g Protein: 4g Carbohydrates: 46g Fiber: 7g Sugar: 9g Sodium: 125mg

417. Smoky Coleslaw

Preparation Time: 10 minutes

Cooking Time: 0 minutes

Servings: 6

Ingredients:

- 1-pound shredded cabbage
- 1/3 cup vegan mayonnaise
- ¼ cup unseasoned rice vinegar
- 3 tablespoons plain vegan yogurt or plain soymilk
- 1 tablespoon vegan sugar
- ½ teaspoon salt
- ¼ teaspoon freshly ground black pepper
- ¼ teaspoon smoked paprika
- ¼ teaspoon chipotle powder

Directions:

1. Put the shredded cabbage in a large bowl. In a medium bowl, whisk the mayonnaise, vinegar, yogurt, sugar, salt, pepper, paprika, and chipotle powder.
2. Pour over the cabbage, mix with a spoon or spatula, and until the cabbage shreds are coated.
3. Divide the coleslaw evenly among 6 single-serving containers.
4. Seal the lids.

Nutrition: Calories: 73 Fat: 4g Protein: 1g Carbohydrates: 8g Fiber: 2g Sugar: 5g Sodium: 283mg

418. Mediterranean Hummus Pizza

Preparation Time: 10 minutes

Cooking Time: 30 minutes

Servings: 2 pizzas

Ingredients:

- ½ zucchini, thinly sliced
- ½ red onion, thinly sliced
- 1 cup cherry tomatoes, halved
- 2 to 4 tablespoons pitted and chopped black olives
- Pinch sea salt
- Drizzle olive oil (optional)
- 2 prebaked pizza crusts
- ½ cup Classic Hummus
- 2 to 4 tablespoons Cheesy Sprinkle

Directions:

1. Preheat the oven to 400°F. Place the zucchini, onion, cherry tomatoes, and olives in a large

bowl, sprinkle them with the sea salt and toss them a bit.

2. Drizzle with a bit of olive oil (if using), to seal in the flavor and keep them from drying out in the oven.

3. 2. Lay the two crusts out on a large baking sheet.

4. Spread half the hummus on each crust, and top with the veggie mixture and some Cheesy Sprinkle.

5. Pop the pizzas in the oven for 20 to 30 minutes or until the veggies are soft.

Nutrition: Calories: 500; Total fat: 25g Carbs: 58g Fiber: 12g

419. **Baked Brussels Sprouts**

Preparation Time: 10 minutes
Cooking Time: 40 minutes
Servings: 4
Ingredients:

- 1-pound Brussels sprouts
- 2 teaspoons extra-virgin olive or canola oil
- 4 teaspoons minced garlic (about 4 cloves)
- 1 teaspoon dried oregano
- ½ teaspoon dried rosemary - ½ teaspoon salt
- ¼ teaspoon freshly ground black pepper
- 1 tablespoon balsamic vinegar

Directions:

1. Preheat the oven to 400°F.

2. Line a rimmed baking sheet with parchment paper.

3. Trim and halve the Brussels sprouts. Transfer to a large bowl. Toss with olive oil, garlic, oregano, rosemary, salt, and pepper to coat well.

3. Transfer to the prepared baking sheet. Bake for 35 to 40 minutes, shaking the pan occasionally to help with even browning until crisp on the outside and tender on the inside.

4. Remove from the oven and transfer to a large bowl. Stir in the balsamic vinegar, coating well.

5. Divide the Brussels sprouts evenly among 4 single-serving containers.

6. Let cool before sealing the lids.

Nutrition: Calories: 77 Fat: 3g Protein: 4g Carbohydrates: 12g Fiber: 5g Sugar: 3g Sodium: 320mg

420. **Basic Baked Potatoes**

Preparation Time: 5 minutes
Cooking Time: 60 minutes
Servings: 5
Ingredients:

- 5 medium Russet potatoes or a variety of potatoes, washed and patted dry

- 1 to 2 tablespoons extra-virgin olive oil
- ¼ teaspoon salt
- ¼ teaspoon freshly ground black pepper

Directions:

1. Preheat the oven to 400°F.

2. Pierce each potato several times with a fork or a knife.

3. Brush the olive oil over the potatoes, then rub each with a pinch of the salt and a pinch of the pepper. Place the potatoes on a baking sheet and bake for 50 to 60 minutes, until tender.

4. Place the potatoes on a baking rack and cool completely. Transfer to an airtight container or 5 single-serving containers.

5. Let cool before sealing the lids.

Nutrition: Calories: 171 Fat: 3g Protein: 4g Carbohydrates: 34g Fiber: 5g Sugar: 3g Sodium: 129mg

421. **Miso Spaghetti Squash**

Preparation Time: 5 minutes
Cooking Time: 40 minutes
Servings: 4
Ingredients:

- 1 (3-pound) spaghetti squash
- 1 tablespoon hot water
- 1 tablespoon unseasoned rice vinegar
- 1 tablespoon white miso

Directions:

1. Preheat the oven to 400°F. Line a rimmed baking sheet with parchment paper. Halve the squash lengthwise and place, cut-side down, on the prepared baking sheet.

2. Bake for 35 to 40 minutes, until tender. Cool until the squash is easy to handle. With a fork, scrape out the flesh, which will be stringy, like spaghetti. Transfer to a large bowl.

1. In a small bowl, combine the hot water, vinegar, and miso with a whisk or fork. Pour over the squash. Gently toss with tongs to coat the squash. Divide the squash evenly among 4 single-serving containers. Let cool before sealing the lids.

Nutrition: Calories: 117 Fat: 2g Protein: 3g Carbohydrates: 25g Fiber: 0g Sugar: 0g Sodium: 218mg

422. **Garlic and Herb Noodles**

Preparation Time: 10 minutes
Cooking Time: 2 minutes
Servings: 4
Ingredients:

- 1 teaspoon extra-virgin olive oil or 2 tablespoons vegetable broth

- 1 teaspoon minced garlic (about 1 clove)
- 4 medium zucchinis, spiral
- ½ teaspoon dried basil
- ½ teaspoon dried oregano
- ¼ to ½ teaspoon red pepper flakes, to taste
- ¼ teaspoon salt (optional)
- ¼ teaspoon freshly ground black pepper

Directions:

1. In a large skillet over medium-high heat, heat the olive oil.
2. Add the garlic, zucchini, basil, oregano, red pepper flakes, salt (if using), and black pepper. Sauté for 1 to 2 minutes, until barely tender.
1. Divide the noodles evenly among 4 storage containers.
2. Let cool before sealing the lids.

Nutrition: Calories: 44 Fat: 2g Protein: 3g Carbohydrates: 7g Fiber: 2g Sugar: 3g Sodium: 20mg

423. Thai Roasted Broccoli

Preparation Time: 5 minutes

Cooking Time: 15 minutes

Servings: 4

Ingredients:

- 1 head broccoli, cut into florets
- 2 tablespoons olive oil
- 1 tablespoon soy sauce or gluten-free tamari

Directions:

1. Preheat the oven to 425°F. Line a baking sheet with parchment paper. In a large bowl, combine the broccoli, oil, and soy sauce. Toss well to combine.
2. Spread the broccoli on the prepared baking sheet. Roast for 10 minutes.
3. Toss the broccoli with a spatula and roast for an additional 5 minutes, or until the edges of the florets begin to brown.

Nutrition: Calories: 44 Fat: 2g Protein: 3g Carbohydrates: 7g Fiber: 2g Sugar: 3g Sodium: 20mg

424. Coconut Curry Noodle

Preparation Time: 10 minutes

Cooking Time: 30 minutes

Servings: 4

Ingredients:

- ½ tablespoon oil
- 3 garlic cloves, minced
- 2 tablespoons lemongrass, minced
- 1 tablespoon fresh ginger, grated
- 2 tablespoons red curry paste
- 1 (14 oz) can coconut milk

- 1 tablespoon brown sugar
- 2 tablespoons soy sauce
- 2 tablespoons fresh lime juice
- 1 tablespoon hot chili paste
- 12 oz linguine
- 2 cups broccoli florets
- 1 cup carrots, shredded
- 1 cup edamame, shelled
- 1 red bell pepper, sliced

Directions:

1. Fill a suitably-sized pot with salted water and boil it on high heat.
2. Add pasta to the boiling water and cook until it is al dente, then rinse under cold water.
3. Now place a medium-sized saucepan over medium heat and add oil.
4. Stir in ginger, garlic, and lemongrass, then sauté for 30 seconds.
5. Add coconut milk, soy sauce, curry paste, brown sugar, chili paste, and lime juice.
6. Stir this curry mixture for 10 minutes or until it thickens.
7. Toss in carrots, broccoli, edamame, bell pepper, and cooked pasta.
8. Mix well, then serve warm.

Nutrition: Calories: 44 Fat: 2g Protein: 3g Carbohydrates: 7g Fiber: 2g Sugar: 3g Sodium: 20mg

425. Collard Green Pasta

Preparation Time: 10 minutes

Cooking Time: 20 minutes

Servings: 4

Ingredients

- 2 tablespoons olive oil
- 4 garlic cloves, minced
- 8 oz whole wheat pasta
- ½ cup panko bread crumbs
- 1 tablespoon nutritional yeast
- 1 teaspoon red pepper flakes
- 1 large bunch collard greens
- 1 large lemon, zest and juiced

Directions:

1. Fill a suitable pot with salted water and boil it on high heat.
2. Add pasta to the boiling water and cook until it is al dente, then rinse under cold water.
3. Reserve ½ cup of the cooking liquid from the pasta.
4. Place a non-stick pan over medium heat and add 1 tablespoon olive oil.

5. Stir in half of the garlic, then sauté for 30 seconds.

6. Add breadcrumbs and sauté for approximately 5 minutes.

7. Toss in red pepper flakes and nutritional yeast, then mix well.

8. Transfer the breadcrumbs mixture to a plate and clean the pan.

9. Add the remaining tablespoon of oil to the nonstick pan.

10. Stir in the garlic clove, salt, black pepper, and chard leaves.

11. Cook for 5 minutes until the leaves are wilted.

12. Add pasta along with the reserved pasta liquid.

13. Mix well, then add garlic crumbs, lemon juice, and zest.

14. Toss well, then serve warm.

Nutrition: Calories: 45 Fat: 2.5g Protein: 4g Carbohydrates: 9g Fiber: 4g Sugar: 3g Sodium: 20mg

426. Jalapeno Rice Noodles

Preparation Time: 10 minutes

Cooking Time: 25 minutes

Servings: 4

Ingredients

- ¼ cup soy sauce
- 1 tablespoon brown sugar
- 2 teaspoons sriracha
- 3 tablespoons lime juice
- 8 oz rice noodles
- 3 teaspoons toasted sesame oil
- 1 package extra-firm tofu, pressed
- 1 onion, sliced
- 2 cups green cabbage, shredded
- 1 small jalapeno, minced
- 1 red bell pepper, sliced
- 1 yellow bell pepper, sliced
- 3 garlic cloves, minced
- 3 scallions, sliced
- 1 cup Thai basil leaves, roughly chopped
- Lime wedges for serving

Directions:

1. Fill a suitably-sized pot with salted water and boil it on high heat.

2. Add pasta to the boiling water and cook until it is al dente, then rinse under cold water.

3. Put the lime juice, soy sauce, sriracha, and brown sugar in a bowl, then mix well.

4. Place a large wok over medium heat, then add 1 teaspoon sesame oil.

5. Toss in tofu and stir for 5 minutes until golden-brown.

6. Transfer the golden-brown tofu to a plate and add 2 teaspoons of oil to the wok.

7. Stir in scallions, garlic, peppers, cabbage, and onion.

8. Sauté for 2 minutes, then add cooked noodles and prepared sauce.

9. Cook for 2 minutes, then garnish with lime wedges and basil leaves.

10. Serve fresh.

Nutrition: Calories: 45 Fat: 2.5g Protein: 4g Carbohydrates: 9g Fiber: 4g Sugar: 3g Sodium: 20mg

427. Rainbow Soba Noodles

Preparation Time: 10 minutes

Cooking Time: 20 minutes

Servings: 4

Ingredients

- 8 oz tofu, pressed and crumbled
- 1 teaspoon olive oil
- ½ teaspoon red pepper flakes
- 10 oz package buckwheat soba noodles, cooked
- 1 package broccoli slaw
- 2 cups cabbage, shredded
- ¼ cup very red onion, thinly sliced

Peanut Sauce

- ¼ cup peanut butter
- ¾ cup hot water
- 2 tablespoons apple cider vinegar
- 1 tablespoon maple syrup
- 1–2 garlic cloves, minced
- 1 lime, zest, and juice
- Salt and crushed red pepper flakes, to taste
- Cilantro, for garnish
- Crushed peanuts, for garnish

Directions:

1. Crumble tofu on a baking sheet and toss in 1 teaspoon oil and 1 teaspoon red pepper flakes.

2. Bake the tofu for 20 minutes at 400°F in a preheated oven.

3. Meanwhile, whisk peanut butter with hot water, garlic cloves, maple syrup, cider vinegar, lime zest, salt, lime juice, and pepper flakes in a large bowl.

4. Toss in cooked noodles, broccoli slaw, cabbages, and onion.

5. Mix well, then stir in tofu, cilantro, and peanuts. Enjoy.

Nutrition: Calories: 45 Fat: 2.5g Protein: 4g Carbohydrates: 9g Fiber: 4g Sugar: 3g Sodium: 20mg

428. Spicy Pad Thai Pasta

Preparation Time: 10 minutes

Cooking Time: 10 minutes

Servings: 4

Ingredients

Spicy Tofu

- 1 lb. extra-firm tofu, sliced
- 1 tablespoon peanut butter
- 3 tablespoons soy sauce
- 2 tablespoons Sriracha
- 2 tablespoons rice vinegar
- 2 teaspoons sesame oil
- 2 teaspoons ginger, grated

Pad Thai

- 8 oz brown rice noodles
- 2 teaspoons coconut oil
- 1 red pepper, sliced
- ½ white onion, sliced
- 2 carrots, sliced
- 1 Thai chili, chopped
- ½ cup peanuts, chopped
- ½ cup cilantro, chopped

Spicy Pad Thai Sauce

- 3 tablespoons soy sauce
- 3 tablespoons fresh lime juice
- 1 tablespoon Sriracha
- 3 tablespoons brown sugar
- 3 tablespoons vegetable broth
- 1 teaspoon garlic-chili paste
- 2 garlic cloves, minced

Directions:

1. Fill a suitably-sized pot with water and soak rice noodles in it.
2. Press the tofu to squeeze excess liquid out of it.
3. Place a non-stick pan over medium-high heat and add tofu.
4. Sear the tofu for 2-3 minutes per side until brown.
5. Whisk all the ingredients for tofu crumbles in a large bowl.
6. Stir in tofu and mix well.
7. Separately mix the pad Thai sauce in a bowl and add to the tofu.
8. Place a wok over medium heat and add 1 teaspoon oil.
9. Toss in chili, carrots, onion, and red pepper, then sauté for 3 minutes.
10. Transfer the veggies to the tofu bowl.
11. Add more oil to the same pan and stir in drained noodles, then stir cook for 1 minute.
12. Transfer the noodles to the tofu and toss it all well.
13. Add cilantro and peanuts.
14. Serve fresh.

Nutrition: Calories: 45 Fat: 2.5g Protein: 4g Carbohydrates: 9g Fiber: 4g Sugar: 3g Sodium: 20mg

429. Linguine with Wine Sauce

Preparation Time: 10 minutes

Cooking Time: 18 minutes

Servings: 4

Ingredients:

- 1 tablespoon olive oil
- 5 garlic cloves, minced
- 16 oz shiitake, chopped
- ¼ teaspoon salt
- ¼ teaspoon ground pepper
- 1 pinch red pepper flakes
- ½ cup dry white wine
- 12 oz linguine
- 2 teaspoons vegan butter
- ¼ cup Italian parsley, finely chopped

Directions:

1. Fill a suitably-sized pot with salted water and bring it to a boil on high heat.
2. Add pasta to the boiling water, then cook until it is al dente, then rinse under cold water.
3. Place a non-stick skillet over medium-high heat, then add olive oil.
4. Stir in garlic and sauté for 1 minute.
5. Stir in mushrooms and cook for 10 minutes.
6. Add salt, red pepper flakes, and black pepper for seasoning.
7. Toss in the cooked pasta and mix well.
8. Garnish with parsley and butter. Enjoy.

Nutrition: Calories: 40; Fat: 2.0g Protein: 5g Carbohydrates: 7g Fiber: 4g Sugar: 3g

430. Cheesy Macaroni with Broccoli

Preparation Time: 10 minutes

Cooking Time: 25 minutes

Servings: 6

Ingredients

- 1/3 cup melted coconut oil
- ¼ cup nutritional yeast
- 1 tablespoon tomato paste
- 1 tablespoon dried mustard
- 2 garlic cloves, minced

- 1 ½ teaspoons salt
- ½ teaspoon ground turmeric
- 4 ½ cups almond milk
- 3 cups cauliflower florets, chopped
- 1 cup raw cashews, chopped
- 1 lb. shell pasta
- 1 tablespoon white vinegar
- 3 cups broccoli florets

Directions:

1. Place a suitably-sized saucepan over medium heat and add coconut oil.
2. Stir in mustard, yeast, garlic, salt, tomato paste, and turmeric.
3. Cook for 1 minute, then add almond milk, cashews, and cauliflower florets.
4. Continue cooking for 20 minutes on a simmer.
5. Transfer the cauliflower mixture to a blender jug, then blend until smooth.
6. Stir in vinegar and blend until creamy.
7. Fill a suitably-sized pot with salted water and bring it to a boil on high heat.
8. Add pasta to the boiling water.
9. Place a steamer basket over the boiling water and add broccoli to the basket.
10. Cook until the pasta is al dente. Drain and rinse the pasta and transfer the broccoli to a bowl.
11. Add the cooked pasta to the cauliflower-cashews sauce.
12. Toss in broccoli florets, salt, and black pepper.
13. Mix well, then serve.

Nutrition: Calories: 40; Fat: 2.0g Protein: 5g Carbohydrates: 7g Fiber: 4g Sugar: 3g Sodium: 18mg

431. **Soba Noodles with Tofu**

Preparation Time: 10 minutes

Cooking Time: 38 minutes

Servings: 4

Ingredients

Marinated Tofu

- 2 tablespoons olive oil
- 8 oz firm tofu, pressed and drained
- ¼ cup cilantro, finely chopped
- ¼ cup mint, finely chopped
- 1-inch fresh ginger, grated

Soba Noodles

- 8 oz soba noodles
- ¾ cup edamame
- 2 cucumbers, peeled and julienned
- 1 large carrot, peeled and julienned
- 2 tablespoons black sesame seeds

- 2 tablespoons white sesame seeds
- 2 scallions, chopped

Ginger-Soy Sauce

- 2 tablespoons fresh lime juice
- 2 tablespoons soy sauce
- 1 tablespoon brown sugar
- 1 tablespoon fresh ginger, grated
- 2 tablespoons sesame oil
- ½ tablespoon garlic chili sauce

Directions:

1. Blend herbs, ginger, salt, black pepper, and olive oil in a blender.
2. Add the spice mixture to the tofu and toss it well to coat.
3. Allow the tofu to marinate for 30 minutes at room temperature.
4. Fill a suitably-sized pot with salted water and bring it to a boil on high heat.
5. Add pasta to the boiling water, then cook until it is al dente, then rinse under cold water.
6. Place a large wok over medium heat and add marinated tofu.
7. Sauté for 5–8 minutes until golden-brown, then transfer to a large bowl.
8. Add veggies to the same wok and stir until veggies are soft.
9. Transfer the veggies to the tofu and add cooked noodles.
10. Toss well, then serve warm. Enjoy.

Nutrition: Calories: 30; Fat: 3.5.0g Protein: 6g Carbohydrates: 6g Fiber: 4g; Sugar: 5g Sodium: 18mg

432. **Plant-Based Keto Lo Mein**

Preparation Time: 10 minutes

Cooking Time: 10 minutes

Servings: 2

Ingredients:

- 2 tablespoons carrots, shredded
- 1 package kelp noodles, soaked in water
- 1 cup broccoli, frozen

For the Sauce

- 1 tablespoon sesame oil
- 2 tablespoons tamari
- ½ teaspoon ground ginger
- ¼ teaspoon Sriracha
- ½ teaspoon garlic powder

Directions:

1. Put the broccoli in a saucepan on medium-low heat and add the sauce ingredients.

2. Cook for about 5 minutes and add the noodles after draining water.

3. Allow simmering for about 10 minutes, occasionally stirring to avoid burning.

4. When the noodles have softened, mix everything well and dish out to serve.

Nutrition: Calories: 30; Fat: 3.5.0g Protein: 6g Carbohydrates: 6g Fiber: 4g

433. Steamed Tomatoes

Preparation Time: 5 minutes
Cooking Time: 10 minutes
Servings: 4
Ingredients

- 1 cup water
- 4 large tomatoes
- 1 tablespoon herbed butter
- 1 cup vegan cheese, shredded

Directions:

1. Place the steamer trivet in the bottom of a pressure cooker and add water.

2. Scoop out the pulp of the tomatoes and stuff with vegan cheese.

3. Put the stuffed tomatoes on the trivet and secure the lid.

4. Cook at high pressure for about 8 minutes and release the pressure naturally.

5. Heat herbed butter in a skillet over medium heat and add stuffed tomatoes.

6. Sauté for about 2 minutes and dish out to serve hot.

Nutrition Per Serving: Calories: 140, net carbs: 5.1g, Fat: 3.7gcarbohydrates: 9.3g, Fiber: 2.2g, sugar: 5g, Protein: 7.4g, sodium: 146mg

434. Baked Tofu

Preparation Time: 20 minutes
Cooking Time: 30 minutes
Servings: 8
Ingredients

- 2/3 cup low-sodium soy sauce
- 1 tablespoon garlic, minced
- 1 teaspoon cayenne pepper
- 1 tablespoon olive oil
- 2 tablespoons fresh cilantro leaves, chopped
- 4 tablespoons balsamic vinegar
- 2 (16-ounce) packages extra-firm tofu, drained, pressed and cubed
- 2 teaspoons white sesame seeds, toasted

Directions:

1. Preheat the oven to 400°F and grease a large baking sheet lightly.

2. Mix soy sauce, vinegar, garlic, and cayenne pepper in a bowl and coat tofu in it.

3. Cover the bowl and refrigerate for at least 3 hours.

4. Place the tofu cubes onto the baking sheet in a single layer and transfer them into the oven.

5. Bake for about 15 minutes on each side and remove from the oven.

6. Dish out on a platter and garnish with sesame seeds and cilantro to serve.

Nutrition: Calories: 132, net carbs: 1.7g, Fat: 0.9g, carbohydrates: 4.2g, Fiber: 0.5g, sugar: 2g, Protein: 12.7g, sodium: 1183mg

CHAPTER 10:

Vegetables & Side Dishes 2

435. Potato Carrot Salad

Preparation Time: 15 minutes
Cooking Time: 10 minutes
Servings: 6
Ingredients:

- Water
- 6 potatoes, sliced into cubes
- 3 carrots, sliced into cubes
- 1 tablespoon milk
- 1 tablespoon Dijon mustard
- ¼ cup mayonnaise
- Pepper to taste
- 2 teaspoons fresh thyme, chopped
- 1 stalk celery, chopped
- 2 scallions, chopped
- 1 slice turkey bacon, cooked crispy and crumbled

Directions:

1. Fill your pot with water.
2. Place it over medium-high heat.
3. Boil the potatoes and carrots for 10 to 15 minutes or until tender.
4. Drain and let cool.
5. In a bowl, mix the milk mustard, mayo, pepper, and thyme.
6. Stir in the potatoes, carrots, and celery.
7. Coat evenly with the sauce.
8. Cover and refrigerate for 4 hours.
9. Top with the scallions and turkey bacon bits before serving.

Nutrition: Calories 106 Fat 5.3 g Saturated fat 1 g Carbohydrates 12.6 g Fiber 1.8g Protein 2 g

436. High Protein Salad

Preparation Time: 5 minutes
Cooking Time: 5 minutes
Servings: 4
Ingredients:
Salad:

- 15-oz can green kidney beans
- 4 tbsp capers
- 4 handfuls arugula
- 15-oz can lentils

Dressing:

- 1 tbsp caper brine
- 1 tbsp tamari
- 1 tbsp balsamic vinegar
- 2 tbsp peanut butter
- 2 tbsp hot sauce
- 1 tbsp tahini

Directions:
For the dressing:

1. In a bowl, stir together all the materials until they come together to form a smooth dressing.

For the salad:

2. Mix the beans, arugula, capers, and lentils. Top with the dressing and serve.

Nutrition: Calories: 205 Fat: 2 g Protein: 13 g Carbs: 31 g Fiber: 17g

437. Vegan Wrap with Apples and Spicy Hummus

Preparation Time: 10 minutes
Cooking Time: 0 minutes
Servings: 2
Ingredients:

- 1 tortilla
- 6-7 tbsp Spicy Hummus (mix it with a few tbsp of salsa)
- Only some leaves of fresh spinach or romaine lettuce
- 1 tsp fresh lemon juice
- 1½ cups broccoli slaw
- ½ apple, sliced thin
- 4 tsp dairy-free plain unsweetened yogurt
- Salt and pepper

Directions:

1. Mix the yogurt and the lemon juice with the broccoli slaw. Add the salt and a dash of pepper for taste. Mix well and set aside.
2. Lay the tortilla flat.
3. Spread the spicy hummus over the tortilla.
4. Lay the lettuce down on the hummus.
5. On one half, pile the broccoli slaw on the lettuce.
6. Place the apple slices on the slaw.
7. Fold the sides of the tortilla up, starting with the end that has the apple and the slaw. Roll tightly.
8. Cut it in half and serve.

Nutrition: Calories: 205 Fat: 2 g Protein: 12 g Carbs: 32 g Fiber: 9g

438. Rice and Veggie Bowl

Preparation Time: 5 minutes
Cooking Time: 15 minutes
Servings: 6
Ingredients:

- 2 tbsp coconut oil
- 1 tsp ground cumin
- 1 tsp ground turmeric
- 1 tsp chili powder

- 1 red bell pepper, chopped
- 1 tsp tomato paste
- 1 bunch of broccoli, cut into bite-sized florets with short stems
- 1 tsp salt, to taste
- 1 large red onion, sliced
- 2 garlic cloves, minced
- 1 head of cauliflower, sliced into bite-sized florets
- 2 cups cooked rice
- Newly ground black pepper to taste

Directions:

1. Heat the coconut grease over medium-high heat in a large pan
2. Wait until the oil is hot, stir in the turmeric, cumin, chili powder, salt, and tomato paste.
3. Cook the content for 1 minute. Stir repeatedly until the spices are fragrant.
4. Add the garlic and onion. Sauté for 3 minutes or until the onions are softened.
5. Add the broccoli, cauliflower, and bell pepper. Cover the pot. Cook for 3 to 4 minutes and stir occasionally.
6. Add the cooked rice. Stir so it will combine well with the vegetables—Cook for 2 to 3 minutes. Stir until the rice is warmed through.
7. Check the seasoning. And make adjustments to taste if desired.
8. Lower the heat and cook on low for 2 to 3 more minutes so the flavors will meld.
9. Serve with freshly ground black pepper.

Nutrition: Calories: 260 Fat: 9 g Protein: 9 g Carbs: 36 g Fiber: 5g

439. Cucumber Tomato Chopped Salad

Preparation Time: 15 minutes

Cooking Time: 0 minutes

Servings: 6

Ingredients:

- ½ cup light mayonnaise
- 1 tablespoon lemon juice
- 1 tablespoon fresh dill, chopped
- 1 tablespoon chive, chopped
- ½ cup feta cheese, crumbled
- Salt and pepper to taste
- 1 red onion, chopped
- 1 cucumber, diced
- 1 radish, diced
- 3 tomatoes, diced
- Chives, chopped as desired

Directions:

1. Combine the mayo, lemon juice, fresh dill, chives, feta cheese, salt, and pepper in a bowl.
2. Mix well.
3. Stir in the onion, cucumber, radish, and tomatoes.
4. Coat evenly.
5. Garnish with the chopped chives.

Nutrition: Calories 187 Fat 16.7 g Saturated fat 4.1 g Carbohydrates 6.7 g Fiber 2 g Protein 3.3 g

440. Zucchini Pasta Salad

Preparation Time: 4 minutes

Cooking Time: 0 minutes

Servings: 15

Ingredients:

- 5 tablespoons olive oil
- 2 teaspoons Dijon mustard
- 3 tablespoons red-wine vinegar
- 1 clove garlic, grated
- 2 tablespoons fresh oregano, chopped
- 1 shallot, chopped
- ¼ teaspoon red pepper flakes
- 16 oz. zucchini noodles
- ¼ cup Kalamata olives pitted
- 3 cups cherry tomatoes, sliced in half
- ¾ cup Parmesan cheese shaved

Directions:

1. Mix the olive oil, Dijon mustard, red wine vinegar, garlic, oregano, shallot, and red pepper flakes in a bowl.
2. Stir in the zucchini noodles.
3. Sprinkle on top the olives, tomatoes, and Parmesan cheese.

Nutrition: Calories 299 Fat 24.7 g Saturated fat 5.1 g Carbohydrates 11.6 g Fiber 2.8 g Protein 7 g

441. Egg Avocado Salad

Preparation Time: 10 minutes

Cooking Time: 0 minutes

Servings: 4

Ingredients:

- 1 avocado
- 6 hard-boiled eggs, peeled and chopped
- 1 tablespoon mayonnaise
- 2 tablespoons freshly squeezed lemon juice
- ¼ cup celery, chopped
- 2 tablespoons chives, chopped
- Salt and pepper to taste

Directions:

1. Add the avocado to a large bowl.
2. Mash the avocado using a fork.
3. Stir in the egg and mash the eggs.
4. Add the mayo, lemon juice, celery, chives, salt, and pepper. Chill in the refrigerator. Wait for at least 30 minutes before serving.

Nutrition: Calories 224 Fat 18 g Saturated fat 3.9 g Carbohydrates 6.1 g Fiber 3.6 g Protein 10.6 g

442. Arugula Salad

Preparation Time: 15 minutes
Cooking Time: 0 minutes
Servings: 4
Ingredients:

- 6 cups fresh arugula leaves
- 2 cups radicchio, chopped
- ¼ cup low-fat balsamic vinaigrette
- ¼ cup pine nuts, toasted and chopped

Directions:

1. Arrange the arugula leaves in a serving bowl.
2. Sprinkle the radicchio on top. Drizzle with the vinaigrette. Sprinkle the pine nuts on top.

Nutrition: Calories 85 Fat 6.6 g Saturated fat 0.5 g Carbohydrates 5.1 g Fiber 1 g Protein 2.2 g

443. Sautéed Cabbage

Preparation Time: 8 minutes
Cooking Time: 12 minutes
Servings: 8
Ingredients:

- ¼ cup butter - 1 onion, sliced thinly
- 1 head cabbage, sliced into wedges
- Salt and pepper to taste
- Crumbled crispy bacon bits as desired

Directions:

1. Add the butter to a pan over medium-high heat.
2. Cook the onion for 1 minute, stirring frequently.
3. Season with salt and pepper.
4. Add the cabbage, then stir it for 12 minutes.
5. Sprinkle with the crispy bacon bits.

Nutrition: Calories 77 Fat 5.9 g Saturated fat 3.6 g Carbohydrates 6.1 g Fiber 2.4 g Protein 1.3 g

444. Avocado Mint Soup

Preparation Time: 10 minutes
Cooking Time: 10 minutes
Servings: 2
Ingredients:

- 1 medium avocado, peeled, pitted, and cut into pieces
- 1 cup of coconut milk
- 2 romaine lettuce leaves
- 20 fresh mint leaves
- 1 tbsp fresh lime juice
- 1/8 tsp salt

Directions:

1. Combine all materials into the blender.
2. The soup should be thick, not as a puree. Wait and blend until it is smooth.
3. Pour into the serving bowls and place in the refrigerator for 10 minutes.
4. Stir well and serve chilled.

Nutrition: Calories 268 Fat 25.6 G Carbohydrates 10.2 G Sugar 0.6 G Protein 2.7 G Cholesterol 0 mg

445. Cucumber Edamame Salad

Preparation Time: 5 minutes
Cooking Time: 8 minutes
Servings: 2
Ingredients:

- 3 tbsp. Avocado oil
- 1 cup cucumber, sliced into thin rounds
- ½ cup fresh sugar snap peas cut up or whole
- ½ cup fresh edamame
- ¼ cup radish, sliced
- 1 large avocado, peeled, pitted, sliced
- 1 nori sheet, crumbled
- 2 tsp. Roasted sesame seeds
- 1 tsp. Salt

Directions:

1. Make a medium-sized pot filled halfway with water to a boil over medium-high heat.
2. Add the sugar snaps and cook them for about 2 minutes.
3. Remove the pot off the heat, drain the excess water, transfer the sugar snaps to a medium-sized bowl, and set aside.
4. Fill the pot with water again, add the teaspoon of salt and bring to a boil over medium-high heat.
5. Add the edamame to the pot and let them cook for about 6 minutes.
6. Take the pot off the heat, drain the excess water, transfer the soybeans to the bowl with sugar snaps, and cool down for about 5 minutes.
7. Combine all ingredients, except for the nori crumbs and roasted sesame seeds, in a medium-sized bowl.
8. Delicately stir, using a spoon, until all ingredients are evenly coated in oil.
9. Top the salad along with the nori crumbs and roasted sesame seeds.

10. Shift the bowl to the fridge and allow the salad to cool for at least 30 minutes.

11. Serve chilled and enjoy!

Nutrition: Calories 409 Carbohydrates 7.1 g Fat 38.25 g Protein 7.6 g

446. Garden Patch Sandwiches on Multigrain Bread

Preparation Time: 15 minutes

Cooking Time: 0 minutes

Servings: 4

Ingredients:

- 1 pound extra-firm tofu drained and patted dry
- 1 medium red bell pepper, finely chopped
- 1 celery rib, finely chopped
- 3 green onions, minced
- 1/4 cup shelled sunflower seeds
- 1/2 cup vegan mayonnaise, homemade or store-bought
- 1/2 teaspoon salt
- 1/2 teaspoon celery salt
- 1/4 teaspoon freshly ground black pepper
- 8 slices whole grain bread
- 4 (1/4-inch) slices ripe tomato
- 4 lettuce leaves

Directions:

1. Grind the tofu put it in a large bowl. Add the bell pepper, celery, green onions, and sunflower seeds.

2. Stir in the mayonnaise, salt, celery salt, and pepper and mix until well combined.

3. Toast the bread, if desired. Spread the mixture evenly onto four slices of the bread.

4. Top each with a tomato slice, lettuce leaf, and the remaining bread.

5. Chop the sandwiches diagonally in half and serve.

Nutrition: Carbohydrates 37g Protein 9g Fat 25g Calories 399

447. Garden Salad Wraps

Preparation Time: 15 minutes

Cooking Time: 10 minutes

Servings: 4

Ingredients:

- 6 tablespoons olive oil
- 1-pound extra-firm tofu, drained, patted dry, and cut into 1/2-inch strips
- 1 tablespoon soy sauce
- 1/4 cup apple cider vinegar
- 1 teaspoon yellow or spicy brown mustard
- 1/2 teaspoon salt
- 1/4 teaspoon freshly ground black pepper
- 3 cups shredded romaine lettuce
- 3 ripe Roma tomatoes, finely chopped
- 1 large carrot, shredded
- 1 medium English cucumber, peeled and chopped
- 1/3 cup minced red onion
- 1/4 cup sliced pitted green olives
- 4 (10-inch) whole-grain flour tortillas or lavash flatbread

Directions:

1. In a large frypan, heat two tablespoons of the oil over medium heat. Add the tofu. Cook it until golden brown, about 10 minutes. Sprinkle with soy sauce and set aside to cool.

2. Combine the vinegar, mustard, salt, and pepper with the remaining four tablespoons of oil, stirring to blend well. Set aside.

3. Mix the lettuce, tomatoes, carrot, cucumber, onion, and olives. Pour on the dressing and flip to coat.

4. To assemble wraps, place one tortilla on a work surface and spread with about one-quarter of the salad.

5. Place a few strips of tofu on the tortilla and roll up tightly. Slice in half

Nutrition: Calories: 89 Total Fat: 8g Carbs: 3g Fiber: 2g Protein: 4g

448. Marinated Mushroom Wraps

Preparation Time: 15 minutes

Cooking Time: 0 minutes

Servings: 2

Ingredients:

- 3 tablespoons soy sauce
- 3 tablespoons fresh lemon juice
- 1 1/2 tablespoons toasted sesame oil
- 2 portobello mushroom caps cut into 1/4-inch strips
- 1 ripe Hass avocado pitted and peeled
- 2 cups fresh baby spinach leaves
- 1 medium red bell pepper cut down into 1/4-inch strips
- 1 ripe tomato, chopped
- Salt and freshly ground black pepper

Directions:

1. Combine the soy sauce, two tablespoons of lemon juice, and the oil.

2. Add the portobello strips, toss to combine, and marinate for 1 hour or overnight. Drain the mushrooms and set them aside.

3. Mash the avocado with the remaining one tablespoon of lemon juice.

4. To assemble wraps, place one tortilla on a work surface and spread with some of the mashed avocados. Topmost with a layer of baby spinach leaves. In the lower third of each tortilla, arrange strips of the soaked mushrooms and some bell pepper strips. Sprinkle with the tomato and salt and black pepper to taste.

5. Roll up tightly and cut in half diagonally. Repeat with the remaining ingredients and serve.

Nutrition: Calories: 89 Total Fat: 8g Carbs: 3g Fiber: 2g Protein: 4g

449. **Green Beans Gremolata**

Preparation Time: 15 minutes

Cooking Time: 5 minutes

Servings: 6

Ingredients:

- 1 Pound Fresh Green Beans, Trimmed, Or Frozen or Canned Green Beans
- 3 Garlic Cloves, Minced
- Zest of 2 Oranges
- 3 Tablespoons Minced Fresh Parsley
- 2 Tablespoons Pine Nuts
- 3 Tablespoons Olive Oil
- Sea Salt
- Freshly Ground Black Pepper

Directions:

1. Fill a large pot about half full with water and bring to a boil over high heat. Add the green beans and cook for 2 to 3 minutes. Drain the beans in a colander and rinse with cold water to stop the cooking.

2. In a small bowl, mix the garlic, orange zest, and parsley.

3. In a large sauté pan over medium-high heat, toast the pine nuts in the dry, hot pan until they are fragrant, 2 to 3 minutes. Remove from the pan and set aside.

4. Heat the olive oil in the same pan until it shimmers. Add the beans and cook, -stirring frequently, until heated through, about 2 minutes.

5. Remove the pan from the heat and add the parsley mixture and pine nuts.

6. Season with salt and pepper. Serve immediately.

Nutrition: Calories: 63 Total Fat: 6.81g Carbs: 0.67g Fiber: 0.1g Protein: 0.17g

450. **Minted Peas**

Preparation Time: 5 minutes

Cooking Time: 5 minutes

Servings: 4

Ingredients:

- 1 Tablespoon Olive Oil
- 4 Cups Peas, Fresh or Frozen (Not Canned)
- ½ Teaspoon Sea Salt
- Freshly Ground Black Pepper
- 3 Tablespoons Chopped Fresh Mint

Directions:

1. In a large sauté pan, heat the olive oil over medium-high heat until hot.

2. Add the peas and cook for about 5 minutes.

3. Remove the pan from heat.

4. Stir in the salt, season with pepper, and stir in the mint. Serve hot.

Nutrition: Calories: 277 Total Fat: 16.4g Carbs: 0.26g Fiber: 0.1g Protein: 30.25g

451. **Sweet and Spicy Brussels Sprout Hash**

Preparation Time: 10 minutes

Cooking Time: 15 minutes

Servings: 4

Ingredients:

- 3 Tablespoons Olive Oil
- 2 Shallots, Thinly Sliced
- 1½ Pound Brussels Sprouts, Trimmed and Cut into Thin Slices
- 3 Tablespoons Apple Cider Vinegar
- 1 Tablespoon Pure Maple Syrup
- ½ Teaspoon Sriracha Sauce (or to taste)
- Sea Salt - Freshly Ground Black Pepper

Directions:

1. In a large sauté pan, heat the olive oil over medium-high heat until it shimmers.

2. Add the shallots and Brussels sprouts and cook, stirring frequently, until the -vegetables soften and begin to turn golden brown, about 10 minutes.

3. Stir in the vinegar, using a spoon to scrape any browned bits from the bottom of the pan.

4. Stir in the maple syrup and Sriracha.

5. Simmer, stirring frequently, until the liquid reduces, 3 to 5 minutes.

6. Season with salt and pepper and serve immediately.

Nutrition: Calories: 111 Total Fat: 10.17g Carbs: 5.35g Fiber: 0.1g Protein: 0.26g

452. Glazed Curried Carrots

Preparation Time: 5 minutes

Cooking Time: 15 minutes

Servings: 6

Ingredients:

- 1 Pound Carrots, Peeled and Thinly Sliced
- 2 Tablespoons Olive Oil
- 2 Tablespoons Curry Powder
- 2 Tablespoons Pure Maple Syrup
- Juice of ½ Lemon
- Sea Salt
- Freshly Ground Black Pepper

Directions:

1. Place the carrots in a large pot and cover them with water.
2. Cook on medium-high heat until tender, about 10 minutes.
3. Drain the carrots and return them to the pan over medium-low heat.
4. Stir in olive oil, curry powder, maple syrup, and lemon juice.
5. Cook, stirring constantly, until the liquid reduces, about 5 minutes.
6. Season with salt and pepper and serve immediately.

Nutrition: Calories: 68 Total Fat: 4.82g Carbs: 6.55g Fiber: 1.4g Protein: 0.38g

453. Carrot-Pineapple Casserole

Preparation Time: 10 minutes

Cooking Time: 50 minutes

Servings: 4

Ingredients:

- 3 large carrots
- 1 large pineapple
- 2 tablespoons all-purpose flour
- 1 tablespoon honey
- ½ teaspoon ground cinnamon
- 1 tablespoon olive oil
- 1/2 cup pineapple juice

Directions:

1. Preheat the oven to 350°F.
2. Peel and slice carrots and pineapples. Bring 1 quart of water to a boil in a medium-sized pot. Boil carrots for 5 minutes or until tender. Drain.
3. Layer carrots and pineapples in a large casserole dish.
4. Using a fork, mix flour, honey and cinnamon in a small bowl. Mix in olive oil to make a crumb topping.
5. Sprinkle flour mixture over carrots and pineapples, then drizzle with juice.
6. Bake for 50 minutes or until pineapples and carrots are tender and the topping is golden brown.

Nutrition: Calories 94, Total Fat 2.9g, Saturated Fat 0.4g, Cholesterol 0mg, Sodium 31mg, Total Carbohydrate 17.4g, Dietary Fiber 1.8g, Total Sugars 11.2g, Protein 0.9g, Calcium 23mg, Iron 0mg, Potassium 206mg, Phosphorus 27 mg

454. Vegetable Medley

Preparation Time: 5 minutes

Cooking Time: 12 minutes

Servings: 3

Ingredients

- 2 carrots, peeled and diced
- 1 small sweet potato, peeled and diced
- 3 pink potatoes, quartered
- 1½ cups butternut squash
- 1 sprig rosemary
- Salt and black pepper, to taste
- 1 tablespoon olive oil
- ½ cup water

Directions:

1. Heat olive oil in a skillet and add a rosemary sprig.
2. Sauté for about 2 minutes and stir in the rest of the ingredients.
3. Cover the lid and cook for about 10 minutes on medium heat.
4. Dish out in a bowl and serve hot.

Nutrition: Calories: 386 net carbs: 68g Fat: 5.2g carbohydrates: 79.8g Fiber: 9.8g sugar: 8.4g Protein: 8.9g sodium: 769mg

CHAPTER 11:

Legumes

455. Sweet Potato Chili with Quinoa

Preparation Time: 15 minutes
Cooking Time: 30 minutes
Servings: 4
Ingredients:

- 1 large onion, finely chopped
- 2 garlic cloves, crushed
- 2 tbsp olive oil
- 1 tablespoon mild chilli powder
- 1 teaspoon ground cumin
- 3 medium sweet potatoes, peeled and cubed
- 1 cup quinoa, and drained
- 1 can of chopped tomatoes
- 2 quarts of vegetable stock
- 1 can of black beans, rinsed and drained
- coriander a small bunch, to serve
- soured cream or yogurt to serve (optional)

Directions:

1. Take a large pot. Dice the onion. Cook the onion and garlic in 1 tablespoon(s) olive oil until soft.
2. Add the chilli powder and cumin, cook for a minute, then add the sweet potato, quinoa, tomatoes, and stock.
3. Let simmer for about 10 minutes, then put in the beans. Half cover the pot with a lid, letting it simmer for maybe 20 to 30 more minutes.
4. The squash and quinoa should be soft enough to poke through with a fork. The liquid should also be noticeably thicker.
5. Sprinkle over the coriander you've chopped up and serve in bowls with a dollop of soured cream or yogurt if you like.

Nutrition: Calories: 388 kcal Protein: 12.1 g Carbs: 65.3 g Fat: 5.8 g (0.7 grams of which saturates)

456. Spicy Sweet Potato Enchiladas

Preparation Time: 10 minutes
Cooking Time: 20 minutes
Servings: 6
Ingredients:

- 1 large sweet potatoes
- 1 red or yellow onion 1
- 1 red bell pepper
- 1 green bell pepper
- 1 teaspoon cumin seeds
- 1 teaspoon dried chilli flakes
- 3 tablespoons olive oil
- 1 small bunch of cilantro/coriander
- 4 large tortillas
- 1 ½ cups grated vegan cheese

- sour cream to serve
- salad to serve

ENCHILADA SAUCE

- 1 can chopped tomatoes
- 1 teaspoon smoked paprika
- 1 teaspoon garlic salt (or use half Himalaya salt, half garlic powder)
- 1 teaspoon dried oregano
- 1 teaspoon sugar

Directions:

1. Heat the oven to 200°C / 400°F /gas mark 6. Chop all of the fresh ingredients, leaving the skins on the potatoes. Finely chop the herbs.
2. Put the potatoes, onion, bell peppers/capsicum and spices on a non-stick baking tray or a baking sheet lined with wax parchment paper.
3. Add the oil and lots of salt and pepper, and toss well. Cook for half an hour or until the potato is tender enough to pierce with a fork (but not mushy).
4. Meanwhile, blend the sauce ingredients in a blender. Take the veg out of the oven and leave to cool a little. Stir through ½ the coriander.
5. Lay out the tortillas flat and spread the veggie mixture evenly between them. Roll up the tortillas; you may want to look up a video on the internet for this, as it helps to watch.
6. Place the tortillas cut-side down into an oiled baking dish.
7. Spoon over the sauce and sprinkle over the cheese, using the nut cheese recipe that we have in this chapter if you'd like.
8. Put them in the oven and bake for about 20 minutes or until bubbling and golden.
9. Serve with vegan sour cream, the other half of the chopped coriander and a fresh side salad.

Nutrition: Calories: 495 kcal Protein: 13.9 g Carbs: 60.7 g Fat: 19.4 g (7.2 grams of which saturates)

457. Raw Nut Cheese

Preparation Time: 10 minutes + 12 hours soak time + 12 hours set / rise time
Cooking Time: 0 minutes
Servings: 3
Ingredients:

- 3 2/3 cups raw cashews
- 1 teaspoon of probiotic powder
- 2 tablespoons onion powder
- 1 tablespoon garlic powder
- 4-5 tablespoons nutritional yeast
- salt and pepper to taste

Directions:

1. Drain the water from the overnight soaked cashews.
2. Put them in a blender with the probiotic powder, blending until smooth.
3. Transfer the mixture into a bowl and cover with plastic wrap or beeswax wrap, being careful to leave a couple of tiny spaces open for air to get in.
4. Leave the bowl at room temperature for 8-12 hours, or until the cheese has risen in size and taken on an aerated quality.
5. Season to taste with onion powder, garlic powder, nutritional yeast, salt, and pepper.
6. It's wonderful on crackers or sprinkled/grated atop any pasta dish to make a vegan, perfectly combined meal.

Nutrition: Calories: 890 kcal Protein: 36 g Carbs: 59.7 g Fat: 65 g (13 grams of which saturates)

458. Artichoke White Bean Sandwich Spread

Preparation Time: 10 minutes
Cooking Time: 15 minutes
Servings: 2
Ingredients:

- ½ cup raw cashews, chopped
- Water
- 1 garlic clove, cut into half
- 1 tablespoon lemon zest
- 1 teaspoon fresh rosemary, chopped
- ¼ teaspoon salt
- ¼ teaspoon pepper
- 6 tablespoons almond, soy or coconut milk
- 1 15.5-ounce can cannellini beans, rinsed and drained well
- 3 to 4 canned artichoke hearts, chopped
- ¼ cup hulled sunflower seeds
- Green onions, chopped, for garnish

Directions:

1. Soak the raw cashews for 15 minutes in enough water to cover them.
2. Drain and dab with a paper towel to make them as dry as possible.
3. Transfer the cashews to a blender and add the garlic, lemon zest, rosemary, salt and pepper.
4. Pulse to break everything up and then add the milk, one tablespoon at a time, until the mixture is smooth and creamy.
5. Mash the beans in a bowl with a fork. Add the artichoke hearts and sunflower seeds.

6. Toss to mix.
7. Pour the cashew mixture on top and season with more salt and pepper if desired.
8. Mix the ingredients well and spread on whole-wheat bread, crackers, or a wrap.

Nutrition: Calories 110 Carbohydrates 14 g Fat 4 g Protein 6 g

459. Lentil Sandwich Spread

Preparation Time: 15 minutes
Cooking Time: 20 minutes
Servings: 3
Ingredients:

- 1 tablespoon water or oil
- 1 small onion, chopped
- 2 cloves garlic, minced
- 1 cup dry lentils
- 2 cups vegetable stock
- 1 tablespoon apple cider vinegar
- 2 tablespoons tomato paste
- 3 sun-dried tomatoes
- 2 tablespoons maple
- 1 teaspoon dried oregano
- ½ teaspoon ground cumin
- 1 teaspoon coriander
- 1 teaspoon turmeric
- ½ lemon, juiced
- 1 tablespoon fresh parsley, chopped

Directions:

1. Warm a Dutch oven over medium heat and add the water or oil.
2. Immediately add the onions and sauté for two to three minutes or until softened.
3. Add more water if this starts to stick to the pan.
4. Add the garlic and sauté for one minute.
5. Add the lentils, vegetable stock, vinegar, and bring to a boil.
6. Turn down to a simmer and cook for 15 minutes or until the lentils are soft and the liquid is almost completely absorbed.
7. Ladle the lentils into a food processor and add the tomato paste, sun-dried tomatoes and syrup; process until smooth.
8. Add the oregano, cumin, coriander, turmeric and lemon; process until thoroughly mixed.
9. Remove the spread to a bowl and apply it to bread, toast, a wrap, or pita.
10. Sprinkle. With toppings as desired.

Nutrition: Calories 360 Carbohydrates 60.7 g Fat 5.4 g Protein 17.5 g

460. Rice and Bean Burritos

Preparation Time: 10 minutes
Cooking Time: 15 minutes
Servings: 8
Ingredients:

- 2 16-ounce cans fat-free refried beans
- 6 tortillas
- 2 cups cooked rice
- ½ cup salsa
- 1 tablespoon olive oil
- 1 bunch green onions, chopped
- 2 bell peppers, finely chopped
- Guacamole

Directions:

1. Preheat the oven to 375°F.
2. Dump the refried beans into a saucepan and place them over medium heat to warm.
3. Heat the tortillas and lay them out on a flat surface.
4. Spoon the beans in a long mound that runs across the tortilla, just a little off from the center.
5. Spoon some rice and salsa over the beans; add the green pepper and onions to taste, along with any other finely chopped vegetables you like.
6. Fold over the shortest edge of the plain tortilla and roll it up, folding in the sides as you go.
7. Place each burrito, seam side down, on a nonstick-sprayed baking sheet.
8. Brush with olive oil and bake for 15 minutes.
9. Serve with guacamole.

Nutrition: Calories 290 Carbohydrates 49 g Fat 6 g Protein 9 g

461. Quinoa Avocado Salad

Preparation Time: 15 minutes
Cooking Time: 4 minutes
Servings: 4
Ingredients:

- 2 tablespoons balsamic vinegar
- ¼ cup cream
- ¼ cup buttermilk
- 5 tablespoons freshly squeezed lemon juice, divided
- 1 clove garlic, grated
- 2 tablespoons shallot, minced
- Salt and pepper to taste
- 2 tablespoons avocado oil, divided
- 1 1/4 cups quinoa, cooked
- 2 heads endive, sliced

- 2 firm pears, sliced thinly
- 2 avocados, sliced
- ¼ cup fresh dill, chopped

Directions:

1. Combine the vinegar, cream, milk, 1 tablespoon lemon juice, garlic, shallot, salt and pepper in a bowl.
2. Pour 1 tablespoon oil into a pan over medium heat.
3. Heat the quinoa for 4 minutes.
4. Transfer quinoa to a plate.
5. Toss the endive and pears in a mixture of remaining oil, remaining lemon juice, salt and pepper.
6. Transfer to a plate.
7. Toss the avocado in the reserved dressing.
8. Add to the plate.
9. Top with the dill and quinoa.

Nutrition: Calories: 431 Total Fat: 28.5g Saturated fat: 8g Cholesterol: 13mg

462. Green Beans with vegan Bacon

Preparation Time: 15 minutes
Cooking Time: 20 minutes
Servings: 8
Ingredients:

- 2 slices of vegan bacon, chopped
- 1 shallot, chopped
- 24 oz. green beans
- Salt and pepper to taste
- ½ teaspoon smoked paprika
- 1 teaspoon lemon juice
- 2 teaspoons vinegar

Directions:

1. Preheat your oven to 450 degrees F.
2. Add the bacon to the baking pan and roast for 5 minutes.
3. Stir in the shallot and beans. Season with salt, pepper and paprika.
4. Roast for 10 minutes. Drizzle with lemon juice and vinegar.
5. Roast for another 2 minutes.

Nutrition: Calories: 49 Total fat: 1.2g Saturated fat: 0.4g Cholesterol: 3mg

463. Chickpea Avocado Sandwich

Preparation Time: 10 minutes
Cooking Time: 5 minutes
Servings: 2
Ingredients:

- Chickpeas – 1 can

- Avocado – 1
- Dill, dried – .25 teaspoon
- Onion powder – .25 teaspoon
- Sea salt – .5 teaspoon
- Celery, chopped – .25 cup
- Green onion, chopped – .25 cup
- Lime juice – 3 tablespoons
- Garlic powder – .5 teaspoon
- Dark pepper, ground – dash
- Tomato, sliced – 1
- Lettuce – 4 leaves
- Bread – 4 slices

Directions:

1. Drain the canned chickpeas and rinse them under cool water.
2. Place them in a bowl along with the herbs, spices, sea salt, avocado, and lime juice. Using a potato masher or fork, mash the avocado and chickpeas together until you have a thick filling.
3. Try not to mash the chickpeas all the way, as they create texture.
4. Stir the celery and green onion into the filling and prepare your sandwiches.
5. Layout two slices of bread, top them with the chickpea filling, some lettuce, and sliced tomato.
6. Top them off with the two remaining slices, slice the sandwiches in half, and serve.

Nutrition: calories 270, fat 15, fiber 3, carbs 5, protein 9

464. **Spicy Chickpeas**

Preparation Time: 15 minutes

Cooking Time: 20 minutes

Servings: 8

Ingredients:

- 1 Tbsp extra-virgin olive oil
- 1 yellow onion, diced •1 tsp curry
- ¼ tsp allspice
- 1 can diced tomatoes
- 2 cans chickpeas, rinsed, drained
- Salt, cayenne pepper, to taste

Directions:

1. Simmer onions in 1 Tbsp oil for 4 minutes.
2. Add allspice and pepper, cook for 2 minutes.
3. Stir in tomatoes, and cook for another 2 minutes.
4. Add chickpeas, and simmer for 10 minutes.
5. Season with salt, and serve.

Nutrition: Calories 146 Carbohydrates 25 g Fat 3 g Protein 5 g

465. **Beans & Greens Bowl**

Preparation Time: 2 minutes

Cooking Time: 2 minutes

Servings: 1

Ingredients:

- 1½ cups curly kale, washed, chopped
- ½ cup black beans, cooked
- ½ avocado
- 2 Tbsp feta cheese, crumbled

Directions:

1. Mix the kale and black beans in a microwavable bowl and heat for about 1 ½ minute.
2. Add the avocado and stir well. Top with feta.

Nutrition: Calories 340 Carbohydrates 32 g Fat 19 g Protein 13 g

466. **Black Beans & Brown Rice**

Preparation Time: 2 minutes

Cooking Time: 45 minutes

Servings: 4

Ingredients:

- 4 cups water
- 2 cups brown rice, uncooked
- 1 can no-salt black beans
- 3 cloves garlic, minced

Directions:

1. Bring the water and rice to boil, simmer for 40 minutes.
2. In a pan, cook the black beans with their liquid and the garlic for 5 minutes.
3. Toss the rice and beans together, and serve.

Nutrition: Calories 220 Carbohydrates 45 g Fat 1.5 g Protein 7 g

467. **Yucatan Bean & Pumpkin Seed Appetizer**

Preparation Time: 10 minutes

Cooking Time: 3 minutes

Servings: 8

Ingredients:

- ¼ cup pumpkin seeds
- 1 can white beans
- 1 tomato, chopped
- 1/3 cup onion, chopped
- 1/3 cup cilantro, chopped
- 4 Tbsp lime juice
- Salt, pepper, to taste

Directions:

1. Toast the pumpkin seeds for 3 minutes to lightly brown.

2. Let cool, and then chop in a food processor.

3. Mix in the remaining ingredients. Season with salt and pepper, and serve.

Nutrition: Calories 12 g Fat 2 g Carbohydrates 12 g Protein 5 g

468. Butter Bean Hummus

Preparation Time: 5 minutes

Cooking Time: 0 minutes

Servings: 4

Ingredients:

- 1 can butter beans, drained, rinsed
- 2 garlic cloves, minced
- ½ lemon, juiced - 1 Tbsp olive oil
- 4 sprigs of parsley, minced
- Sea salt, to taste

Directions:

1. Blend all ingredients in a food processor into a creamy mixture.

2. Serve as a dip for bread, crackers, or any type of vegetables.

Nutrition: Calories 150 Carbohydrates 23 g Fat 4 g Protein 8 g

469. Greek-style Gigante Beans

Preparation Time: 8 hours 5 minutes

Cooking Time: 10 hours

Servings: 10

Ingredients:

- 12 ounces Gigante beans
- 1 can tomatoes with juice, chopped
- 2 stalks celery, diced
- 1 onion, diced
- 4 garlic cloves, minced
- Salt, to taste

Directions:

1. Soak beans in water for 8 hours.

2. Combine drained beans with the remaining ingredients. Stir, and pour water to cover.

3. Cook for 10 hours on low. Season with salt, and serve.

Nutrition: Calories 63 Carbohydrates 13 g Fat 2 g Protein 4 g

470. Brown Rice & Red Beans & Coconut Milk

Preparation Time: 10 minutes

Cooking Time: 1 hour

Servings: 6

Ingredients:

- 2 cups brown rice, uncooked

- 4 cups water
- 1 Tbsp olive oil
- 1 onion, diced
- 3 cloves garlic, minced
- 2 cans red beans
- 1 can coconut milk

Directions:

1. Bring brown rice in water to a boil, then simmer for 30 minutes.

2. Sauté onion in olive oil. Add garlic and cook until golden.

3. Mix the onions and garlic, beans, and coconut milk into the rice.

4. Simmer for 15 minutes.

5. Serve hot.

Nutrition: Calories 280 Carbohydrates 49 g Fat 3 g Protein 8 g

471. Black-Eyed Peas with Herms

Preparation Time: 10 minutes

Cooking Time: 1 hour

Servings: 8

Ingredients:

- 2 cans no-sodium black-eyed beans
- ½ cup extra-virgin olive oil
- 1 cup parsley, chopped
- 4 green onions, sliced
- 2 carrots, grated
- 2 Tbsp tomato paste
- 2 cups water
- Salt, pepper, to taste

Directions:

1. Drain the beans, reserve the liquid.

2. Sauté beans, parsley, onions, and carrots in oil for 3 minutes.

3. Add remaining ingredients, 2 cups reserved beans liquid, and water.

4. Cook for 30 minutes.

5. Season with salt, pepper and serve.

Nutrition: Calories 230 Carbohydrates 23 g Fat 15 g Protein 11 g

472. Curry Lentil Soup

Preparation Time: 5 minutes

Cooking Time: 40 minutes

Servings: 6

Ingredients:

- 1 cup brown lentils
- 1 medium white onion, peeled, chopped
- 28 ounces diced tomatoes

- 1 ½ teaspoon minced garlic
- 1 inch of ginger, grated
- 3 cups vegetable broth
- 1/2 teaspoon salt
- 2 tablespoons curry powder
- 1 teaspoon cumin
- 1/2 teaspoon cayenne
- 1 tablespoon olive oil
- 1 1/2 cups coconut milk, unsweetened
- ¼ cup chopped cilantro

Directions:

1. Take a soup pot, place it over medium-high heat, add oil and when hot, add onion, stir in garlic and ginger and cook for 5 minutes until golden brown.
2. Then add all the ingredients except for milk and cilantro, stir until mixed and simmer for 25 minutes until lentils have cooked.
3. When done, stir in milk, cook for 5 minutes until thoroughly heated, and then garnish the soup with cilantro.
4. Serve straight away

Nutrition: Calories: 269 Fat: 15 g Carbs: 26 g Protein: 10 g Fiber: 10 g

473. Mexican Lentil Soup

Preparation Time: 5 minutes
Cooking Time: 45 minutes
Servings: 6
Ingredients:

- 2 cups green lentils
- 1 medium red bell pepper, cored, diced
- 1 medium white onion, peeled, diced
- 2 cups diced tomatoes
- 8 ounces diced green chilies
- 2 celery stalks, diced
- 2 medium carrots, peeled, diced
- 1 ½ teaspoon minced garlic
- 1/2 teaspoon salt
- 1 tablespoon cumin
- 1/4 teaspoon smoked paprika
- 1 teaspoon oregano
- 1/8 teaspoon hot sauce
- 2 tablespoons olive oil
- 8 cups vegetable broth
- ¼ cup cilantro, for garnish

- 1 avocado, peeled, pitted, diced, for garnish

Directions:

1. Take a large pot over medium heat, add oil and when hot, add all the vegetables, reserving tomatoes and chilies, and cook for 5 minutes until softened.
2. Then add garlic, stir in oregano, cumin, and paprika, and continue cooking for 1 minute.
3. Add lentils, tomatoes and green chilies, season with salt, pour in the broth, and simmer the soup for 40 minutes until cooked.
4. When done, ladle soup into bowls, top with avocado and cilantro, and serve straight away

Nutrition: Calories: 235 Fat: 9 g Carbs: 32 g Protein: 9 g Fiber: 10 g

474. Tex-Mex Tofu & Beans

Preparation Time: 25 minutes
Cooking Time: 12 minutes
Servings: 2
Ingredients

- 1 cup dry black beans
- 1 cup dry brown rice
- 1 14-oz. Package firm tofu, drained
- 2 tbsp. Olive oil
- 1 small purple onion, diced
- 1 medium avocado, pitted, peeled
- 1 garlic clove, minced
- 1 tbsp. Lime juice
- 2 tsp. Cumin
- 2 tsp. Paprika
- 1 tsp. Chili powder
- ¼ tsp salt
- ¼ tsp pepper

Directions:

1. Cut the tofu into ½-inch cubes.
2. Heat the olive oil in a large skillet over high heat. Add the diced onions and cook until soft, for about 5 minutes.
3. Add the tofu and cook for an additional 2 minutes, flipping the cubes frequently.
4. Meanwhile, cut the avocado into thin slices and set them aside.
5. Lower the heat to medium and mix in the garlic, cumin, and cooked black beans.
6. Stir until everything is incorporated thoroughly, and then cook for an additional 5 minutes.
7. Add the remaining spices and lime juice to the mixture in the skillet. Mix thoroughly and remove the skillet from the heat.

8. Serve the tex-mex tofu and beans with a scoop of rice and garnish with the fresh avocado.

9. Enjoy immediately, or store the rice, avocado, and tofu mixture separately.

Nutrition: Calories 1175, total fat 46.8g, saturated fat 8.8g, cholesterol 0mg, sodium 348mg, total carbohydrate 152.1g, dietary fiber 28.8g, total sugars 5.7g, protein 47.6g, vitamin d 0mcg, calcium 601mg, iron 13mg, potassium 2653mg

CHAPTER 12:

Legumes 2

475. Black Bean Burgers

Preparation Time: 10 minutes
Cooking Time: 15 minutes
Servings: 6
Ingredients:

- 1 Onion, diced
- ½ cup Corn Nibs
- 2 Cloves Garlic, minced
- ½ teaspoon Oregano, dried
- ½ cup Flour
- 1 Jalapeno Pepper, small
- 2 cups Black Beans, mashed & canned ¼ cup Breadcrumbs (Vegan)
- 2 teaspoons Parsley, minced ¼ teaspoon cumin
- 1 tablespoon Olive Oil
- 2 teaspoons Chili Powder
- ½ Red Pepper, diced
- Sea Salt to taste

Directions:

1. Set your flour on a plate, and then get out your garlic, onion, peppers and oregano, throwing it in a pan.
2. Cook over medium-high heat, and then cook until the onions are translucent. Place the peppers in, and sauté until tender.
3. Cook for two minutes, and then set it to the side.
4. Use a potato masher to mash your black beans, then stir in the vegetables, cumin, breadcrumbs, parsley, salt, and chili powder, and then divide it into six patties.
5. Coat each side, and then cook until it is fried on each side.

Nutrition:
Calories: 357 Protein: 17.9g Fat: 5.1 g Carbohydrates: 61.1 g

476. Hearty Black Lentil Curry

Preparation Time: 30 minutes
Cooking Time: 6 hours and 15 minutes
Servings: 4
Ingredients:

- 1 cup of black lentils, rinsed and soaked overnight
- 14 ounces of chopped tomatoes
- 2 large white onions, peeled and sliced
- 1 1/2 teaspoon of minced garlic
- 1 teaspoon of grated ginger
- 1 red chili
- 1 teaspoon of salt
- 1/4 teaspoon of red chili powder

- 1 teaspoon of paprika
- 1 teaspoon of ground turmeric
- 2 teaspoons of ground cumin
- 2 teaspoons of ground coriander
- 1/2 cup of chopped coriander
- 4-ounce of vegetarian butter
- 4 fluid of ounce water
- 2 fluid of ounce vegetarian double cream

Directions:

1. Place a large pan over moderate heat, add butter and let heat until melted.
2. Add the onion and garlic and ginger and cook for 10 to 15 minutes or until the onions are caramelized.
3. Then stir in salt, red chili powder, paprika, turmeric, cumin, ground coriander, and water.4. Transfer this mixture to a 6-quarts slow cooker and add tomatoes and red chili.
4. Drain lentils, add to slow cooker and stir until just mix.
5. Plugin slow cooker; adjust cooking time to 6 hours and let cook on low heat setting.
6. When the lentils are done, stir in cream and adjust the seasoning.
7. Serve with boiled rice or whole wheat bread.

Nutrition: Calories: 299 Protein: 5.5 g Fat: 27.9 g Carbohydrates: 9.8 g

477. Flavorful Refried Beans

Preparation Time: 15 minutes
Cooking Time: 8 hours
Servings: 8
Ingredients:

- 3 cups of pinto beans, rinsed
- 1 small jalapeno pepper, seeded and chopped
- 1 medium-sized white onion, peeled and sliced
- 2 tablespoons of minced garlic
- 5 teaspoons of salt
- 2 teaspoons of ground black pepper
- 1/4 teaspoon of ground cumin
- 9 cups of water

Directions:

1. Using a 6-quarts slow cooker, place all the ingredients and stir until it mixes properly.
2. Cover the top, plug in the slow cooker, adjust the cooking time to 6 hours, let it cook on the high heat setting, and add more water if the beans get too dry.
3. When the beans are done, drain them, then reserve the liquid.

4. Mash the beans using a potato masher and pour in the reserved cooking liquid until it reaches your desired mixture.

5. Serve immediately.

Nutrition:

Calories: 268 Protein: 16.5 g Fat: 1.7 g Carbohydrates: 46.6g

478. Smoky Red Beans and Rice

Preparation Time: 15 minutes
Cooking Time: 6 minutes
Servings: 6
Ingredients:

- 30 ounces of cooked red beans
- 1 cup of brown rice, uncooked
- 1 cup of chopped green pepper
- 1 cup of chopped celery
- 1 cup of chopped white onion
- 1 1/2 teaspoon of minced garlic 1/2 teaspoon of salt
- 1/4 teaspoon of cayenne pepper
- 1 teaspoon of smoked paprika
- 2 teaspoons of dried thyme
- 1 bay leaf
- 2 1/3 cups of vegetable broth

Directions:

1. Using a 6-quarts slow cooker, place all the ingredients except for the rice, salt, and cayenne pepper.

2. Stir until it mixes properly and then cover the top.

3. Plug in the slow cooker, adjust the cooking time to 4 hours, and steam on a low heat setting.

4. Then pour in and stir the rice, salt, cayenne pepper and continue cooking for an additional 2 hours at a high heat setting.

5. Serve straight away.

Nutrition: Calories: 791 Protein: 3.2 g Fat: 86.4 g Carbohydrates: 9.6 g

479. Spicy Black-Eyed Peas

Preparation Time: 12 minutes
Cooking Time: 8 hours and 8 minutes
Servings: 8
Ingredients:

- 32-ounce black-eyed peas, uncooked
- 1 cup of chopped orange bell pepper
- 1 cup of chopped celery
- 8-ounce of chipotle peppers, chopped
- 1 cup of chopped carrot
- 1 cup of chopped white onion

- 1 teaspoon of minced garlic 3/4 teaspoon of salt
- 1/2 teaspoon of ground black pepper
- 2 teaspoons of liquid smoke flavoring
- 2 teaspoons of ground cumin
- 1 tablespoon of adobo sauce
- 2 tablespoons of olive oil
- 1 tablespoon of apple cider vinegar
- 4 cups of vegetable broth

Directions:

1. Place a medium-sized non-stick skillet pan over an average temperature of heat; add the bell peppers, carrot, onion, garlic, oil, and vinegar.

2. Stir until it mixes properly and let it cook for 5 to 8 minutes or until it gets translucent.

3. Transfer this mixture to a 6-quarts slow cooker and add the peas, chipotle pepper, adobo sauce, and vegetable broth.

4. Stir until mixed properly and cover the top.

5. Plug in the slow cooker, adjust the cooking time to 8 hours, and let it cook on the low heat setting or until peas are soft. Serve right away.

Nutrition:

Calories: 1071 Protein: 5.3 g Fat: 13.6 g Carbohydrates: 18.5 g

480. Bean and Carrot Spirals

Preparation Time: 10 minutes
Cooking Time: 40 minutes
Servings: 24
Ingredients:

- 4 8-inch flour tortillas
- 1 ½ cup of Easy Mean White Bean dip
- 10 ounces spinach leaves
- ½ cup diced carrots - ½ cup diced red peppers

Directions:

1. Start by preparing the bean dip, seen above. Next, spread out the bean dip on each tortilla, making sure to leave about a ¾ inch white border on the tortillas' surface.

2. Next, place spinach in the center of the tortilla, followed by carrots and red peppers.

3. Roll the tortillas into tight rolls, and cover every roll with plastic wrap or aluminum foil.

4. Let them chill in the fridge for twenty-four hours.

5. Afterward, remove the wrap from the spirals and remove the very ends of the rolls.

6. Slice the rolls into six individual spiral pieces, and arrange them on a platter for serving. Enjoy!

Nutrition: Calories: 205 kcal Protein: 6.41 g Fat: 4.16 g Carbohydrates: 35.13 g

481. Peppered Pinto Beans

Preparation Time: 10 minutes
Cooking Time: 15 minutes
Servings: 6
Ingredients:

- 1 tsp. Chili powder
- 1 tsp. ground cumin
- .5 cup Vegetable
- 2 cans Pinto beans
- 1 Minced jalapeno
- 1 Diced red bell pepper
- 1 tsp. Olive oil

Directions:

1. Take out a pot and heat the oil.
2. Cook the jalapeno and pepper for a bit before adding in the pepper, salt, cumin, broth, and beans.
3. Place to a boil and then reduce the heat to cook for a bit.
4. After 10 minutes, let it cool and serve.

Nutrition: Calories: 183 Carbs: 32g Fat: 2g Protein: 11g

482. Pesto and White Bean Pasta

Preparation Time: 10 minutes
Cooking Time: 10 minutes
Servings: 4
Ingredients:

- 5 cup Chopped black olives
- 25 Diced red onion
- 1 cup Chopped tomato
- 5 cup Spinach pesto
- 1.5 cup Cannellini beans
- 8 oz. Rotini pasta, cooked

Directions:

1. Bring out a bowl and toss together the pesto, beans, and pasta.
2. Add in the olives, red onion, and tomato, and toss around a bit more before serving.

Nutrition: Calories 544 Carbs 83g Fat 17g Protein 23g

483. Lentil Tacos

Preparation Time: 10 minutes;
Cooking Time: 12 minutes
Servings: 8 tacos
Ingredients:

- 2 cups cooked lentils
- ½ cup chopped green bell pepper
- ½ cup chopped white onion

- ½ cup halved grape tomatoes
- 1 teaspoon minced garlic
- ½ teaspoon garlic powder
- 1 teaspoon red chili powder
- ½ teaspoon smoked paprika
- ½ teaspoon ground cumin
- 8 whole-grain tortillas

Directions:

1. Take a large skillet pan, place it over medium heat, add oil, and let it heat.
2. Add onion, bell pepper, and garlic, stir until mixed, and then cook for 5 minutes until vegetables begin to soften.
3. Add lentils and tomatoes, stir in all the spices and then continue cooking for 5 minutes until hot.
4. Assemble the tacos and for this, heat the tortillas until warmed, and then fill each tortilla with ¼ cup of the cooked lentil mixture.
5. Serve straight away.

Nutrition: Calories: 315 Cal; Fat: 7.8 g; Protein: 13 g; Carbs: 49.8 g; Fiber: 16.2 g

484. Red Lentil and Chickpea Bowl

Preparation Time: 5 minutes
Cooking Time: 25 minutes
Servings: 4
Ingredients:

- 1 teaspoon salt
- ½ curry powder
- 2 teaspoons Garam masala seasoning
- 15 oz drained chickpeas
- 2 Diced Roma tomatoes
- 1 cup water
- 2 cups vegetable broth
- 1 cup vegan milk
- ½ cup dried red lentils
- ½ cup diced onion
- 1 cup chopped carrots

Directions:

1. To start this recipe, take out a pot and start boiling some water and carrots on the stove. After 5 minutes, you can drain these and set them to one side.
2. As the carrots are boiling, you can Heat a bit of oil in a frying pan and cook the onion for a bit. It will take about ten minutes.
3. In a big pan, add the chickpeas, carrots, milk, water, vegetable broth, lentils, and onion, along with the seasonings and spices.

4. Bring all of this to a boil before reducing the heat and letting it simmer for a bit.

5. After twenty minutes of cooking, you can take it off the heat before serving and enjoying it.

Nutrition: Calories: 189 Carbs: 22g Fat: 11g Protein: 16g

485. Bean and Rice Burritos

Preparation Time: 10 minutes

Cooking Time: 20 minutes

Servings: 6

Ingredients:

- 32 ounces refried beans - 2 cups cooked rice
- 2 cups chopped spinach
- 1 tablespoon olive oil
- 1/2 cup tomato salsa
- 6 tortillas, whole-grain, warm
- Guacamole as needed for serving

Directions:

1. Switch on the oven, then set it to 375 degrees F and let it preheat.

2. Take a medium saucepan, place it over medium heat, add beans, and cook for 3 to 5 minutes until softened, remove the pan from heat.

3. Place one tortilla on a clean working space, spread some of the beans on it into a log, leaving 2-inches of the edge, top beans with spinach, rice and salsa, and then tightly wrap the tortilla to seal the filling like a burrito.

4. Repeat with the remaining tortillas, place these burritos on a baking sheet, brush them with olive oil and then bake for 15 minutes until golden.

5. Serve burritos with guacamole.

Nutrition: Calories: 421 Fat: 9 g Carbs: 70 g Protein: 15 g

486. Spicy Nut-Butter Noodles

Preparation Time: 15 minutes

Cooking Time: 15 minutes

Servings: 4

Ingredients:

- 1 package soba noodles
- ½ cup vegetable stock
- 1 tablespoon minced fresh ginger
- 2 garlic cloves, minced
- ¼ cup soy sauce
- ¼ cup peanut butter or another nut butter
- 1 teaspoon sriracha or chili paste
- 4 green onions (white and green parts), chopped
- chopped peanuts (optional)

Directions:

1. Prepare the soba noodles according to the package direction. Drain and set aside.

2. In a small saucepan, combine the vegetable stock, ginger, garlic, soy sauce, peanut butter, and Sriracha, over medium-high heat, stirring until the peanut butter is melted and the sauce is heated through.

3. Toss the sauce with the hot noodles.

4. Top with chopped green onions and peanuts if using.

5. Serve immediately.

Nutrition: Calories: 401 Fat: 36.83 g Carbs: 15.61 g Protein: 6.76 g

487. Lentil and Turnip Soup

Preparation Time: 10 minutes

Cooking Time: 25 minutes

Servings: 4

Ingredients:

- 1 cup red lentils
- 2 medium white onions, peeled, sliced
- 14 ounces turnip, peeled, cubed
- 2 tablespoons lemon juice
- 2 ½ teaspoons salt
- 2 bay leaves
- 2 tablespoons lemon zest
- 4 tablespoons olive oil
- 6 cups boiling water

Directions:

1. Take a large pot, place it over medium heat, add oil, and then let it heat.

2. Add onions, cook for 5 minutes until onions turn tender, and then add turnip pieces along with red lentils and bay leaves.

3. Pour in the water, stir until mixed, and then boil the soup for 15 minutes until lentils and turnip turn tender.

4. Add salt, lemon juice, and zest into the juice, stir until mixed, and then cook for 3 minutes.

5. Serve straight away.

Nutrition Per Serving: Calories: 111.7 Cal; Fat: 2 g; Protein: 6.7 g; Carbs: 18.2 g; Fiber: 6.4 g

488. Tomato and Chickpea Curry

Preparation Time: 5 minutes

Cooking Time: 15 minutes

Servings: 4

Ingredients:

- 28 ounces cooked chickpeas
- 2 medium white onions, peeled, sliced

- 4 medium tomatoes, chopped
- 1 teaspoon salt
- 4 tablespoons olive oil
- 2 teaspoons curry powder
- 1 tablespoon soy sauce
- 1 teaspoon ground cumin
- 2 bay leaves
- 14 ounces coconut milk, unsweetened

Directions:

1. Take a large pot, place it over medium-high heat, add oil and then let it heat until hot.
2. Add onion, stir in salt and then cook for 2 minutes.
3. Add bay leaves and all the spices, stir until mixed, and then cook for 1 minute.
4. Add chickpeas, cook for another minute, add tomatoes and then continue cooking for 3 minutes.
5. Add milk, simmer for 5 minutes until thoroughly hot, stir in milk and soy sauce and then cook for 1 minute.
6. Serve straight away.

Nutrition Per Serving: Calories: 177.3 Cal; Fat: 5 g; Protein: 6 g; Carbs: 29 g; Fiber: 6.2 g

489. Lentil Stroganoff

Preparation Time: 10 minutes;
Cooking Time: 50 minutes;
Servings: 4;
Ingredients:

- 1 cup brown lentils
- 1 medium white onion, peeled, chopped
- 2 dill pickles - 1 teaspoon salt
- ¼ teaspoon ground nutmeg
- 1 tablespoon paprika
- 1 tablespoon soy sauce
- 5 tablespoons tomato sauce
- 2 tablespoons cashew cream
- 3 cups of water

Directions:

1. Take a medium pot, place it over medium-high heat, add lentil, and then pour in water.
2. Add onion, stir until mixed, bring the mixture to a boil and then continue boiling the lentils for 40 minutes until lentils turn soft.
3. Add pickles and tomato sauce, stir in salt, paprika, nutmeg, soy sauce, and cashew cream and bring the mixture to a boil.
4. Serve straight away.

Nutrition Per Serving: Calories: 240 Cal; Fat: 100 g; Protein: 24.5 g; Carbs: 33 g; Fiber: 4 g

490. Kung Pao Lentils

Preparation Time: 10 minutes
Cooking Time: 45 minutes
Servings: 3
Ingredients:
For the Lentils:

- ½ cup brown lentils
- 1 ½ cups water
- ¼ teaspoon salt

For the Sauce:

- 3 tablespoons soy sauce
- 2 tablespoons of rice wine vinegar
- 1 tablespoon rice wine
- 1 teaspoon hoisin sauce
- 1 teaspoon toasted sesame oil
- 2 tablespoons maple syrup
- ¼ teaspoon lime zest
- 2 teaspoons cornstarch
- 3 tablespoons water

For the Vegetables:

- ¾ cup chopped celery
- 3 tablespoons cashews
- 1 medium green bell pepper, cored, chopped
- ½ cup chopped red onion
- 1 medium red bell pepper, cored, chopped
- 1 tablespoon minced garlic
- ½ teaspoon ground black pepper
- 1 teaspoon red pepper flakes
- 1-inch piece of ginger, grated
- 2 tablespoons lemon juice
- 2 teaspoon grapeseed oil

Directions:

1. Prepare the lentils and for this, take a medium saucepan, place it over medium-high heat, add lentils in it, pour in water, and then stir in salt.
2. Bring the lentils to boil, cook for 6 minutes, then switch heat to medium level, and then continue boiling for 25 minutes until lentils turn tender.
3. When done, let the lentil rest for 5 minutes, drain excess liquid from the pan, and then set aside until required.
4. Prepare the sauce and for this, take a medium bowl, place all of its ingredients in it and then stir until combined, set aside until required.
5. Prepare the vegetables and for this, take a large skillet pan, place it over medium-high heat, add oil and then let it heat until hot.
6. Add onion, cook for 3 minutes, add cashews and then cook for 1 minute.

7. Stir in bell peppers, celery garlic, and ginger, cook for 4 minutes, add lentils, pour in the sauce, and then stir until mixed.

8. Switch heat to the low level and then cook the lentils for 4 minutes until the sauce has thickened.

9. Stir in red pepper flakes, black pepper, and lemon juice, and then serve.

Nutrition Per Serving: Calories: 283 Cal; Fat: 9 g; Protein: 12 g; Carbs: 37 g; Fiber: 12 g

491. Lentil Brown Rice Soup

Preparation Time: 10 minutes

Cooking Time: 50 minutes

Servings: 4

Ingredients:

- ½ cup diced carrots
- ½ cup brown lentils, soaked
- 1 cup broccoli florets
- 1/3 cup brown rice, soaked
- ½ cup diced red bell pepper
- ½ of a medium white onion, peeled, chopped
- 1 cup baby spinach
- 1 ½ cup diced tomatoes
- 1 green chili, chopped
- 1 tablespoon minced garlic
- 1-inch piece of ginger, grated
- ¾ teaspoon salt
- ½ teaspoon turmeric powder
- ¼ teaspoon ground black pepper
- ½ teaspoon cumin seeds
- 1 bay leaf
- ½ teaspoon mustard seeds
- ½ teaspoon paprika
- 1 teaspoon coriander powder
- ½ teaspoon curry powder
- ¼ teaspoon chipotle pepper
- 1 teaspoon lemon juice
- 1 teaspoon olive oil
- 2 teaspoons ketchup
- 4 cups of water

Directions:

1. Take a large saucepan, place it over medium heat, add oil and then let it heat until hot.

2. Add mustard and cumin seeds, cook for 1 minute until golden, add onion, ginger, garlic, and bay leaf, and then continue cooking for 5 minutes.

3. Add all the spices, stir until mixed, cook for 1 minute, add tomatoes, and then cook for 5 minutes until mixture turn saucy.

4. Add all the vegetables, season with salt, add ketchup and then stir until mixed.

5. Add rice and lentils, pour in the water, stir until mixed, cover the pan with its lid and then cook for 40 minutes until lentils and vegetables have thoroughly cooked.

6. When done, add spinach into the soup, stir until mixed, and then continue cooking for 5 minutes until spinach leaves wilt.

7. Serve straight away.

Nutrition Per Serving: Calories: 205 Cal; Fat: 2 g; Protein: 9.5 g; Carbs: 37 g; Fiber: 10 g

492. Peanut and Lentil Soup

Preparation Time: 5 minutes

Cooking Time: 35 minutes

Ingredients:

- ½ cup red lentils
- ½ cup diced zucchini
- ½ cup diced sweet potato
- ½ cup diced potato
- ½ cup chopped broccoli florets
- ½ of a medium onion, peeled, chopped
- 2 tomatoes
- ½ cup baby spinach
- 2 tablespoons peanuts
- 4 cloves of garlic, peeled
- 1-inch piece of ginger
- 1 ½ teaspoon ground cumin
- ¾ teaspoon salt
- ¼ teaspoon ground black pepper
- 2 teaspoons ground coriander
- 1 ½ teaspoon Harissa Spice Blend
- 1 tablespoon sambal oelek
- 1 teaspoon lemon juice
- ¼ cup peanut butter
- 1 tablespoon tomato paste
- 1 teaspoon olive oil
- 2 ½ cups vegetable stock
- 2 tablespoons chopped cilantro

Directions:

1. Take a large saucepan, place it over medium heat, add oil and then let it heat.

2. Add onion, stir until coated in oil, and then cook for 5 minutes.

3. Place tomatoes in a blender, add garlic, ginger, all the spices, tomato paste, and chili sauce, and then pulse until pureed.

4. Pour the tomato mixture into the onion mixture, stir until mixed, and then cook for 5 minutes.

5. Add half of the nuts, lentils, and all the vegetables, stir in salt, peanut butter, and lemon juice, pour in the stock, cover the pan with its lid and then cook for 20 minutes until vegetables turn tender.

6. Add spinach, continue cooking for 5 minutes, garnish with cilantro, and then serve.

Nutrition Per Serving: Calories: 411 Cal; Fat: 17 g; Protein: 20 g; Carbs: 50 g; Fiber: 18 g

493. Lentil with Spinach
Preparation Time: 5 minutes
Cooking Time: 25 minutes
Servings: 2
Ingredients:

- ½ cup red lentils
- 1 cup chopped spinach
- ½ teaspoon mustard seeds
- ½ teaspoon ground turmeric
- 1/3 teaspoon cumin seeds
- 1/3 teaspoon cayenne
- 1/3 teaspoon nigella seeds
- 2/3 teaspoon salt
- 1/8 teaspoon fennel seeds
- 1/8 teaspoon fenugreek seeds
- 1 teaspoon olive oil
- 2 ½ cups water

Directions:

1. Take a large saucepan, place it over medium heat, add oil and then let it heat until hot.
2. Add all the seeds, stir until coated in oil, and then cook for 1 to 2 minutes until seeds begin to pop.
3. Stir in cayenne pepper and turmeric, stir in lentils and then cook for 1 minute until roasted.
4. Season with salt, pour in the water, and then cook for 20 minutes until lentils have thoroughly cooked; cover the pan partially with its lid.
5. Stir in spinach, simmer for 2 minutes until spinach leaves wilt, and then serve.

Nutrition Per Serving: Calories: 193 Cal; Fat: 3 g; Protein: 12 g; Carbs: 28 g; Fiber: 14 g

494. Beans and Lentils Soup
Preparation Time: 10 minutes
Cooking Time: 48 minutes
Servings: 4
Ingredients

- 2 tbsp water
- 1½ cups onion, diced
- 3 cups potatoes, cut into chunks
- ½ cup celery, diced
- 1 cup carrots, diced
- 4 cloves garlic, minced
- 1½ tsp dried rosemary leaves
- 1 tsp dried thyme leaves
- 1½ tsp ground mustard
- 1 tsp sea salt
- ¼ tsp ground black pepper
- 1 cup green lentils, rinsed
- 2 cups vegetable stock
- 5 cups water
- 1 tbsp red miso
- 1½ tbsp blackstrap molasses
- 2 dried bay leaves
- 15-oz white beans

Directions:

1. Heat a large pot over medium heat.
2. Add all ingredients to it and cook for 8 minutes, stirring occasionally.
3. Increase heat and bring it to a boil.
4. Once it is boiled, let it cook for 40 minutes.
5. Remove bay leaf.
6. Serve and enjoy.

Nutrition: Calories 810, total fat 3.8g, saturated fat 0.6g, cholesterol 0mg, sodium 762mg, total carbohydrate 156.3g, dietary fiber 40.5g, total sugars 29.3g, protein 43.6g, vitamin d 0mcg, calcium 481mg, iron 19mg, potassium 3663mg

CHAPTER 13:

Sauce, Condiments & Dressing

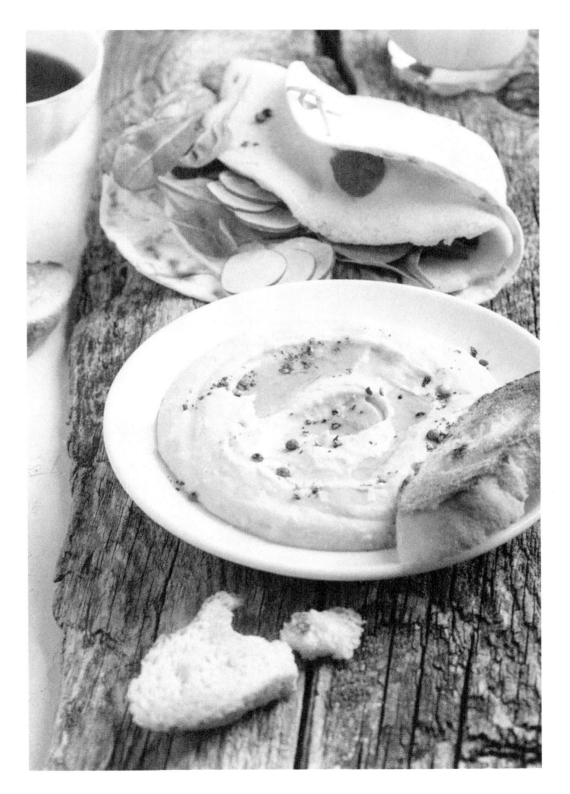

495. White Beans Dip

Preparation Time: 15 minutes

Cooking Time: 0 minutes

Servings: 6

Ingredients

- ½ cup olive oil
- 2 tablespoons garlic cloves, chopped
- 2 (15.8-ounce) cans white beans, drained and rinsed
- ¼ cup fresh lemon juice
- 4 tablespoons fresh parsley, chopped and divided
- 1 teaspoon ground cumin
- ½ tablespoon salt
- 1 teaspoon ground white pepper

Directions:

1. In a small saucepan, place the olive oil and garlic over medium-low heat and cook for about 2 minutes, stirring continuously.
2. Remove the pan of garlic oil from heat and let it cool slightly.
3. Strain the garlic oil, reserving both the oil and garlic in separate bowls.
4. In a food processor, place the beans, garlic, lemon juice, 2 tablespoons of parsley, and cumin, and pulse until smooth.
5. While the motor is running, add the reserved oil and pulse until light and smooth.
6. Transfer the dip into a bowl and stir in salt and white pepper.
7. Serve with the garnishing of remaining parsley.

Nutrition: Calories 263 Total Fat 18.1 g Saturated Fat 2.5 g Cholesterol 0 mg Sodium 630 mg Total Carbs 20.2 g Fiber 5.7 g Sugar 0.3 g Protein 7 g

496. Edamame Hummus

Preparation Time: 15 minutes

Cooking Time: 15 minutes

Servings: 8

Ingredients

- 10 ounces frozen edamame pods
- 1 ripe avocado, peeled, pitted, and chopped roughly
- ½ cup fresh cilantro, chopped
- ¼ cup scallion, chopped
- 1 jalapeño pepper
- 1 garlic clove, peeled
- 2–3 tablespoons fresh lime juice
- Salt and ground black pepper, to taste
- ¼ cup avocado oil
- 2 tablespoons fresh basil leaves

Directions:

1. In a small pot of boiling water, cook the edamame pods for 6–8 minutes.
2. Drain the edamame pods and let them cool completely.
3. Remove soybeans from the pods.
4. In a food processor, add edamame and remaining ingredients (except for oil) and pulse until mostly pureed.
5. While the motor is running, add the reserved oil and pulse until light and smooth.
6. Transfer the hummus into a bowl and serve with the garnishing of remaining basil leaves.

Nutrition: Calories 339 Total Fat 33.8 g Saturated Fat 4.3 g Cholesterol 0 mg Sodium 27 mg Total Carbs 6.3 g Fiber 3.1 g Sugar 0.3 g Protein 5.1 g

497. Beans Mayonnaise

Preparation Time: 10 minutes

Cooking Time: 0 minutes

Servings: 4

Ingredients

- 1 (15-ounce) can white beans, drained and rinsed
- 2 tablespoons apple cider vinegar
- 1 tablespoon fresh lemon juice
- 2 tablespoons yellow mustard
- ¾ teaspoon salt
- 2 garlic cloves, peeled
- 2 tablespoons aquafaba (liquid from the can of beans)

Directions:

1. In a food processor, add all ingredients (except for oil) and pulse until mostly pureed.
2. While the motor is running, add the reserved oil and pulse until light and smooth.
3. Transfer the mayonnaise into a container and refrigerate to chill before serving.

Nutrition: Calories 8 Total Fat 1.1 g Saturated Fat 0.1 g Cholesterol 0 mg Sodium 559 mg Total Carbs 14.3 g Fiber 4.1 g Sugar 0.2 g Protein 5.2 g

498. Cashew Cream

Preparation Time: 10 minutes

Cooking Time: 0 minutes

Servings: 5

Ingredients

- 1 cup raw, unsalted cashews, soaked for 12 hours and drained - ½ cup water
- 1 tablespoon nutritional yeast
- 1 teaspoon fresh lemon juice
- 1/8 teaspoon salt

Directions:

1. In a food processor, add all ingredients and pulse at high speed until creamy and smooth.
2. Serve immediately.

Nutrition: Calories 165 Total Fat 12.8 g Saturated Fat 2.5 g Cholesterol 0 mg Sodium 65 mg Total Carbs 9.9 g Fiber 1.3 g Sugar 1.4 g Protein 5.1 g

499. Lemon Tahini

Preparation Time: 15 minutes

Cooking Time: 0 minutes

Servings: 4

Ingredients

- ¼ cup fresh lemon juice
- 4 medium garlic cloves, pressed
- ½ cup tahini
- ½ teaspoon fine sea salt
- Pinch of ground cumin
- 6 tablespoons ice water

Directions:

1. In a medium bowl, combine the lemon juice and garlic and set aside for 10 minutes.
2. Through a fine-mesh sieve, strain the mixture into another medium bowl, pressing the garlic solids.
3. Discard the garlic solids.
4. In the bowl of lemon juice, add the tahini, salt, and cumin, and whisk until well blended.
5. Slowly, add water, 2 tablespoons at a time, whisking well after each addition.

Nutrition: Calories 187 Total Fat 16.3 g Saturated Fat 2.4 g Cholesterol 0 mg Sodium 273 mg Total Carbs 7.7 g Fiber 2.9 g Sugar 0.5 g Protein 5.4 g

500. Avocado Dill Dressing

Preparation Time: 20 minutes

Cooking Time: 0 minutes

Servings: 1 cup

Ingredients:

- 2 ounces raw, unsalted cashews (about ½ cup)
- ½ cup water
- 3 tablespoons lemon juice
- ½ medium, ripe avocado, chopped
- 1 medium clove garlic
- 2 tablespoons chopped fresh dill
- 2 green onions, white and green parts, chopped

Directions:

1. Put the cashews, water, lemon juice, avocado, and garlic into a blender. Keep it aside for at least 15 minutes to soften the cashews.

2. Blend until everything is fully mixed. Fold in the dill and green onions, and blend briefly to retain some texture.
3. Store in an airtight container in the fridge for up to 3 days and stir well before serving.

Nutrition: Calories: 312; Fat: 21g; Protein: 8g; Carbohydrates: 23g

501. Cilantro Chili Dressing

Preparation Time: 5 minutes

Cooking Time: 0 minutes

Servings: ¾ cup

Ingredients:

- 1 (4-ounce) can chopped green chilies
- 1 to 2 cloves garlic
- ¼ cup fresh lime juice
- ¼ cup water
- ¼ cup chopped fresh cilantro
- 2 teaspoons maple syrup (optional)
- Freshly ground pepper, to taste

Directions:

1. Combine all the ingredients in a food processor and pulse until creamy and smooth.

Nutrition: Calories: 54; Fat: 2g; Protein: 2g; Carbohydrates: 6g

502. Spinach and Avocado Dressing

Preparation Time: 10 minutes

Cooking Time: 0 minutes

Servings: 1 cup

Ingredients:

- 2 ounces spinach leaves (about 1 cup chopped and packed) - ¼ medium, ripe avocado
- ¼ cup water, plus more as needed
- 1 small clove garlic
- 1 tablespoon Dijon mustard
- 1 green onion, white and green parts, sliced

Directions:

1. Blitz all the ingredients in a blender until thoroughly mixed.
2. Add a little more water if a thinner consistency is desired.

Nutrition: Calories: 146; Fat: 1g; Carbohydrates: 1g; Protein: 2g

503. Maple Dijon Dressing

Preparation Time: 5 minutes

Cooking Time: 0 minutes

Servings: ½ cup

Ingredients:

- ¼ cup apple cider vinegar

- 2 teaspoons Dijon mustard
- 2 tablespoons maple syrup
- 2 tablespoons low-sodium vegetable broth
- ¼ teaspoon black pepper
- Salt, to taste (optional)

Directions:
1. Mix the apple cider vinegar, Dijon mustard, maple syrup, vegetable broth, and black pepper in a resealable container until well incorporated.
2. Season with salt, if desired.

Nutrition: Calories: 82; Fat: 0g; Carbohydrates: 19g; Protein: 1g

504. Orange Mango Dressing

Preparation Time: 5 minutes
Cooking Time: 0 minutes
Servings: ¾ cup
Ingredients:
- 1 medium mango, peeled and cut into chunks
- 1 clove garlic, crushed
- ½ cup orange juice
- 1 teaspoon soy sauce
- ¼ teaspoon curry powder

Directions:
1. Place all the ingredients in a blender and blend until creamy and smooth.

Nutrition: Calories: 51; Fat: 1g; Carbohydrates: 11g; Protein: 1g

505. Cashew Mustard Dressing

Preparation Time: 20 minutes
Cooking Time: 0 minutes
Servings: 1 cup
Ingredients:
- 2 ounces raw, unsalted cashews (about ½ cup)
- ½ cup water
- 3 tablespoons lemon juice
- 2 teaspoons apple cider vinegar
- 2 tablespoons Dijon mustard
- 1 medium clove garlic

Directions:
1. Put all the ingredients in a food processor and keep them aside for at least 15 minutes.
2. Purée until the ingredients are combined into a smooth and creamy mixture.
3. Thin the dressing with a little extra water as needed to achieve your preferred consistency.

Nutrition: Calories: 187; Fat: 13g; Carbohydrates: 11g; Protein: 6g

506. Vinegary Maple Syrup Dressing

Preparation Time: 5 minutes
Cooking Time: 0 minutes
Servings: 2/3 cup
Ingredients:
- ¼ cup rice vinegar
- ¼ cup balsamic vinegar
- 2½ tablespoons maple syrup (optional)
- 1½ tablespoons Dijon mustard
- Freshly ground pepper, to taste

Directions:
1. Combine all the ingredients in a jar.
2. Cover and shake until well blended.

Nutrition: Calories: 49; Fat: 0g; Carbohydrates: 12g; Protein: 0g

507. Garlic Cilantro Dressing

Preparation Time: 10 minutes
Cooking Time: 0 minutes
Servings: 1 cup
Ingredients:
- 1/2 cup almonds
- 1/2 cup water
- 1 bunch cilantro
- 1 red chili pepper, chopped
- 2 cloves garlic, crushed
- 2 tablespoons fresh lime juice
- 1 teaspoon lime zest
- Sea salt and ground black pepper
- 5 tablespoons extra-virgin olive oil

Directions:
1. Place the almonds and water in your blender and mix until creamy and smooth.
2. Add in the cilantro, chili pepper, garlic, lime juice, lime zest, salt and black pepper; blitz until everything is well combined.
3. Then, gradually add in the olive oil and mix until smooth.

Nutrition: Calories: 181; Fat: 18g; Carbohydrates: 5g; Protein: 3g

508. Cranberry Dressing

Preparation Time: 5 minutes
Cooking Time: 0 minutes
Servings: 2 cups
Ingredients:
- ¼ cup rice vinegar
- ¼ cup Dijon mustard
- ¼ cup cranberry sauce

- ¼ cup apple cider vinegar
- ¼ cup walnut oil
- 1 cup vegetable oil
- 1 garlic clove, chopped
- Salt and ground black pepper, as required

Directions:

1. Put rice vinegar, Dijon mustard, cranberry sauce, apple cider vinegar, garlic, salt and black pepper in a blender and pulse until smooth.
2. Add walnut oil and vegetable and pulse to form a creamy mixture.
3. Dish out in a bowl and serve to enjoy.

Nutrition: Calories: 220; Fat: 12g; Protein: 5g; Carbohydrates: 7g

509. Thai Peanut Dressing

Preparation Time: 10 minutes

Cooking Time: 0 minutes

Servings: ½ cup

Ingredients:

- 2 tbsp. Water
- ¼ cup Natural Peanut Butter
- Pinch of Cayenne
- 2 tbsp. Sesame Oil
- Juice of ½ of 1 Lemon
- 2 tbsp. Soy Sauce
- 1 tsp. Maple Syrup
- 1 tbsp. Rice Vinegar
- 2 Garlic cloves, minced
- 2 tsp. Ginger, fresh & grated

Directions:

1. Mix all the ingredients in a large bowl, excluding the water, with an immersion blender or blend in a high-speed blender.
2. Blend until you get a smooth, thickened sauce.
3. Add water as needed to get the consistency you desire.

Nutrition: Calories: 75; Total fat: 1g; Carbohydrates: 15g; Protein: 4g

510. Herb Avocado Salad Dressing

Preparation Time: 10 minutes

Cooking Time: 0 minutes

Servings: 2 cups

Ingredients:

- 1 medium-sized avocado, pitted, peeled and mashed
- 4 tablespoons extra-virgin olive oil
- 4 tablespoons almond milk
- 2 tablespoons cilantro, minced

- 2 tablespoons parsley, minced
- 1 lemon, juiced
- 2 garlic cloves, minced
- 1/2 teaspoon mustard seeds
- 1/2 teaspoon red pepper flakes
- Kosher salt and cayenne pepper, to taste

Directions:

1. Mix all the above ingredients in your food processor or blender.
2. Blend until uniform, smooth and creamy.

Nutrition: Calories: 101; Protein: 1g; Carbohydrates: 4g; Fat: 9g

511. Cesar Style Dressing

Preparation Time: 5 minutes

Cooking Time: 0 minutes

Servings: 1 ½ cup

Ingredients:

- 3 tablespoons vegan mayonnaise
- 2 tablespoons vegan Worcestershire sauce
- 1 tablespoon Dijon mustard
- 1 teaspoon red wine vinegar
- 4 teaspoons minced garlic (about 4 cloves)
- ¾ cup extra-virgin olive oil
- ¼ cup nutritional yeast
- ¼ teaspoon salt
- ¼ teaspoon freshly ground black pepper

Directions:

1. In a blender or food processor, combine the mayonnaise, Worcestershire, mustard, vinegar, and garlic.
2. Blend until the ingredients are well combined.
3. You might need to stop and scrape down the sides during this process to ensure all ingredients are mixed well.
4. With the blender running, slowly add the olive oil until the dressing begins to thicken.
5. Continue to add olive oil until desired consistency. Add the nutritional yeast, and pulse a few times to incorporate.
6. Season with salt and pepper, and do a final pulse or two.

Nutrition: Calories: 127; Fat: 14g; Carbohydrates: 2g; Protein: 1g

512. Vegan Thousand Island

Preparation Time: 10 minutes

Cooking Time: 0 minutes

Servings: 2 cups

Ingredients:

- 1¼ cup vegan mayonnaise

- 2 tablespoons unsweetened almond milk or soymilk, plus more if needed
- 1/4 cup ketchup
- 2 teaspoons vegan Worcestershire sauce
- ¼ teaspoon salt, plus more if needed
- 4 to 6 tablespoons sweet pickle relish, to taste

Directions:

1. In a blender or food processor, combine the mayonnaise, milk, ketchup, Worcestershire sauce, and ¼ teaspoon salt.
2. Pulse until smooth, about 30 seconds.
3. Add more nut milk if you prefer a smoother consistency.
4. Transfer the dressing to a bowl.
5. Stir in the relish, and add additional salt to taste.

Nutrition: Calories: 96; Fat: 8g; Carbohydrates: 4g; Protein: 0g

513. Strawberry Peach Vinaigrette

Preparation Time: 5 minutes
Cooking Time: 0 minutes
Servings: 1 ¼ cup
Ingredients:

- 1 peach, pitted
- 4 strawberries
- ¼ cup water
- 2 tablespoons balsamic vinegar

Directions:

1. In a blender, combine the peach, strawberries, water, and vinegar.
2. Blend on high for 1 to 2 minutes, or until the dressing has a smooth consistency.

Nutrition: Calories: 10; Protein: 0g; Carbohydrates: 2g; Fat: 0g

CHAPTER 14:

Sauce, Condiments & Dressing 2

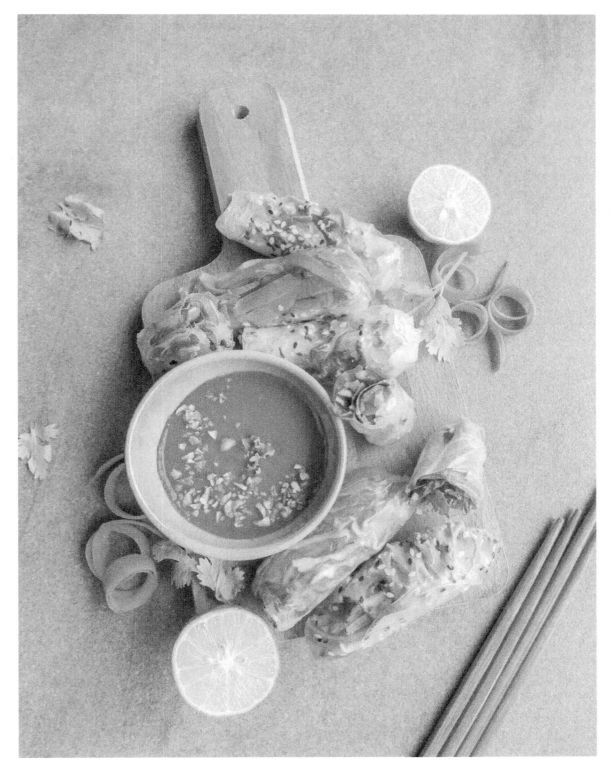

514. Raspberry Vinaigrette

Preparation Time: 5 minutes

Cooking Time: 0 minutes

Servings: 1

Ingredients:

- ½ cup raspberries
- ½ cup olive oil
- ¼ cup balsamic vinegar or white wine vinegar
- 2 to 3 tablespoons sugar, maple syrup, or Simple Syrup
- ¼ cup water
- Pinch salt

Directions:

1. In a small blender or food processor, combine the raspberries, olive oil, vinegar, sugar, water, and salt.
2. Purée until smooth.
3. Store in an airtight container in the refrigerator for up to 1 week.
4. Shake before using.

PRO TIP: Add ¼ cup fresh basil leaves for a truly special flavor.

Nutrition Per Serving (2 tablespoons) Calories: 139; Protein: 0g; Total fat: 14g; Saturated fat: 2g; Carbohydrates: 10g; Fiber: 1g

515. Creamy Tahini Dressing

Preparation Time: 5 minutes

Cooking Time: 0 minutes

Servings: 1

Ingredients:

- ½ cup tahini
- ¼ cup freshly squeezed lemon juice or apple cider vinegar
- 1 tablespoon olive oil (optional)
- 1 garlic clove, minced, or ½ teaspoon garlic powder (optional)
- 1 tablespoon sugar or maple syrup (optional)
- ¼ cup water, plus more as needed

Directions:

1. In a small bowl, mix the tahini and lemon juice, stirring until it becomes very thick and creamy.
2. Stir in the olive oil (if using), garlic (if using), sugar (if using), and water. If it's too thick for your liking, add more water, 1 tablespoon at a time, until you get the consistency you desire.
3. Store in an airtight container in the refrigerator for up to 1 week.

4. It will thicken to a spreadable consistency as it sits, so, if using it as a dressing, add 2 tablespoons of water and stir well.

Nutrition Per Serving (2 tablespoons) Calories: 111; Protein: 3g; Total fat: 10g; Saturated fat: 1g; Carbohydrates: 4g; Fiber: 1g

516. Peanut Sauce

Preparation Time: 10 minutes

Cooking Time: 0 minutes

Servings: 1

Ingredients:

- ½ cup creamy peanut butter
- 3 tablespoons apple cider vinegar or freshly squeezed lime juice
- 2 tablespoons soy sauce
- 1 to 2 teaspoons toasted sesame oil
- 1 tablespoon sugar or maple syrup (optional)
- Pinch red pepper flakes (optional)
- ¼ cup water, plus more as needed

Directions:

1. In a small bowl, mix the peanut butter, vinegar, and soy sauce, stirring until it becomes light in color and very thick and creamy.
2. Stir in the sesame oil, sugar (if using), red pepper flakes (if using), and water. Add more water if you like, 1 tablespoon at a time, until you get the consistency you desire.
3. Store in an airtight container in the refrigerator for up to 1 week. It will thicken to a spreadable consistency as it sits, so, if you're using it as a dressing, add 2 tablespoons of water and stir until smooth.

SUBSTITUTION TIP: If you use chunky peanut butter, add 1 extra tablespoon to make up for the chunks.

Nutrition Per Serving (2 tablespoons) Calories: 110; Protein: 4.5g; Total fat: 9g; Saturated fat: 2g; Carbohydrates: 5g; Fiber: 1g

517. Cilantro-Lime Dressing

Preparation Time: 10 minutes

Cooking Time: 0 minutes

Servings: 1

Ingredients:

- ¼ cup chopped fresh cilantro
- ¾ cup canned coconut milk
- 1 tablespoon tahini or ¼ cup plain nondairy yogurt
- 3 tablespoons freshly squeezed lime juice
- 1 tablespoon sugar
- Salt

Directions:

1. In a small blender or food processor, combine the cilantro, coconut milk, tahini, lime juice, and sugar, and season to taste with salt.
2. Blend for about 1 minute until smooth.
3. Taste, and add more salt as needed.
4. Store in an airtight container in the refrigerator for up to 1 week.

PRO TIP: Add some minced jalapeño pepper for a spicy boost—up to one whole pepper, depending on your preferred spice level. Remove the seeds if you like; they're very spicy.

Nutrition Per Serving (2 tablespoons) Calories: 59; Protein: 1g; Total fat: 6g; Saturated fat: 4g; Carbohydrates: 2g; Fiber: 0g

518. Caesar Dressing

Preparation Time: 5 minutes

Cooking Time: 0 minutes

Servings: 1

Ingredients:

- ½ cup plain non-dairy yogurt plus ¼ cup tahini, or ¾ cup plain non-dairy yogurt, or ½ cup tahini plus ¼ cup water
- 2 tablespoons nutritional yeast
- 2 to 3 tablespoons freshly squeezed lemon juice
- 3 or 4 pitted green olives
- 2 teaspoons Dijon mustard
- 1 garlic clove or ½ teaspoon garlic powder
- Pinch salt

Directions:

1. In a small blender, combine the yogurt, tahini, nutritional yeast, lemon juice, olives, mustard, garlic, and salt.
2. Purée until smooth, adding water as needed to thin it to your desired consistency.
3. Store in an airtight container in the refrigerator for up to 1 week.
4. It will thicken to a spreadable consistency as it sits, so, if you're using it as a dressing, add 2 tablespoons of water and stir until smooth.

Nutrition Per Serving (2 tablespoons) Calories: 71; Protein: 3g; Total fat: 5g; Saturated fat: 1g; Carbohydrates: 5g; Fiber: 2g

519. Coconut Curry Sauce

Preparation Time: 5 minutes

Cooking Time: 0 minutes

Servings: 1

Ingredients:

- ¾ cup canned coconut milk
- 1 tablespoon curry paste or 1 to 2 teaspoons curry powder
- 1 tablespoon sugar
- 1 tablespoon freshly squeezed lime juice or lemon juice
- Salt

Directions:

1. In a small bowl, whisk together the coconut milk, curry paste, sugar, and lime juice.
2. Season to taste with salt.
3. Store in an airtight container in the refrigerator for up to 1 week.

A CLOSER LOOK: Curry paste is available in the Asian section of most grocery stores; the red variety is slightly spicier than the green.

Nutrition Per Serving (2 tablespoons) Calories: 56; Protein: 1g; Total fat: 5g; Saturated fat: 4g; Carbohydrates: 2g; Fiber: 0g

520. Herbed Croutons

Preparation Time: 5 minutes

Cooking Time: 10 minutes

Servings: 4

Ingredients:

- 2 tablespoons olive oil or vegan margarine, melted
- 1 teaspoon dried herbs
- Salt
- 1 slice bread, cut into bite-size cubes

Directions:

1. Preheat the oven or toaster oven to 400°F or heat a small skillet over medium-high heat.
2. In a small bowl, stir together the olive oil and dried herbs, season to taste with salt.
3. Add the bread cubes and toss to coat in the oil. Transfer to a small rimmed baking sheet, toaster oven tray, or skillet.
4. Bake or fry for 10 minutes, turning occasionally, until lightly browned.
5. Store in an airtight container in the refrigerator for up to 5 days.

Nutrition Per Serving Calories: 77; Protein: 1g; Total fat: 7g; Saturated fat: 1g; Carbohydrates: 3g; Fiber: 1g

521. Spinach Pesto

Preparation Time: 5 minutes

Cooking Time: 0 minutes

Servings: 1

Ingredients:

- ½ cup unsalted raw pumpkin seeds
- 2 cups packed raw spinach

- ¼ cup fresh parsley or fresh basil
- 3 tablespoons olive oil, plus more as needed
- 2 to 4 tablespoons nutritional yeast (optional)
- 1 tablespoon freshly squeezed lemon juice, plus more as needed
- 1 small garlic clove, peeled
- 3 to 4 tablespoons water, plus more as needed (depending on how much nutritional yeast you use)
- Salt

Directions:

1. In a food processor or small blender, process the pumpkin seeds until they're broken up quite a bit.
2. Add the spinach, parsley, olive oil, nutritional yeast (if using), lemon juice, garlic, and water, and process until smooth.
3. Season to taste with salt. If necessary, stir in an extra drizzle of olive oil, lemon juice, and/or water to get a creamy texture.
4. Store in an airtight container in the refrigerator for up to 5 days or in the freezer indefinitely.

PREP TIP: If you prefer a softer garlic flavor, when you have the oven on for something else (between 350°F and 400°F), put some garlic cloves, in their skins, in a small oven-proof dish and bake for about 10 minutes, until soft. Squeeze them out of their skins to use—they're great spread on bread or mashed into potatoes.

Nutrition Per Serving (2 tablespoons) Calories: 133; Protein: 5g; Total fat: 12g; Saturated fat: 2g; Carbohydrates: 4g; Fiber: 1g

522. Refried Beans

Preparation Time: 10 minutes

Cooking Time: 10 minutes

Servings: 3

Ingredients:

- 1 tablespoon olive oil
- ¼ onion, finely diced, or 1 teaspoon onion powder
- Salt
- 1 garlic clove, minced, or ½ teaspoon garlic powder
- ½ to 1 teaspoon chili powder
- 1 (15-ounce) can pinto beans or black beans, drained and rinsed
- 1 tablespoon freshly squeezed lime juice (optional)
- Freshly ground black pepper

Directions:

1. Heat the olive oil in a skillet over medium heat.
2. Add the onion and a pinch of salt, and sauté for about 3 minutes, until the onion is soft.

3. Stir in the garlic and chili powder, and sauté for 1 to 2 minutes more.
4. Stir in the pinto beans, and cook for about 2 minutes to heat them through.
5. Using a fork or potato masher, mash the beans to your desired consistency.
6. Stir in the lime juice (if using) and season to taste with pepper. Taste, and add more salt and pepper as needed.
7. Store in an airtight container in the refrigerator for up to 1 week.

Nutrition Per Serving (½ cup) Calories: 61; Protein: 3g; Total fat: 2g; Saturated fat: 0g; Carbohydrates: 8g; Fiber: 3g

523. Simple Barbecue Sauce

Preparation Time: 5 minutes

Cooking Time: 5 minutes

Servings: 1

Ingredients:

- 2/3 cup ketchup
- 1/3 cup apple cider vinegar
- ¼ cup packed brown sugar
- 2 tablespoons soy sauce or tamari
- ¼ teaspoon garlic powder (optional, but highly recommended)
- Pinch red pepper flakes, or to taste

Directions:

1. In a medium saucepan, stir together the ketchup, vinegar, brown sugar, soy sauce, garlic powder (if using), and red pepper flakes.
2. Bring to a simmer over medium-low heat, and cook for about 5 minutes.
3. Alternatively, stir together the ingredients in a microwave-safe bowl, cover, and heat on high power for 1 minute. Let cool.
4. Store in an airtight container in the refrigerator for up to 1 week.

PRO TIP: For a smoky flavor, add 1 to 2 teaspoons of smoked paprika and/or a few drops of liquid smoke.

Nutrition Per Serving (2 tablespoons) Calories: 44; Protein: 1g; Total fat: 0g; Saturated fat: 0g; Carbohydrates: 10g; Fiber: 0g

524. Garlic Butter

Preparation Time: 5 minutes

Cooking Time: 0 minutes

Servings: ¼ CUP

Ingredients:

- ¼ cup coconut oil or vegan margarine, softened
- 2 teaspoons garlic powder or 4 small garlic cloves, minced

- 4 teaspoons nutritional yeast (optional)
- Large pinch salt

Directions:

1. In a small bowl, stir together the coconut oil, garlic powder, nutritional yeast (if using), and salt.
2. Store in an airtight container in the refrigerator.
3. If you used fresh garlic, it will keep for up to 2 weeks.
4. It will keep for a while longer if you used garlic powder.

Nutrition Per Serving (1 tablespoon) Calories: 134; Protein: 2g; Total fat: 14g; Saturated fat: 12g; Carbohydrates: 3g; Fiber: 1g

525. Pram Sprinkle

Preparation Time: 5 minutes

Cooking Time: 0 minutes

Servings: ½ Cup

Ingredients:

- ½ cup seeds or nuts, such as sunflower, pumpkin, sesame, or hemp seeds, or walnuts, cashews, or almonds
- ¼ cup nutritional yeast
- Pinch salt

Directions:

1. In a small blender or clean coffee grinder, pulse the seeds or nuts until crumbly.
2. Add the nutritional yeast and salt, and pulse a few more times.
3. Store in an airtight container at room temperature for up to 1 week.

Nutrition Per Serving (2 tablespoons) Calories: 203; Protein: 11g; Total fat: 15g; Saturated fat: 2g; Carbohydrates: 11g; Fiber: 6g

526. Sour Cream

Preparation Time: 5 minutes

Cooking Time: 0 minutes

Servings: 1

Ingredients:

- 8 ounces silken tofu, or 1 cup plain non-dairy yogurt, or 6 ounces firm tofu plus 2 tablespoons water
- 2 tablespoons freshly squeezed lemon juice
- 1 tablespoon olive oil
- 1 tablespoon apple cider vinegar
- 1 teaspoon onion powder
- 1/2 teaspoon garlic powder
- 1/8 to ¼ teaspoon salt, plus more as needed

Directions:

1. In a small blender or food processor, combine the tofu, lemon juice, olive oil, vinegar, onion powder, garlic powder, and salt.
2. Purée until smooth and creamy.
3. Taste and add more salt as needed.
4. Store in an airtight container in the refrigerator for up to 1 week.

Nutrition Per Serving (2 tablespoons) Calories: 63; Protein: 5g; Total fat: 4g; Saturated fat: 1g; Carbohydrates: 2g; Fiber: 1g

527. Simple Syrup

Preparation Time: 5 minutes

Cooking Time: 5 To 10 minutes

Servings: 1

Ingredients:

- ¾ cup water
- ¾ cup packed dark brown sugar, granulated sugar, unrefined coconut sugar, or muscovite sugar

Directions:

1. In a small saucepan, bring the water to a light boil over medium heat.
2. Add the brown sugar, and stir to dissolve.
3. Reduce the heat to low and simmer for a few minutes or longer if you want a thicker syrup.
4. Alternatively, put the water in a microwave-safe container and heat it on high power for 2 minutes.
5. Stir in the sugar and let sit.
6. Or, boil the water in a kettle and combine it with the sugar in a small heat-proof bowl. Let stand for a few minutes.
7. Store in an airtight container in the refrigerator or at room temperature for up to 2 weeks.

PRO TIP: Look for maple extract in the baking aisle, and add a drop or two to give the syrup a maple flavor.

Nutrition Per Serving (1 tablespoon) Calories: 27; Protein: 0g; Total fat: 0g; Saturated fat: 0g; Carbohydrates: 6g; Fiber: 0g

528. Chocolate Icing

Preparation Time: 5 minutes

Cooking Time: 0 minutes

Servings: 1

Ingredients:

- 1 tablespoon unsweetened cocoa powder
- 1 tablespoon sugar
- 2 teaspoons non-dairy milk

Directions:
1. In a small bowl, stir together the cocoa powder and sugar.
2. Slowly add the milk, 1 teaspoon at a time, stirring to bring the icing together.

SUBSTITUTION TIP: Swap carob powder for the cocoa powder. It doesn't taste like chocolate, but it has a similar vibe and more calcium and natural sweetness than cocoa.

Nutrition Per Serving Calories: 49; Protein: 1g; Total fat: 1g; Saturated fat: 0g; Carbohydrates: 12g; Fiber: 2g

529. Vanilla Icing

Preparation Time: 5 minutes
Cooking Time: 0 minutes
Servings: ½ cup
Ingredients:
- 1 tablespoon coconut oil or unsalted vegan margarine, softened
- ¾ cup powdered sugar or
- ½ cup granulated sugar plus
- ¼ cup cornstarch, plus more as needed
- 1 tablespoon nondairy milk
- ½ teaspoon vanilla extract (optional)

Directions:
1. In a medium bowl, stir together the coconut oil, powdered sugar, milk, and vanilla (if using) until smooth.
2. Add more powdered sugar as needed, 1 tablespoon at a time, to get a spreadable consistency.

Per Serving Nutrition (2 tablespoons) Calories: 137; Protein: 0g; Total fat: 4g; Saturated fat: 3g; Carbohydrates: 25g; Fiber: 0g

530. General Tso Sauce

Preparation Time: 5 minutes
Cooking Time: 10 minutes
Servings: 4
Ingredients
- ¼ cup Rice Vinegar
- ½ cup water
- 1 ½ T Sriracha Sauce
- ¼ cup soy sauce
- 1 ½ T Corn Starch
- ½ cup sugar

Directions:
1. General Tso Sauce is a classic, and you can now make a healthier version of it! All you must do is take out your saucepan and place all the ingredients in it.
2. Once in place, bring everything over medium heat and whisk together for ten minutes or until the sauce begins to get thick.
3. Finally, remove from the heat and enjoy!

Nutrition: Calories: 150 Carbs: 30g Fat: 0g Proteins: 2g

531. Cashew Cheese Sauce

Preparation Time: 5 minutes
Cooking Time: 0 minutes
Servings: 8
Ingredients
- 1 Tbsp Olive Oil
- ½ cup Water
- ¾ cup Raw Cashews
- 1 Tbsp Lemon Juice
- ½ tsp Tamari Sauce
- Salt, to taste

Directions:
1. As you begin a plant-based diet, you may be thinking you will miss your cheese.
2. Luckily, this cashew cheese is an excellent replacement!
3. All you will have to do is take the rest of the components, place them into a blender, and combine until completely smoothed out.
4. Once you are done, place it in the fridge and enjoy!

Nutrition: Calories: 90 Carbs: 5g Fat: 10g Proteins: 5g

532. Ranch Dressing

Preparation Time: 10 minutes
Cooking Time: 0 minutes
Servings: 8
Ingredients
- 1 cup Water (1 C.)
- 1/2 tsp Dried Dill (.)
- 1 tsp Garlic Powder
- 2 Tbsp Chives, Chopped
- 2 Tbsp Lemon Juice
- Salt, to Taste
- 1 tsp Dried Parsley
- 1 1/3 cup Raw Cashews
- 1 tsp Onion Powder

Directions:
1. Before you begin this recipe, you will want to soak your cashews for at least one hour. This will make the next step much easier!
2. Once the cashews are done, place them into your blender along with the garlic, onion, lemon, and water.

3. Go ahead and blend these ingredients on high until the sauce gets creamy.

4. When this is all set, you can gently stir in the chives, dill, and parsley, and then enjoy your vegan dressing!

Nutrition: Calories: 140 Carbs: 9g Fat: 10g Proteins: 3g

533. Minty Lime Dressing

Preparation Time: 10 minutes

Cooking Time: 0 minutes

Servings: 4

Ingredients

- 6 Tbsp Olive Oil
- 1 Tbsp Fresh Chives
- 1 Tbsp Fresh Mint
- 1 Lime
- Salt, to taste
- 2 Tbsp White Wine Vinegar

Directions:

1. For a salad dressing that is cool and refreshing, this recipe will certainly hit the spot! You will want to start by getting a small mixing bowl out and adding the fresh herbs with the vinegar, salt, and juice from your lime.

2. When these are combined well, you will slowly want to add in the olive oil while continuously whisking the ingredients together.

3. Once all the olive oil is in, season to your liking, and then enjoy over your favorite salad

Nutrition: Calories: 10 Carbs: 2g Fat: 0g Proteins: 0g

CHAPTER 15:

Gluten free Recipes

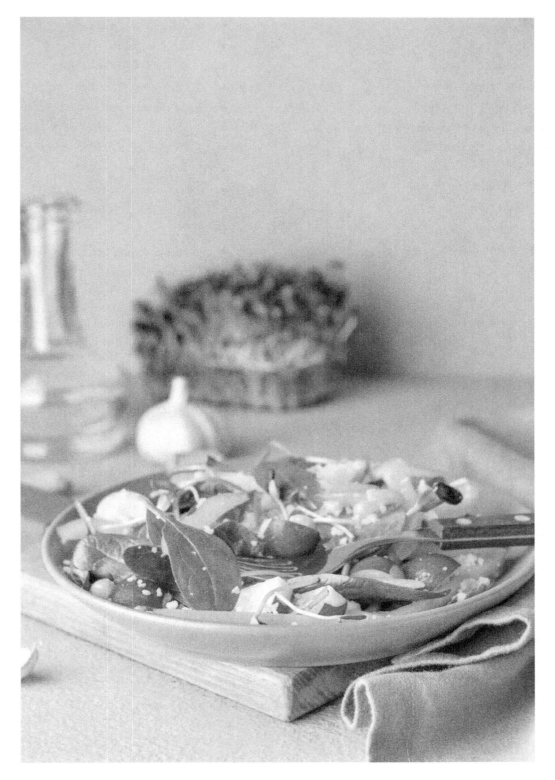

534. Eggplant and Rice Casserole

Preparation Time: 30 minutes
Cooking Time: 35 minutes
Servings: 4
Ingredients:

For sauce

- ½ cup olive oil
- 1 small onion
- 4 garlic cloves
- 6 ripe tomatoes
- 2 tablespoons tomato paste
- 1 teaspoon dried oregano
- ¼ teaspoon ground nutmeg
- ¼ teaspoon ground cumin

For casserole

- 4 (6-inch) Japanese eggplants
- 2 tablespoons olive oil
- 1 cup cooked rice
- 2 tablespoons pine nuts
- 1 cup water

Directions:

For sauce

1. In a heavy-bottomed saucepan over medium heat, heat the olive oil. Add the onion and cook for 5 minutes.
2. Stir in the garlic, tomatoes, tomato paste, oregano, nutmeg, and cumin. Bring to a boil. Cover, reduce heat to low, and simmer for 10 minutes. Remove and set aside.

For casserole

3. Preheat the broiler.
4. While the sauce simmers, drizzle the eggplant with the olive oil and place them on a baking sheet. Broil for about 5 minutes until golden. Remove and let cool.
5. Turn the oven to 375°F. Arrange the cooled eggplant, cut-side up, in a 9-by-13-inch baking dish. Gently scoop out some flesh to make room for the stuffing.
6. In a bowl, combine half the tomato sauce, the cooked rice, and pine nuts. Fill each eggplant half with the rice mixture.
7. In the same bowl, combine the remaining tomato sauce and water. Pour over the eggplant.
8. Bake, covered, for 20 minutes.

Nutrition:
453 calories 39g fat
6g protein 14g Carbohydrates

535. Many Vegetable Couscous

Preparation Time: 15 minutes
Cooking Time: 45 minutes
Servings: 8
Ingredients:

- ¼ cup olive oil
- 1 onion, chopped
- 4 garlic cloves, minced
- 2 jalapeño peppers
- ½ teaspoon ground cumin
- ½ teaspoon ground coriander
- 1 (28-ounce) can crushed tomatoes
- 2 tablespoons tomato paste
- 1/8 teaspoon salt - 2 bay leaves
- 11 cups water, divided
- 4 carrots, peeled and cut into 2-inch pieces
- 2 zucchinis - 1 acorn squash
- 1 (15-ounce) can chickpeas
- ¼ cup chopped Preserved Lemons (optional)
- 3 cups couscous

Directions:

1. In a large heavy-bottomed pot over medium heat, heat the olive oil. Stir in the onion and cook for 4 minutes. Stir in the garlic, jalapeños, cumin, and coriander. Cook for 1 minute.
2. Add the tomatoes, tomato paste, salt, bay leaves, and 8 cups of water. Bring the mixture to a boil.
3. Add the carrots, zucchini, and acorn squash and return to a boil. Reduce the heat slightly, cover, and cook for about 20 minutes until the vegetables are tender but not mushy. Remove 2 cups of the cooking liquid and set aside. Season as needed. Add the chickpeas and preserved lemons (if using). Cook for 2 to 3 minutes, and turn off the heat.
4. In a medium pan, bring the remaining 3 cups of water to a boil over high heat. Stir in the couscous, cover, and turn off the heat. Let the couscous rest for 10 minutes. Drizzle with 1 cup of reserved cooking liquid. Using a fork, fluff the couscous. Mound it on a large platter. Drizzle it with the remaining cooking liquid. Remove the vegetables from the pot and arrange on top. Serve the remaining stew in a separate bowl.

Nutrition:
415 calories
7g fat
14g protein
17g Carbohydrates

536. Kushari

Preparation Time: 25 minutes

Cooking Time: 80 minutes

Servings: 8

Ingredients:

For sauce

- 2 tablespoons olive oil
- 2 garlic cloves, minced
- 1 (16-ounce) can tomato sauce
- ¼ cup white vinegar
- ¼ cup Harissa, or store-bought
- 1/8 teaspoon salt

For rice

- 1 cup olive oil
- 2 onions, thinly sliced
- 2 cups dried brown lentils
- 4 quarts plus ½ cup water
- 2 cups short-grain rice
- 1 teaspoon salt
- 1-pound short elbow GF pasta
- 1 (15-ounce) can chickpeas

Directions:

For sauce

1. In a saucepan over medium heat, heat the olive oil.
2. Add the garlic and cook for 1 minute.
3. Stir in the tomato sauce, vinegar, harissa, and salt. Increase the heat to bring the sauce to a boil. Reduce the heat to low and cook for 20 minutes or until the sauce has thickened. Remove and set aside.

For rice

4. Line a plate with paper towels and set aside.
5. In a large pan over medium heat, heat the olive oil.
6. Add the onions and cook for 7 to 10 minutes, stirring often, until crisp and golden. Transfer the onions to the prepared plate and set aside. Reserve 2 tablespoons of the cooking oil. Reserve the pan.
7. In a large pot over high heat, combine the lentils and 4 cups of water. Bring to a boil and cook for 20 minutes. Drain, transfer to a bowl, and toss with the reserved 2 tablespoons of cooking oil. Set aside. Reserve the pot.
8. Place the pan you used to fry the onions over medium-high heat and add the rice, 4½ cups of water, and the salt to it. Bring to a boil. Reduce

the heat to low, cover the pot, and cook for 20 minutes. Turn off the heat and let the rice rest for 10 minutes.6.

9. In the pot used to cook the lentils, bring the remaining 8 cups of water, salted, to a boil over high heat. Drop in the pasta and cook for 6 minutes or according to the package instructions. Drain and set aside.
10. To assemble: Spoon the rice onto a serving platter. Top it with the lentils, chickpeas, and pasta. Drizzle with the hot tomato sauce and sprinkle with the crispy fried onions.

Nutrition:

668 calories

13g fat

25g protein

21g Carbohydrates

537. Bulgur with Tomatoes and Chickpeas

Preparation Time: 10 minutes

Cooking Time: 35 minutes

Servings: 6

Ingredients:

- ½ cup olive oil
- 1 onion, chopped
- 6 tomatoes
- 2 tablespoons tomato paste
- 2 cups water
- 1 tablespoon Harissa
- 1/8 teaspoon salt
- 2 cups coarse bulgur #3
- 1 (15-ounce) can chickpeas

Directions:

1. In a heavy-bottomed pot over medium heat, heat the olive oil.
2. Add the onion and sauté for 5 minutes.
3. Add the tomatoes with their juice and cook for 5 minutes.
4. Stir in the tomato paste, water, harissa, and salt. Bring to a boil.
5. Stir in the bulgur and chickpeas. Return the mixture to a boil. Reduce the heat to low, cover the pot, and cook for 15 minutes. Let rest for 15 minutes before serving.

Nutrition:

413 calories

19g fat

11g protein

15g Carbohydrates

538. Portobello Caprese

Preparation Time: 15 minutes
Cooking Time: 30 minutes
Servings: 2
Ingredients:

- 1 tablespoon olive oil
- 1 cup cherry tomatoes
- 4 large fresh basil leaves, thinly sliced, divided
- 3 medium garlic cloves, minced
- 2 large portobello mushrooms, stems removed
- 4 pieces mini Mozzarella balls
- 1 tablespoon Parmesan cheese, grated

Directions:

1. Prep oven to 350°F (180°C). Grease a baking pan with olive oil.
2. Drizzle 1 tablespoon olive oil in a nonstick skillet, and heat over medium-high heat.
3. Add the tomatoes to the skillet, and sprinkle salt and black pepper to season. Prick some holes on the tomatoes for juice during the cooking. Put the lid on and cook the tomatoes for 10 minutes or until tender.
4. Reserve 2 teaspoons of basil and add the remaining basil and garlic to the skillet. Crush the tomatoes with a spatula, then cook for half a minute. Stir constantly during the cooking. Set aside.
5. Arrange the mushrooms in the baking pan, cap side down, and sprinkle with salt and black pepper to taste.
6. Spoon the tomato mixture and Mozzarella balls on the gill of the mushrooms, then scatter with Parmesan cheese to coat well.
7. Bake for 20 minutes
8. Remove the stuffed mushrooms from the oven and serve with basil on top.

Nutrition:
285 calories
21.8g fat
14.3g protein
14.2g Carbohydrates

539. Mushroom and Cheese Stuffed Tomatoes

Preparation Time: 15 minutes
Cooking Time: 20 minutes
Servings: 4
Ingredients:

- 4 large ripe tomatoes
- 1 tablespoon olive oil
- ½ pound white or cremini mushrooms
- 1 tablespoon fresh basil, chopped
- ½ cup yellow onion, diced
- 1 tablespoon fresh oregano, chopped
- 2 garlic cloves, minced
- ½ teaspoon salt
- ¼ teaspoon freshly ground black pepper
- 1 cup part-skim Mozzarella cheese, shredded
- 1 tablespoon Parmesan cheese, grated

Directions:

1. Set oven to 375°F (190°C).
2. Chop a ½-inch slice off the top of each tomato. Scoop the pulp into a bowl and leave ½-inch tomato shells. Arrange the tomatoes on a baking sheet lined with aluminum foil.
3. Heat the olive oil in a nonstick skillet over medium heat.
4. Add the mushrooms, basil, onion, oregano, garlic, salt, and black pepper to the skillet and sauté for 5 minutes
5. Pour the mixture to the bowl of tomato pulp, then add the Mozzarella cheese and stir to combine well.
6. Spoon the mixture into each tomato shell, then top with a layer of Parmesan.
7. Bake for 15 minutes
8. Remove the stuffed tomatoes from the oven and serve warm.

Nutrition:
254 calories
14.7g fat
17.5g protein
18.6g Carbohydrates

540. Tabbouleh

Preparation Time: 15 minutes
Cooking Time: 5 minutes
Servings: 6
Ingredients:

- 4 tablespoons olive oil
- 4 cups riced cauliflower
- 3 garlic cloves
- ½ large cucumber
- ½ cup Italian parsley
- Juice of 1 lemon
- 2 tablespoons red onion
- ½ cup mint leaves, chopped

- ½ cup pitted Kalamata olives
- 1 cup cherry tomatoes
- 2 cups baby arugula
- 2 medium avocados

Directions:

1. Warm 2 tablespoons olive oil in a nonstick skillet over medium-high heat.
2. Add the rice cauliflower, garlic, salt, and black pepper to the skillet and sauté for 3 minutes or until fragrant. Transfer them to a large bowl.
3. Add the cucumber, parsley, lemon juice, red onion, mint, olives, and remaining olive oil to the bowl. Toss to combine well. Reserve the bowl in the refrigerator for at least 30 minutes.
4. Remove the bowl from the refrigerator. Add the cherry tomatoes, arugula, and avocado to the bowl. Sprinkle with salt and black pepper, and toss to combine well. Serve chilled.

Nutrition:

198 calories

17.5g fat

4.2g protein

8.9g Carbohydrates

541. Spicy Broccoli Rabe and Artichoke Hearts

Preparation Time: 5 minutes

Cooking Time: 15 minutes

Servings: 4

Ingredients:

- 3 tablespoons olive oil, divided
- 2 pounds fresh broccoli rabe
- 3 garlic cloves, finely minced
- 1 teaspoon red pepper flakes
- 1 teaspoon salt, plus more to taste
- 13.5 ounces artichoke hearts
- 1 tablespoon water
- 2 tablespoons red wine vinegar

Directions:

1. Warm 2 tablespoons olive oil in a nonstick skillet over medium-high skillet.
2. Add the broccoli, garlic, red pepper flakes, and salt to the skillet and sauté for 5 minutes or until the broccoli is soft.
3. Add the artichoke hearts to the skillet and sauté for 2 more minutes or until tender.
4. Add water to the skillet and turn down the heat to low. Put the lid on and simmer for 5 minutes.

5. Meanwhile, combine the vinegar and 1 tablespoon of olive oil in a bowl.
6. Drizzle the simmered broccoli and artichokes with oiled vinegar, and sprinkle with salt and black pepper. Toss to combine well before serving.

Nutrition:

272 calories

21.5g fat

11.2g protein

12.3g Carbohydrates

542. Shakshuka

Preparation Time: 10 minutes

Cooking Time: 25 minutes

Servings: 4

Ingredients:

- 5 tablespoons olive oil, divided
- 1 red bell pepper, finely diced
- ½ small yellow onion, finely diced
- 14 ounces crushed tomatoes, with juices
- 6 ounces frozen spinach
- 1 teaspoon smoked paprika
- 2 garlic cloves
- 2 teaspoons red pepper flakes
- 1 tablespoon capers
- 1 tablespoon water
- 6 large eggs
- ¼ teaspoon freshly ground black pepper
- ¾ cup feta or goat cheese
- ¼ cup fresh flat-leaf parsley

Directions:

1. Prep oven to 300°F (150°C).
2. Cook 2 tablespoons olive oil in an oven-safe skillet over medium-high heat.
3. Cook bell pepper and onion to the skillet for 6 minutes.
4. Add the tomatoes and juices, spinach, paprika, garlic, red pepper flakes, capers, water, and 2 tablespoons olive oil to the skillet. Stir and boil.
5. Turn down the heat to low, then put the lid on and simmer for 5 minutes.
6. Crack the eggs over the sauce, and keep a little space between each egg, leave the egg intact and sprinkle with freshly ground black pepper.
7. Cook for another 8 minutes
8. Scatter the cheese over the eggs and sauce, and bake in the preheated oven for 5 minutes

9. Drizzle 1 tablespoon olive oil and spread the parsley on top before serving warm.

Nutrition:

335 calories 26.5g fat

16.8g protein 23.4g Carbohydrates

543. Spring Sandwich

Preparation Time: 10 minutes

Cooking Time: 25 minutes

Servings: 4

Ingredients:

- 1 pinch of salt
- 1 pinch of black pepper
- 4 teaspoons of extra-virgin olive oil
- 4 eggs
- 4 multigrain sandwich thins
- 1 onion, finely diced
- 1 tomato, sliced thinly
- 2 cups of fresh baby spinach leaves
- 4 tablespoons of crumbled feta
- 1 sprig of fresh rosemary

Directions:

1. Preheat your oven to 375 F.
2. Slice the multigrain sandwich thins open and brush each side with one teaspoon of olive oil. Place them into the oven and toast for five minutes. Remove and set aside.
3. Situate non-stick skillet over medium heat, add the remaining 2 teaspoons of olive oil and strip the leaves of rosemary off into the pan. Add in the eggs, one by one.
4. Cook until the eggs have whitened, and the yolks stay runny. Flip once using a spatula and then remove from the heat.
5. Place the multigrain thins onto serving plates, then place the spinach leaves on top, followed by sliced tomato, one egg, and a sprinkling of feta cheese. Add salt and pepper, then close your sandwich using the remaining multigrain thins.

Nutrition:

150 calories 15g fat

3g protein 5g Carbohydrates

544. Lemon-Tahini Sauce

Preparation Time: 10 Minutes

Cooking Time: 0 Minutes

Servings: 1 Cup

Ingredients:

- ½ cup tahini
- One garlic clove, minced
- Juice and zest of 1 lemon
- ½ teaspoon salt, plus more as needed
- ½ cup warm water, plus more as needed

Directions:

1. Combine the tahini and garlic in a small bowl.
2. Add the lemon juice and zest, and salt to the bowl and stir to mix well.
3. Fold in the warm water and whisk until well combined and creamy. Feel free to add more warm water if you like a thinner consistency.
4. Taste and add additional salt as needed.
5. Stock the sauce in a sealed vessel in the refrigerator for up to 5 days.

Nutrition:

Calories: 179

Fat: 15.5g

Protein: 5.1g

Carbs: 6.8g

Fiber: 3.0g

Sodium: 324mg

545. Springtime Quinoa Salad

Preparation Time: 10 minutes

Cooking Time: 25 minutes

Servings: 4

Ingredients:

For vinaigrette:

- 1 pinch of salt
- 1 pinch of black pepper
- ½ teaspoon of dried thyme
- ½ teaspoon of dried oregano
- ¼ cup of extra-virgin olive oil
- 1 tablespoon of honey
- juice of 1 lemon
- 1 clove of garlic, minced
- 2 tablespoons of fresh basil, diced

For salad:

- 1 ½ cups of cooked quinoa
- 4 cups of mixed leafy greens
- ½ cup of kalamata olives, halved and pitted
- ¼ cup of sun-dried tomatoes, diced
- ½ cup of almonds, raw, unsalted and diced

Directions:

1. Combine all the vinaigrette ingredients together, either by hand or using a blender or food processor. Set the vinaigrette aside in the refrigerator.

2.   In a large salad bowl, combine the salad ingredients.

3.   Drizzle the vinaigrette over the salad, then serve.

Nutrition:

201 calories 13g fat

4g protein 4g Carbohydrates

546. Tomato Poached Fish with Herbs and Chickpeas

Preparation Time: 20 minutes

Cooking Time: 20 minutes

Servings: 2

Ingredients:

- 1 pinch of salt
- 1 pinch of black pepper
- 4 sprigs of fresh oregano
- 4 sprigs of fresh dill
- 1 ½ cups of water
- 1 cup of white wine
- 2 tablespoons of extra-virgin olive oil
- 1 tablespoon of tomato paste
- 2 cloves of garlic
- 2 shallots
- 1 lemon
- zest of 1 lemon
- 14 g can of chickpeas
- 8 g of cherry tomatoes
- 1 Fresno pepper
- 1 lb. of cod

Directions:

1.   Situate saucepan over high heat, cook olive oil, garlic, and shallots for two minutes.

2.   Add the salt, pepper, tomato paste, cherry tomatoes, chickpeas, and Fresno pepper.

3.   Stir in the water and wine. Place the fish into the center of the pan, ensuring it is submerged in the liquid. Sprinkle the lemon zest over the broth, then add the lemon slices and fresh herbs.

4.   Place a lid onto the saucepan and allow the broth to simmer for five to ten minutes, depending on the thickness of the cut of fish.

5.   When cooked, remove from the heat and serve over basmati rice. Top with a few toasted pistachios for added texture.

Nutrition:

351 calories 21g fat

9g protein 6g Carbohydrates

547. Garlic Prawn and Pea Risotto

Preparation Time: 15 minutes

Cooking Time: 30 minutes

Servings: 4

Ingredients:

- 1 pinch of salt
- 1 pinch of black pepper
- 1 red chili
- 3 tablespoons of extra-virgin olive oil
- g of butter
- Juice of 1 lemon
- Zest of 1 lemon
- 50 Fl g of fish stock
- 1 cup of white wine
- 1 clove of garlic, finely diced
- 1 onion, diced
- 7 g of frozen peas
- 14 g of raw prawns
- g of Arborio rice

Directions:

1.   Rinse the prawns under running water and then remove their heads and shells. Keep these aside and keep the prawn meat aside.

2.   Situate saucepan over medium heat, add one tablespoon of olive oil, garlic, half of the finely diced chili, prawn heads, and shells. Cook until the shells change color. Boil stock, then turn the heat down to a simmer.

3.   In a separate medium saucepan over medium heat, add half the butter and the onions. Cook until the onions have softened. Add the risotto into the pan and stir continuously until you notice that the rice has become transparent in appearance.

4.   Stir wine to the rice and cook

5.   Begin to ladle the stock over the rice, one spoonful at a time. Ensure that the ladle of stock has evaporated before continuing to add the next. Stir in the peas and prawns.

6.   Continue adding stock until the rice has reached an al dente texture, soft with a starchy center, around 20 to 30 minutes. Continue to cook until the prawn meat has changed color.

7.   Remove the risotto from the heat, then add the remaining chili, olive oil, and lemon juice.

8.   Top with salt, pepper, lemon zest and serve.

Nutrition:

341 calories 16g fat 7g protein5g Carbohydrates

548. Mediterranean Tostadas

Preparation Time: 15 minutes

Cooking Time: 10 minutes

Servings: 4

Ingredients:

- 1 pinch salt
- 1 pinch black pepper
- 1 pinch oregano
- 1 pinch garlic powder
- 4 tostadas
- 1 tablespoon of extra-virgin olive oil
- ½ cup of milk
- ½ cup of roasted red pepper hummus
- 8 eggs, beaten
- ½ cup of green onion, finely diced
- ½ cup of red bell peppers, finely diced
- ½ cup of diced cucumber
- ½ cup of diced tomato
- ¼ cup of crumbled feta
- 1 handful of fresh basil

Directions:

1. Position non-stick skillet over medium heat, cook olive oil and red peppers. Cook until these have softened, then add the salt, pepper, oregano, garlic powder, milk, eggs, and onion.

2. Gently stir the mixture until you reach a scrambled egg consistency.

3. Once cooked through, remove from the heat.

4. Place a tostada onto each place, and top with the hummus, egg, tomato, cucumber, feta, and fresh basil leaves.

Nutrition:

251 calories

19g fat

6g protein

4g Carbohydrates

549. Vegetable Ratatouille

Preparation Time: 15 minutes

Cooking Time: 40 minutes

Servings: 8

Ingredients:

- 1 pinch salt
- 1 pinch black pepper
- 1 pinch brown sugar
- ¼ cup extra-virgin olive oil
- ¼ cup of white wine
- 3 cloves of garlic
- 1 onion, diced
- 1 lb. of eggplant
- 1 cup of zucchini
- 1 ½ cups of canned tomato
- 1 red bell pepper, diced
- 1 green bell pepper, diced
- ½ cup of fresh basil

Directions:

1. Place saucepan over medium heat, cook olive oil and finely diced garlic and onion.

2. Add the cubed eggplant and continue to cook for a further 5 minutes.

3. Add the salt, pepper, and diced bell peppers. Allow to cook for another 3 minutes.

4. Add the sliced zucchini to the saucepan and cook for 3 minutes.

5. Mix white wine and canned tomatoes.

6. Allow to simmer for another five minutes. Taste the ratatouille.

7. Pull away from the heat, add the basil, and serve with a side portion of barley or brown rice.

Nutrition:

401 calories

19g fat

7g protein

8g Carbohydrates

CHAPTER 16:

Snacks & Appetizers

550. Nori Snack Rolls

Preparation Time: 5 minutes

Cooking Time: 10 minutes

Servings: 4 Rolls

Ingredients

- 2 tablespoons almond, cashew, peanut, or another nut butter
- 2 tablespoons tamari, or soy sauce
- 4 standard nori sheets
- 1 mushroom, sliced
- 1 tablespoon pickled ginger
- ½ cup grated carrots

Directions:

1. Preheat the oven to 350°F.
2. Mix the nut butter and tamari until smooth and very thick. Lay out a nori sheet, rough side up, the long way.
3. Spread a thin line of the tamari mixture on the far end of the nori sheet, from side to side. Lay the mushroom slices, ginger, and carrots in a line at the other end (the end closest to you).
4. Fold the vegetables inside the nori, rolling toward the tahini mixture, which will seal the roll. Repeat to make 4 rolls.
5. Finish and serve
6. Put on a baking sheet and bake for 8-10 minutes, or until the rolls are slightly browned and crispy at the ends. Let the rolls cool for a few minutes, then slice each roll into 3 smaller pieces.

Nutrition Per Serving (1 roll) Calories: 79; Total fat: 5g; Carbs: 6g; Fiber: 2g; Protein: 4g

551. Risotto Bites

Preparation Time: 15 minutes

Cooking Time: 20 minutes

Servings: 12 Bites

Ingredients

- ½ cup panko bread crumbs
- 1 teaspoon paprika
- 1 teaspoon chipotle powder or ground cayenne pepper
- 1½ cups cold Green Pea Risotto
- Nonstick cooking spray

Directions:

1. Preheat the oven to 425°F.
2. Line a baking sheet with parchment paper.
3. On a large plate, combine the panko, paprika, and chipotle powder. Set aside.
4. Roll 2 tablespoons of the risotto into a ball.

5. Gently roll in the bread crumbs and place on the prepared baking sheet. Repeat to make a total of 12 balls.
6. Bake
7. Spritz the tops of the risotto bites with nonstick cooking spray and bake for 15-20 minutes until they begin to brown.
8. Finish and Serve
9. Cool completely before storing in a large airtight container in a single layer (add a piece of parchment paper for a second layer), or in a plastic freezer bag.

Nutrition Per Serving (6 bites): Calories: 100; Fat: 2g; Protein: 6g; Carbohydrates: 17g; Fiber: 5g; Sugar: 2g; Sodium: 165mg

552. Black Sesame Wonton Chips

Preparation Time: 5 minutes

Cooking Time: 5 minutes

Servings: 24 Chips

Ingredients

- 12 Vegan Wonton Wrappers
- Toasted sesame oil
- 1/3 cup black sesame seeds
- Salt

Directions:

1. Preheat the oven to 450°F. Lightly oil a baking sheet and set it aside.
2. Cut the wonton wrappers in half crosswise, brush them with sesame oil, and arrange them in a single layer on the prepared baking sheet.
3. Sprinkle wonton wrappers with sesame seeds and salt.
4. Bake
5. Bake until crisp and golden brown.
6. Finish and Serve
7. Cool completely before serving.
8. These are best eaten on the day they are made, but once cooled, they can be covered and stored at room temperature for 1-2 days.

Nutrition Per Serving (6 bites): Calories: 60; Fat: 1.5g; Protein: 1.99g; Carbohydrates: 9.51g; Fiber: 0.5g; Sugar: 0.01g; Sodium: 92mg

553. Tamari Toasted Almonds

Preparation Time: 2 minutes

Cooking Time: 8 minutes

Servings: ½ Cup

Ingredients

- ½ cup raw almonds, or sunflower seeds
- 2 tablespoons tamari, or soy sauce
- 1 teaspoon toasted sesame oil

Directions:

1. Heat a dry skillet to medium-high heat, then add the almonds, stirring frequently to keep them from burning.
2. Once the almonds are toasted—7-8 minutes for almonds, or 34 minutes for sunflower seeds—pour the tamari and sesame oil into the hot skillet and stir to coat. You can turn off the heat, and as the almonds cool, the tamari mixture will stick and dry onto the nuts.

Nutrition Per Serving (1 tablespoon) Calories: 89; Total fat: 8g; Carbs: 3g; Fiber: 2g; Protein: 4g

554. Avocado and Tempeh Bacon Wraps

Preparation Time: 10 minutes

Cooking Time: 8 minutes

Servings: 4 Wraps

Ingredients

- 2 tablespoons extra-virgin olive oil
- 8 ounces tempeh bacon, homemade or store-bought
- 4 (10-inch) soft flour tortillas or lavash flatbread
- ¼cup vegan mayonnaise, homemade or store-bought - 4 large lettuce leaves
- 2 ripe Hass avocados, pitted, peeled, and cut into ¼-inch slices
- 1 large ripe tomato, cut into ¼-inch slices

Directions:

1. In a large skillet, heat the oil over medium heat.
2. Add the tempeh bacon and cook until browned on both sides, about 8 minutes.
3. Remove from the heat and set aside.
4. Place 1 tortilla on a work surface.
5. Spread with some of the mayonnaise and one-fourth of the lettuce and tomatoes.
6. Finish and Serve
7. Pit, peel, and thinly slice the avocado and place the slices on top of the tomato.
8. Add the reserved tempeh bacon and roll up tightly. Repeat with remaining ingredients and serve.

Nutrition Per Serving: Calories: 590; Total fat: 32,45g; Carbs: 60.98g; Fiber: 17.2g; Protein: 24g

555. Tempeh-Pimiento Cheese Ball

Preparation Time: 5 minutes

Cooking Time: 30 minutes

Servings: 8

Ingredients

- 8 ounces tempeh, cut into ½ -inch pieces
- 1 (2-ounce) jar chopped pimientos, drained
- ¼ cup nutritional yeast
- ¼ cup vegan mayonnaise, homemade or store-bought
- 2 tablespoons soy sauce
- ¾ cup chopped pecans

Directions:

1. In a medium saucepan of simmering water, cook the tempeh for 30 minutes. Set aside to cool.
2. In a food processor, combine the cooled tempeh, pimientos, nutritional yeast, mayo, and soy sauce.
3. Process until smooth.
4. Transfer the tempeh mixture to a bowl and refrigerate until firm and chilled for at least 2 hours or overnight.
5. Finish and Serve
6. In a dry skillet, toast the pecans over medium heat until lightly toasted.
7. Set aside to cool.
8. Shape the tempeh mixture into a ball, and roll it in the pecans, pressing the nuts lightly into the tempeh mixture so that they stick.
9. Refrigerate for at least 1 hour before serving. If not using right away, cover and keep refrigerated until needed.
10. Properly stored, it will keep for 2-3 days.

Nutrition Per Serving: Calories: 171; Total fat: 12.93g; Carbs: 7.06g; Fiber: 1.7g; Protein: 9g

556. Peppers and Hummus

Preparation Time: 15 minutes

Cooking Time: 0 minutes

Servings: 4

Ingredients

- one 15-ounce can chickpeas, drained and rinsed
- juice of 1 lemon, or 1 tablespoon prepared lemon juice
- ¼ cup tahini
- 3 tablespoons extra-virgin olive oil
- ½ teaspoon ground cumin
- 1 tablespoon water
- ¼ teaspoon paprika
- 1 red bell pepper, sliced
- 1 green bell pepper, sliced
- 1 orange bell pepper, sliced

Directions:

1. In a food processor, combine chickpeas, lemon juice, tahini, 2 tablespoons of olive oil, cumin, and water.
2. Finish and Serve
3. Process on high speed until blended for about 30 seconds.

4. Scoop the hummus into a bowl and drizzle with the remaining tablespoon of olive oil.

5. Sprinkle with paprika and serve with sliced bell peppers.

Nutrition Per Serving: Calories: 294; Total fat: 15.37g; Carbs: 31.72g; Fiber: 8.7g; Protein: 10.86g

557. Savory Roasted Chickpeas

Preparation Time: 5 minutes

Cooking Time: 25 minutes

Servings: 1 Cup

Ingredients

- 1 (14-ounce) can chickpeas, rinsed and drained, or 1½ cups cooked
- 2 tablespoons tamari or soy sauce
- 1 tablespoon nutritional yeast
- 1 teaspoon smoked paprika or regular paprika
- 1 teaspoon onion powder
- ½ teaspoon garlic powder

Directions:

1. Preheat the oven to 400°F.

2. Toss the chickpeas with all the other ingredients, and spread them out on a baking sheet.

3. Bake

4. Bake for 20-25 minutes, tossing halfway through.

5. Bake these at a lower temperature until fully dried and crispy if you want to keep them longer.

6. You can easily double the batch, and if you dry them out, they will keep about a week in an airtight container.

Nutrition Per Serving (¼ cup) Calories: 121; Total fat: 2g; Carbs: 20g; Fiber: 6g; Protein: 8g

558. Savory Seed Crackers

Preparation Time: 5 minutes

Cooking Time: 50 minutes

Servings: 20 Crackers

Ingredients:

- ¾ cup pumpkin seeds (pepitas)
- ½ cup sunflower seeds
- ½ cup sesame seeds
- ¼ cup chia seeds
- 1 teaspoon minced garlic (about 1 clove)
- 1 teaspoon tamari or soy sauce
- 1 teaspoon vegan Worcestershire sauce
- ½ teaspoon ground cayenne pepper
- ½ teaspoon dried oregano
- ½ cup water

Directions:

1. Preheat the oven to 325°F.

2. Line a rimmed baking sheet with parchment paper.

3. In a large bowl, combine the pumpkin seeds, sunflower seeds, sesame seeds, chia seeds, garlic, tamari, Worcestershire sauce, cayenne, oregano, and water. Bake

4. Transfer to the prepared baking sheet and spread it out to all sides.

5. Bake for 25 minutes. Remove the pan from the oven, and flip the seed "dough" over so the wet side is up.

6. Bake for another 20-25 minutes until the sides are browned. Finish and Serve

7. Cool completely before breaking up into 20 pieces. Divide evenly among 4 glass jars and close tightly with lids.

Nutrition Per Serving (5 crackers): Calories: 339; Fat: 29g; Protein: 14g; Carbohydrates: 17g; Fiber: 8g; Sugar: 1g; Sodium: 96mg

559. Tomato and Basil Bruschetta

Preparation Time: 10 minutes

Cooking Time: 6 minutes

Servings: 12 Bruschetta

Ingredients

- 3 tomatoes, chopped
- ¼ cup chopped fresh basil
- 1 tablespoon extra-virgin olive oil
- A pinch of sea salt - 1 baguette, cut into 12 slices
- 1 garlic clove, sliced in half

Directions:

1. In a small bowl, combine the tomatoes, basil, olive oil, and salt, and stir to mix. Set aside. Preheat the oven to 425°F.

2. Place the baguette slices in a single layer on a baking sheet and toast in the oven until brown for about 6 minutes. Finish and Serve Flip the bread slices over once during cooking.

3. Remove from the oven and rub the bread on both sides with the sliced clove of garlic.

4. Top with the tomato-basil mixture and serve immediately.

Nutrition Per Serving: Calories: 11; Total fat: 0.57g; Carbs: 1.29g; Fiber: 0.4g; Protein: 0.39g

560. Refried Bean and Salsa Quesadillas

Preparation Time: 5 minutes

Cooking Time: 6 minutes

Servings: 4 Quesadillas

Ingredients

- 1 tablespoon canola oil, plus more for frying

- 1½ cups cooked or 1 (15.5-ounce) can pinto beans, drained and mashed
- 1 teaspoon chili powder
- 4 (10-inch) whole-wheat flour tortillas
- 1 cup tomato salsa, homemade or store-bought
- ½ cup minced red onion (optional)

Directions:

1. In a medium saucepan, heat the oil over medium heat.
2. Add the mashed beans and chili powder and cook, stirring, until hot, about 5 minutes. Set aside.
3. To assemble, place 1 tortilla on a work surface and spoon about ¼ cup of the beans across the bottom half.
4. Top the beans with the salsa and onion if using.
5. Fold the top half of the tortilla over the filling and press slightly.
6. In a large skillet, heat a thin layer of oil over medium heat.
7. Place folded quesadillas, 1 or 2 at a time, into the hot skillet and heat until hot, turning once, about 1 minute per side.
8. Cut quesadillas into 3 or 4 wedges and arrange them on plates.
9. Serve immediately.

Nutrition Per Serving: Calories: 264; Total fat: 8.1g; Carbs: 38.76g; Fiber: 10.7g; Protein: 10.36g

561. **Jicama and Guacamole**

Preparation Time: 15 minutes

Cooking Time: 0 minutes

Servings: 4

Ingredients

- juice of 1 lime, or 1 tablespoon prepared lime juice
- 2 hass avocados, peeled, pits removed, and cut into cubes
- ½ teaspoon sea salt
- ½ red onion, minced
- 1 garlic clove, minced
- ¼ cup chopped cilantro (optional)
- 1 jicama bulb, peeled and cut into matchsticks

Directions:

1. In a medium bowl, squeeze the lime juice over the top of the avocado and sprinkle with salt.
2. Lightly mash the avocado with a fork. Stir in the onion, garlic, and cilantro, if using.
3. Finish and Serve
4. Serve with slices of jicama to dip in guacamole.

5. To store, place plastic wrap over the bowl of guacamole and refrigerate.
6. The guacamole will keep for about 2 days.

Nutrition Per Serving: Calories: 189; Total fat: 14.88g; Carbs: 15.34g; Fiber: 8.9g; Protein: 3g

562. **Sesame- Wonton Crisps**

Preparation Time: 10 minutes

Cooking Time: 10 minutes

Servings: 12 Crisps

Ingredients

- 12 Vegan Wonton Wrappers
- 2 tablespoons toasted sesame oil
- 12 shiitake mushrooms, lightly rinsed, patted dry, stemmed, and cut into 1/4-inch slices
- 4 snow peas, trimmed and cut crosswise into thin slivers
- 1 teaspoon soy sauce
- 1 tablespoon fresh lime juice
- ½ teaspoon brown sugar
- 1 medium carrot, shredded
- Toasted sesame seeds or black sesame seeds, if available

Directions:

1. Preheat the oven to 350°F.
2. Lightly oil a baking sheet and set it aside. Brush the wonton wrappers with 1 tablespoon of the sesame oil and arrange them on the baking sheet.
3. Bake until golden brown and crisp for about 5 minutes. Set aside to cool. (Alternately, you can tuck the wonton wrappers into mini-muffin tins to create cups for the filling. Brush with sesame oil and bake them until crisp.)
4. In a large skillet, heat the extra olive oil over medium heat.
5. Add the mushrooms and cook until softened.
6. Stir in the snow peas and the soy sauce and cook for 30 seconds. Set aside to cool.
7. In a large bowl, combine the lime juice, sugar, and the remaining 1 tablespoon of sesame oil.
8. Stir in the carrot and cooled shiitake mixture.
9. Finish and Serve
10. Top each wonton crisp with a spoonful of the shiitake mixture.
11. Sprinkle with sesame seeds and arrange on a platter to serve.

Nutrition Per Serving: Calories: 128; Total fat: 2.88g; Carbs: 22.09g; Fiber: 1.1g; Protein: 3.53g

563. Macadamia-Cashew Patties

Preparation Time: 10 minutes
Cooking Time: 10 minutes
Servings: 4 Patties
Ingredients

- ¾ cup chopped macadamia nuts
- ¾ cup chopped cashews
- 1 medium carrot, grated
- 1 small onion, chopped
- 1 garlic clove, minced
- 1 jalapeño or other green chile, seeded and minced
- ¾ cup old-fashioned oats
- ¾ cup dry unseasoned bread crumbs
- 2 tablespoons minced fresh cilantro
- ½ teaspoon ground coriander
- Salt and freshly ground black pepper
- 2 teaspoons fresh lime juice
- Canola or grapeseed oil, for frying
- 4 sandwich rolls
- Lettuce leaves and condiment of choice

Directions:

1. In a food processor, combine the macadamia nuts, cashews, carrot, onion, garlic, chile, oats, bread crumbs, cilantro, coriander, and salt and pepper.
2. Process until well mixed.
3. Add the lime juice and process until well blended.
4. Taste, adjusting the seasonings if necessary.
5. Shape the mixture into 4 equal patties.
6. In a large skillet, heat a thin layer of oil over medium heat.
7. Add the patties and cook until golden brown on both sides, turning once, for about 10 minutes in total.
8. Finish and Serve
9. Serve on sandwich rolls with lettuce and condiments of choice.

Nutrition Per Serving: Calories: 1033; Total fat: 58.96g; Carbs: 97.98g; Fiber: 10.1g; Protein: 39.84g

564. Lemon Coconut Cilantro Rolls

Preparation Time: 30 minutes
Cooking Time: 30 minutes
Servings: 16 Pieces
Ingredients

- ½ cup fresh cilantro, chopped
- 1 cup sprouts (clover, alfalfa)
- 1 garlic clove, pressed
- 2 tablespoons ground Brazil nuts or almonds
- 2 tablespoons flaked coconut
- 1 tablespoon coconut oil
- Pinch cayenne pepper
- Pinch sea salt
- Pinch freshly ground black pepper
- Zest and juice of 1 lemon
- 2 tablespoons ground flaxseed
- 1 to 2 tablespoons water
- 2 whole-wheat wraps, or corn wraps

Directions:

1. Put everything but the wraps in a food processor and pulse to combine. Or combine the ingredients in a large bowl.
2. Add the water, if needed, to help the mix come together.
3. Spread the mixture out over each wrap, roll it up, and place it in the fridge for 30 minutes to set.
4. Finish and Serve
5. Remove the rolls from the fridge and slice each into 8 pieces to serve as appetizers or sides with a soup or stew.
6. Get the best flavor by buying whole raw Brazil nuts or almonds, toasting them lightly in a dry skillet or toaster oven, then grinding them in a coffee grinder.

Nutrition: Per Serving (1 piece) Calories: 66; Total fat: 4g; Carbs: 6g; Fiber: 1g; Protein: 2g

565. Seeded Crackers

Preparation Time: 1 hour
Cooking Time: 10 minutes
Servings: 36 crackers
Ingredients:

- ½ cup pumpkin seeds
- ½ cup sunflower seeds
- ¼ cup sesame seeds
- ¼ cup chia seeds
- ¾ cup water
- ¾ teaspoon salt
- 1 teaspoon rosemary
- 1 teaspoon onion powder

Directions:

1. Preheat oven to 350°F. Set aside two large pieces of parchment paper.
2. Combine all ingredients in a large bowl. Set aside to rest for 15 minutes.

3. Oil one side of each of the two sheets of parchment paper to avoid sticking in the next step.

4. Place the dough between the two pieces of parchment paper. Roll out the dough thin using a rolling pin (roll to approximately 10 x 14-inch rectangle).

5. Slide the rolled-out dough onto a baker's half sheet.

6. Bake for 20 minutes.

7. Remove from oven and cut into large pieces. Flip each piece over when finished.

8. Bake for an additional 14 minutes.

9. Let cool and store in an airtight container.

Nutrition: 26 calories, 2 g fat, 1 gram's protein, 1 gram's fiber, 2 g carbs

566. Banana Bites

Preparation Time: 15 minutes
Cooking Time: 15 minutes
Servings: 4 servings
Ingredients:

- 2 bananas
- ½ cup vegan chocolate, melted
- 1 cup roasted pistachios, in pieces or finely crushed

Directions:

1. Set aside a parchment-lined baking sheet.

2. Peel the bananas and stick a toothpick in both ends to make the next step easier.

3. Dip and fully coat the bananas in the melted chocolate. Set onto the parchment paper.

4. If using whole pistachios, place the nuts into a food processor and pulse until fine. Leave some pistachios intact.

5. Sprinkle the pistachios on top of the banana.

6. Freeze the bananas to set the chocolate and pistachios for 5 minutes.

7. Remove the bananas and cut them into bites. Return to the freezer in a glass container.

8. When ready to consume, remove bananas from the freezer and thaw for 10 minutes to soften.

Nutrition: 273 calories, 14 g fat, 6 g protein, 5 g fiber, 37 g carbs

CHAPTER 17:

Snacks & Appetizers 2

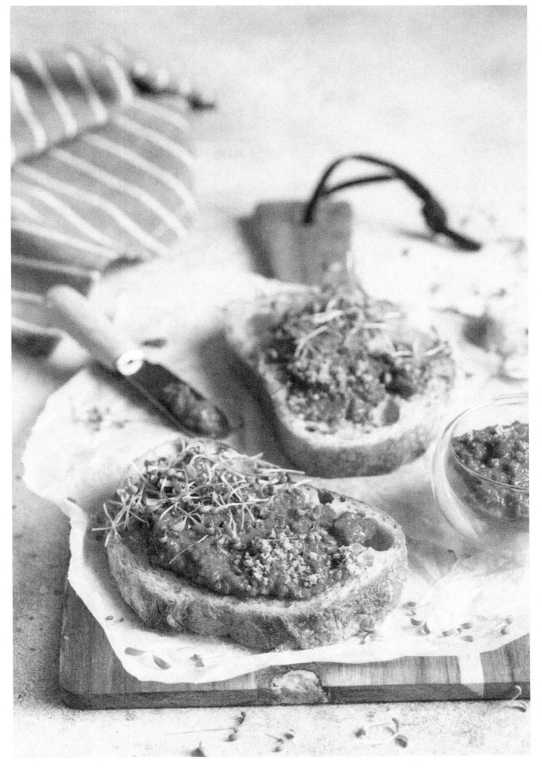

567. Sweet Potato Toast

Preparation Time: 5 minutes
Cooking Time: 10 minutes
Servings: 1
Ingredients:

- ½ of 1 Avocado, ripe
- 2 tbsp. Sun-dried Tomatoes
- 1 Sweet Potato, sliced into ¼-inch thick slices
- ½ cup Chickpeas
- Salt & Pepper, as needed
- 1 tsp. Lemon Juice
- Pinch of Red Pepper
- 2 tbsp. Vegan Cheese

Directions:

1. Start by slicing the sweet potato into five ¼ inch wide slices.
2. Next, toast the sweet potato in the toaster for 9 to 11 minutes.
3. Then, place the chickpeas in a medium-sized bowl and mash with the avocado.
4. Stir in the crushed red pepper, lemon juice, pepper, and salt.
5. Stir until everything comes together.
6. Finally, place the mixture on the top of the sweet potato toast.
7. Top with cheese and sun-dried tomatoes.

Nutrition: Calories: 452 Kcal Protein: 19g Carbohydrates: 77g Fat: 11g

568. Hummus Toast

Preparation Time: 5 minutes
Cooking Time: 5 minutes
Servings: 1
Ingredients:

- 1 tbsp. Hemp Seeds
- 1 tbsp. Sunflower Seeds, roasted & unsalted
- 2 Vegan Bread Slices
- ¼ cup Hummus

For the hummus:

- 15 oz. Chickpeas
- ¾ tsp. Salt
- 2 tbsp. Lime Juice, fresh
- 2 tbsp. Extra Virgin Olive Oil
- 2 Garlic cloves - ½ cup Tahini

Directions:

1. To begin with, toast the bread for 1 to 1 ½ minutes or until lightly toasted.

2. Meanwhile, to make the hummus place the undrained chickpeas and garlic cloves in a medium bowl.
3. Microwave for 2 to 3 minutes on a high heat.
4. After that, put the lime juice, tahini, and salt along with the cooked chickpeas into a food processor.
5. Blend for 2 to 3 minutes or until smooth.
6. While blending, spoon in the olive oil gradually. Combine. Taste the mixture for seasoning. If needed, add more salt and pepper.
7. Next, top the toast with hummus, hemp and sunflower seeds.
8. Serve and enjoy.

Nutrition: Calories: 316 Kcal Protein: 19g Carbohydrates: 24g; Fat: 16g

569. Tacos

Preparation Time: 10 minutes
Cooking Time: 30 minutes
Servings: 4
Ingredients:

- 6 Taco Shells

For the slaw:

- 1 cup Red Cabbage, shredded
- 3 Scallions, chopped
- 1 cup Green Cabbage, shredded
- 1 cup Carrots, sliced

For the dressing:

- 1 tbsp. Sriracha
- ¼ cup Apple Cider Vinegar
- ¼ tsp. Salt
- 2 tbsp. Sesame Oil
- 1 tbsp. Dijon Mustard
- 1 tbsp. Lime Juice
- ½ tbsp. Tamari
- 1 tbsp. Maple Syrup
- ¼ tsp. Salt

Directions:

1. To start with, make the dressing, whisk all the ingredients in a small bowl until mixed well.
2. Next, combine the slaw ingredients in another bowl and toss well.
3. Finally, take a taco shell and place the slaw in it.
4. Serve and enjoy.

Nutrition: Calories: 216Kcal Protein: 10g Carbohydrates: 15g Fat: 13g

570. Kale Chips

Preparation Time: 10 minutes
Cooking Time: 1 Hour 30 minutes
Servings: 10
Ingredients:

- ½ tsp. Smoked Paprika
- 2 bunches of Curly Kale
- 1 tsp. Garlic Powder
- ½ cup Nutritional Yeast
- 2 cups Cashew, soaked for 2 hours
- 1 tsp. Salt
- ½ cup Nutritional Yeast

Directions:

1. To make these tasty, healthy chips place the kale in a large mixing bowl.
2. Now, combine all the remaining ingredients in the high-speed blender and blend for 1 minute or until smooth.
3. Next, pour this dressing over the kale chips and mix well with your hands.
4. Then, preheat your oven to 225°F or 107°C.
5. Once heated, arrange the kale leaves on a large baking sheet leaving ample space between them.
6. Bake the leaves for 80 to 90 minutes, flipping them once in between.
7. Finally, allow them to cool completely and then store them in an air-tight container.

Nutrition: Calories: 191Kcal Protein: 9g Carbohydrates: 16g Fat: 12g

571. Spicy Roasted Chickpeas

Preparation Time: 10 minutes
Cooking Time: 25 minutes
Servings: 6
Ingredients:

- ½ tsp. Cumin
- 2 × 15 oz. Chickpeas
- ¼ tsp. Cayenne Pepper
- ¼ cup Olive Oil
- ½ tsp. Onion Powder
- 1 tsp. Sea Salt
- ¾ tsp. Garlic Powder
- ½ tsp. Chili Powder
- ¾ tsp. Paprika
- Sea Salt, as needed

Directions:

1. Preheat the oven to 425 °F.
2. After that, put the chickpeas in a strainer lined with a paper towel and allow them to dry for 10 to 15 minutes.
3. Then, transfer the chickpeas onto a baking paper-lined baking sheet and then spoon some olive oil over it.
4. Coat the chickpeas with the oil. Sprinkle a dash of salt over it.
5. Now, put the baking sheet in the oven and bake for 23 to 25 minutes, tossing them every 5 minutes or until they are golden brown.
6. Once they have become crispy, remove the sheet from the oven.
7. Next, mix all the remaining seasoning ingredients in another bowl until combined well.
8. Finally, stir the chickpeas into this mixture and toss well.
9. Serve immediately.

Nutrition: Calories: 212 Kcal Protein: 9.3g; Carbohydrates: 28.9g; Fat: 7.4g

572. Nuts Trail Mix

Preparation Time: 10 minutes
Cooking Time: 10 minutes
Servings: 2
Ingredients:

- 1 cup Walnuts, raw
- 2 cups Tart Cherries, dried
- 1 cup Pumpkin Seeds, raw
- 1 cup Almonds, raw
- 1 cup Cashew

Directions:

1. First, mix all the ingredients needed to make the trail mix in a large mixing bowl until combined well.
2. Store in an air-tight container.

Nutrition: Calories: 596 Kcal Protein: 17.5g Carbohydrates: 46.1g Fat: 39.5g

573. Crispy Cauliflower

Preparation Time: 10 minutes
Cooking Time: 30 minutes
Servings: 6
Ingredients:

- 1 head cauliflower, cut into florets
- 2 tbsp potato starch
- 1/2 tsp salt
- 1/4 tsp black pepper
- 1/2 tsp turmeric
- 1 tbsp nutritional yeast, optional

- 1/2 tsp chili powder or paprika
- 1 tbsp avocado oil

Directions:

1. Start by preheating the oven to 450 degrees F.
2. Grease a baking sheet with a tablespoon of oil.
3. Add cauliflower to the baking sheet and toss in oil and the rest of the ingredients.
4. Mix well, then bake for 30 minutes.
5. Serve.

Nutrition: Calories 172 Total Fat 11.8 g Saturated Fat 4.4 g Cholesterol 62 mg Sodium 871 mg Total Carbs 45.8 g Fiber 0.6 g Sugar 2.3 g Protein 4 g

574. Spinach Mushroom Pockets

Preparation Time: 10 minutes
Cooking Time: 23 minutes
Servings: 4
Ingredients:

- 1 package puff pastry
- 16 oz mushrooms, sliced
- 2 bags spinach
- 1 1/2 tbsp garlic, minced
- 1 pinch salt
- 1 block extra-firm tofu, pressed
- 1 tsp onion powder
- 1 tsp basil
- 1 tsp oregano
- Black pepper, to taste
- 1/4 tsp salt
- 2 1/2 tbsp nutritional yeast
- 2 tbsp lemon juice
- 1 tsp mustard - 1 tbsp milk

Directions:

1. Place mushrooms in a large pot and heat until they release their liquid.
2. Stir in 1.5 teaspoons garlic and spinach, then cover with a lid.
3. Cook for 3 minutes until spinach wilts.
4. Toss the rest of the ingredients into a bowl and set it aside.
5. Spread the pastry into a thin sheet and cut circles out of it. Divide the filling in the circles and fold the circle, then pinch the edges closed.
6. Bake them for 20 minutes approximately in the oven at 375 degrees. Serve.

Nutrition: Calories 246; Total Fat 7.4 g; Saturated Fat 4.6 g; Cholesterol 105 mg; Sodium 353 mg; Total Carbs 29.4 g; Sugar 6.5 g; Fiber 2.7 g; Protein 7.2 g

575. Breaded Tofu

Preparation Time: 10 minutes
Cooking Time: 10 minutes
Servings: 4
Ingredients:

- 1 (14-oz) package extra-firm tofu
- ½ cup cornstarch
- ½ cup breadcrumbs
- ¼ cup of water
- ¼ cup of vegetable oil
- 2 tbsp soy sauce
- 1 tbsp nutritional yeast
- 1 pinch salt
- ½ cup BBQ sauce

Directions:

1. Drain the tofu, then slice it into finger-length strips.
2. Whisk water, soy sauce, and cornstarch in a small bowl.
3. Mix breadcrumbs with salt and yeast in a shallow bowl.
4. Pour vegetable oil into a large pan and heat over medium-high heat.
5. First, dip the tofu in the cornstarch mixture, then coat them with the breadcrumbs mixture.
6. Shallow fry the tofu for 3 minutes per side.
7. Serve.

Nutrition: Calories 293 Total Fat 16 g Saturated Fat 2.3 g Cholesterol 75 mg Sodium 386 mg Total Carbs 25.2 g Sugar 2.6 g Fiber 1.9 g; Protein 4.2 g

576. Raisin Protein Balls

Preparation Time: 10 minutes
Cooking Time: 30 minutes
Servings: 6
Ingredients:

- 1 cup dry oats
- ½ cup creamy peanut butter
- ¼ cup raisins

Directions:

1. Start by thoroughly mixing all the ingredients in a bowl.
2. Make golf ball sized fat bombs out of it.
3. Place them on a baking sheet and freeze for 30 minutes. Serve.

Nutrition: Calories 169 Total Fat 10.6 g Saturated Fat 3.1 g Cholesterol 131 mg Sodium 834 mg Total Carbs 31.4 g Fiber 0.2 g Sugar 0.3 g Protein 4.6 g

577. Cheese Cucumber Bites

Preparation Time: 10 minutes

Cooking Time: 0 minutes

Servings: 8

Ingredients:

- 4 large cucumbers
- 1 cup raw sunflower seeds
- 1/2 tsp salt
- 2 tbsp raw red onion, chopped
- 1 handful fresh chives, chopped
- 1 clove fresh garlic, chopped
- 2 tbsp nutritional yeast
- 2 tbsp fresh lemon juice - 1/2 cup water

Directions:

1. Start by blending sunflower seeds with salt in a food processor for 20 seconds.
2. Toss in remaining ingredients except for the cucumber and chives and process until smooth.
3. Slice the cucumber into 1.5-inch thick rounds.
4. Top each slice with sunflower mixture.
5. Garnish with sumac and chives.
6. Serve.

Nutrition: Calories 211 Total Fat 25.5 g Saturated Fat 12.4 g Cholesterol 69 mg Sodium 58 mg Total Carbs 32.4 g Fiber 0.7 g Sugar 0.3 g Protein 1.4 g

578. Hummus without Oil

Preparation Time: 5 minutes

Cooking Time: 5 minutes

Servings: 6

Ingredients:

- 2 tablespoons of lemon juice
- 1 15-ounce can of chickpeas
- 2 tablespoons of tahini
- 1-2 freshly chopped/minced garlic cloves
- Red pepper hummus
- 2 tablespoons of almond milk pepper

Directions:

1. Rinse the chickpeas and put them in a high-speed blender with garlic.
2. 2Blend them until they break into fine pieces.
3. Add the other ingredients and blend everything until you have a smooth paste. Add some water if you want a less thick consistency.
4. Your homemade hummus dip is ready to be served with eatables!

Nutrition: Calories: 202 per serving Fat – 3 g Carbohydrates – 35 g Protein – 11 g

579. Tempting Quinoa Tabbouleh

Preparation Time: 10 minutes

Cooking Time: 10 minutes

Servings: 6

Ingredients:

- 1 cup of well-rinsed quinoa
- 1 finely minced garlic clove
- ½ teaspoon of kosher salt
- ½ cup of extra virgin olive oil
- 2 tablespoons of fresh lemon juice
- Freshly ground black pepper
- 2 Persian cucumbers, cut into ¼-inch pieces
- 2 thinly sliced scallions
- 1 pint of halved cherry tomatoes
- ½ cup of chopped fresh mint
- 2/3 cup of chopped parsley

Directions:

1. Put a medium saucepan on high heat and boil the quinoa mixed with salt in 1 ¼ cups of water.
2. Decrease the heat to medium-low, cover the pot, and simmer everything until the quinoa is tender. The entire process will take 10 minutes.
3. Remove the quinoa from heat and allow it to stand for 5 minutes. Fluff it with a fork.
4. In a small bowl, whisk the garlic with the lemon juice. Add the olive oil gradually.
5. Mix the salt and pepper to taste.
6. On a baking sheet, spread the quinoa and allow it to cool. Shift it to a large bowl and mix ¼ of the dressing.
7. Add the tomatoes, scallions, herbs, and cucumber.
8. Give them a good toss and season everything with pepper and salt.
9. Add the remaining dressing.

Nutrition: Calories: 292 per serving Fat – 20 g Carbohydrates – 25 g; Protein – 5 g

580. Quick Peanut Butter Bars

Preparation Time: 10 minutes

Cooking Time: 15 minutes

Servings: 10

Ingredients:

- 20 soft-pitted Medjool dates
- 1 cup of raw almonds
- 1 ¼ cup of crushed pretzels
- 1/3 cup of natural peanut butter

Directions:

1. Put the almonds in a food processor and mix them until they are broken.

2. Add the peanut butter and the dates. Blend them until you have a thick dough

3. Crush the pretzels and put them in the processor. Pulse enough to mix them with the rest of the ingredients. You can also give them a good stir with a spoon.

4. Take a small, square pan and line it with parchment paper. Press the dough onto the pan, flattening it with your hands or a spoon.

5. Put it in the freezer for about 2 hours or in the fridge for about 4 hours.

6. Once it is fully set, cut it into bars. Store them and enjoy them when you are hungry. Just remember to store them in a sealed container.

Nutrition: Calories: 343 per serving Fat – 23 g Carbohydrates – 33 g Protein – 5 g

581. Hummus Made with Sweet Potato

Preparation Time: 15 minutes
Cooking Time: 55 minutes
Servings: 3-4 cups
Ingredients:

- 2 cups of cooked chickpeas
- 2 medium sweet potatoes
- 3 tablespoons of tahini
- 3 tablespoons of olive oil
- 3 freshly peeled garlic gloves
- Freshly squeezed lemon juice
- Ground sea salt
- ¼ teaspoon of cumin
- Zest from half a lemon
- ½ teaspoon of smoked paprika
- 1 ½ teaspoon of cayenne pepper

Directions:

1. Preheat the oven to 400°F. Put the sweet potatoes on the middle rack of the oven and bake them for about 45 minutes. You can also bake the potatoes in a baking dish. You will know that they are ready when they become soft and squishy.

2. Allow the sweet potatoes to cool down. Blend all the other ingredients in a food processor.

3. After the sweet potatoes have sufficiently cooled down, use a knife to peel off the skin.

4. Add the sweet potatoes to a blender and blend well with the rest of the ingredients.

5. Once you have a potato mash, sprinkle some sesame seeds and cayenne pepper, and serve it!

Nutrition: Calories: 33.6 per serving Fat – 0.9 g; Carbohydrates – 5,6 g; Protein – 1 g

582. Crisp Balls Made with Peanut Butter

Preparation Time: 29 minutes
Cooking Time: 20 minutes
Servings: 16 balls
Ingredients:

- ¼ cup of wheat germ
- ½ cup of natural peanut butter
- 1/3 cup of rolled oats
- ¼ cup of unsweetened flaked coconut
- ¼ cup of whole quick oats
- ½ teaspoon of ground cinnamon
- ¼ cup of brown rice crisp cereal
- 1 tablespoon of maple syrup
- ¼ cup of apple cider vinegar

Directions:

1. In a bowl, mix all the ingredients apart from the rice cereal. Combine everything properly.

2. Create 16 balls out of the mixture. Each ball should be 1 inch in diameter.

3. In a shallow dish, add the rice cereal and roll each ball on the crispiest. See that the balls are properly coated.

4. Enjoy your no-bake crisp balls.

5. Store them in a refrigerator for later use.

Nutrition: Calories: 79 per serving Fat – 4.8 g Carbohydrates – 6.3 g Protein – 3.5 g

583. Healthy Protein Bars

Preparation Time: 19 minutes
Cooking Time: 15 minutes
Servings: 12 balls
Ingredients:

- 1 large banana
- 1 cup of rolled oats
- 1 serving of vegan vanilla protein powder

Directions:

1. In a food processor, blend the protein powder and rolled oats.

2. Blend them for 1 minute until you have a semi-coarse mixture. The oats should be slightly chopped but not powdered.

3. Add the banana and form a pliable and coarse dough.

4. Shape into either balls or small bars and store them in a container.

5. Eat one and store the rest in an airtight container in the refrigerator!

Nutrition: Calories: 47 per serving Fat – 0.7 g Carbohydrates – 8 g Protein – 2.7 g

584. Tofu Saag

Preparation Time: 25 minutes
Cooking Time: 20 minutes
Servings: 6
Ingredients:

- 21 Ounces Water Packed Tofu, Fir & Cubed into 1 Inch Pieces
- 10 Ounces Baby Spinach, Torn
- 2 Tablespoons Canola Oil, Divided
- 10 Ounces Baby Kale, Stemmed
- 1 Teaspoon Cumin
- 1 Teaspoon Fennel
- 8 Green Cardamom Pods
- 6 Whole Cloves
- 3 Red Chilies, Red
- 2 Tablespoon Ginger, Fresh & Minced
- Sea Salt to Tate
- 1 Teaspoon Water
- 1/8 Teaspoon Red Pepper

Directions:

1. Cook your tofu in two batches, making sure to drain it on paper towels. Your tofu should be golden.

2. Get out a Dutch oven, and then bring two inches of water to a boil, adding in your kale and spinach. Cover and cook until wilted. This should take four minutes, and then stir occasionally.

3. Drain well, and reserve the cooking liquid. Place your spinach and kale into a blender, and blend until smooth. Use your cooking liquid as needed to blend.

4. Combine a tablespoon of oil, a teaspoon of cumin seeds, fennel, and red chilies in a skillet. Cook for two minutes until golden brown and fragrant. Make sure to stir frequently.

5. Stir in your ginger, and cook for thirty seconds.

6. Remove your cardamom and cloves, and then discard them.

7. Stir in your spinach, and then add a quarter cup of cooking liquid into a blender, making a puree. Scrape it down, and then put it in the pan. Stir in your salt, and then cook for five more minutes.

8. Put your tofu on top of your spinach mix, and then cover. Cook for another five more minutes.

9. Combine your ghee, cumin, fennel, and remaining red chilies. Cook for two minutes, and then add in your ground red pepper. Add in a teaspoon of water, and then stir to mix before serving.

Nutrition: Calories: 210 Protein: 12 Grams Fat: 13.7 Grams Carbs: 13 Grams

585. Mango Sticky Rice

Preparation Time: 15 minutes
Cooking Time: 20 minutes
Servings: 3
Ingredients:

- ½ Cup Sugar
- 1 Mango, Sliced
- 14 Ounces Coconut Milk, Canned
- ½ Cup Basmati Rice

Directions:

1. Cook your rice per package instructions, and add half of your sugar. When cooking your rice, substitute half of your water for half of your coconut milk.

2. Boil your remaining coconut milk in a saucepan with your remaining sugar.

3. Boil on high heat until it's thick, and then add in your mango slices.

Nutrition: Calories: 571 Protein: 6 Grams Fat: 29.6 Grams Carbs: 77.6 Grams

586. Oatmeal Sponge Cookies

Preparation Time: 25 minutes
Cooking Time: 15 minutes
Servings: 12
Ingredients:

- ¼ Cup Applesauce
- ½ Teaspoon Cinnamon
- 1/3 Cup Raisins
- ½ Teaspoon Vanilla Extract, Pure
- 1 Cup Ripe Banana, Mashed
- 2 Cups Oatmeal

Directions:

1. Start by heating your oven to 350.
2. Mix everything together. It should be gooey.
3. Drop it onto an ungreased baking sheet by the tablespoon, and then flatten.
4. Bake for fifteen minutes.

Nutrition: Calories: 79.1 Protein: 2 Grams Fat: 1 Gram Carbs: 16.4 Grams

CHAPTER 18:

Desserts

587. Zesty orange-cranberry energy bites

Preparation Time: 10 minutes

Cooking Time: 0 minutes

Servings: 12 bites

Ingredients

- 2 tablespoons almond butter, or cashew or sunflower seed butter
- 2 tablespoons maple syrup or brown rice syrup
- 3/4 cup cooked quinoa
- 1/4 cup sesame seeds, toasted
- 1 tablespoon chia seeds
- ½ teaspoon almond extract, or vanilla extract
- Zest of 1 orange
- 1 tablespoon dried cranberries
- ¼ cup ground almonds

Directions:

1. Mix the nut or seed butter and syrup until smooth and creamy in a medium bowl. Stir in the rest of the ingredients, and mix to make sure the consistency is holding together in a ball. Form the mix into 12 balls.
2. Place them on a baking sheet lined with parchment or waxed paper and put them in the fridge to set for about 15 minutes.
3. If your balls aren't holding together, it's likely because of the moisture content of your cooked quinoa. Add more nut or seed butter mixed with syrup until it all sticks together.

Nutrition: (1 bite) Calories: 109; total fat: 7g; carbs: 11g; fiber: 3g; protein: 3g

588. Chocolate and walnut farfalle

Preparation Time: 10 minutes

Cooking Time: 0 minutes

Servings: 4 servings

Ingredients

- 1/2 cup chopped toasted walnuts
- 1/4 cup vegan semisweet chocolate pieces
- 8 ounces farfalle
- 3 tablespoons vegan margarine
- 1/4 cup light brown sugar

Directions:

1. Grind the walnuts and chocolate pieces in a food processor or blender until crumbly. Do not over process. Set aside.
2. In a pot of boiling salted water, cook the farfalle, occasionally stirring, until al dente, about 8 minutes. Drain well and return to the pot.

3. Add the margarine and sugar and toss to combine and melt the margarine.
4. Transfer the noodle mixture to a serving

Nutrition: Calories: 81; total fat: 37.64g; carbs: 42.38g; fiber: 4.8g; protein: 8.68g

589. Almond-date energy bites

Preparation Time: 5 minutes

Servings: 24 bites

Ingredients

- 1 cup dates, pitted
- 1 cup unsweetened shredded coconut
- ¼ cup chia seeds
- ¾ cup ground almonds
- ¼ cup cocoa nibs, or non-dairy chocolate chips

Directions:

1. Purée everything in a food processor until crumbly and sticking together, pushing down the sides whenever necessary to keep it blending. If you don't have a food processor, you can mash soft Medjool dates. But if you're using harder baking dates, you'll have to soak them and then try to purée them in a blender.
2. Form the mix into 24 balls and place them on a baking sheet lined with parchment or waxed paper. Put in the fridge to set for about 15 minutes.
3. Use the softest dates you can find. Medjool dates are the best for this purpose. The hard dates you see in the baking aisle of your supermarket are going to take a long time to blend up. If you use those, try soaking them in water for at least an hour before starting and then draining.

Nutrition: (1 bite) Calories: 152; total fat: 11g; carbs: 13g; fiber: 5g; protein: 3g

590. Pumpkin Pie Cups (Pressure Cooker)

Preparation Time: 5 minutes

Cooking Time: 6 minutes

Servings: 4-6

Ingredients

- 1 cup canned pumpkin purée
- 1 cup nondairy milk
- 6 tablespoons unrefined sugar or pure maple syrup (less if using sweetened milk), plus more for sprinkling
- ¼ cup spelt flour or all-purpose flour
- ½ teaspoon pumpkin pie spice
- Pinch salt

Directions:

1. Stir together the pumpkin, milk, sugar, flour, pumpkin pie spice, and salt in a medium bowl. Pour the mixture into 4 heat-proof ramekins. Sprinkle a bit more sugar on the top of each, if you like.

2. Put a trivet in the bottom of your electric pressure cooker's cooking pot and pour in a cup or two of water. Place the ramekins onto the trivet, stacking them if needed (3 on the bottom, 1 on top).

3. High pressure for 6 minutes.

4. Close and lock the lid and ensure the pressure valve is sealed, then select high pressure and set the time for 6 minutes.

5. Pressure release. Once the cooking time is complete, quickly release the pressure, and be careful not to get your fingers or face near the steam release. Once all the pressure has been released, carefully unlock and remove the lid. Let cool for a few minutes before carefully lifting out the ramekins with oven mitts or tongs. Let cool for at least 10 minutes before serving.

Nutrition: Calories: 129; total fat: 1g; protein: 3g; sodium: 39mg; fiber: 3g

591. Granola-stuffed baked apples

Preparation Time: 10 minutes
Cooking Time: 60 minutes
Servings: 4
Ingredients

- 1/2 cup vegan granola, homemade or store-bought
- 2 tablespoons creamy peanut butter or almond butter
- 1 tablespoon vegan margarine
- 1 tablespoon pure maple syrup
- 1/2 teaspoon ground cinnamon
- 4 granny smith or other firm baking apples
- 1 cup apple juice

Directions:

1. Preheat the oven to 350°f. Grease a 9 x 13-inch baking pan and set it aside. Combine the granola, peanut butter, margarine, maple syrup, and cinnamon in a medium bowl and mix well.

2. Core the apples and stuff the granola mixture into the centers of the apples, packing tightly.

3. Place the apples upright in the prepared pan. Pour the apple juice over the apples and bake until tender, about 1 hour. Serve warm.

Nutrition: Calories: 361; total fat: 13.65g; protein: 7.69g; sodium: 62mg; fiber: 8.4g

592. Better pecan bars

Preparation Time: 5 minutes
Cooking Time: 20 minutes
Servings: 12 bars
Ingredients

- 1 cup whole-grain flour
- 1 cup light brown sugar, divided
- 1/2 cup plus 1/4 cup vegan margarine, softened
- 1 cup pecan pieces
- 1/4 cup pure maple syrup
- 1/3 cup vegan semisweet chocolate chips

Directions:

1. Preheat the oven to 350°F. Lightly oil an 8-inch square baking pan and set it aside. In a food processor, combine the flour, 1/2 cup of sugar, and 1/2 cup of margarine. Process to mix well.

2. Transfer the mixture to the prepared baking pan and press it firmly into the bottom. Bake for 12 minutes. Remove from the oven and set aside.

3. Combine the remaining 1/2 cup of sugar and the remaining 1/4 cup of margarine in a saucepan. Cook over medium heat, constantly stirring, until mixture boils. Add the pecans and maple syrup and boil for about 30 seconds, stirring constantly. Pour the mixture evenly over the crust.

4. Bake until the caramel layer is bubbly and the crust is lightly browned, about 7 minutes. Remove from oven and sprinkle with chocolate chips. Allow chips to melt slightly, then drag a fork through them to swirl into the top. Cool slightly, then refrigerate to set the topping before cutting into bars. Store in an airtight container.

Nutrition Calories: 373; total fat: 26.12g; protein: 2.96g; sodium: 16mg; fiber: 2.7g

593. Chocolate-almond bars

Preparation Time: 5 minutes
Cooking Time: 30 minutes
Servings: 12 bars
Ingredients

- 2/3 cup vegan margarine, melted
- 1/2 cup almond butter
- 1 teaspoon pure vanilla extract
- 1/2 teaspoon salt
- 1 cup light brown sugar
- 2 cups whole-grain flour
- 1 cup vegan semisweet chocolate chips
- 3/4 cup slivered almonds

Directions:

1. Preheat the oven to 375°f. Lightly grease an 8-inch square baking pan and set it aside. Combine the margarine, almond butter, vanilla, and salt in a large bowl. Add the sugar and stir until well blended. Add the flour and stir until well blended.

2. Fold in the chocolate chips and half of the almonds. Press the dough into the prepared pan. Sprinkle the remaining almonds over the top and press them into the dough.

3. Bake until browned, 25 to 30 minutes. Cool completely before cutting into bars. Store in an airtight container.

Nutrition: Calories: 546; total fat: 47.18g; protein: 7.94g; sodium: 259mg; fiber: 5.1

594. Coconut and almond truffles

Preparation Time: 15 minutes

Cooking Time: 0 minutes

Servings: 8 truffles

Ingredients

- 1 cup pitted dates
- 1 cup almonds
- ½ cup sweetened cocoa powder, plus extra for coating
- ½ cup unsweetened shredded coconut
- ¼ cup pure maple syrup
- 1 teaspoon vanilla extract
- 1 teaspoon almond extract
- ¼ teaspoon sea salt

Directions:

1. In the bowl of a food processor, combine all the ingredients and process until smooth. Chill the mixture for about 1 hour.

2. Roll the mixture into balls, and then roll the balls in cocoa powder to coat.

3. Serve immediately or keep chilled until ready to serve.

Nutrition: Calories: 95; total fat: 0.96g; protein: 1.6g; sodium: 91mg; fiber: 3.3

595. Pecan and date-stuffed roasted pears

Preparation Time: 10 minutes

Cooking Time: 30 minutes

Servings: 4

Ingredients

- 4 firm ripe pears, cored
- 1 tablespoon fresh lemon juice
- 1/2 cup finely chopped pecans
- 4 dates, pitted and chopped
- 1 tablespoon vegan margarine
- 1 tablespoon pure maple syrup
- 1/4 teaspoon ground cinnamon
- 1/8 teaspoon ground ginger
- 1/2 cup pear, white grape, or apple juice

Directions:

1. Preheat the oven to 350°f. Grease a shallow baking dish and set it aside. Halve the pears lengthwise and use a melon baller to scoop out the cores. Rub the exposed part of the pears with lemon juice to avoid discoloration.

2. In a medium bowl, combine the pecans, dates, margarine, maple syrup, cinnamon, and ginger and mix well.

3. Stuff the mixture into the centers of the pear halves and arrange them in the prepared baking pan. Pour the juice over the pears. Bake until tender, 30 to 40 minutes. Serve warm.

Nutrition Calories: 283 total Fat: 20.81g; protein: 2.67g; sodium: 5mg; fiber: 4.4

596. Lime-macerated mangos

Preparation Time: 10 minutes

Cooking Time: 0 minutes

Servings: 4 to 6

Ingredients

- 3 ripe mangos
- 1/3 cup light brown sugar
- 2 tablespoons fresh lime juice
- 1/2 cup dry white wine
- Fresh mint sprigs

Directions:

1. Peel, pit, and cut the mangos into 1/2-inch dice. Layer the diced mango in a large bowl, sprinkling each layer with about 1 tablespoon of sugar. Cover with plastic wrap and refrigerate for 2 hours.

2. Pour in the lime juice and wine, mixing gently to combine with the mango. Cover and refrigerate for 4 hours.

3. About 30 minutes before serving time, bring the fruit to room temperature. To serve, spoon the mango and the liquid into serving glasses and garnish with mint.

Nutrition Calories: 103 total Fat: 5.62g; protein: 4.55g; sodium: 303mg; fiber: 0.2

597. Fudgy brownies (pressure cooker)

Preparation Time: 10 minutes

Cooking Time: 11 minutes

Servings: 4-6

Ingredients

- 3 ounces dairy-free dark chocolate
- 1 tablespoon coconut oil or vegan margarine
- ½ cup applesauce
- 2 tablespoons unrefined sugar
- 1/3 cup all-purpose flour
- ½ teaspoon baking powder
- Pinch salt

Directions:

1. Put a trivet in your electric pressure cooker's cooking pot and pour in a cup or two of water.
2. Select sauté or simmer. Combine the chocolate and coconut oil in a large heat-proof glass or ceramic bowl. Place the bowl over the top of your pressure cooker, as you would a double boiler.
3. Stir occasionally until the chocolate is melted, then turn off the pressure cooker. Stir the applesauce and sugar into the chocolate mixture.
4. Add the flour, baking powder, and salt and stir just until combined.
5. Pour the batter into 3 heat-proof ramekins. Put them in a heat-proof dish and cover with aluminum foil.
6. Lower the dish onto the trivet using a foil sling or silicone helper handles. (alternately, cover each ramekin with foil and place them directly on the trivet, without the dish.)
7. High pressure for 6 minutes. Close and lock the lid and ensure the pressure valve is sealed, then select high pressure and set the time for 5 minutes.
8. Pressure release. Once the cooking time is complete, quick release the pressure, being careful not to get your fingers or face near the steam release. Once all the pressure has been released, carefully unlock and remove the lid.
9. Let cool for a few minutes before carefully lifting out the dish, or ramekins, with oven mitts or tongs. Let cool for a few minutes more before serving.
10. Top with fresh raspberries and an extra drizzle of melted chocolate.

Nutrition: Calories: 316; total fat: 14g; protein: 5g; sodium: 68mg; fiber: 5g

598. Chocolate-banana fudge

Preparation Time: 10 minutes

Cooking Time: 0 minutes

Servings: about 36 pieces

Ingredients

- 1 ripe banana
- ¾ cup vegan semisweet chocolate chips
- 4 cups confectioners' sugar
- 1 teaspoon pure vanilla extract

Directions:

1. Line an 8-inch square baking pan with enough waxed paper or aluminum foil so that the ends hang over the edge of the pan. (this will help you get the fudge out of the pan later.) Set aside. Place the banana in a food processor and blend until smooth.
2. Melt the chocolate chips in a double boiler or microwave, then add to the pureed banana along with the sugar and vanilla and process until smooth.
3. Scrape the mixture into the prepared pan. Smooth the top and refrigerate until firm, at least 2 hours.
4. Once chilled, grip the waxed paper, lift the fudge from the pan, and transfer it to a cutting board. Remove and discard the waxed paper.
5. Cut the fudge into small pieces and serve.
6. Cover and refrigerate any leftovers.

Nutrition Calories: 65; total fat: 1.24g; protein: 0.18g; sodium: 1mg; fiber: 0.3g

599. Chocolate–almond butter truffles

Preparation Time: 15 minutes

Cooking Time: 0 minutes

Servings: about 24 truffles

Ingredients

- 1 cup vegan semisweet chocolate chips
- 1/2 cup almond butter
- 2 tablespoons plain or vanilla soy milk
- 1 tablespoon pure vanilla extract
- 1 cup confectioners' sugar
- 2 tablespoons unsweetened cocoa powder
- 1/2 cup finely chopped toasted almonds

Directions:

1. Melt the chocolate in a double boiler or microwave.
2. Combine the almond butter, soy milk, and vanilla in a food processor and blend until smooth. Add

the sugar, cocoa, and melted chocolate and blend until smooth and creamy.

3. Transfer the mixture to a bowl and refrigerate until chilled, at least 45 minutes.

4. Roll the chilled mixture into 1-inch balls and place them on an ungreased baking sheet.

5. Place the ground almonds in a shallow bowl and roll the balls in them, turning to coat. Place the truffles on a serving platter, refrigerate for 30 minutes, and serve.

Nutrition Calories: 118; total fat: 8.03g; protein: 2.58g; sodium: 25mg; fiber: 1.6g

600. Chocolate macaroons

Preparation Time: 10 minutes

Cooking Time: 15 minutes

Servings: 8

Ingredients

- 1 cup unsweetened shredded coconut
- 2 tablespoons cocoa powder
- 2/3 cup coconut milk
- ¼ cup agave
- Pinch of sea salt

Directions:

1. Preheat the oven to 350°F. Line a baking sheet with parchment paper. In a medium saucepan, cook all the ingredients over -medium-high heat until a firm dough is formed. Scoop the dough into balls and place it on the baking sheet.

2. Bake it for 15 minutes, remove it from the oven and let cool on the baking sheet.

3. Serve cooled macaroons or store in a tightly sealed container for up to

Nutrition: Calories: 55; total fat: 5.03g; protein: 0.92g; sodium: 35mg; fiber: 1.2g

601. Chocolate pudding

Preparation Time: 5 minutes

Cooking Time: 0 minutes

Servings: 1

Ingredients

- 1 banana
- 2 to 4 tablespoons nondairy milk
- 2 tablespoons unsweetened cocoa powder
- 2 tablespoons sugar (optional)
- ½ ripe avocado or 1 cup silken tofu (optional)

Directions:

1. In a small blender, combine the banana, milk, cocoa powder, sugar (if using), and avocado (if using). Purée until smooth.

2. Alternatively, in a small bowl, mash the banana very well, and stir in the remaining ingredients.

Nutrition: Calories: 244; protein: 4g; total fat: 3g; saturated fat: 1g; carbohydrates: 59g; fiber: 8g

602. Avocado pudding

Preparation Time: 10 minutes

Cooking Time: 0 minutes

Servings: 8

Ingredients:

- 2 ripe avocados, peeled, pitted and cut into pieces
- 1 tbsp fresh lime juice
- 14 oz can coconut milk
- 80 drops of liquid stevia
- 2 tsp vanilla extract

Directions:

1. Add all ingredients into the blender and blend until smooth.

2. Serve and enjoy.

Nutrition: calories 317; fat 30.1 g; carbohydrates 9.3 g; sugar 0.4 g; protein 3.4 g; cholesterol 0 mg

603. Almond butter brownies

Preparation Time: 30 minutes

Cooking Time: 0 minutes

Servings: 4

Ingredients:

- 1 scoop protein powder
- 2 tbsp cocoa powder
- 1/2 cup almond butter, melted
- 1 cup bananas, overripe

Directions:

1. Preheat the oven to 350°F/176°C

2. Spray brownie tray with cooking spray.

3. Add all ingredients into the blender and blend until smooth.

4. Pour batter into the prepared dish and bake in preheated oven for 20 minutes.

5. Serve and enjoy.

Nutrition: calories 82; fat 2.1 g; carbohydrates 11.4 g; protein 6.9 g; sugars 5 g; cholesterol 16 mg

604. Raspberry chia pudding

Preparation Time: 3 hours 10 minutes

Cooking Time: 0 minutes

Servings: 2

Ingredients:

- 4 tbsp chia seeds
- 1 cup coconut milk
- 1/2 cup raspberries

Directions:

1. Add raspberry and coconut milk in a blender and blend until smooth.
2. Pour the mixture into the mason jar.
3. Add chia seeds in a jar and stir well.
4. Close the jar tightly with a lid and shake well.
5. Place in refrigerator for 3 hours.
6. Serve chilled and enjoy.

Nutrition: calories 361; fat 33.4 g; carbohydrates 13.3 g; sugar 5.4 g; protein 6.2 g; cholesterol 0 mg

605. Chocolate fudge

Preparation Time: 10 minutes

Cooking Time: 0 minutes

Servings: 12

Ingredients:

- 4 oz unsweetened dark chocolate
- 3/4 cup coconut butter
- 15 drops liquid stevia
- 1 tsp vanilla extract

Directions:

1. Melt coconut butter and dark chocolate.
2. Add ingredients to the large bowl and combine well.
3. Pour the mixture into a silicone loaf pan and place in refrigerator until set.
4. Cut into pieces and serve.

Nutrition: calories 157; fat 14.1 g; carbohydrates 6.1 g; sugar 1 g; protein 2.3 g; cholesterol 0 mg

606. Quick Chocó brownie

Preparation Time: 10 minutes

Cooking Time: 0 minutes

Servings: 1

Ingredients:

- 1/4 cup almond milk
- 1 tbsp cocoa powder
- 1 scoop chocolate protein powder
- 1/2 tsp baking powder

Directions:

1. In a microwave-safe mug, blend together baking powder, protein powder, and cocoa.
2. Add almond milk in a mug and stir well.
3. Place mug in microwave and microwave for 30 seconds.
4. Serve and enjoy.

Nutrition: calories 207; fat 15.8 g; carbohydrates 9.5 g; sugar 3.1 g; protein 12.4 g; cholesterol 20 mg

607. Cinnamon Coconut Chips

Preparation Time: 7 minutes

Cooking Time: 25 minutes

Servings: 2

Ingredients:

- ¼ cup coconut chips, unsweetened
- ¼ teaspoon of sea salt
- ¼ cup cinnamon

Directions:

1. Add cinnamon and salt to a mixing bowl and set it aside. Heat a pan over medium heat for 2 minutes.
2. Place the coconut chips in the hot pan and stir until coconut chips are crisp and lightly brown.
3. Toss toasted coconut chips with cinnamon and salt. Serve and enjoy!

Nutrition: Calories: 228 Fat: 21 grams Net Carbs: 7.8 grams Protein: 1.9 grams

608. Peach Cobbler

Preparation Time: 20 minutes

Cooking Time: 4 hours

Servings: 4

Ingredients:

- 4 cups peaches, peeled and sliced
- ¼ cup of coconut sugar
- ½ teaspoon cinnamon powder
- 1 ½ cups vegan sweet crackers, crushed
- ¼ cup stevia - ¼ teaspoon nutmeg, ground
- ½ cup almond milk
- 1 teaspoon vanilla extract
- Cooking spray

Directions:

1. In a bowl, mix peaches with coconut sugar and cinnamon and stir.
2. Mix crackers with stevia, nutmeg, almond milk, and vanilla extract in a separate bowl and stir.
3. Shower your slow cooker with cooking spray and spread peaches on the bottom. Add crackers mix, spread, cover, and cook on Low for 4 hours. Divide cobbler between plates and serve. Enjoy!

Nutrition: Calories: 212 Fat: 4 grams Net Carbs: 7 grams Protein: 3 grams

609. Chocolate Brownies

Preparation Time: 10 minutes

Cooking Time: 20 minutes

Servings: 4

Ingredients:

- 2 tablespoons cocoa powder

- 1 scoop protein powder
- 1 cup bananas, over-ripe
- ½ cup almond butter, melted

Directions:

1. Preheat the oven to 350°F.
2. Spray the brownie pan with cooking spray.
3. Add the real ingredients to your blender and blend until smooth.
4. Pour the batter into the prepared pan.
5. Put in the oven for 20 minutes.
6. Serve and enjoy!

Nutrition: Calories: 82 Fat: 2.1 grams Net Carbs: 11.4 grams Protein: 6.9 grams

610. The Keto Lovers "Magical" Grain-Free Granola

Preparation Time: 30 minutes
Cooking Time: 1 Hour and 15 minutes
Servings:
Ingredients:

- ½ cup of raw sunflower seeds
- ½ cup of raw hemp hearts
- ½ cup of flaxseeds
- ¼ cup of chia seeds
- 2 tablespoons of Psyllium Husk powder
- 1 tablespoon of cinnamon
- Stevia
- ½ teaspoon of baking powder
- ½ teaspoon of salt - 1 cup of water

Directions:

1. Preheat your oven to 300 F. Make sure to line a baking page with a parchment piece.
2. Take your food processor and grind all the seeds.
3. Add the dry ingredients and mix well.
4. Stir in water until fully incorporated.
5. Let the mixture sit for a while. Wait until it thickens up. Spread the mixture evenly-giving a thickness of about ¼ inch. Bake for 45 minutes.
6. Break apart the granola and keep baking for another 30 minutes until the pieces are crunchy.
7. Remove and allow them to cool. Enjoy!

Nutrition: Calories: 292 Fat: 25 grams Net Carbs: 12 grams Protein: 8 grams

611. Keto Ice Cream

Preparation Time: 10 minutes
Cooking Time: 3-4 Hours to Freeze
Servings: 4-5
Ingredients:

- 1 ½ teaspoon of natural vanilla extract

- 1/8 teaspoon of salt
- 1/3 cup of erythritol
- 2 cups of artificial coconut milk, full fat

Directions:

1. Stir together the vanilla extract, salt, sweetener, and milk.
2. If you do not come up with an ice cream machine, freeze the mixture in ice cube trays, then use a high-speed blender to blend the frozen cubes or thaw them enough to meld in a regular blender or food processor.
3. If you have an ice cream machine, just blend according to the manufacturer's directions.
4. Eat as it is or freeze for a firmer texture.

Nutrition: Calories: 184 Fat: 19.1 grams Net Carbs: 4.4 grams Protein: 1.8 grams

612. Apple Mix

Preparation Time: 10 minutes
Cooking Time: 4 Hours
Servings: 6
Ingredients:

- 6 apples, cored, peeled, and sliced
- 1½ cups almond flour
- Cooking spray
- 1 cup of coconut sugar
- 1 tablespoon cinnamon powder
- ¾ cup cashew butter, melted

Directions:

1. Add apple slices to your slow cooker after you have greased it with cooking spray.
2. Add flour, sugar, cinnamon, and coconut butter, stir gently, cover, cook on High for 4 hours, divide into bowls and serve cold. Enjoy!

Nutrition: Calories: 200 Fat: 5 grams Net Carbs: 8 grams Protein: 4 grams

613. Almond Butter Fudge

Preparation Time: 17 minutes
Cooking Time: 2-3 Hours to Freeze
Servings: 8
Ingredients:

- 2 ½ tablespoons coconut oil
- 2 ½ tablespoons honey
- ½ cup almond butter

Directions:

1. In a saucepan, pour almond butter, then add coconut oil warm for 2 minutes or until melted.
2. Add honey and stir.
3. Pour the mixture into a candy container and store it in the fridge until set.

4. Serve and enjoy!

Nutrition: Calories: 63 Fat: 4.8 grams Net Carbs: 5.6 grams Protein: 0.2 grams

614. The Vegan Pumpkin Spicy Fat Bombs

Preparation Time: 20 minutes
Cooking Time: 1 Hour and 20 minutes
Servings: 12
Ingredients:

- ¾ cup of pumpkin puree
- ¼ cup of hemp seeds
- ½ cup of coconut oil
- 2 teaspoons of pumpkin pie spice
- 1 teaspoon of vanilla extract
- Liquid Stevia

Directions:

1. Take a blender and add together all the ingredients.
2. Blend them well and portion the mixture out into silicon molds.
3. Allow them to chill and enjoy!

Nutrition: Calories: 103 Fat: 10 grams Net Carbs: 2 grams Protein: 1 gram

615. Orange Cake

Preparation Time: 25 minutes
Cooking Time: 5 Hours and 10 minutes
Servings: 4
Ingredients:

- Cooking spray
- 1 teaspoon baking powder
- 1 cup almond flour
- 1 cup of coconut sugar
- ½ teaspoon cinnamon powder
- 3 tablespoons coconut oil, melted
- ½ cup almond milk
- ½ cup pecans, chopped
- ¾ cup of water
- ½ cup raisins
- ½ cup orange peel, grated
- ¾ cup of orange juice

Directions:

1. In a bowl, mix flour with half of the sugar, baking powder, cinnamon, two tablespoons oil, milk, pecans, and raisins, stir and pour this in your slow cooker after you have sprayed it with cooking spray.
2. Warm a small pan over medium heat. Add water, orange juice, orange peel, the rest of the oil, and the remainder of the sugar, stir, bring to a boil,

pour over the blend in the slow cooker, cover, and cook on Low for 5 hours.

3. Divide into dessert bowls and serve cold. Enjoy!

Nutrition: Calories: 182 Fat: 3 grams Net Carbs: 4 grams Protein: 3 grams

616. Chia Raspberry Pudding

Preparation Time: 10 minutes
Cooking Time: 3 Hours
Servings: 2
Ingredients:

- 4 tablespoons chia seeds
- ½ cup raspberries
- 1 cup of coconut milk

Directions:

1. Add the raspberry and coconut milk into your blender and blend until smooth.
2. Pour the mixture into a mason jar.
3. Add chia seeds and stir.
4. Cap jar and shake.
5. Set in the fridge for 3 hours.
6. Serve and enjoy!

Nutrition: Calories: 408 Fat: 38.8 grams Net Carbs: 22.3 grams Protein: 9.1 grams

617. Pumpkin Cake

Preparation Time: 20 minutes
Cooking Time: 2 Hours and 10 minutes
Servings: 10
Ingredients:

- 1 ½ teaspoons baking powder
- Cooking spray
- 1 cup pumpkin puree
- 2 cups almond flour
- ½ teaspoon baking soda
- 1 ½ teaspoons cinnamon, ground
- ¼ teaspoon ginger, ground
- 1 tablespoon coconut oil, melted
- 1 tablespoon flaxseed mixed with two tablespoons water
- 1 tablespoon vanilla extract
- 1/3 cup maple syrup
- 1 teaspoon lemon juice

Directions:

1. In a bowl, flour with baking powder, baking soda, cinnamon, and ginger, then stir.
2. Add flaxseed, coconut oil, vanilla, pumpkin puree, maple syrup, and lemon juice, stir and pour in your slow cooker after spraying it with cooking spray parchment paper.

3. Cover Up pot and cook on Low for 2 hours and 20 minutes.

4. Leave the cake to cool down, slice, and serve. Enjoy!

Nutrition: Calories: 182 Fat: 3 grams Net Carbs: 3 grams Protein: 1 gram

618. Banana Bread

Preparation Time: 10 minutes

Cooking Time: 50 minutes

Servings: 6 to 8

Ingredients:

- 1½ cups flour
- 1 teaspoon baking soda
- 1 teaspoon baking powder
- ¼ cup brown sugar - ½ teaspoon salt
- ½ cup rolled oats
- 3 large ripe bananas
- 2 tablespoons ground flaxseed
- 1/3 cup unsweetened soy milk
- 1/3 cup vegetable oil
- 2 tablespoon maple syrup
- 1 tablespoon vanilla extract
- 1 cup mini dairy-free chocolate chips, divided

Directions:

1. Preheat the oven to 350°F. Fat a loaf pan or line with parchment paper covering all four sides.

2. Combine the flour, baking soda, baking powder, brown sugar, salt, and rolled oats in a large bowl. Set aside. Mash the bananas until almost no chunks remain. Add the flaxseed, milk, oil, maple syrup, and vanilla extract. Stir to combine.

3. Steadily pour down the wet ingredients into dry materials and stir until just combined. Stir in 1/2 f the mini chocolate chips.

4. Drench the cake batter into the greased or lined pan and spread it out evenly. Sprinkle the remaining chocolate chips on top in an even layer—Bake for 50 minutes. You may also wait until a toothpick incorporated in the center of the cake comes out clean. Cool it for 10 minutes.

5. Move it to a wire rack to continue cooling.

Nutrition: Calories: 420 Total Fat: 19 G Carbs: 57 G Fiber: 5 G Protein: 7 G

619. Apple Crisp

Preparation Time: 10 minutes

Cooking Time: 40 minutes

Servings: 6

Ingredients:

- ½ cup vegan butter

- 6 large apples, diced large
- 1 cup dried cranberries
- 2 tablespoons granulated sugar
- 2 teaspoons ground cinnamon, divided
- ¼ teaspoon ground nutmeg
- ¼ teaspoon ground ginger
- 2 teaspoons lemon juice
- 1 cup all-purpose flour
- 1 cup rolled oats
- 1 cup brown sugar
- 1/4 teaspoon salt

Directions:

1. Preheat the oven to 350°F. Gently grease an 8-inch square baking dish with butter or cooking spray.

2. Make the filling. In a large bowl, combine the apples, cranberries, granulated sugar, one teaspoon of cinnamon, nutmeg, ginger, and lemon juice. Toss to coat. Move the apple mixture to the prepared baking dish.

3. Make the topping. In the same large bowl, now empty, combine the all-purpose flour, oats, brown sugar, and salt. Stir to combine. Add Up the butter and, using a pastry cutter (or two knives moving in a crisscross pattern), cut back the butter into the flour and oat mixture until the butter is small.

4. Spread the topping over the apples evenly, patting down slightly—Bake for 35 minutes or until golden and bubbly.

Nutrition: Calories: 488 Total Fat: 9 G Carbs: 101 G Fiber: 10 G Protein: 5 G Calcium: 50 Mg Vitamin D: 0 Mcg Vitamin B12: 0 Mcg Iron: 2 Mg Zinc: 1 Mg

620. Secret Ingredient Chocolate Brownies

Preparation Time: 10 minutes

Cooking Time: 35 minutes

Servings: 6 to 8

Ingredients:

- ¾ cup flour
- ¼ teaspoon baking soda
- ¼ teaspoon salt
- 1/3 Cup vegan butter
- ¾ cup of sugar
- 2 tablespoon water
- 1¼ cups semi-sweet or dark dairy-free chocolate chips
- 6 tablespoons aquafaba, divided
- 1 Teaspoon Vanilla Extract

Directions:

1. Preheat the oven to 325°F. Line Up a 9-inch square baking pan with parchment or grease well.

2. In a large bowl, combine the flour, baking soda, and salt. Set aside.

3. Mix up the butter, sugar, and water in a medium saucepan. Bring to a boil, stirring occasionally. Reduce heat and stir in the chocolate chips.

4. Whisk in 3 tablespoons of aquafaba until thoroughly combined. Add the vanilla extract and the remaining three tablespoons of aquafaba, and whisk until mixed.

5. Add the chocolate mixture into the flour mixture and stir until mixed. Pour down an even layer into the prepared pan. Bake for 35 minutes until the top is set, but the brownie jiggles when slightly shaken. Allow for 45 minutes to 1 hour of cooling before removing and serving.

Nutrition: Calories: 369 Total Fat: 19 G Carbs: 48 G Fiber: 1 G Protein: 4 G Calcium: 1 Mg Vitamin D: 0 Mcg Vitamin B12: 0 Mcg Iron: 1 Mg Zinc: 0 Mg

621. Chocolate Chip Pecan Cookies

Preparation Time: 10 minutes
Cooking Time: 16 minutes
Servings: 30 Small Cookies
Ingredients:

- ¾ cup pecan halves, toasted
- 1 cup vegan butter
- ½ teaspoon salt
- ½ cup powdered sugar
- 2 teaspoons vanilla extract
- 2 cups all-purpose flour
- 1 cup mini dairy-free chocolate chips

Directions:

1. Preheat the oven to 350°F. Line a large rimmed baking page with parchment paper.

2. In a small skillet over medium heat, toast the pecans until warm and fragrant, about 2 minutes. Remove from the pan. Once these are cool, chop them into small pieces.

3. Make use of an electric hand mixer or a stand mixer fitted with a paddle attachment, combine the butter, salt, and powdered sugar, and cream together on high speed for 3 to 4 minutes, until light and fluffy. Add the vanilla extract and beat for 1 minute.

4. Turn the mixer on low and slowly add the flour, ½ cup at a time, until a dough form. Combine the chocolate chips and pecans and mix until just incorporated.

5. Using your hands, a large spoon, or a 1-inch ice cream scoop, drop 1-inch balls of dough on the baking sheet, spread out 1 inch apart. Gently press down on the cookies to flatten them slightly.

6. Bake for 10 to 15 minutes. Wait until just yellow around the edges. Let it cool for 5 minutes.

7. Transfer them to a wire rack. Serve or store in an airtight container.

Nutrition: Calories: 152 Total Fat: 11 G Carbs: 13 G Fiber: 1 G Protein: 2 G Calcium: 2 Mg Vitamin D: 0 Mcg Vitamin B12: 0 Mcg Iron: 0 Mg Zinc: 0 Mg

622. No-Bake Chocolate Coconut Energy Balls

Preparation Time: 15 minutes
Cooking Time: 3 to 4 Hours for Chilling
Servings: 9 Energy Balls
Ingredients:

- ¼ cup dry roasted or raw pumpkin seeds
- ¼ cup dry roasted or raw sunflower seeds
- ½ cup unsweetened shredded coconut
- 2 tablespoons chia seeds - ¼ teaspoon salt
- 1½ tablespoons Dutch-process cocoa powder
- ¼ cup rolled oats
- 2 tablespoons coconut oil, melted
- 6 pitted dates
- 2 tablespoons all-natural almond butter

Directions:

1. Mix the pumpkin seeds, sunflower seeds, coconut, chia seeds, salt, cocoa powder, and oats in a food processor. Pulse until the mix is coarsely crumbled.

2. Add the coconut oil, dates, and almond butter. Pulse until the mixture is fused and sticks together when squeezed between your fingers.

3. Scoop out two tablespoons of the mix at a time and roll them into 1½-inch balls with your hands. Place them spaced apart on a freezer-safe plate and freeze for 15 minutes. Remove from the freezer and keep refrigerated in an airtight container for up to 4 days.

Nutrition: Calories: 230 Total Fat: 12 G Carbs: 27 G Fiber: 5 G Protein: 5 G

623. Blueberry Hand Pies

Preparation Time: 6 to 8 minutes
Cooking Time: 20 minutes plus Chill Time
Servings: 6 to 8
Ingredients:

- 3 cups all-purpose flour, plus extra for sifting work surface

- ½ teaspoon salt
- ¼ cup, plus two tablespoons granulated sugar, divided
- 1 cup vegan butter
- ½ cup of cold water
- 1 cup fresh blueberries
- 2 teaspoons lemon zest
- 2 teaspoons lemon juice
- ¼ teaspoon ground cinnamon
- 1 teaspoon cornstarch
- ¼ cup unsweetened soy milk
- Coarse sugar, for sprinkling

Directions:

1. Preheat the oven to 375°F. Set aside.
2. In a large bowl, merge the flour, salt, two tablespoons of granulated sugar, and vegan butter. Using a pastry cutter or two knives moving in a crisscross pattern, cut the butter into the other ingredients until the butter is small peas.
3. Add the cold water and knead to form a dough. Tear the dough in half and wrap the halves separately in plastic wrap. Refrigerate for 15 minutes.
4. Make the blueberry filling. In a medium bowl, mix the blueberries, lemon zest, lemon juice, cinnamon, cornstarch, and the remaining ¼ cup of sugar.
5. Remove one half of the dough. On a floured side, roll out the dough to ¼- to ½-inch thickness. Turn a 5-inch bowl upside down, and, using it as a guide, cut the dough into circles to make mini pie crusts. Reroll scrap dough to cut out more circles. Repeat with the second half of the dough. You should come to an end up with 8 to 10 circles. Place the circles on the prepared sheet pan.
6. Spoon 1½ tablespoons of blueberry filling onto each circle, leaving a ¼-inch border and folding the circles in half to cover the filling, forming a half-moon shape. Use a fork to press the edges of the dough to seal the pies.
7. When all the pies are assembled, use a paring knife to score the pies by cutting three lines through the top crusts. Brush each pie with soy milk and sprinkle with coarse sugar. Bake for 20 minutes or until the filling is bubbly and the tops are golden. Let cool before serving.

Nutrition: Calories: 416 Total Fat: 23 G Carbs: 46 G Fiber: 5 G Protein: 6 G

624. Date Squares

Preparation Time: 20 minutes
Cooking Time: 25 minutes
Servings: 12
Ingredients:

- Cooking spray for greasing
- 1½ cups rolled oats
- 1½ cups all-purpose flour
- ¾ cup, plus 1/3 cup brown sugar, divided
- ½ teaspoon ground cinnamon
- ¼ teaspoon ground nutmeg
- 1 teaspoon baking soda
- ¼ teaspoon salt
- ¾ cup vegan butter
- 18 pitted dates
- 1 teaspoon lemon zest
- 1 teaspoon lemon juice
- 1 cup of water

Directions:

1. Preheat the oven to 350°F. Lightly grease or shower an 8-inch square baking plate. Set aside.
2. Make the base and topping mixture. In a large bowl, blend the rolled oats, flour, and ¾ cup of brown sugar, cinnamon, nutmeg, baking soda, and salt. Combine the butter and, using a pastry cutter or two knives working in a crisscross motion, cut the butter into the blend to form a crumbly dough. Press half of the dough into the prepared baking dish and set the remaining half aside.
3. To make a date filling, place a small saucepan over medium heat. Add the dates, the remaining 1/3 cup of sugar, the lemon zest, lemon juice, and water. Bring to a boil and cook for 7 to 10 minutes, until thickened.
4. When cooked, pour the date mixture over the dough base in the baking dish and top with the remaining crumb dough. Gently press down and spread evenly to cover all the filling. Bake for 25 minutes until lightly golden on top. Cool before serving. Store in an airtight container.

Nutrition: Calories: 443 Total Fat: 12 G Carbs: 81 G Fiber: 7 G Protein: 5 G

625. Homemade Chocolates with Coconut and Raisins

Preparation Time: 10 minutes
Cooking Time: Chilling time
Servings: 20
Ingredients:

- 1/2 cup cacao butter, melted

- 1/3 cup peanut butter
- 1/4 cup agave syrup
- A pinch of grated nutmeg
- A pinch of coarse salt
- 1/2 teaspoon vanilla extract
- 1 cup dried coconut, shredded
- 6 ounces dark chocolate, chopped
- 3 ounces raisins

Directions:

1. Carefully combine all the ingredients, not including the chocolate, in a mixing bowl.
2. Spoon the mixture into molds. Leave to set hard in a cool place.
3. Melt the dark chocolate in your microwave. Pour in the melted chocolate until the fillings are covered. Leave to set hard in a cool place. Enjoy!

Nutrition: Calories: 130 Fat: 9.1g Carbs: 12.1g Protein: 1.3g

626. Easy Mocha Fudge

Preparation Time: 10 minutes
Cooking Time: 60 minutes
Servings: 20
Ingredients:

- 1 cup cookies, crushed
- 1/2 cup almond butter
- 1/4 cup agave nectar
- 6 ounces dark chocolate, broken into chunks
- 1 teaspoon instant coffee
- A pinch of grated nutmeg
- A pinch of salt

Directions:

1. Line a large baking layer with parchment paper.
2. Melt the chocolate in your microwave and add in the remaining ingredients; stir to combine well.
3. Scrape the batter into a parchment-lined baking sheet. Put it in your freezer for a minimum of 1 hour to set.
4. Cut into squares and serve. Bon appétit!

Nutrition: Calories: 105 Fat: 5.6g Carbs: 12.9g Protein: 1.1g

627. Key Lime Pie

Preparation Time: 3 hours and 15 minutes
Cooking Time: 0 minutes
Servings: 12
Ingredients:
For the Crust:

- ¾ cup coconut flakes, unsweetened
- 1 cup dates, soaked in warm water for 10 minutes in water, drained

- For the Filling:
- ¾ cup of coconut meat
- 1 ½ avocado, peeled, pitted
- 2 tablespoons key lime juice
- ¼ cup agave

Directions:

1. Prepare the crust, and for this, place all its ingredients in a food processor and pulse for 3 to 5 minutes until the thick paste comes together.
2. Take an 8-inch pie pan, grease it with oil, pour crust mixture in it and spread and press the mixture evenly in the bottom and along the sides, and freeze until required.
3. Prepare the filling and for this, place all its ingredients in a food processor, and pulse for 2 minutes until smooth.
4. Pour the filling into the prepared pan, smooth the top and freeze for 3 hours until set.
5. Cut pie into slices and then serve.

Nutrition: Calories: 213 Fat: 10 g Carbs: 29 g Protein: 1200 g Fiber: 6 g

628. Chocolate Mint Grasshopper Pie

Preparation Time: 4 hours and 15 minutes
Cooking Time: 0 minutes
Servings: 4
Ingredients:
For the Crust:

- 1 cup dates, soaked in warm water for 10 minutes in water, drained
- 1/8 teaspoons salt
- 1/2 cup pecans
- 1 teaspoons cinnamon
- 1/2 cup walnuts
- For the Filling:
- ½ cup mint leaves
- 2 cups of cashews, soaked in warm water for 10 minutes in water, drained
- 2 tablespoons coconut oil
- 1/4 cup and 2 tablespoons of agave
- 1/4 teaspoons spirulina
- 1/4 cup water

Directions:

1. Prepare the crust, and for this, place all its ingredients in a food processor and pulse for 3 to 5 minutes until the thick paste comes together.
2. Take a 6-inch springform pan, grease it with oil, place crust mixture in it and spread and press the mixture evenly in the bottom and along the sides, and freeze until required.

3. Prepare the filling and for this, place all its ingredients in a food processor, and pulse for 2 minutes until smooth.

4. Pour the filling into the prepared pan, smooth the top, and freeze for 4 hours until set.

5. Cut pie into slices and then serve.

Nutrition: Calories: 223.7 Fat: 7.5 g Carbs: 36 g Protein: 2.5 g Fiber: 1 g

629. Peanut Butter Energy Bars

Preparation Time: 5 hours and 15 minutes

Cooking Time: 5 minutes

Servings: 16

Ingredients:

- 1/2 cup cranberries
- 12 Medjool dates, pitted
- 1 cup roasted almond
- 1 tablespoon chia seeds
- 1 1/2 cups oats
- 1/8 teaspoon salt
- 1/4 cup and 1 tablespoon agave nectar
- 1/2 teaspoon vanilla extract, unsweetened
- 1/3 cup and 1 tablespoon peanut butter, unsalted
- 2 tablespoons water

Directions:

1. Place an almond in a food processor, pulse until chopped, and then transfer into a large bowl.

2. Add dates into the food processor along with oats, pour in water, and pulse for dates are chopped.

3. Add dates mixture into the almond mixture, add chia seeds and berries and stir until mixed.

4. Take a saucepan, place it over medium heat, add the remaining butter and remaining ingredients, stir until the mixture reaches a liquid consistency.

5. Pour the butter mixture over the date mixture, and then stir until well combined.

6. Take an 8 by 8 inches baking tray, line it with a parchment sheet, add date mixture in it, spread and press it evenly and refrigerate for 5 hours.

7. Cut it into sixteen bars and serve.

Nutrition: Calories: 187 Fat: 7.5 g Carbs: 27.2 g Protein: 4.7 g Fiber: 2 g

630. Black Bean Brownie Pops

Preparation Time: 45 minutes

Cooking Time: 2 minutes

Servings: 12

Ingredients:

- 3/4 cup chocolate chips
- 15-ounce cooked black beans
- 1 tablespoon maple syrup
- 5 tablespoons cacao powder
- 1/8 teaspoon sea salt
- 2 tablespoons sunflower seed butter

Directions:

1. Place black beans in a food processor, add remaining ingredients, except for chocolate, and pulse for 2 minutes until combined and the dough starts to come together.

2. Shape the dough into twelve balls, arrange them on a baking sheet lined with parchment paper, then insert a toothpick into each ball and refrigerate for 20 minutes.

3. Then meat chocolate in the microwave for 2 minutes, and dip brownie pops in it until covered.

4. Return the pops into the refrigerator for 10 minutes until set and then serve.

Nutrition: Calories: 130 Fat: 6 g Carbs: 17 g Protein: 4 g Fiber: 1 g

631. Lemon Cashew Tart

Preparation Time: 3 hours and 15 minutes

Cooking Time: 0 minutes

Servings: 12

Ingredients:

For the Crust:

- 1 cup almonds
- 4 dates, pitted, soaked in warm water for 10 minutes in water, drained
- 1/8 teaspoon crystal salt
- 1 teaspoon vanilla extract, unsweetened
- For the Cream:
- 1 cup cashews, soaked in warm water for 10 minutes in water, drained
- 1/4 cup water
- 1/4 cup coconut nectar
- 1 teaspoon coconut oil
- 1 teaspoon vanilla extract, unsweetened
- 1 lemon, Juiced
- 1/8 teaspoon crystal salt
- For the Topping:
- Shredded coconut as needed

Directions:

1. Prepare the cream, and for this, place all its ingredients in a food processor, pulse for 2 minutes until smooth, and then refrigerate for 1 hour.

2. Then prepare the crust, and for this, place all its ingredients in a food processor and pulse for 3 to 5 minutes until the thick paste comes together.

3. Take a tart pan, grease it with oil, place crust mixture in it and spread and press the mixture evenly in the bottom and along the sides, and freeze until required.

4. Pour the filling into the prepared tart, smooth the top, and refrigerate for 2 hours until set.

5. Cut tart into slices and then serve.

Nutrition: Calories: 166 Fat: 10 g Carbs: 15 g Protein: 5 g Fiber: 1 g

632. Peppermint Oreos

Preparation Time: 2 hours
Cooking Time: 0 minutes
Servings: 12
Ingredients:
For the Cookies:
- 1 cup dates
- 2/3 cup brazil nuts
- 3 tablespoons carob powder
- 2/3 cup almonds
- 1/8 teaspoon sea salt
- 3 tablespoons water

For the Crème:
- 2 tablespoons almond butter
- 1 cup coconut chips
- 2 tablespoons melted coconut oil
- 1 cup coconut shreds
- 3 drops of peppermint oil
- 1/2 teaspoon vanilla powder

For the Dark Chocolate:
- 3/4 cup cacao powder
- 1/2 cup date paste
- 1/3 cup coconut oil, melted

Directions:
1. Prepare the cookies, and for this, place all the ingredients in a food processor and pulse for 3 to 5 minutes until the dough comes together.

2. Then place the dough between two parchment sheets, roll the dough, then cut out twenty-four cookies of the desired shape and freeze until solid.

3. Prepare the crème, and for this, place all its ingredients in a food processor and pulse for 2 minutes until smooth.

4. When cookies have hardened, sandwich crème in between the cookies by placing dollops on top of a cookie and then pressing it with another cookie.

5. Freeze the cookies for 30 minutes and in the meantime, prepare chocolate and for this, place all the ingredients in a bowl and whisk until combined.

6. Dip frouncesen cookie sandwich into chocolate, at least two times, and then freeze for another 30 minutes until chocolate has hardened.

7. Serve straight away.

Nutrition: Calories: 470 Fat: 32 g Carbs: 51 g Protein: 7 g Fiber: 12 g

633. Snickers Pie

Preparation Time: 4 hours
Cooking Time: 0 minutes
Servings: 16
Ingredients:
For the Crust:
- 12 Medjool dates, pitted
- 1 cup dried coconut, unsweetened
- 5 tablespoons cocoa powder
- 1/2 teaspoon sea salt
- 1 teaspoon vanilla extract, unsweetened
- 1 cup almonds

For the Caramel Layer:
- 10 Medjool dates, pitted, soaked for 10 minutes in warm water, drained
- 2 teaspoons vanilla extract, unsweetened
- 3 teaspoons coconut oil
- 3 tablespoons almond butter, unsalted

For the Peanut Butter Mousse:
- 3/4 cup peanut butter
- 2 tablespoons maple syrup
- 1/2 teaspoon vanilla extract, unsweetened
- 1/8 teaspoon sea salt
- 28 ounces coconut milk, chilled

Directions:
1. Prepare the crust, and for this, place all its ingredients in a food processor and pulse for 3 to 5 minutes until the thick paste comes together.

2. Take a baking pan, line it with parchment paper, place crust mixture in it, and spread and press the mixture evenly in the bottom, and freeze until required.

3. Prepare the caramel layer, and for this, place all its ingredients in a food processor and pulse for 2 minutes until smooth.

4. Pour the caramel on top of the prepared crust, smooth the top and freeze for 30 minutes until set.

5. Prepare the mousse and for this, separate coconut milk and its solid, then add solid from coconut milk into a food processor, add remaining ingredients and then pulse for 1 minute until smooth.

6. Top prepared mousse over caramel layer, and then freeze for 3 hours until set.

7. Serve straight away.

Nutrition: Calories: 456 Fat: 33 g Carbs: 37 g Protein: 8.3 g Fiber: 5 g

634. Double Chocolate Orange Cheesecake

Preparation Time: 4 hours
Cooking Time: 0 minutes
Servings: 12
Ingredients:
For the Base:
- 9 Medjool dates, pitted
- 1/3 cup Brazil nuts
- 2 tablespoons maple syrup
- 1/3 cup walnuts
- 2 tablespoons water
- 3 tablespoons cacao powder

For the Chocolate Cheesecake:
- 1/2 cup cacao powder
- 1 1/2 cups cashews, soaked for 10 minutes in warm water, drained
- 1/3 cup liquid coconut oil
- 1 teaspoon vanilla extract, unsweetened
- 1/3 cup maple syrup
- 1/3 cup water

For the Orange Cheesecake:
- 2 oranges, juiced
- 1/4 cup maple syrup
- 1 cup cashews, soaked for 10 minutes in warm water, drained
- 1 teaspoon vanilla extract, unsweetened
- 2 tablespoons coconut butter
- 1/2 cup liquid coconut oil
- 2 oranges, zested
- 4 drops of orange essential oil

For the Chocolate Topping:
- 3 tablespoons cacao powder
- 3 drops of orange essential oil
- 2 tablespoons liquid coconut oil
- 3 tablespoons maple syrup

Directions:
1. Prepare the base, and for this, place all its ingredients in a food processor and pulse for 3 to 5 minutes until the thick paste comes together.

2. Take a cake tin, place crust mixture in it and spread and press the mixture evenly in the bottom, and freeze until required.

3. Prepare the chocolate cheesecake, and for this, place all its ingredients in a food processor and pulse for 2 minutes until smooth.

4. Pour the chocolate cheesecake mixture on top of the prepared base, smooth the top and freeze for 20 minutes until set.

5. Then prepare the orange cheesecake and for this, place all its ingredients in a food processor, and pulse for 2 minutes until smooth

6. Top orange cheesecake mixture over chocolate cheesecake, and then freeze for 3 hours until hardened.

7. Then prepare the chocolate topping and for this, take a bowl, add all the ingredients in it and stir until well combined.

8. Spread chocolate topping over the top, freeze the cake for 10 minutes until the topping has hardened, and then slice to serve.

Nutrition: Calories: 508 Fat: 34.4 g Carbs: 44 g Protein: 8 g Fiber: 3 g

635. Coconut Ice Cream Cheesecake

Preparation Time: 3 hours
Cooking Time: 0 minutes
Servings: 4
Ingredients:
For the First Layer:
- 1 cup mixed nuts
- 3/4 cup dates, soaked for 10 minutes in warm water
- 2 tablespoons almond milk

For the Second Layer:
- 1 medium avocado, diced
- 1 cup cashew nuts, soaked for 10 minutes in warm water
- 3 cups strawberries, sliced
- 1 tablespoon chia seeds, soaked in 3 tablespoons soy milk
- 1/2 cup agave
- 1 cup melted coconut oil
- 1/2 cup shredded coconut
- 1 lime, juiced

Directions:
1. Prepare the first layer, and for this, place all its ingredients in a food processor and pulse for 3 to 5 minutes until the thick paste comes together.

2. Take a springform pan, place crust mixture in it and spread and press the mixture evenly in the bottom, and freeze until required.

3. Prepare the second layer, and for this, place all its ingredients in a food processor and pulse for 2 minutes until smooth.

4. Pour the second layer on top of the first layer, smooth the top, and freeze for 4 hours until hard.

5. Serve straight away.

Nutrition: Calories: 411.3 Fat: 30.8 g Carbs: 28.7 g Protein: 4.7 g Fiber: 1.3 g

636. Matcha Coconut Cream Pie

Preparation Time: 5 minutes

Cooking Time: 0 minutes

Servings: 4

Ingredients:

For the Crust:

- 1/2 cup ground flaxseed
- 3/4 cup shredded dried coconut
- 1 cup Medjool dates, pitted
- 3/4 cup dehydrated buckwheat groats
- 1/4 teaspoons sea salt

For the Filling:

- 1 cup dried coconut flakes
- 4 cups of coconut meat
- 1/4 cup and 2 Tablespoons coconut nectar
- 1/2 Tablespoon vanilla extract, unsweetened
- 1/4 teaspoons sea salt
- 2/3 cup and 2 Tablespoons coconut butter
- 1 tablespoon matcha powder
- 1/2 cup coconut water

Directions:

1. Prepare the crust, and for this, place all its ingredients in a food processor and pulse for 3 to 5 minutes until the thick paste comes together.

2. Take a 6-inch springform pan, grease it with oil, place crust mixture in it and spread and press the mixture evenly in the bottom and along the sides, and freeze until required.

3. Prepare the filling and for this, place all its ingredients in a food processor, and pulse for 2 minutes until smooth.

4. Pour the filling into the prepared pan, smooth the top, and freeze for 4 hours until set.

5. Cut pie into slices and then serve.

Nutrition: Calories: 209 Fat: 18 g Carbs: 10 g Protein: 1 g Fiber: 2 g

637. Chocolate Peanut Butter Cake

Preparation Time: 5 minutes

Cooking Time: 0 minutes

Servings: 8

Ingredients:

For the Base:

- 1 tablespoon ground flaxseeds
- 1/8 cup millet

- 3/4 cup peanuts
- 1/4 cup and 2 tablespoons shredded coconut unsweetened
- 1 teaspoon hemp oil
- 1/2 cup flake oats

For the Date Layer:

- 1 tablespoon ground flaxseed
- 1 cup dates
- 1 tablespoon hemp hearts
- 2 tablespoons coconut
- 3 tablespoons cacao

For the Chocolate Layer:

- 3/4 cup coconut flour
- 2 tablespoons and 2 teaspoons cacao
- 1 tablespoon maple syrup
- 8 tablespoons warm water
- 2 tablespoons coconut oil
- 1/2 cup coconut milk
- 2 tablespoons ground flaxseed

For the Chocolate Topping:

- 7 ounces coconut cream
- 2 1/2 tablespoons cacao - 1 teaspoon agave

For Assembly:

- 1/2 cup almond butter

Directions:

1. Prepare the crust, and for this, place all its ingredients in a food processor and pulse for 3 to 5 minutes until the thick paste comes together.

2. Take a loaf tin, grease it with oil, place crust mixture in it and spread and press the mixture evenly in the bottom and along the sides, and freeze until required.

3. Prepare the date layer, and for this, place all its ingredients in a food processor and pulse for 2 minutes until smooth.

4. Prepare the chocolate layer, and for this, place flour and flax in a bowl and stir until combined.

5. Take a saucepan, add the remaining ingredients, stir until mixed, and Cooking Time for 5 minutes until melted and smooth.

6. Add it into the flour mixture, stir until dough comes together, and set aside.

7. Prepare the chocolate topping, place all its ingredients in a food processor, and pulse for 3 to 5 minutes until smooth.

8. Press date layer into the base layer, refrigerate for 1 hour, then press chocolate layer on its top, finish with chocolate topping, refrigerate for 3 hours and serve.

Nutrition: Calories: 390 Fat: 24.3 g Carbs: 35 g Protein: 10.3 g Fiber: 2 g

638. Chocolate Raspberry Brownies

Preparation Time: 4 hours
Cooking Time: 0 minutes
Servings: 4
Ingredients:
For the Chocolate Brownie Base:
- 12 Medjool Dates, pitted
- 3/4 cup oat flour
- 3/4 cup almond meal
- 3 tablespoons cacao
- 1 teaspoon vanilla extract, unsweetened
- 1/8 teaspoon sea salt
- 3 tablespoons water
- 1/2 cup pecans, chopped

For the Raspberry Cheesecake:
- 3/4 cup cashews, soaked, drained
- 6 tablespoons agave nectar - 1/2 cup raspberries
- 1 teaspoon vanilla extract, unsweetened
- 1 lemon, juiced
- 6 tablespoons liquid coconut oil

For the Chocolate Coating:
- 2 1/2 tablespoons cacao powder
- 3 3/4 tablespoons coconut Oil
- 2 tablespoons maple syrup
- 1/8 teaspoon sea salt

Directions:
1. Prepare the crust, and for this, place all its ingredients in a food processor and pulse for 3 to 5 minutes until the thick paste comes together.
2. Take a 6-inch springform pan, grease it with oil, place crust mixture in it and spread and press the mixture evenly in the bottom and along the sides, and freeze until required.
3. Prepare the cheesecake topping, and for this, place all its ingredients in a food processor and pulse for 2 minutes until smooth.
4. Pour the filling into the prepared pan, smooth the top, and freeze for 8 hours until solid.
5. Prepare the chocolate coating and for this, whisk together all its ingredients until smooth, drizzle on top of the cake and then serve.

Nutrition: Calories: 371 Fat: 42.4 g Carbs: 42 g Protein: 5.5 g Fiber: 2 g

639. Brownie Batter

Preparation Time: 5 minutes
Cooking Time: 0 minutes
Servings: 4
Ingredients:
- 4 Medjool dates, pitted, soaked in warm water
- 1.5 ounces chocolate, unsweetened, melted
- 2 tablespoons maple syrup - 4 tablespoons tahini
- ½ teaspoon vanilla extract, unsweetened
- 1 tablespoon cocoa powder, unsweetened
- 1/8 teaspoon sea salt - 1/8 teaspoon espresso powder
- 2 to 4 tablespoons almond milk, unsweetened

Directions:
2. Place all the ingredients in a food processor and process for 2 minutes until combined.
3. Set aside until required.

Nutrition: Calories: 44 Fat: 1 g Carbs: 6 g Protein: 2 g Fiber: 0 g

640. Strawberry Mousse

Preparation Time: 5 minutes
Cooking Time: 15 minutes
Servings: 4
Ingredients:
- 8 ounces coconut milk, unsweetened
- 2 tablespoons honey - 5 strawberries

Directions:
1. Place berries in a blender and pulse until the smooth mixture comes together.
2. Place milk in a bowl, whisk until whipped, and then add remaining ingredients and stir until combined. Refrigerate the mousse for 10 minutes and then serve.

Nutrition: Calories: 145 Fat: 23 g Carbs: 15 g Protein: 5 g Fiber: 1 g

641. Blueberry Mousse

Preparation Time: 20 minutes
Cooking Time: 0 minutes
Servings: 2
Ingredients:
- 1 cup wild blueberries
- 1 cup cashews, soaked for 10 minutes, drained
- 1/2 teaspoon berry powder
- 2 tablespoons coconut oil, melted
- 1 tablespoon lemon juice
- 1 teaspoon vanilla extract, unsweetened
- 1/4 cup hot water

Directions:
1. Place all the ingredients in a food processor and process for 2 minutes until smooth.
2. Set aside until required.

Nutrition: Calories: 433 Fat: 32.3 g Carbs: 44 g Protein: 5.1 g Fiber: 0 g

642. Black Bean Balls

Preparation Time: 10-20 minutes

Cooking Time: 20 minutes

Servings: 12 balls, 3 per serving

Ingredients:

- 420 g can black beans, rinsed
- 80 g raw cacao powder
- 30 g almond butter
- 15 ml maple syrup

Directions:

1. In a food processor, combine 420g black beans, 60g cacao powder, almond butter, and maple syrup.
2. Process until the mixture is well combined.
3. Shape the mixture into 12 balls.
4. Roll the balls through the remaining cacao powder.
5. Place the balls in a refrigerator for 10 minutes.
6. Serve.

Nutrition: Calories 245 Total Fat 3g Total Carbohydrate 41.4g Dietary Fiber 17.1g Total Sugars 3.1g Protein 13.1g

643. Chia Soy Pudding

Preparation Time: 10-20 minutes

Cooking Time: 5 minutes

Servings: 2

Ingredients:

- 45 g almond butter
- 15 ml maple syrup
- ¼ teaspoon vanilla paste
- 235 ml soy milk
- 45 g chia seeds
- 1 small banana, sliced
- 10 g crushed almonds

Directions:

1. Combine almond butter, maple syrup, vanilla, and soy milk in a jar.
2. Stir in chia seeds.
3. Cover and refrigerate for 3 hours.
4. After 3 hours, open the jar.
5. Top the chia pudding with banana and crushed almonds.
6. Serve.

Nutrition: Calories 298 Total Fat 13.8g Total Carbohydrate 37.2g Dietary Fiber 10.8g Total Sugars 17.4g Protein 10.1g

644. Blueberry Ice Cream

Preparation Time: 10-20 minutes

Cooking Time: 10 minutes

Servings: 4

Ingredients:

- 140 g raw cashews, soaked overnight
- 125 g silken tofu
- 230 g fresh blueberries
- 5 g lemon zest
- 100 ml maple syrup
- 100 ml coconut oil
- 15 g almond butter

Directions:

1. Rinse and drain cashews.
2. Place the cashews, blueberries, pale syrup, coconut oil, and almond butter in a food processor.
3. Process until smooth.
4. Transfer the mixture into the freezer-friendly container.
5. Cover with a plastic foil and freeze for 4 hours.
6. Remove the ice cream from the fridge 15 minutes before serving.
7. Scoop the ice creams and transfer into a bowl.
8. Serve.

Nutrition: Calories 544 Total Fat 40.7g Total Carbohydrate 43.4g Dietary Fiber 2.6g Total Sugars 28g Protein 8.1g

645. Chickpea Choco Slices

Preparation Time: 10-20 minutes

Cooking Time: 50 minutes

Servings: 12 slices, 2 per r serving

Ingredients:

- 400 g can chickpeas, rinsed, drained
- 250 g almond butter
- 70 ml maple syrup
- 15 ml vanilla paste
- 1 pinch salt
- 2 g baking powder
- 2 g baking soda
- 40 g vegan chocolate chips

Directions:

1. Preheat oven to 180°C/350°F.
2. Grease a large baking pan with coconut oil.
3. Combine chickpeas, almond butter, maple syrup, vanilla, salt, baking powder, and baking soda in a food blender.

4. Blend until smooth. Stir in half the chocolate chips-
5. Spread the batter into the prepared baking pan.
6. Sprinkle with reserved chocolate chips.
7. Bake for 45-50 minutes or until an inserted toothpick comes out clean.
8. Cool on a wire rack for 20 minutes. slice and serve.

Nutrition: Calories 426 Total Fat 27.2g Total Carbohydrate 39.2g Dietary Fiber 4.9g Total Sugars 15.7g Protein 10g

646. Chocolate Orange Mousse

Preparation Time: 10-20 minutes
Cooking Time: 10 minutes
Servings: 4
Ingredients:

- 450g can black beans, rinsed, drained
- 55 g dates, pitted, soaked in water for 15 minutes
- 30 ml coconut oil
- 110 ml maple syrup
- 60 ml soy milk
- 1 orange, zested

Directions:

1. Place the black bean in a food processor.
2. Add drained dates and process until smooth.
3. Add coconut oil, maple syrup, and soy milk. Process for 1 minute.
4. Finally, stir in lemon zest.
5. Spoon the mixture into four dessert bowls.
6. Chill for 1 hour before serving.

Nutrition: Calories 375 Total Fat 8g Total Carbohydrate 68.5g Dietary Fiber 12.1g Total Sugars 35.9g Protein 11.3g

Conclusion

The word vegan has some pretty heavy connotations. You might picture a grumpy, judgmental person with braces and unshaven armpits or the guy who yelled at you that your leather shoes were unethical. People usually connect veganism with a huge list of restrictions and rigid dietary rules. But this is simply not the case! A plant-based diet can actually be really flexible and inclusive to all sorts of palates, so I'm hoping for this article to debunk some myths and shed light on what's going on in the world of plants.

There are likely many reasons why someone chooses to go plant-based: for the animals, for the environment, for people in poor countries where livestock farming is a huge problem. Whatever your reason is, you probably already know that it doesn't have to be complicated. Eating plants is just eating plants.

A lot of people think that reducing or eliminating animal products has to be a long and difficult process, but that's really not the case! I used to think the same thing: "I'm going to try being vegan for a week." The first hour was awesome, then I got hungry and caved and had a steak sandwich, then I got sad and grossed out. Then while watching videos of animals being murdered for their skin by my shoes, I was like, "Screw this. I'm going back to cheeseburgers. And non-organic wine. " But that's not to say that eating vegan is a short and easy process. It might take some time to get used to it, but the alternatives are just so unappealing. You'll probably end up going back and forth, but most people make a significant change after just a couple of weeks. All that being said, there are many people who are vegan for life.

Even those who were formerly vegetarian find it difficult switching over to veganism, so it's no surprise that many people have some hesitations about changing their diet in this way. The first problem that comes to mind is: "Where do you get your protein?" People are often afraid of a protein deficiency. This is pretty non-sense, if you haven't guessed already. There's so much protein in plant-based milks, beans, and other products that any herbivore would be jealous. But if you're still worried about meeting your protein quota, companies like Vega sell mixes with all the essential amino acids (for vegans).

Another thing people are worried about is the complete lack of protein. This is extremely untrue, especially considering all the delicious sources of protein that are available. While nobody can tell you exactly how much protein you'll need, a lot of people do end up being a bit too hungry after switching to a plant-based diet.

The main concern that many have regarding not eating meat and dairy products is that they will be missing out on essential nutrients, especially calcium. However, just like for humans (and probably most animals), milk in all its forms has been considered unnecessary for some time now. By going plant-based, you don't have to eliminate all dairy products from your diet. You can still eat yogurt, cheese, and cream cheese, milk chocolate, ice cream, and even ice cream sandwiches.

However, many people find that they do feel a bit more satisfied after switching to a plant-based diet. Other than calcium and protein, there are many other essential vitamins that we get from animal products: lutein (which is important for eye health), vitamin B12 (needed by red blood cells), DHA (essential for brain development in children), and many more.

Printed in Great Britain
by Amazon

44845291R00143